AF321492

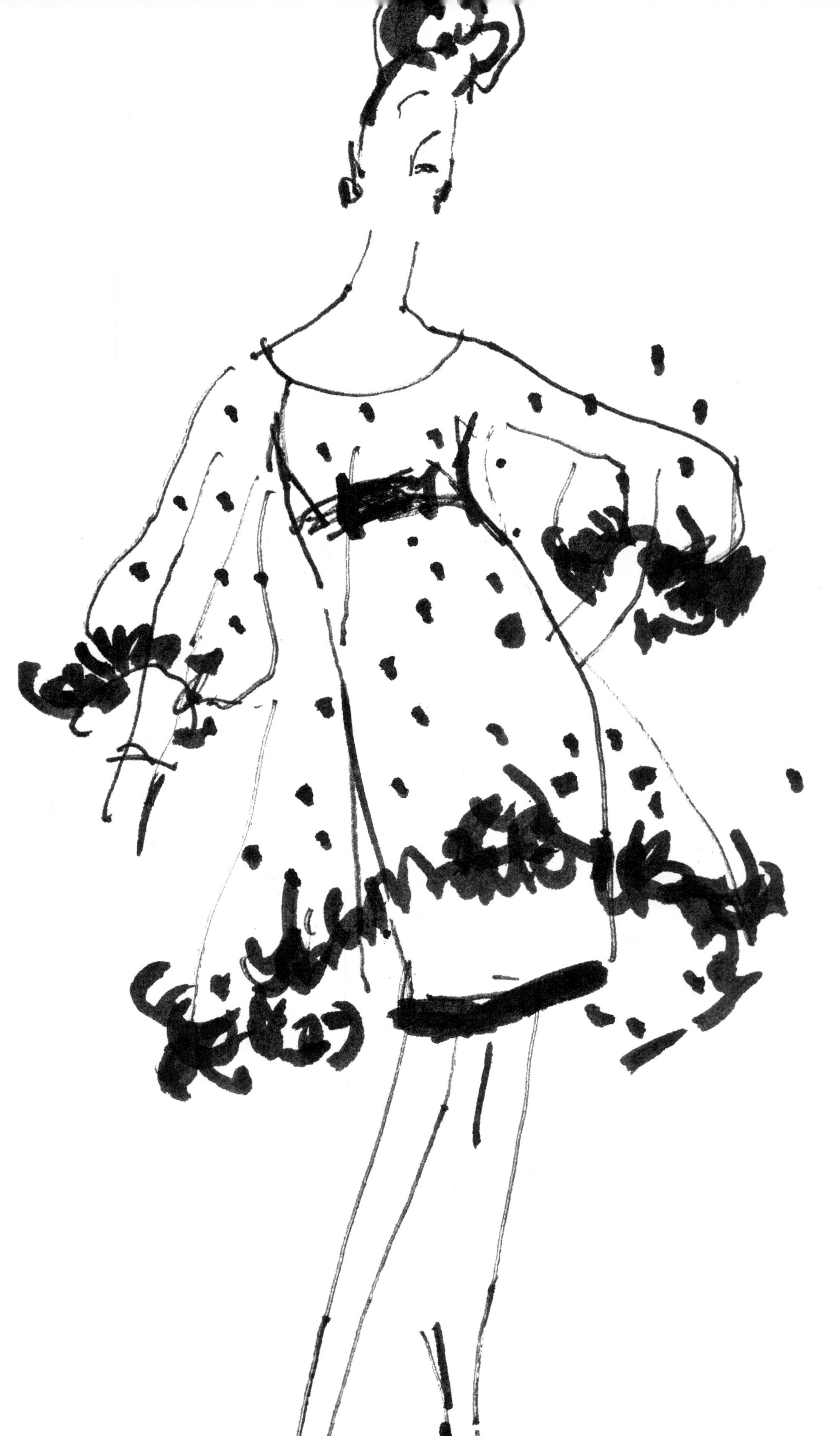

JOE EULA

Master of Twentieth-Century Fashion Illustration

CATHY HORYN

Images curated by
Melisa Gosnell and Dagon James

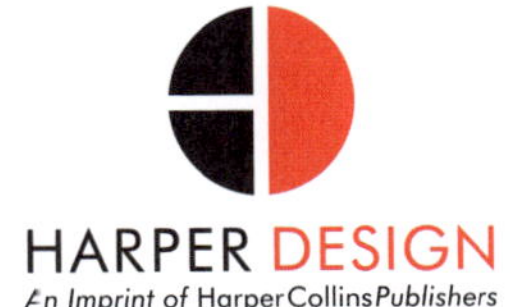

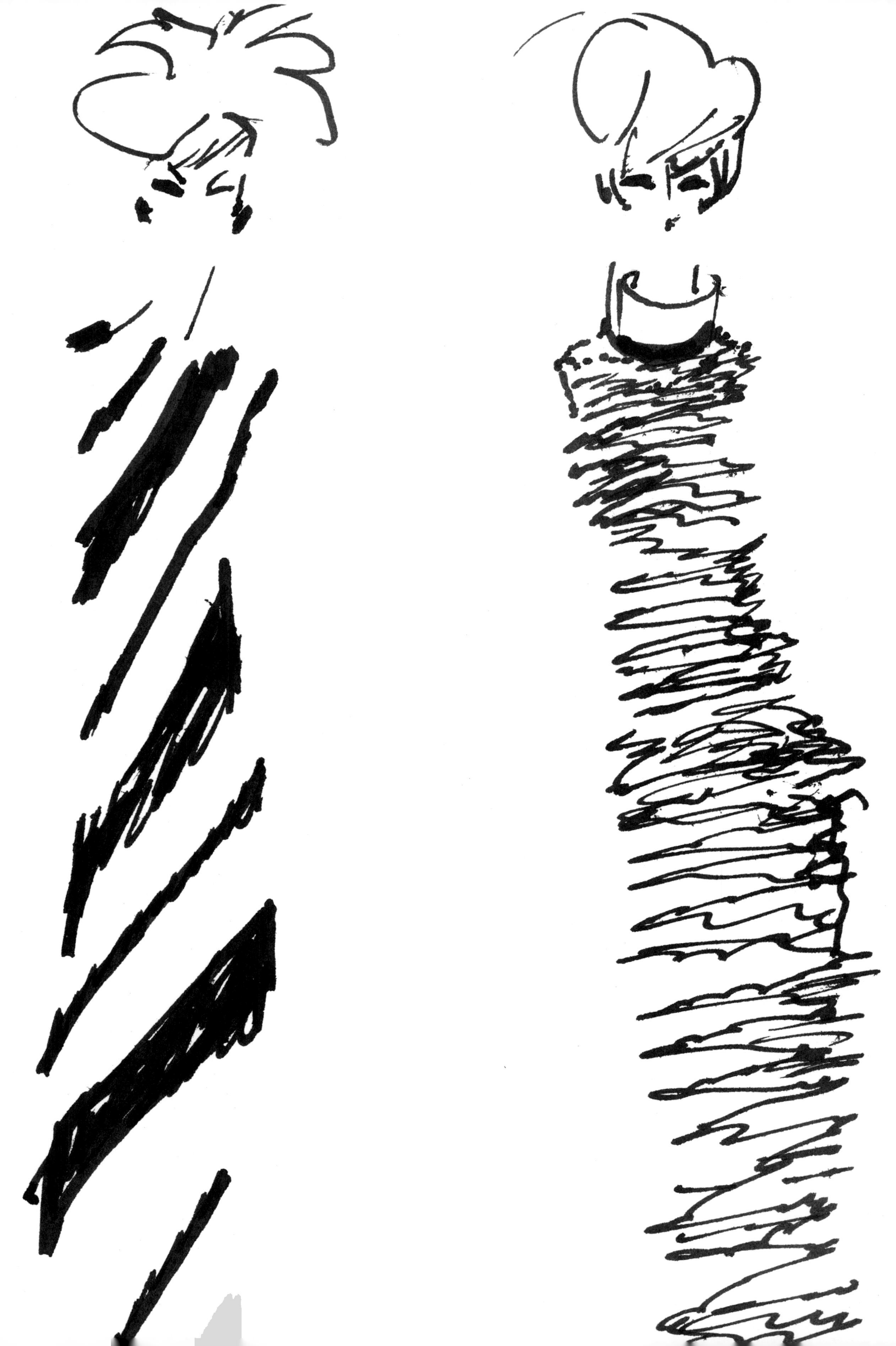

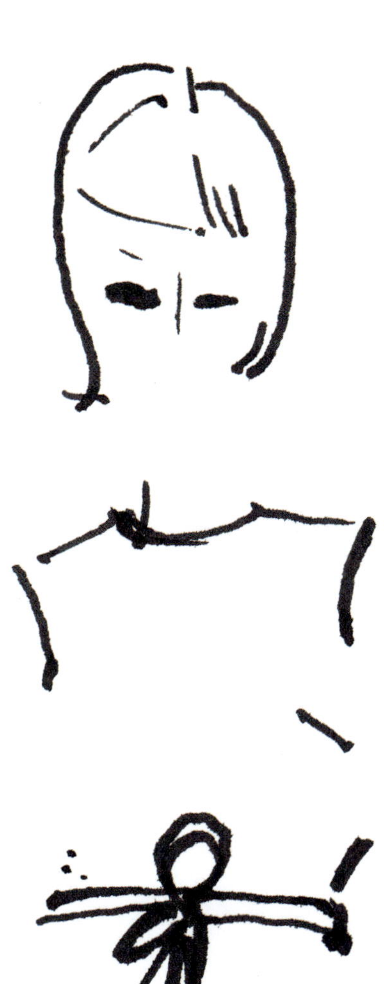

Contents

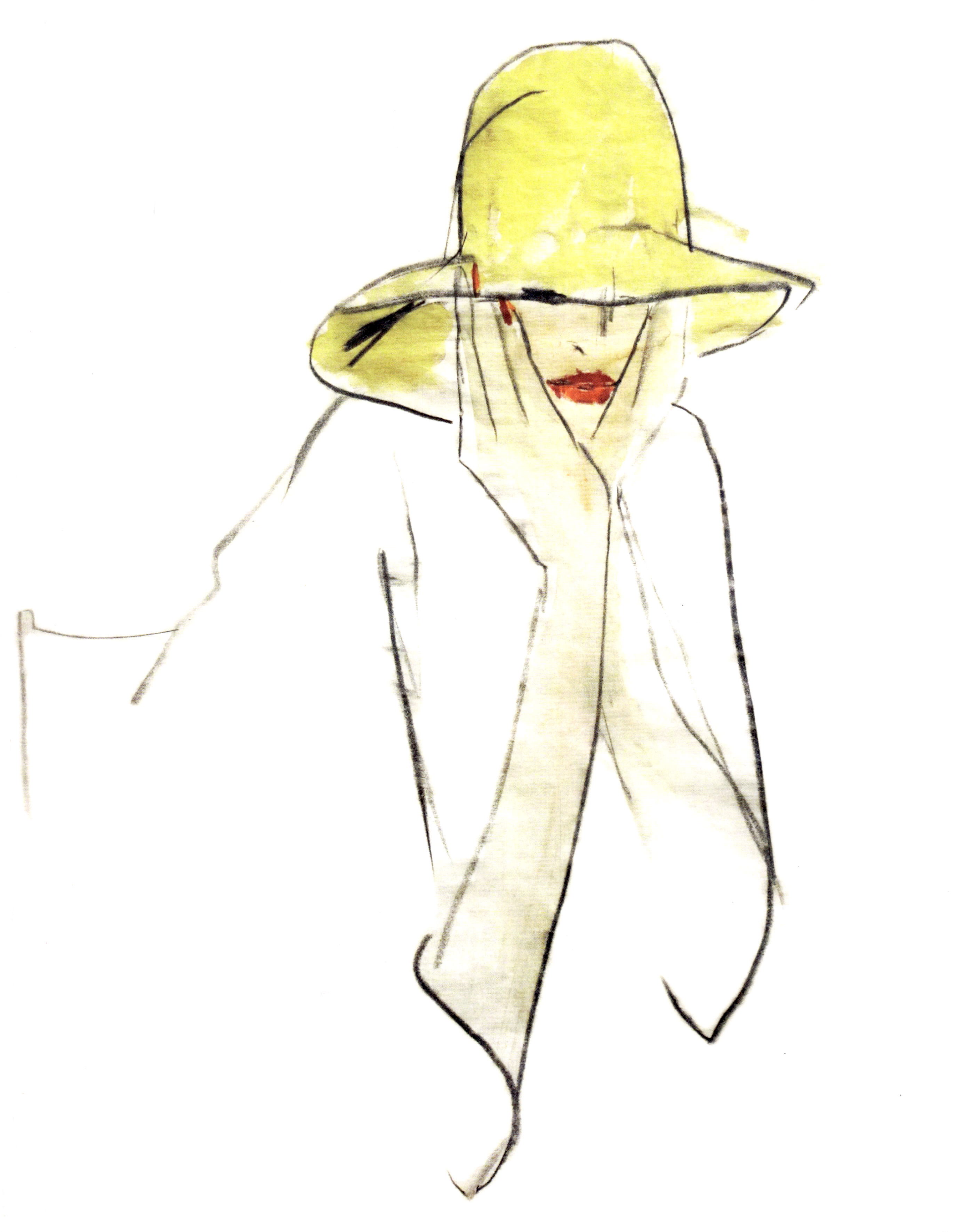

Introduction

One day in 1962, Joe Eula was sitting in Chanel's Paris salon, quickly getting off some sketches before the models returned to their dressing room. The French houses didn't want anyone sketching their clothes; they complained incessantly about copies. However, Eula had no time for such rules. He had a deadline to meet—for the *New York Herald Tribune*, for which he illustrated Eugenia Sheppard's columns. In the late 1950s, Sheppard had resurrected the idea of the fashion report loaded with society names and gossip just as a new group of idols emerged, women like Jacqueline Kennedy, Babe Paley, and Gloria Vanderbilt. Sheppard and Eula covered the Kennedy Inauguration together in that frozen, prideful January of 1961. They were an unbeatable team: both short and feisty, Sheppard from the swells of Columbus, Ohio; Eula, a war hero from working-class South Norwalk, Connecticut. And because Sheppard adored fashion and her column was so popular in the United States and Europe, the French designers gradually rolled over once she began publishing Eula's spirited drawings.

OPPOSITE: American brilliance. In spare lines and sunny colors, Eula evoked the attitude in sportswear. Watercolor and pen illustration, late 1950s.

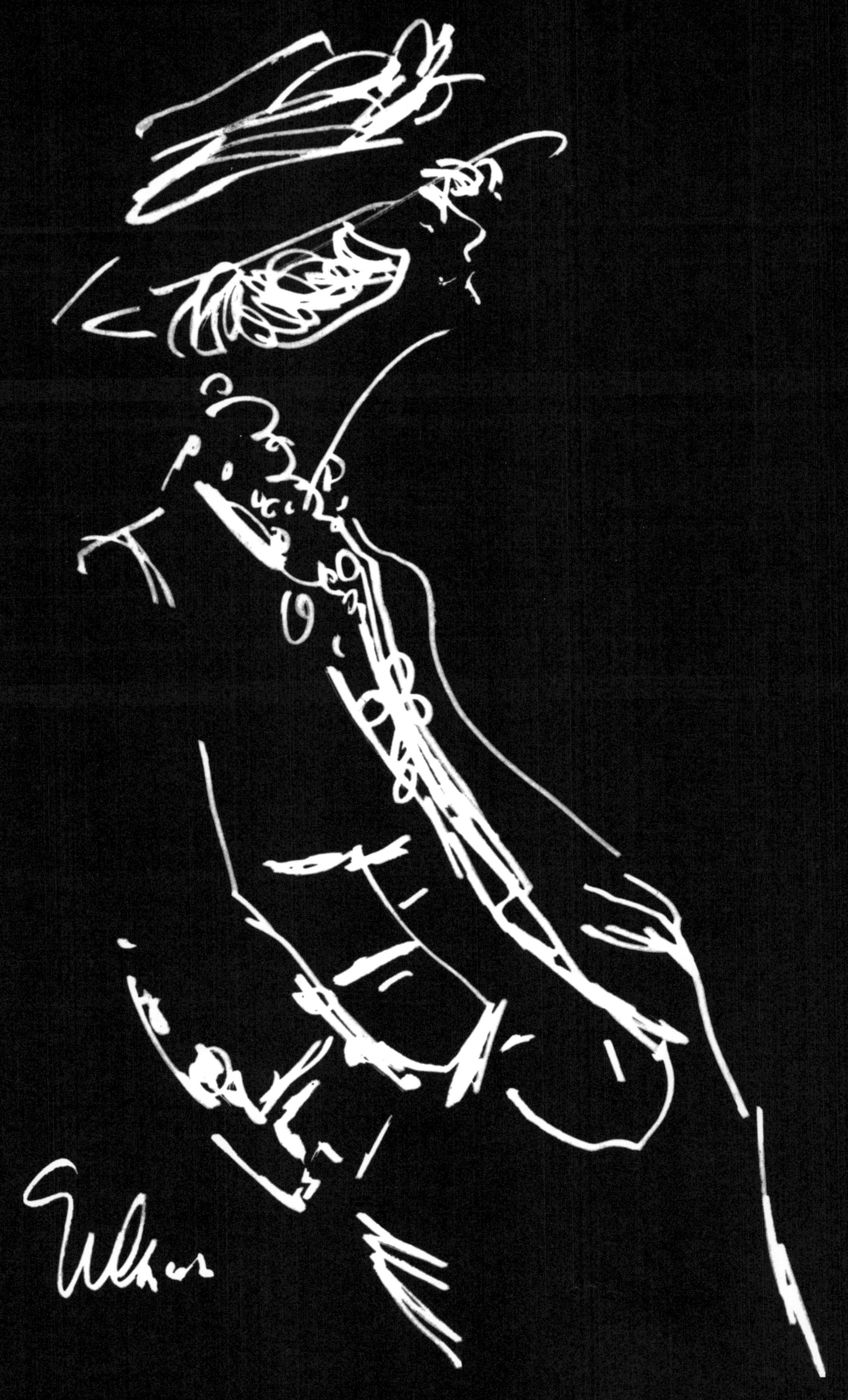

But not Chanel. She refused to give in to the press. "I had heard about this woman all my life," Eula said years later. "She was just like a knife in everyone's gut and brain." So there he was in the couturiere's salon, drawing the models after the show, telling them to be quick, when he looked up and saw Chanel coming down the staircase. "She was heading straight toward me," he said. However, he continued to draw, his hand gliding almost imperceptibly to a clean square of paper, and by the time the terror reached him he had finished her portrait. From then on, until Chanel's death in 1971, the two were good friends, Eula often lunching at her Rue Cambon studio. And every time he was in Paris, which was usually twice a year to sketch the collections, he took her to *West Side Story*, a long-running attraction in the city. "It was the only show she liked," he said.

That story, preserved among some loose typed pages that Eula once intended for a memoir but then abandoned, does not appear in any of the Chanel biographies, which would validate not only her surprising taste in musical theater but also Eula's friendship with the legend. It's also an example of how the illustrator achieved his insider perch in the fashion world and in New York society—without apparent effort, design, or care. Since he was not in the habit of making things up and often cut people down with his brutal honesty, it's safe to assume the story is true. What makes Eula such a difficult figure to grasp in the fashion and cultural scene of the past seventy-five years is that he sticks out like a sore thumb, and yet in another sense, he seems nowhere to be found. Andy Warhol once called Eula "the most important person" in New York, saying, "He knows everybody who's anybody. Anybody who's somebody. . . . All the really chic people."

This was unquestionably true. On the summer night in 1971 when Warhol made that remark to the writer Bob Colacello, Eula was having one of his weekly parties at

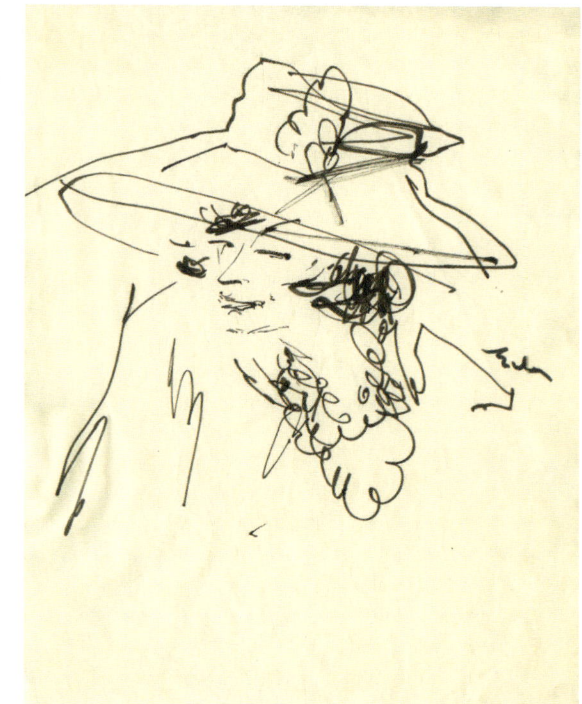

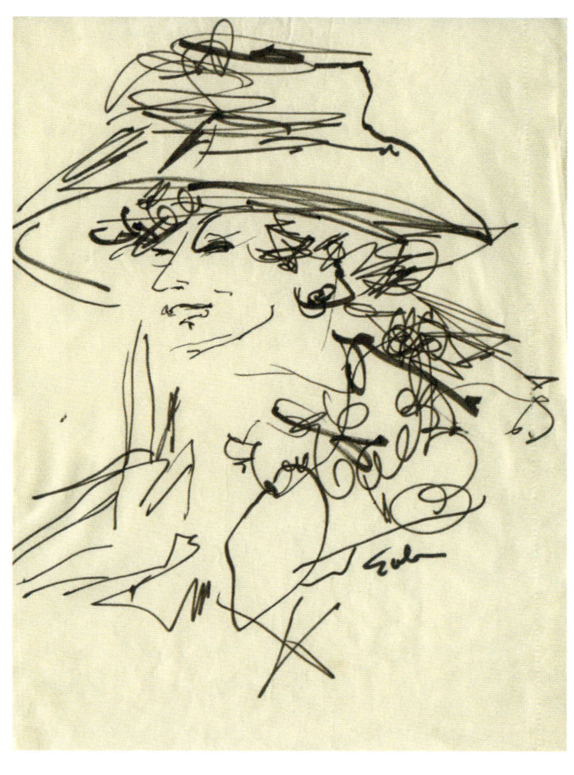

his floor-through apartment at 41 West Fifty-Fourth Street. In attendance were Elsa Peretti, Loulou de la Falaise, Marisa Berenson, Berry Berenson, Anjelica Huston, Liza Minnelli, Marina Schiano, and the designers Halston, Giorgio di Sant'Angelo, Stephen Burrows, and Fernando Sánchez. The photographer Charles Tracy, a regular guest, recalls meeting Diana Vreeland and Lily Auchincloss at Eula's. The model Nancy North, who was part of Halston's gang, says of these gatherings, "They were packed with people, like the party scenes in *Breakfast at Tiffany's*."

But for someone who was in the middle of the riot, who in fact had an outrageous personality, an extraordinary eye, and, plainly, a gift for friendship, Eula occupies at

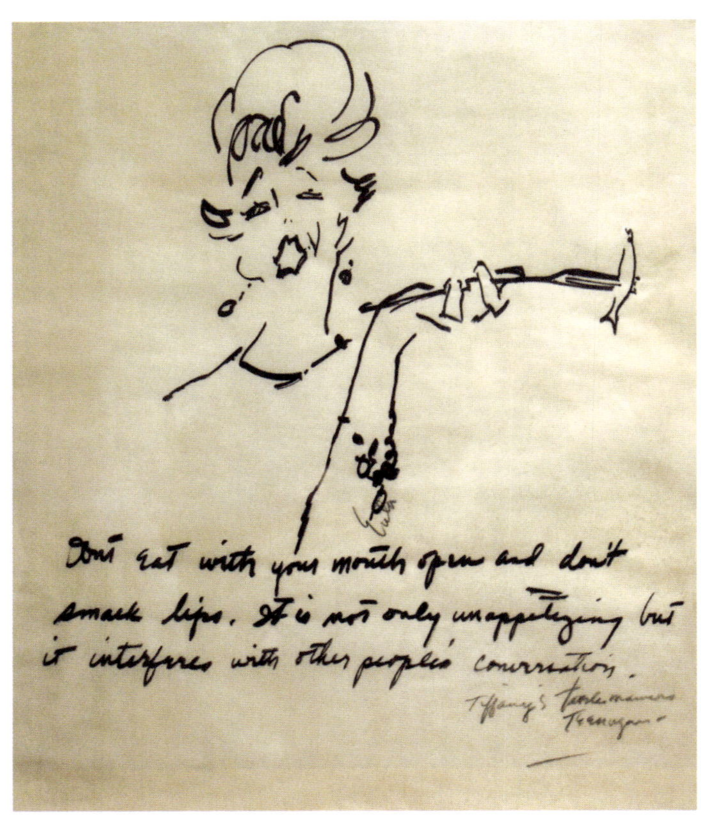

best a marginal place in most published accounts of the years between 1950 and 1985, when his career was flourishing. More curious, considering his remarkable output, is that he is barely acknowledged in surveys of twentieth-century fashion illustrators alongside Eric, René Bouché, and Antonio Lopez. Was he a minor player, or a too-little-known original overshadowed by superstars?

To a large degree, the problem lies with Eula himself, and the kind of career he had. It's unclassifiable. It's off the charts, actually. He worked primarily as a fashion illustrator, but he also turned out drawings for album covers, show posters, and nightclub logos, many of them iconic. These include the drawing of Minnelli for her 1972 concert *Liza with a "Z,"* a springy poster advertising a 1965 performance by the Supremes at Lincoln Center, and the spare, Giacometti-like figures that haunt the cover of Miles Davis's 1961 album, *Sketches of Spain*. That same year, *Tiffany's Table Manners for Teenagers* by Tiffany & Co. chairman Walter Hoving was published, with Eula's offhand drawings of various courses and the proper ways to attack them relieving much of the confusion and ceremony around etiquette. The book, like many examples of his commercial work, remains in use today.

ABOVE: One of Eula's sketches from *Tiffany's Table Manners for Teenagers* by Walter Hoving, 1961. OPPOSITE: Eula's album cover for Miles Davis's *Sketches of Spain*, 1961. PAGES 12–13 AND 14–15: Drawings for show posters for Liza Minnelli (1972) and the Supremes (1965).

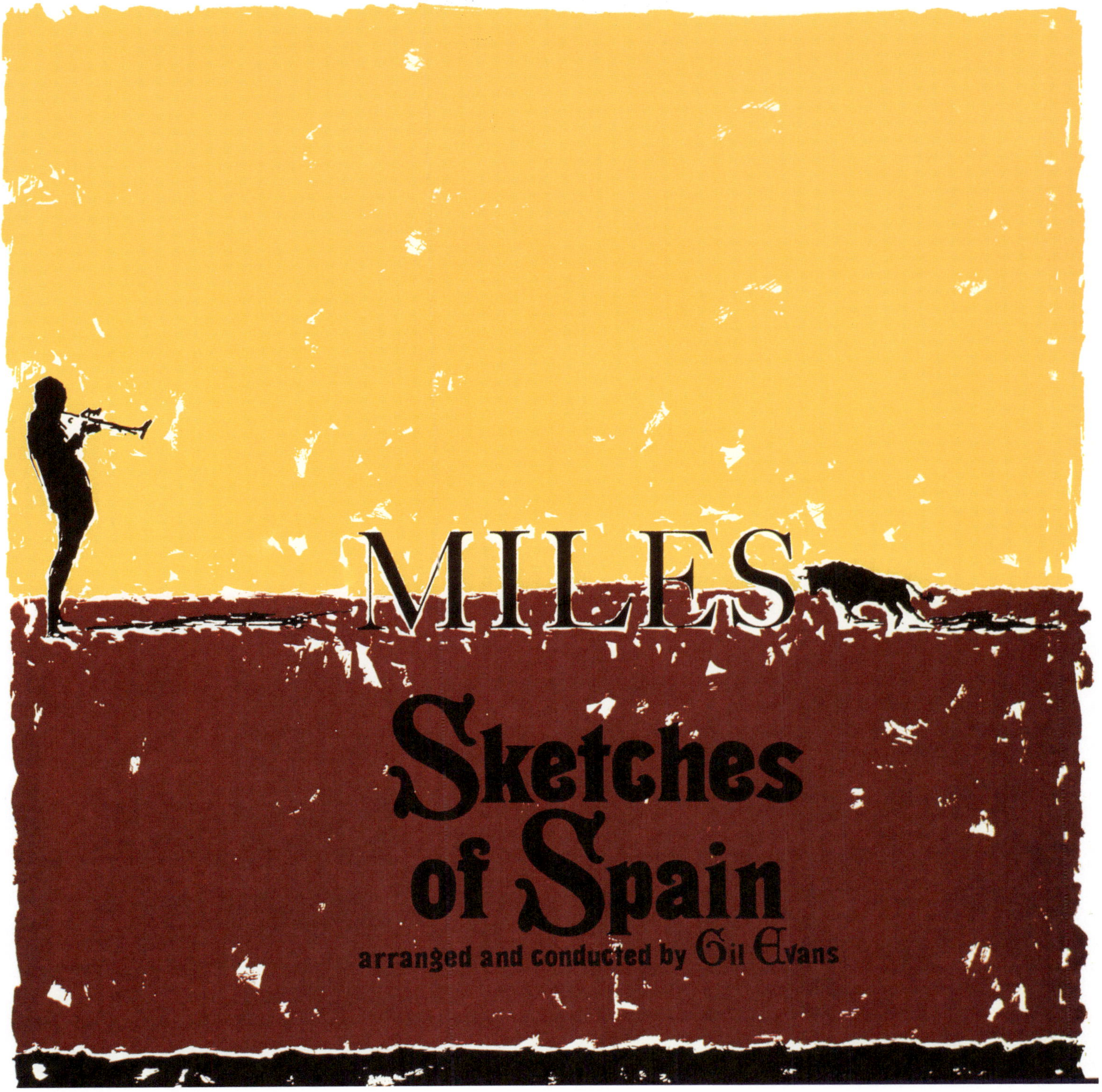

MILES

Sketches of Spain

arranged and conducted by Gil Evans

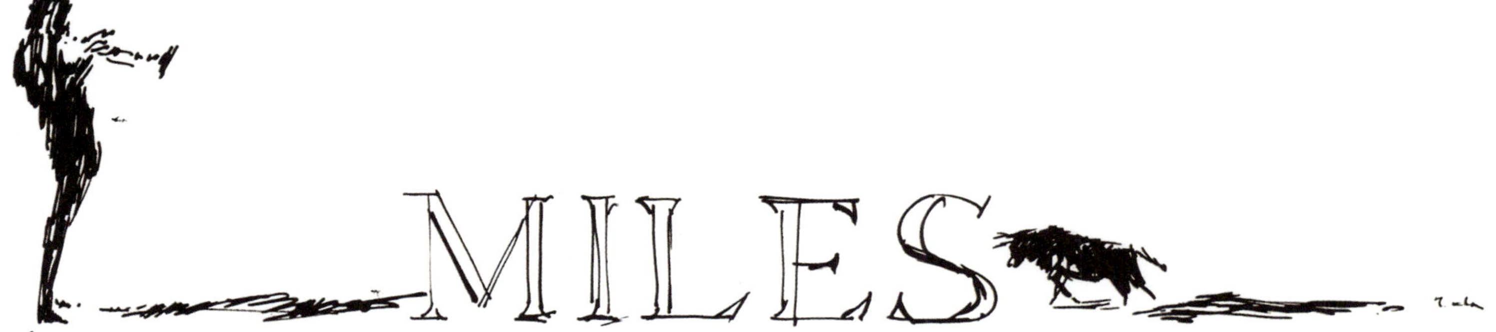

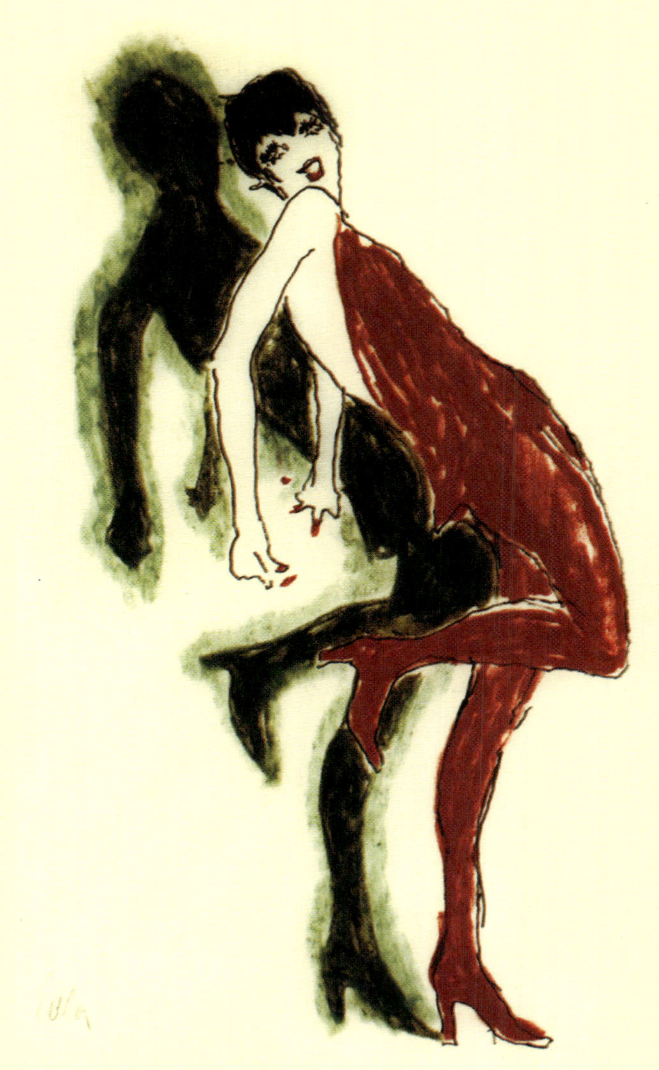

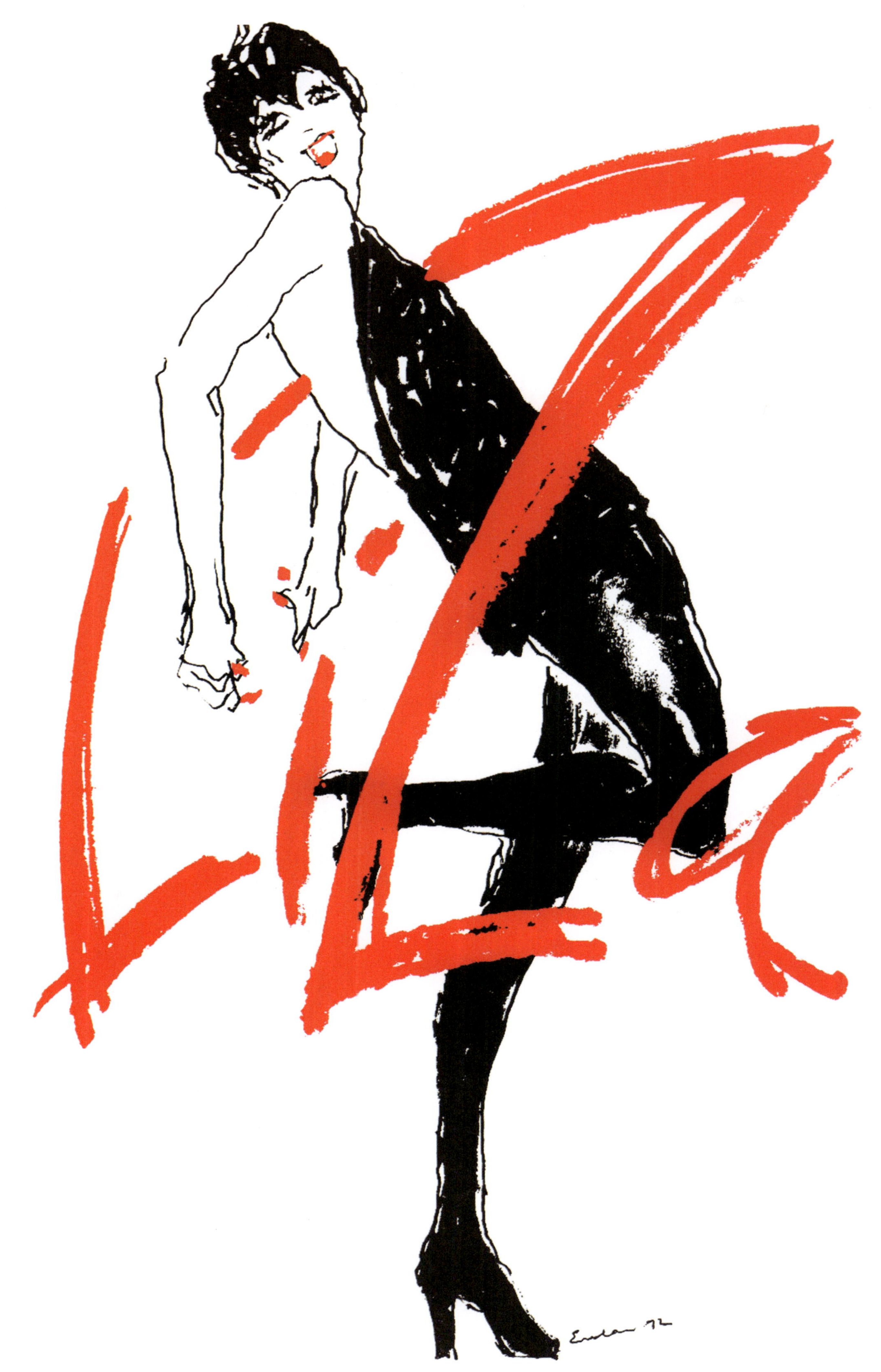

LIZA

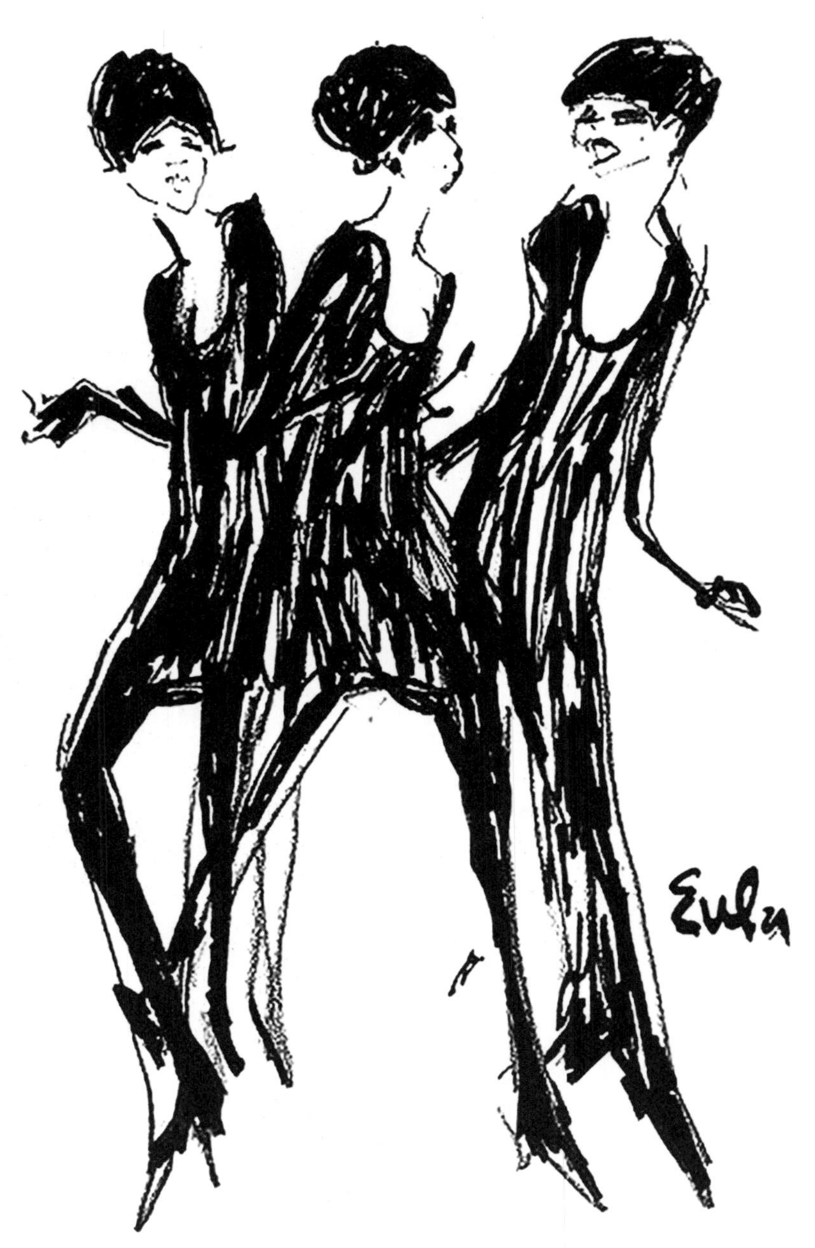

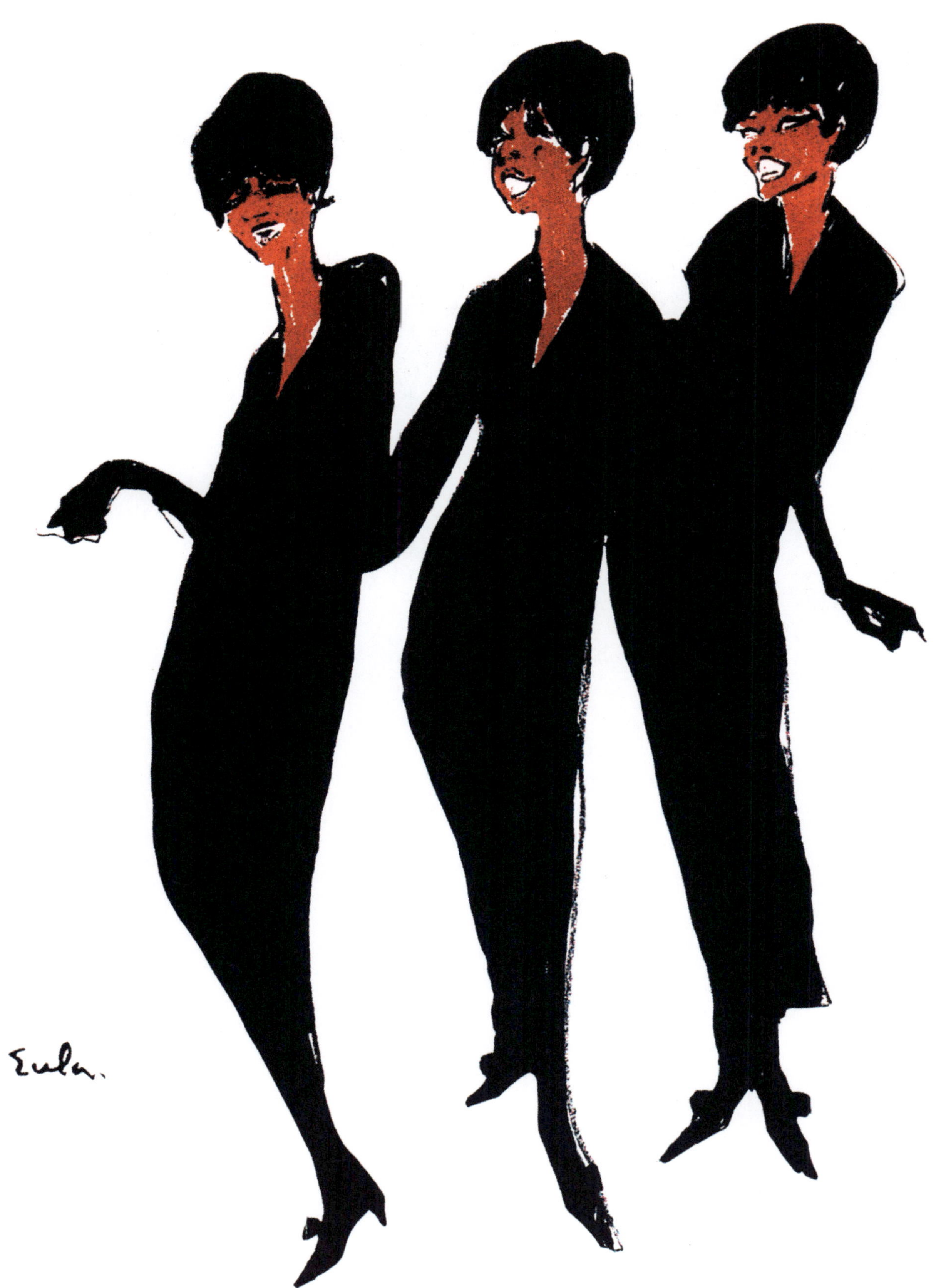

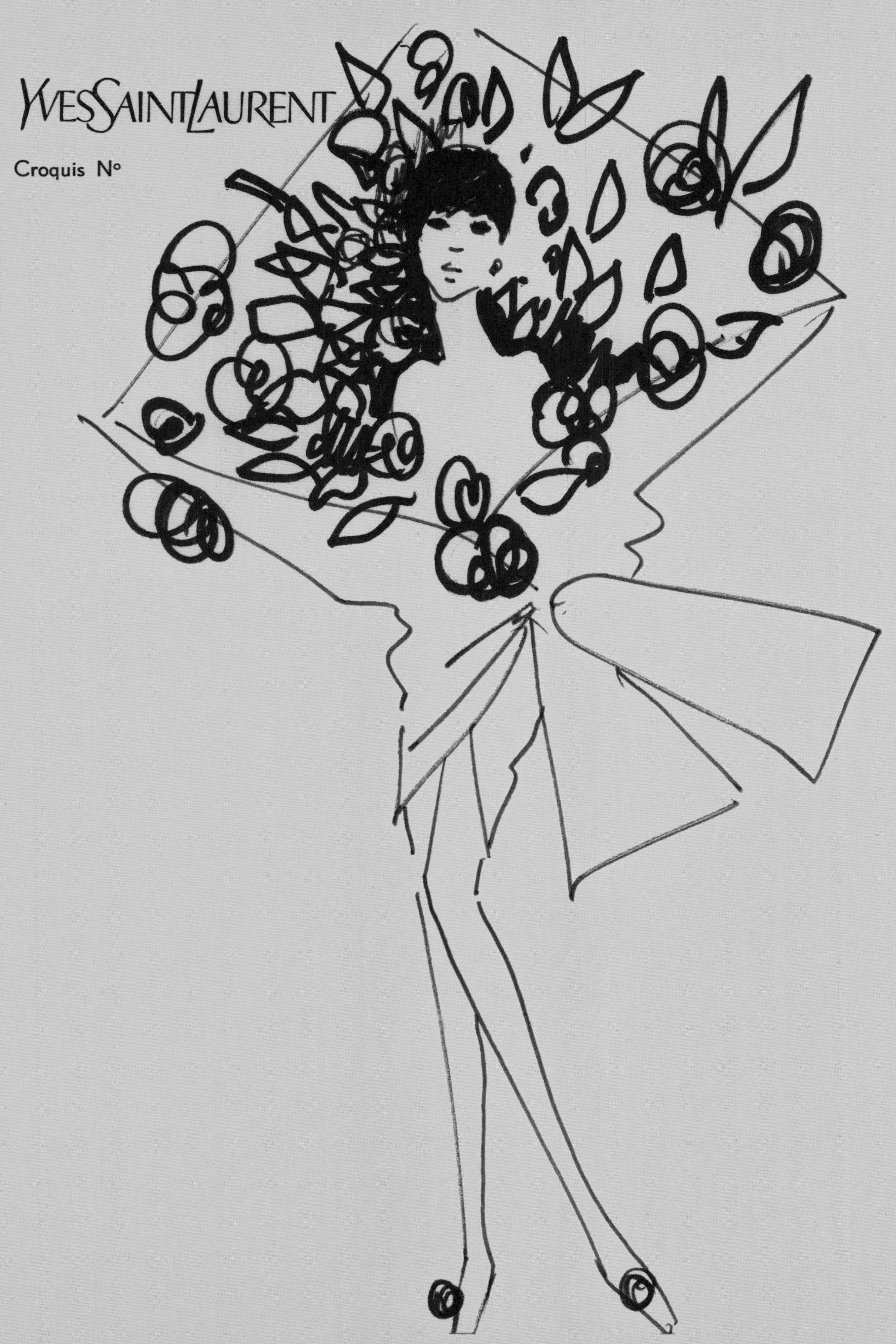

YVESSAINTLAURENT
Croquis Nº

Eula was a great crossover artist, though this, too, made it tough to define his achievement. While covering the collections with Sheppard, he also worked with the photographer Milton H. Greene, best known for his portraits of Marilyn Monroe. During the 1960s, the Greene-Eula studio produced a steady flow of layouts for *Life* and other magazines, with Eula acting as stylist and set designer. Eula and Greene traveled the world for *Life*, doing photo essays on celebrities, film stars, and fashion, often in collaboration with the magazine's singular fashion editor, Sally Kirkland. In addition, they created a CBS special called *Bacall and the Boys*. Shot in Paris, the film followed actress Lauren Bacall as she led viewers on a tour of fashion houses while designers such as Yves Saint Laurent talked about their collections. It was the first time a mainstream audience was given an inside glimpse into haute couture. Around this time Eula tried his hand at costume design, for Jerome Robbins's ballet *Dances at a Gathering*. According to Eula, Robbins was inspired by a drawing Eula did for an invitation to a benefit for Cesar Chavez and the National Farm Workers Association.

In every sense, Eula was light and fast. His drawings were graphic, sharp, minimal, and, as with the portrait of the Chanel model, usually executed in a matter of seconds. He almost never revised—it bored him to do so. To the model China Machado, who met Eula in the late 1950s, it was as though what he saw went straight down his arm to the paper. She says, "It was immediate, it was spontaneous, it was of the moment. He was the only one who really had that quality." Minnelli says, "Joe didn't go into great detail in his drawings, but he showed you what the object was about. It's the damnedest thing."

As Minnelli suggests, Eula's work had a quality that was at once essential and mysterious, and it found its most sympathetic ally in Roy Halston Frowick, the thin, elegant modernist who, as Colacello observed at Eula's party, had an "Olympian grandness" that belied his Midwestern upbringing. Through most of the 1970s, Eula was Halston's creative director, another testimony to his eclectic talents. The late Fernando Sánchez, who had a reservoir of insight into his fellow designers, maintained that Halston's clothes would never have hit their note of informal luxury were it not for the influence of Eula and Elsa Peretti, a zesty personality who knew

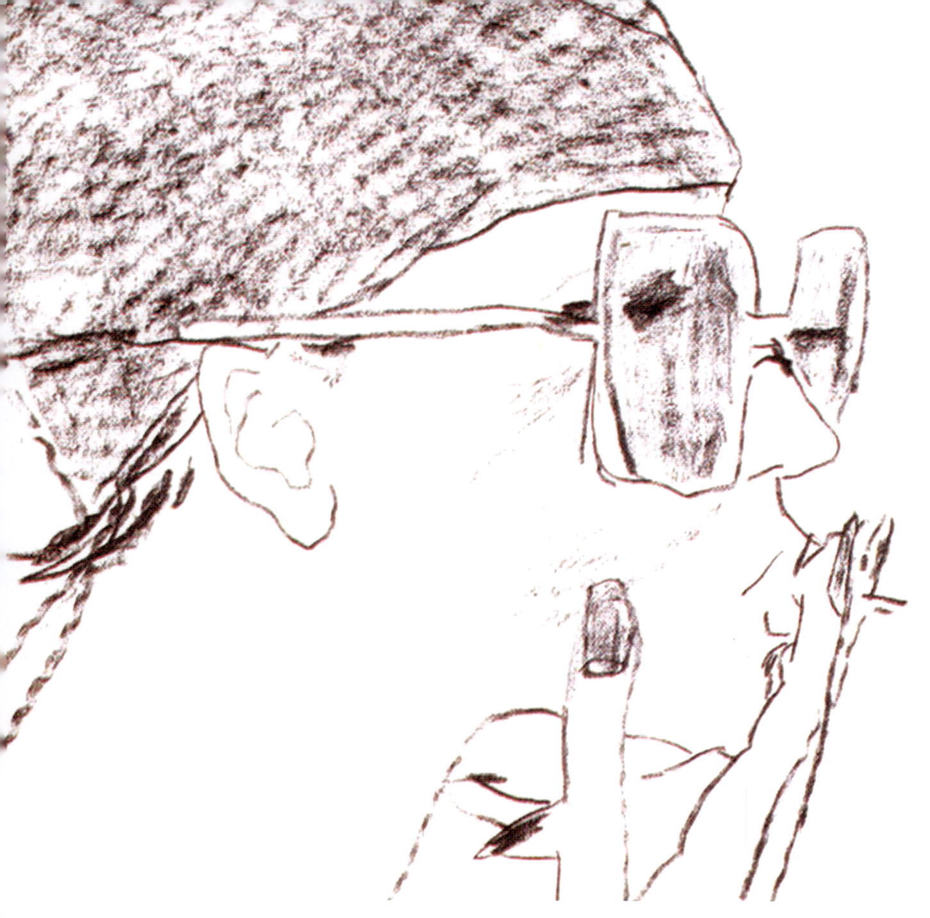

her own mind about clothes—the simpler the better. "They really defined Halston's style and the idea that chic doesn't necessarily imply money," Sánchez said. There is considerable debate about how much influence Eula had in the Halston studio, but one thing is sure: he always had that modern, less-is-more attitude. It arose out of a need to seek the essence of a thing, whether the character registered in a human face or the movement of a dress, and then express it in a form that stood up to that ideal. For Eula, this was watercolor and the incisive line—or, as he once said, "If you could do it with one line, why put down fifty?" How could he not have influenced the ravishing simplicity of Halston?

Other illustrators, notably Eric, René Gruau, and Tom Keogh, were far better draftsmen—more evocative and consistent—than Eula. As David Downton, the most authoritative fashion illustrator today, says, "You can get a really bad Joe Eula and you can't get a really bad Eric, and you probably can't get a really bad Kenneth Paul Bloch." (Bloch drew for *Women's Wear Daily*, covering the collections as well as the social scene.) And in terms of scope, Eula's career absolutely dims in comparison to that of the Hungarian Marcel Vertès, who designed advertisements for Elsa Schiaparelli's perfumes and won two Academy Awards for costume and set design for *Moulin Rouge* (1952). And Keogh, an American and one of the most captivating postwar illustrators, distinguished himself in different ways as well: he created a dance sequence for the 1955 Fred Astaire classic, *Daddy Long Legs*. One reason that Eula, and to an extent Bloch, never achieved international stature is that his work ran in newspapers, which are read and then thrown away. "The great illustrators that people know are, frankly, the ones that were in *Vogue*," says Downton, the author of *Masters of Fashion Illustration*, a survey of twentieth-century artists. "People kept *Vogue*. It was covetable."

ABOVE: Elsa Peretti, 1970s. OPPOSITE: The frenetic party scene: Halston, Peretti, and Andy Warhol, 1970s.

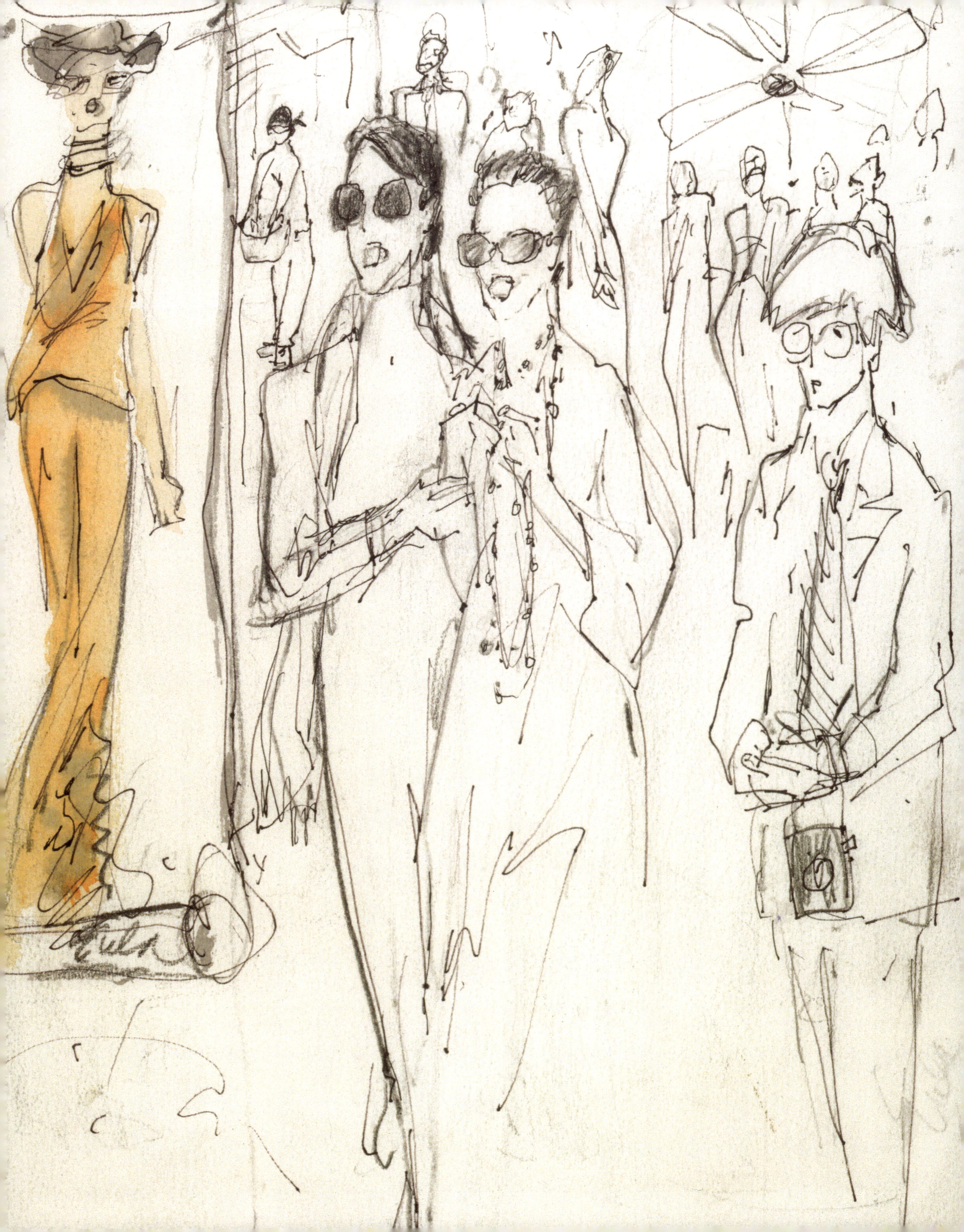

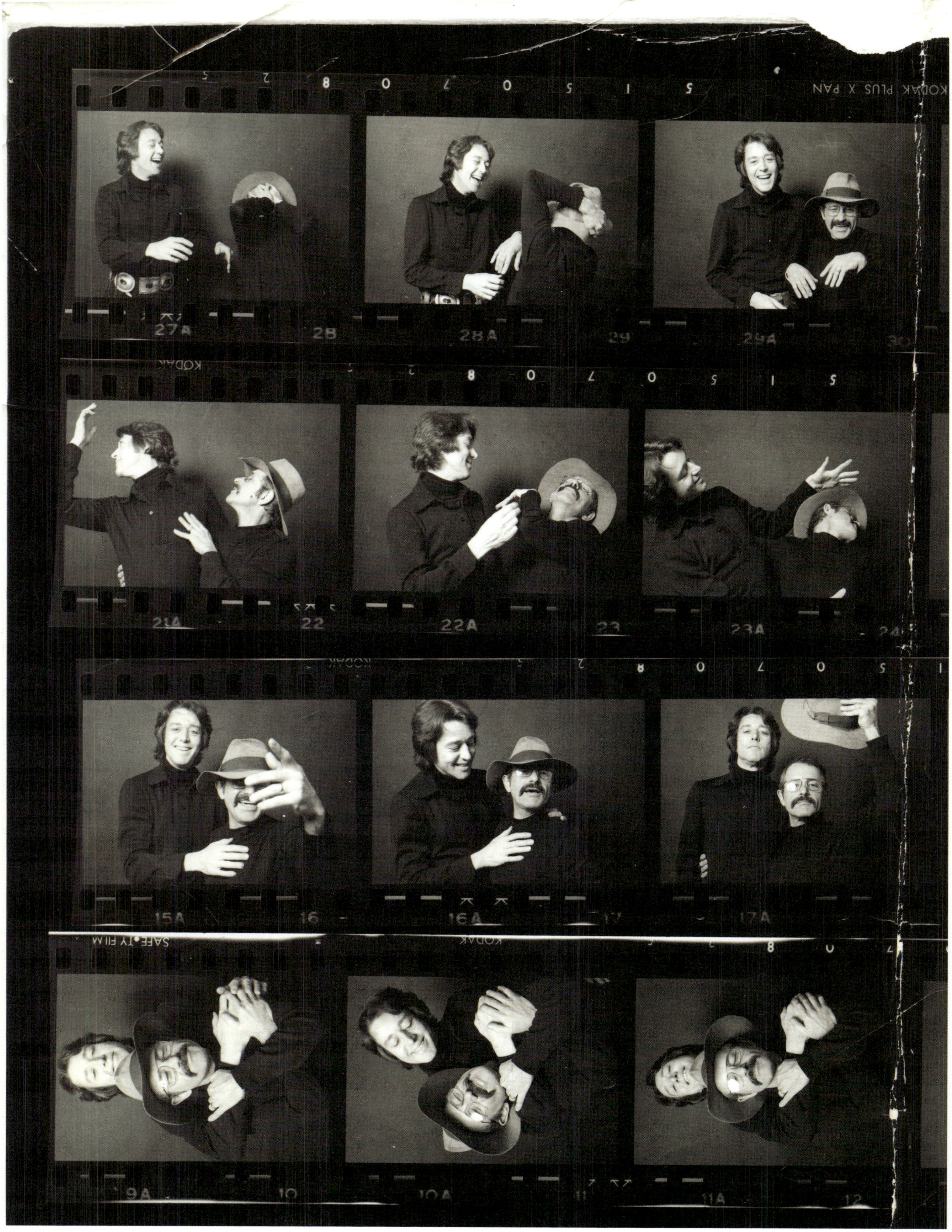
KODAK PLUS X PAN
27A
28
28A
29
29A
30
KODAK
21A
22
22A
23
23A
24
KODAK
15A
16
16A
17
17A
SAFETY FILM
KODAK
9A
10
10A
11
11A
12

In any case, comparisons have a limited value because Eula, with his diverse talents, was in his own class as an artist. Downton remarks, "To the best of my knowledge, no [other] fashion illustrator ever sat and drew Marilyn Monroe." Eula drew the actress in 1957, during the filming of *The Prince and the Showgirl* in England, which Milton Greene produced with Sir Laurence Olivier, who also directed and costarred in the movie. "It's on a really torn old piece of paper," says Downton. "It's her and Olivier." Not that Eula ever gave importance to such encounters. In fact, while generous and wisely funny in conversation, he usually sidestepped questions about his celebrated friends or his own life, or he responded with a mischievous jab. Either way, you didn't get much satisfaction.

His friend, photographer Charles Tracy, says, "I loved Joe, loved him like a brother, but there's so much I didn't know about him." He recalls a fairly typical exchange: "I said to him, 'Tell me about Marilyn.' 'Well, she sat in bed eating a pork chop.' I said, 'Joe, please don't talk about Marilyn Monroe that way.' And he said, 'Well, she did!'" Tracy, after a pause, says, "He didn't really care, did he? I mean, he did care, but he showed like he didn't."

All the same, Eula was a presence. He knew that his opinions counted, that he had helped shape a dynamic era in fashion. He was also aware that being his own man gave him an edge in that clubby world. "He was a magician in a way, someone stirring things up," says Downton. "I think fashion illustration was the least of it. If you put Joe's drawings of Halston up against Kenneth Paul Bloch's, Kenneth's are much better. That's the truth of it, but it's also only a small part of it."

When I met Eula, in the fall of 2001, he was winding down his career, and would only live another three years. I never saw the outrageous side of Joe, who could be cocky and seductive—"a little Mussolini," in the words of his close friend, artist Ron Ferri—and who, despite saying exactly what was on his mind regardless of whom he was speaking to, seemed to have a magnetic hold over people. "You should have heard him talking to these society dames," says Tracy, laughing. "'Just sit down!' 'I've heard enough from you!'" I knew next to nothing about Eula—only that his name carried weight with a lot of stylish people.

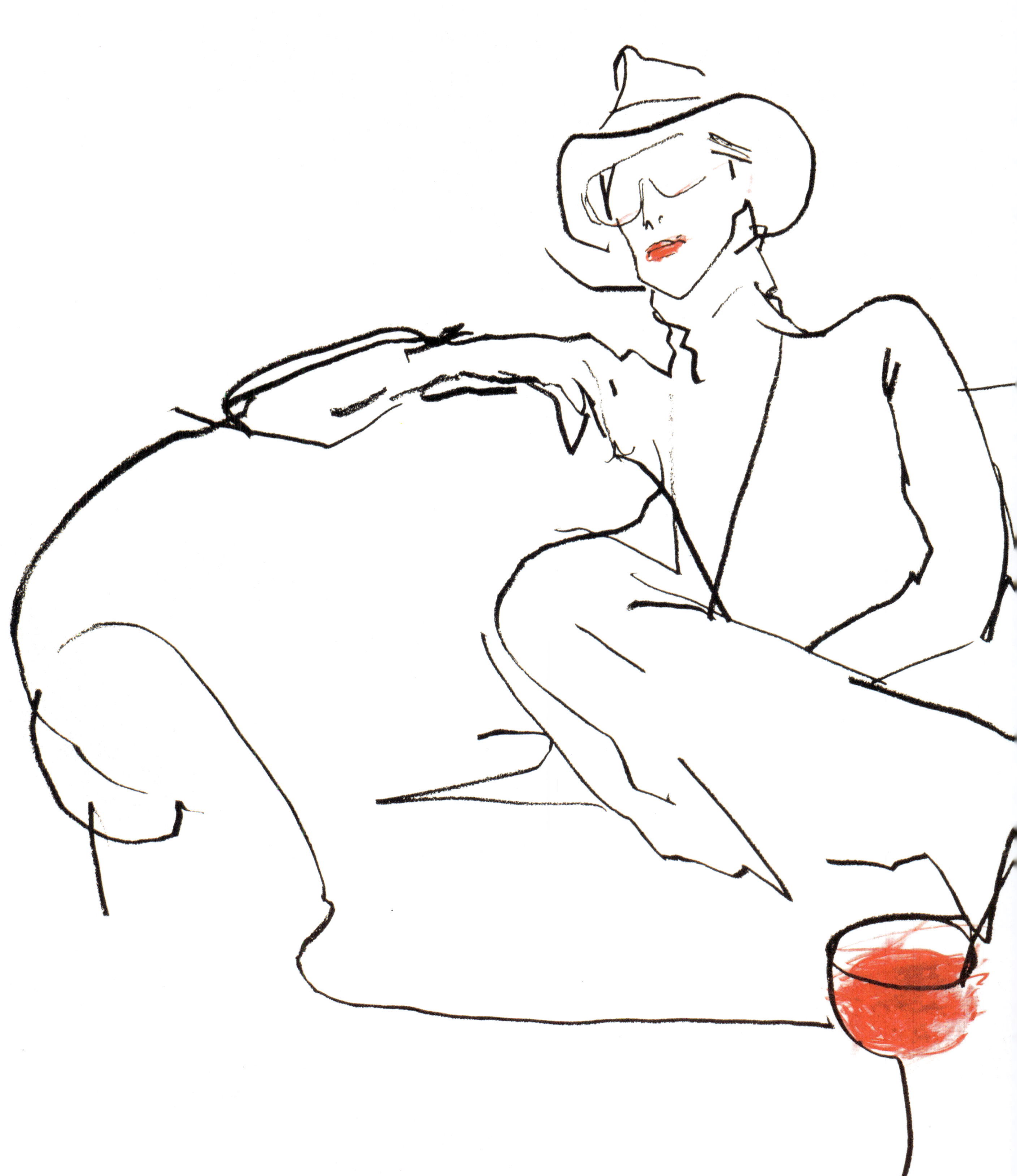

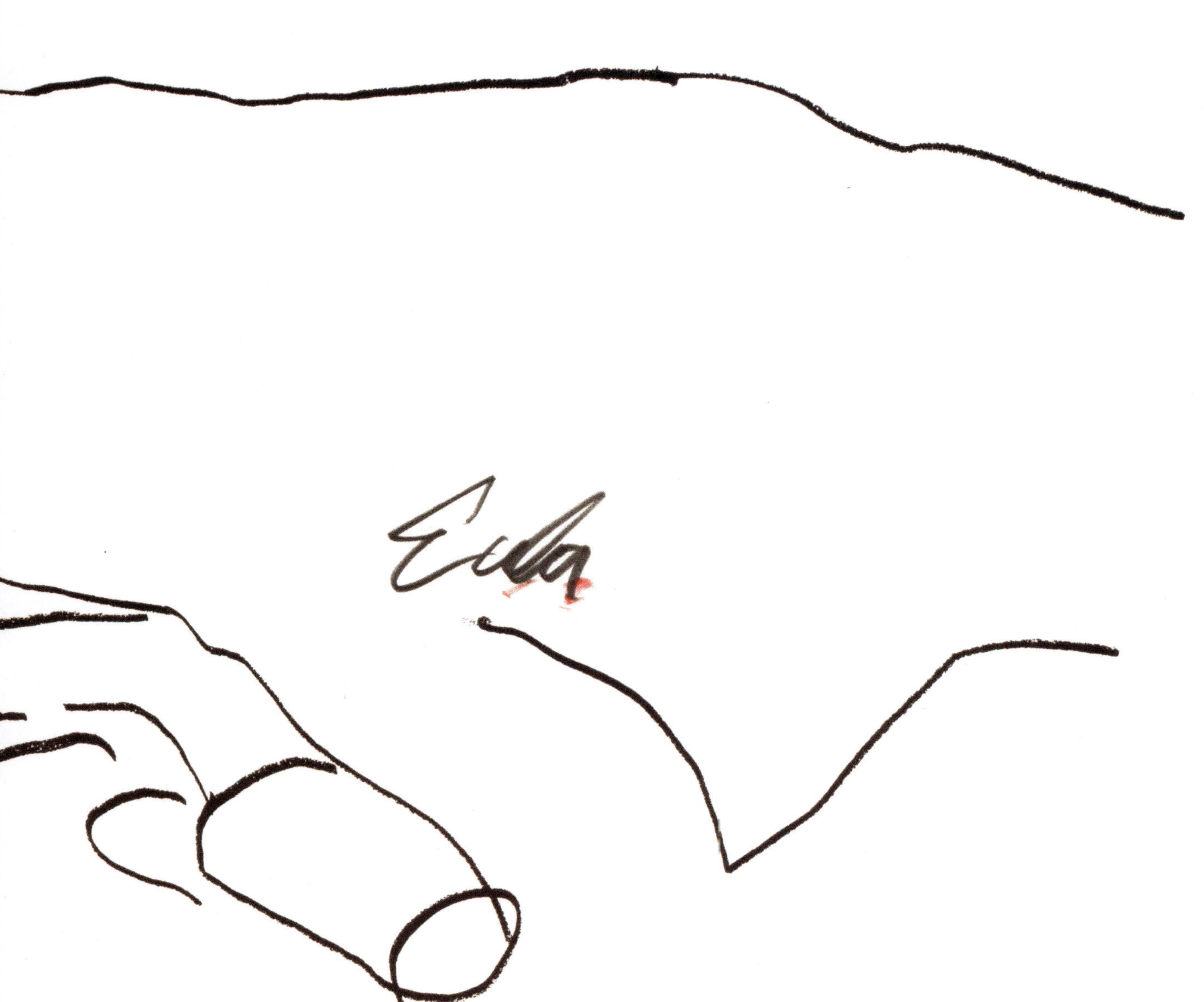

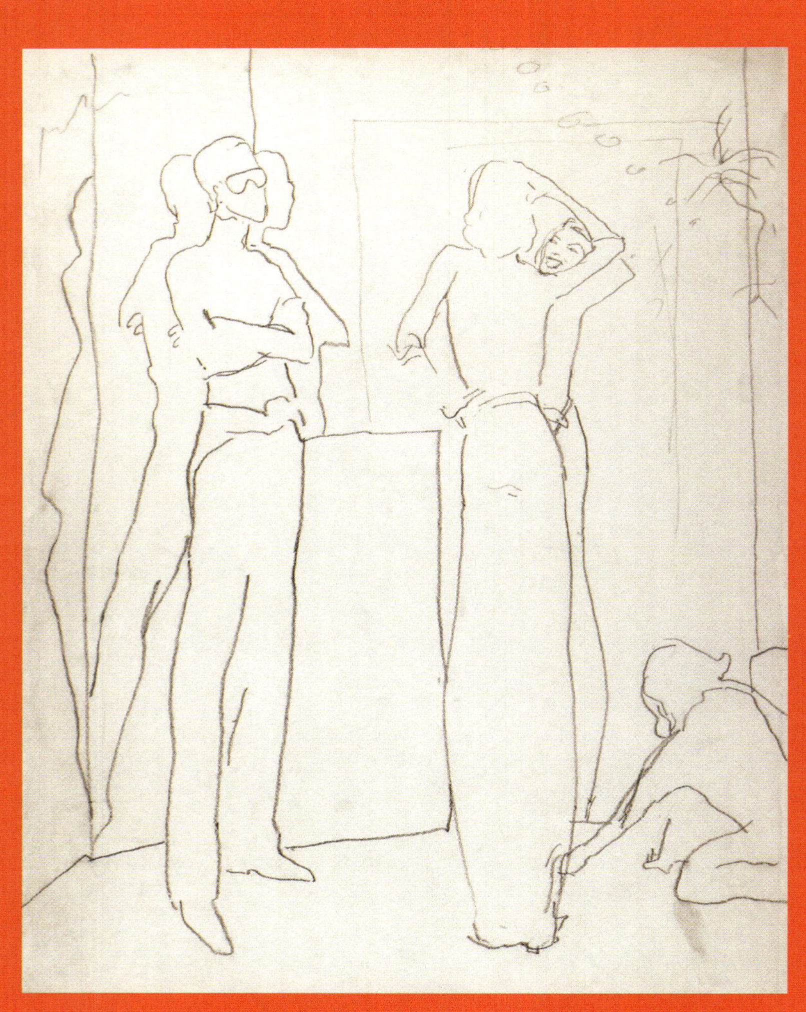

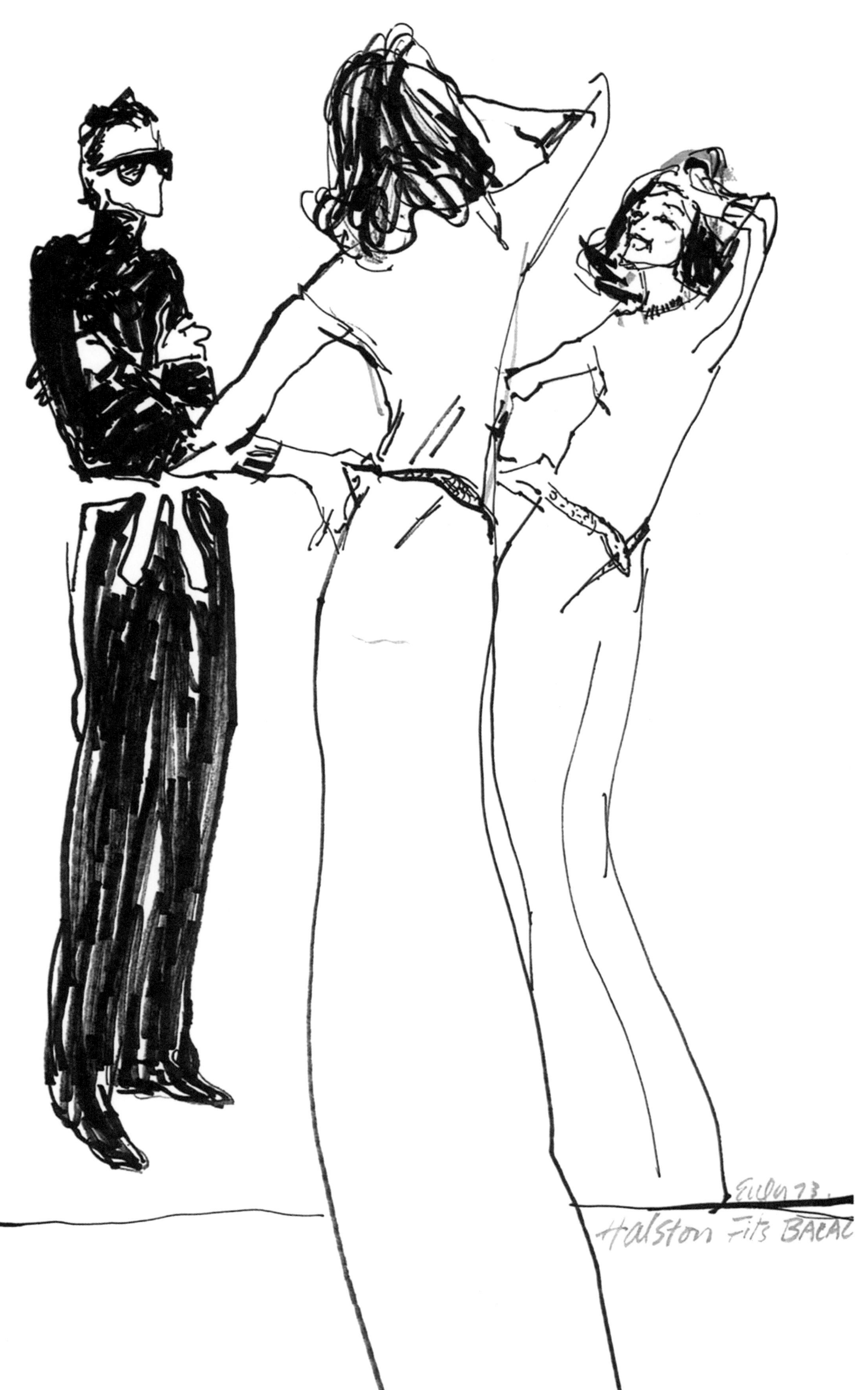

Eula 73.
Halston Fits Bacal

All through 2001, while working at the *New York Times*, I helped Bill Blass with his memoir, *Bare Blass*. As Bill's book was partly an oral history, I arranged to interview Eula at his apartment, which was then in the Osborne, a gloomy dowager of a building on West Fifty-Seventh Street. Eula and Bill had been buddies in the mid-1950s; they had spent a number of summers together on Fire Island, with a group that included the designer Jacques Tiffeau, a good-looking man who had been Christian Dior's lover; Glenn Bernbaum, who later opened the society café Mortimer's; Stevie Kaufmann, whose family owned the eponymous Pittsburgh department store; and the actor Tony Randall and his wife, Florence, who modeled for Bill. I also knew that Eula had been involved in the staging of the 1973 landmark fashion show at Versailles, when five squabbling American designers—including Blass—were pitted against the five best French couturiers of the day.

When I stepped off the elevator in the Osborne, I saw Eula waiting for me at the door of his apartment. He was short and wiry, about five-foot-six. His face was square, with a droopy salt-and-pepper mustache and a pleasant but skeptical expression. He wore large wire-rimmed glasses, an old polo shirt, khaki shorts, and, if I recall correctly, shower sandals. He led me into a long, high-ceilinged hallway, where I was immediately confronted with a career's worth of work on the walls, all in their original form—the drawings for *Sketches of Spain* and the Supremes poster, various fashion portraits, Broadway posters, and the incredibly erotic logo for the Cheetah club. I stood for a moment, gazing at the art that covered the hall from ceiling to floor. Then I followed Eula into the living room of the L-shaped apartment. The atmosphere was bohemian, with low leather couches and eclectic tables, and the artwork in this room felt more personal, with early fashion sketches and blown-out watercolors of flowers.

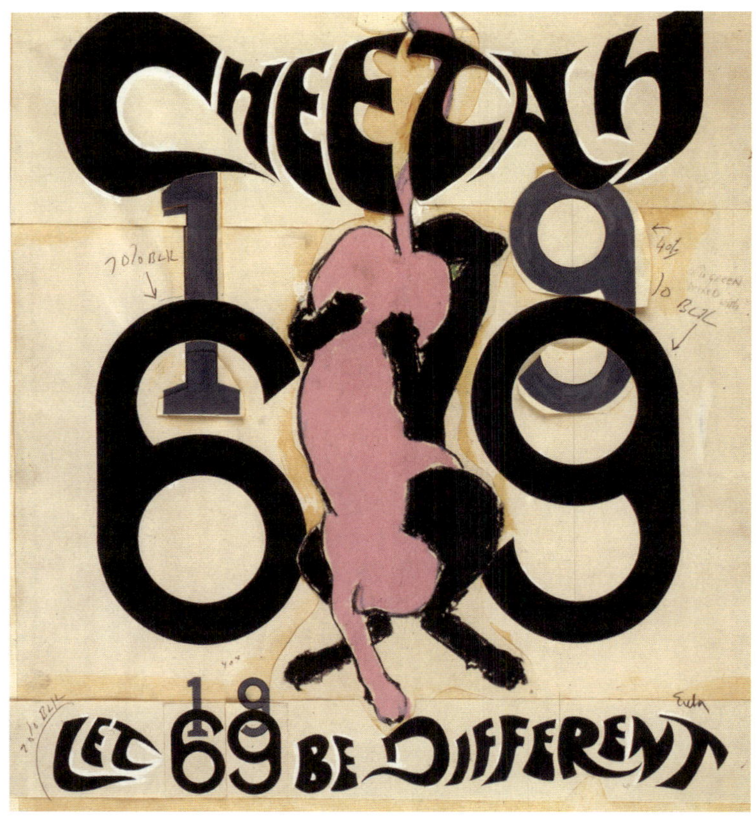

ABOVE: Logo for the Cheetah Club, 1960s. OPPOSITE: Eula sketched fashion in the moment, rarely revising. Here, a 1960s ensemble, possibly Balenciaga.

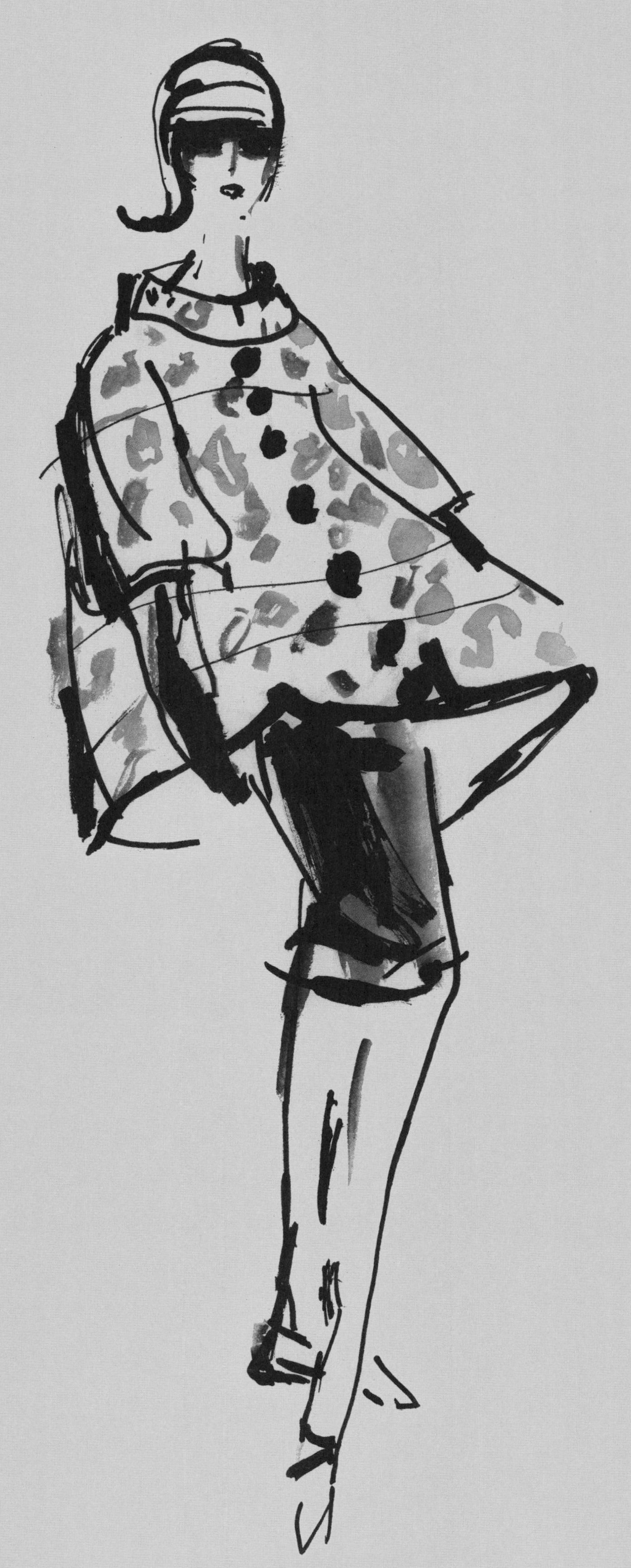

We sat and talked for about an hour. Eula had an earthy, tough way of speaking, and I could easily see why people, including Bill, enjoyed being around him. He was truthful but not a bore about it. He spoke fondly of those Fire Island summers, recalling: "None of us had much money then. Bill was well-known, but we were all the bright young boys of the world. Halston wasn't anywhere near the scene. I don't think he had even arrived in New York yet. It was another world, because it really was not that sissy crap stuff. I mean, we were a gang. God, we laughed like crazy."

When I stood up to leave, I wandered over to the little galley kitchen, whose window overlooked Seventh Avenue.

Suddenly, Eula barked, "Stand there! Don't move!"

I turned my head slightly and saw that he had a sketch pad in front of him on the counter. His hand flew across the paper as he snatched glances at me. I did as I was told, and perhaps a minute later he tore the page from the pad and handed it to me, a slight smirk on his face.

"Here," he said, "to remember the day."

I was stunned by what I saw. He had captured not so much my likeness, though he had done that, as much as a quality I'd always felt in myself but which no photograph had ever caught. It was a chin-up yet overcast beauty. I was deeply touched. I thought, *You old devil, you were observing me all along.*

Eula and I saw a lot of each other afterward. He illustrated several stories for the *New York Times*, including a feature I wrote about Belmont Park. We tramped all over the place while Eula drew exercise boys breezing horses. He was wonderful at drawing horses. And though his lungs were failing from years of smoking and drug use, he kept going. Several times I drove to his country house, a stone cottage in Hurley, New York, built in 1733 by a Dutch farmer. Eula had bought the five-acre property, which fronted the cornfields of his neighbor's farm, in the mid-1970s. The house was initially a weekend retreat and later became his permanent home. Halston spent Independence Day weekend there in 1977, according to *The Warhol Diaries*, and Eula's great friend Elsa Peretti came there often to unwind and for the casual, fend-for-yourself hospitality. Eula once said, "In the country, I put on my Italian

OPPOSITE: Eula's portrait of Cathy Horyn in his New York City kitchen, 2001.

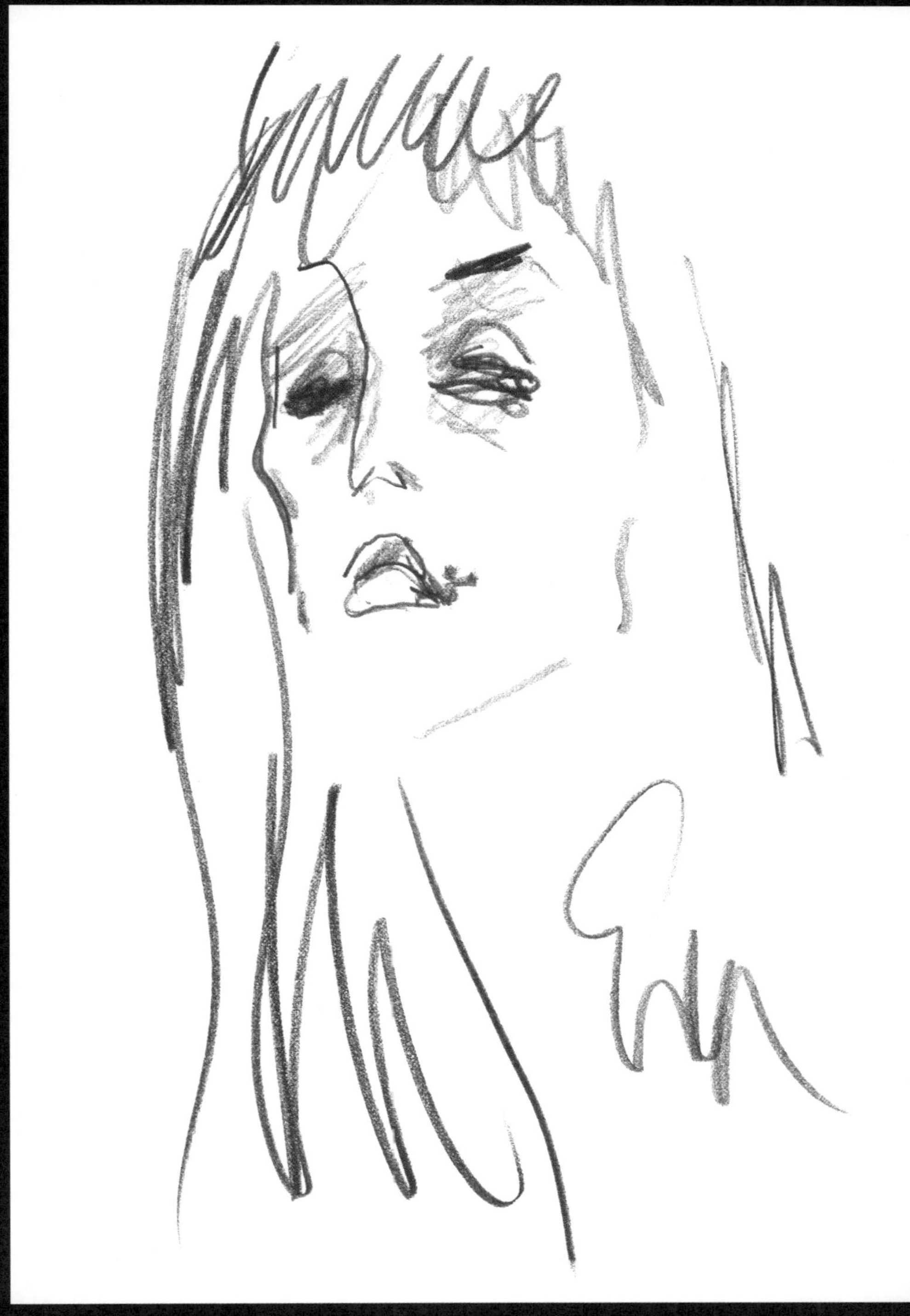

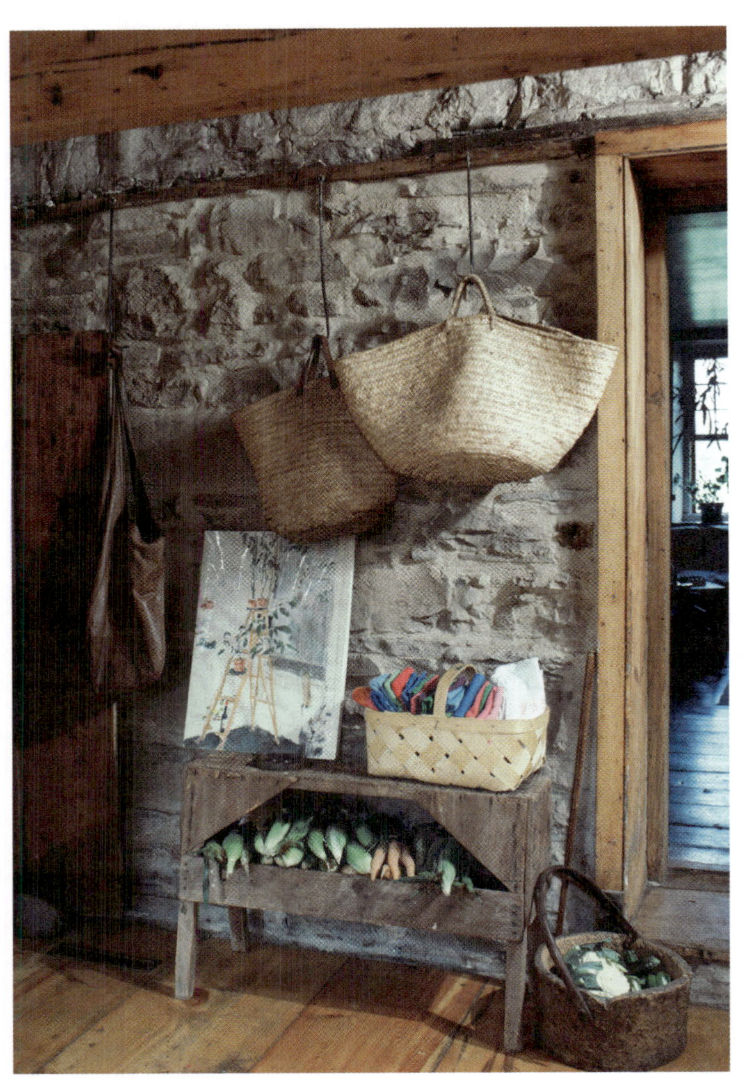
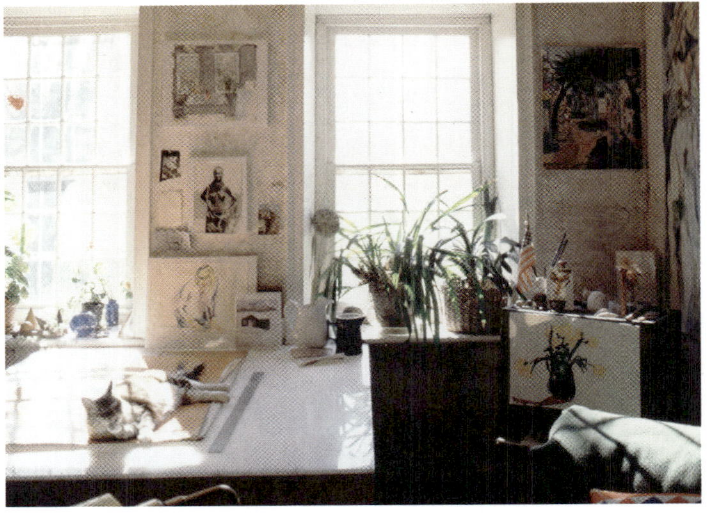
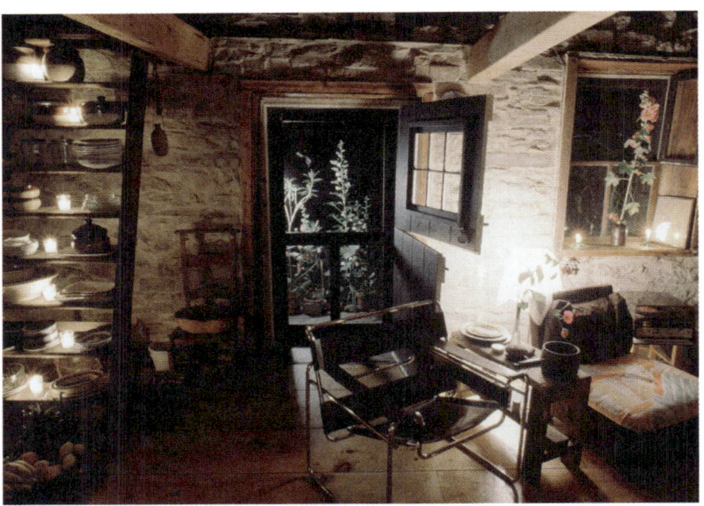
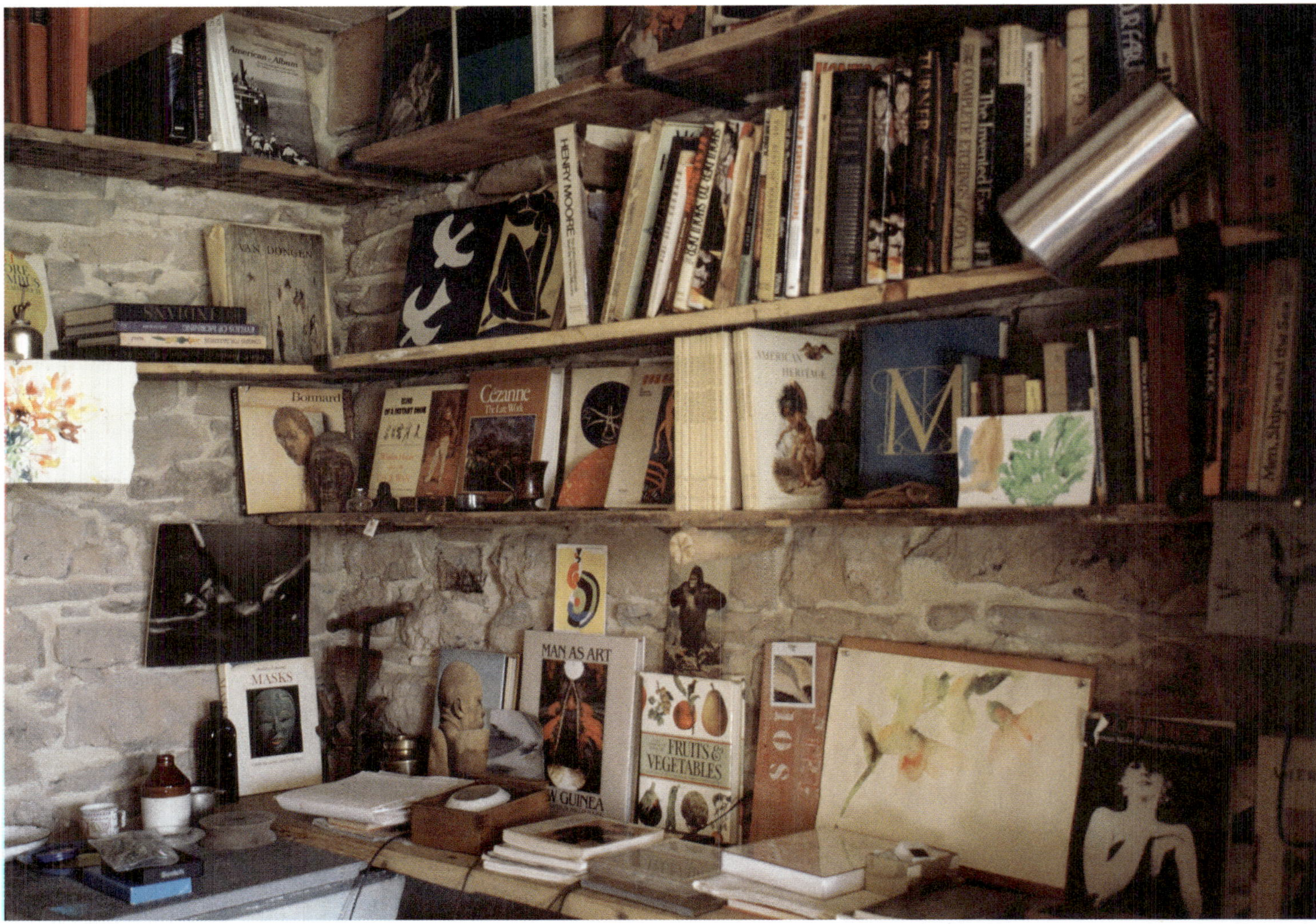

act—lots of fresh grown things, and plenty of people to enjoy them." Among those he welcomed were his eleven nieces and nephews.

Ron Ferri recalls the drive with Eula to the farm, a ritual in itself: "Every Friday we'd get in the truck—Joe never had a car—and go up the back way. He was a little cheap and didn't want to pay the tolls. We'd leave the city at two or three in the afternoon with a bottle of tequila, and by the time we got to Hurley, we had finished the bottle. We knew every flower and every church on the way up. We did this for forty years. The corncrib was my studio."

The house was Eula's domain, and it summed up his aesthetic in every broken-in old chair, rough stone wall, and improvised arrangement of flowers, paintings, and chipped pottery. His studio was in the room on the right as you entered the house, with watercolors pinned on the walls, a drafting table, and an elegant wardrobe; on the left was the living room, with its large fireplace and odd bits of furniture found

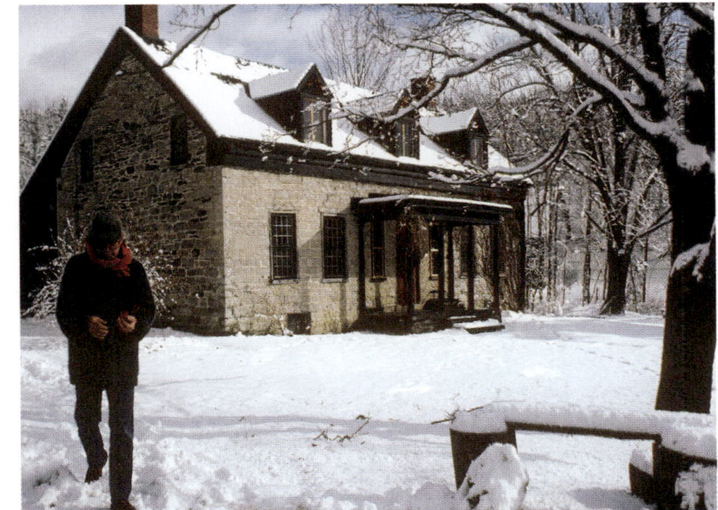

in Hudson Valley estate sales or brought from Europe, all arranged seemingly willy-nilly. The kitchen was at the back of the cottage. An old chaise longue was tucked into a corner, near a stone fireplace that Eula had re-created from memories of time spent in Italy. Propped by the back door was a wooden ladder holding plates and mugs, including the flower- and rooster-patterned dishes that he made for Tiffany in his later years, at Peretti's suggestion. There was another studio out in the garden, along with a swimming pool that had been a gift from Halston.

Eula's drawings give clear insight into his tastes and priorities. In explaining why he preferred watercolor to oil paints, Eula said, "I like the immediate. I like the essence of its having been there and gone and then stopped. That's watercolor, clothes, a moving figure, a beautiful flower that blooms, and at the height of its breath the goddamned falling petals are its most gorgeous moment." That was the sense of the house, too. It had a gone-to-pot beauty, and right away it put you in a good mood. You wanted to bottle its essence. Milton Greene's son Joshua, who was

OPPOSITE: The interior of Eula's home in Hurley, New York. ABOVE: Eula outside the Hurley house, 1990s. PAGES 32–33: Eula often painted watercolors in his garden in Hurley.

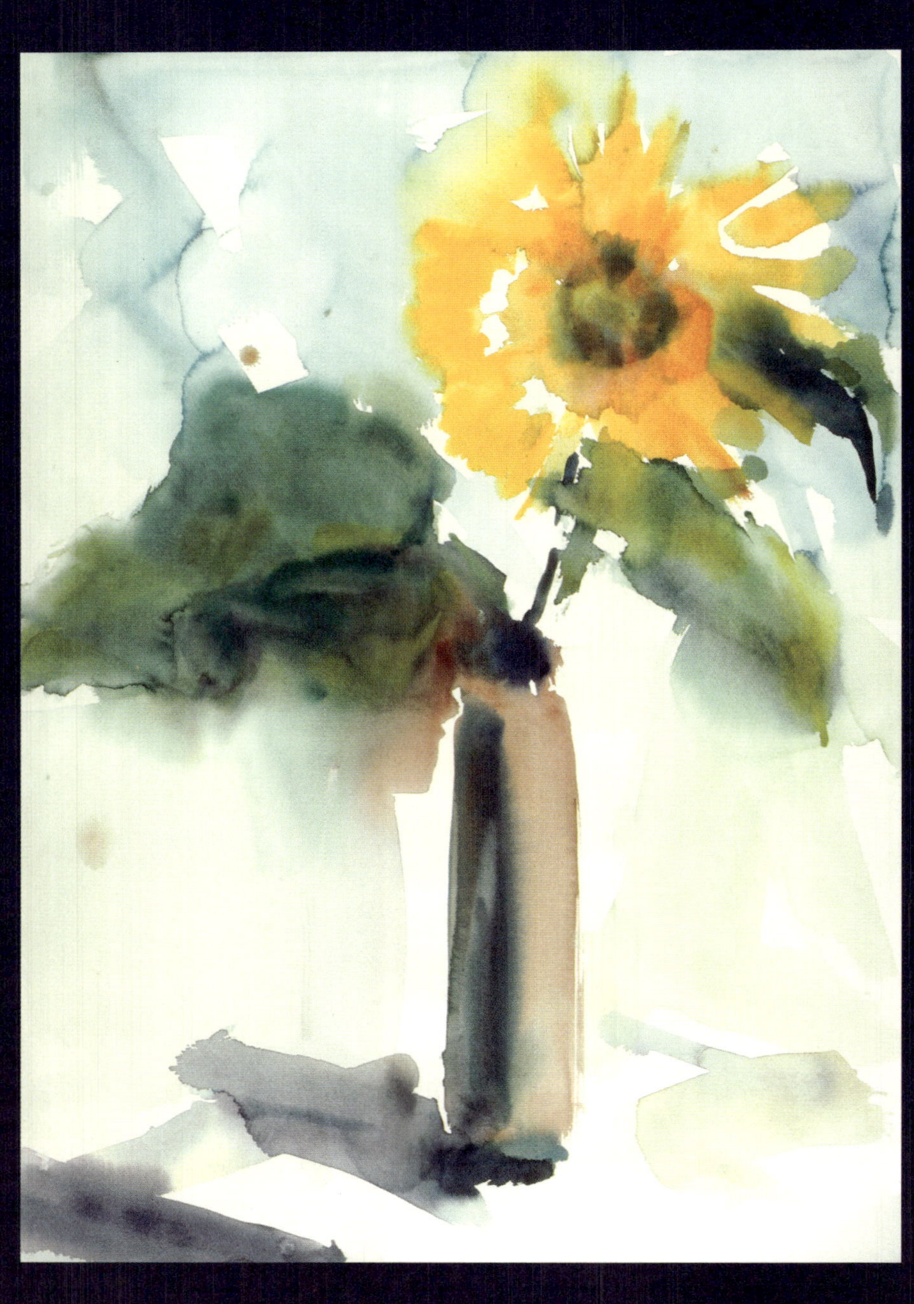

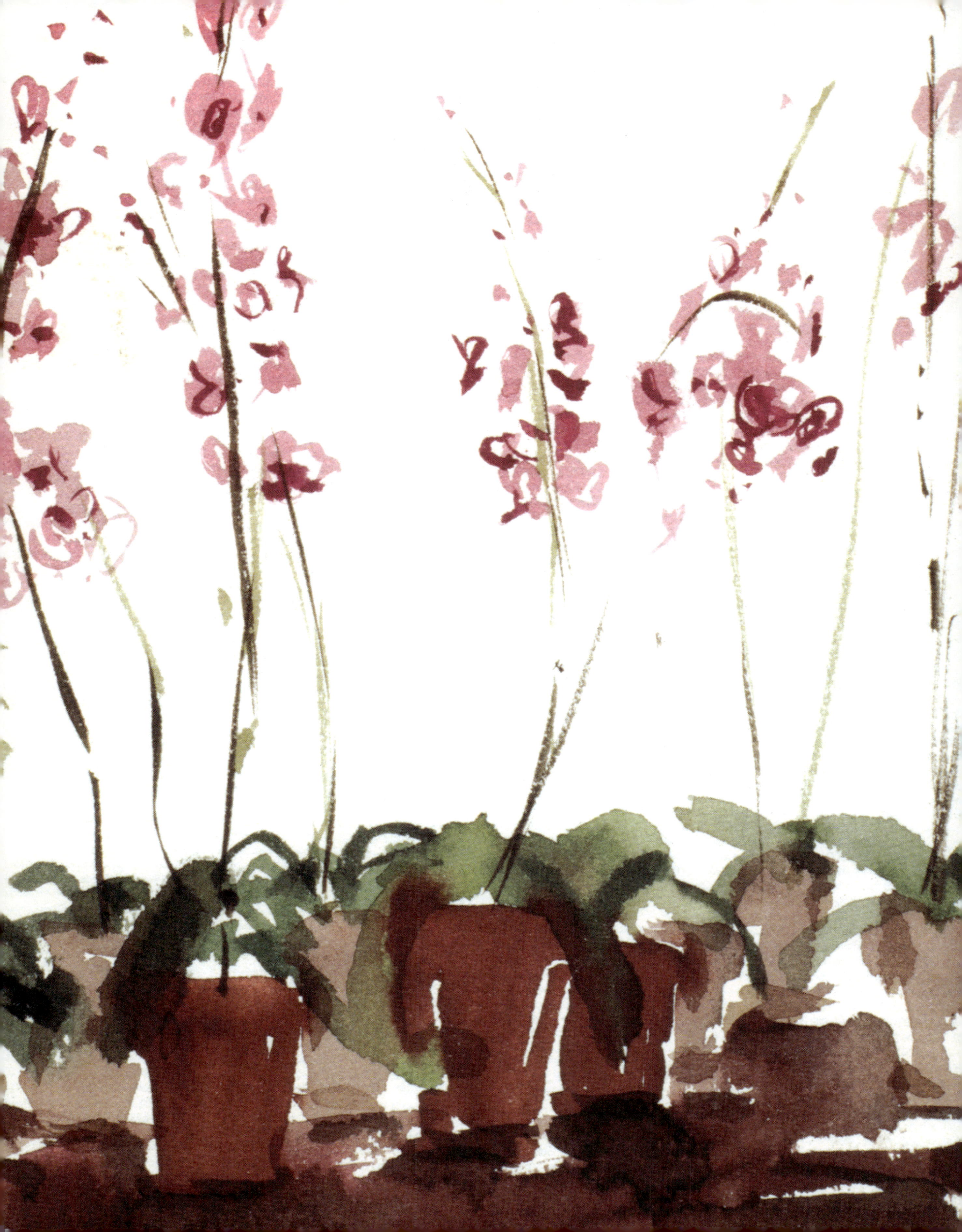

as close to Eula as he was to his own father, made dozens of visits. He says, "To me, everything about that house was an ongoing visual game that Joe played to amuse himself. He excelled in that ability—it wasn't just the painting. But if all of that could have translated into being a real fine-art painter, and being known for it, then Joe would be the superstar we wished he had become. He was doing the work for everyone else." And not his own work.

There is some truth in what Greene says. It is one of the puzzles of Eula's career that "the most important person in New York," to quote Warhol, never made it bigger than he did. He never stopped working, but he preferred the infinitely immediate to the carefully revised, and he couldn't find a way to bridge the two. And as Greene concedes, Eula would have been a very poor boss if he had had a large art or design studio. "He could never have people working for him without their being slaves," he says with a laugh. "He didn't know how to be appropriate or politically correct. Nobody was going to tell Joe what to do."

Eula had a way of sizing up people or situations with a single deft remark, and, equally, cutting them down if they were grand or a windbag. No one was immune. China Machado says, "Joe would bullshit, but he didn't let anyone else do it. He would just get you. He knew how to chop you off if there was any bullshit." One particularly hair-raising episode occurred at a Saint Laurent couture show in the early 1980s. Eula was there by contract to sketch the collection for Lizzette Kattan, then editor of Italian *Harper's Bazaar*. Kattan, in her twenties at the time, had grown to rely on his company to get couturiers to take her seriously. "I brought him everywhere," she says. "He was like my shadow. When I would go to appointments to see Yves or Karl Lagerfeld, he would always be with me. To have somebody like Joe with me, aside from being an inspiration, gave them trust. He was extremely protective of me. He respected my views, and at the same time . . ." Kattan pauses, smiling. "Sometimes I had to walk away from him." Recalling the Saint Laurent show, she says, "After the third dress had come down the runway, Joe stood up and started screaming, 'This is couture? These are the worst fucking clothes I've seen in my life, and we're leaving.' He took me and we left. I thought I was going to die of embarrassment." Amends had to be made to the designer and his partner, Pierre Bergé; and Giuseppe Della Schiava, the publisher of Italian and French *Harper's Bazaar*, had to get involved to turn things around. Eula continued to work for the magazine until well into the 1990s, and he and Kattan remained close for the rest of his life. Still, I said to her, it was a wonder he wasn't fired that day. "Yes, he could have lost his job," she says. "But Joe was that kind of man. Did he care? No."

I didn't see that side of Eula, as I said. He was older when I met him, though when I visited him in the country I used to think that it was he who was very young and I who was old. He would be on the other side of the butcher-block island that served as his kitchen table, giving a final stir to the pasta he had made. He often wore shorts, an old sweatshirt, and a faded red kerchief at his neck. If it was autumn, a fire would be blazing in the fireplace.

He would ask me about the stories I was working on and make helpful suggestions. He had great curiosity. I suppose I could have asked him about Chanel and Halston—there was plenty of wine and opportunity. But the truth is that it never crossed my mind to ask Eula about the past, because he had such a contemporary outlook. All of his thoughts and energy flowed in one direction, allowing him to refresh himself with the new and to begin again and yet again.

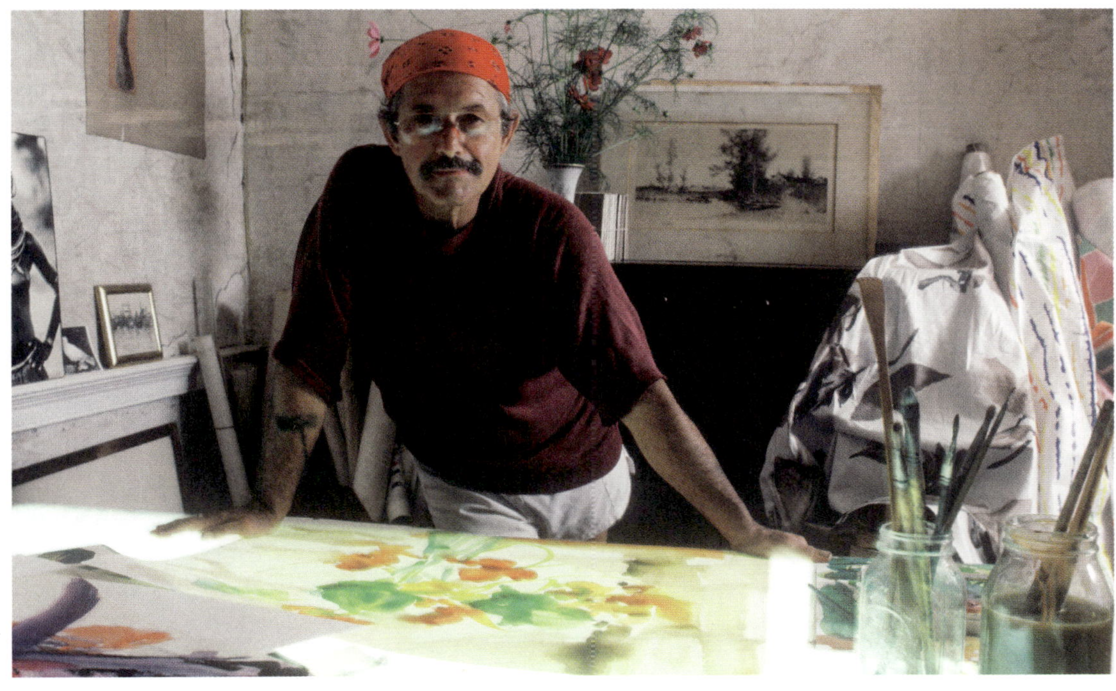

LEFT: Eula in his Hurley studio.

Joseph Benedict Eula was born on January 16, 1925, in South Norwalk, Connecticut. His father, Dominick, was a civil engineer. Perhaps as early as 1919, when Joe's older sister, Margaret ("Marge"), was born, Dominick left his wife, Lena, to supervise a roads project in the Dominican Republic, staying in touch with her by letters. After his return in 1924, he and Lena had three boys, all with January birthdays. Joe, whom his father nicknamed Gig, or Giggy, was followed by Anthony ("Toe") and Dominick ("Babe"). Then, in March 1927, Dominick Sr. died of heart disease. He was thirty-four.

For Lena, this must have been a terrible blow. Somehow, though, she had the wherewithal to open a grocery store in South Norwalk, and while she was working, Marge looked after her three brothers in their house on Couch Street. "Marge was very instrumental in our growing up," Anthony says. When he was nine, Joe went to work in the store on Saturdays and for a few hours after church on Sundays so that his mother could prepare lunch for a family gathering. You never knew whether it was going to be for ten or fifty people, Joe used to say. He was deeply devoted to Lena and often said of her, "I was born to the greatest free-spirited gypsy the world has ever known."

Nonetheless, while her boys were still young, Lena remarried—to a man named Joe Paqua, who owned a liquor store. "We could never figure out why Mother married him," Anthony says. "He wasn't much of a father." Financial security was no doubt one reason; the country was in the midst of the Depression. Whatever his feelings toward his stepfather, who moved into the house on Couch Street, Joe had plans of his own. In 1942, a few months shy of his eighteenth birthday, he enlisted in the army. He was assigned to the 10th Mountain Division, a ski outfit that saw some of its heaviest action in the Apennines and in Italy's Po Valley. Joe had been a good skier in high school. In later years, he made light of his war experience, saying, "I never had so many men in my life," and that the only things he liked about his army uniform were "the boots, the skis, and the parkas."

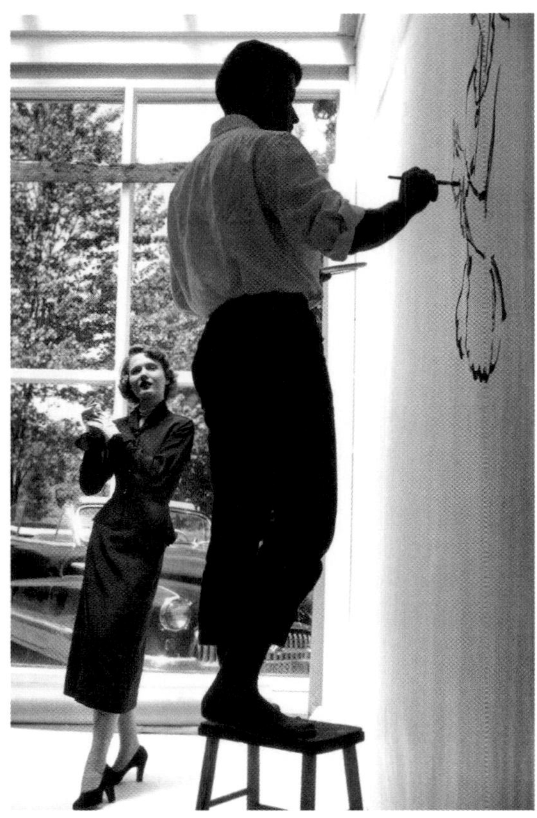

ABOVE: Eula sketching a model in New York for a backdrop, 1950s.
OPPOSITE: A drawing of a tailored ensemble, probably for *Harper's Bazaar*, early 1950s.

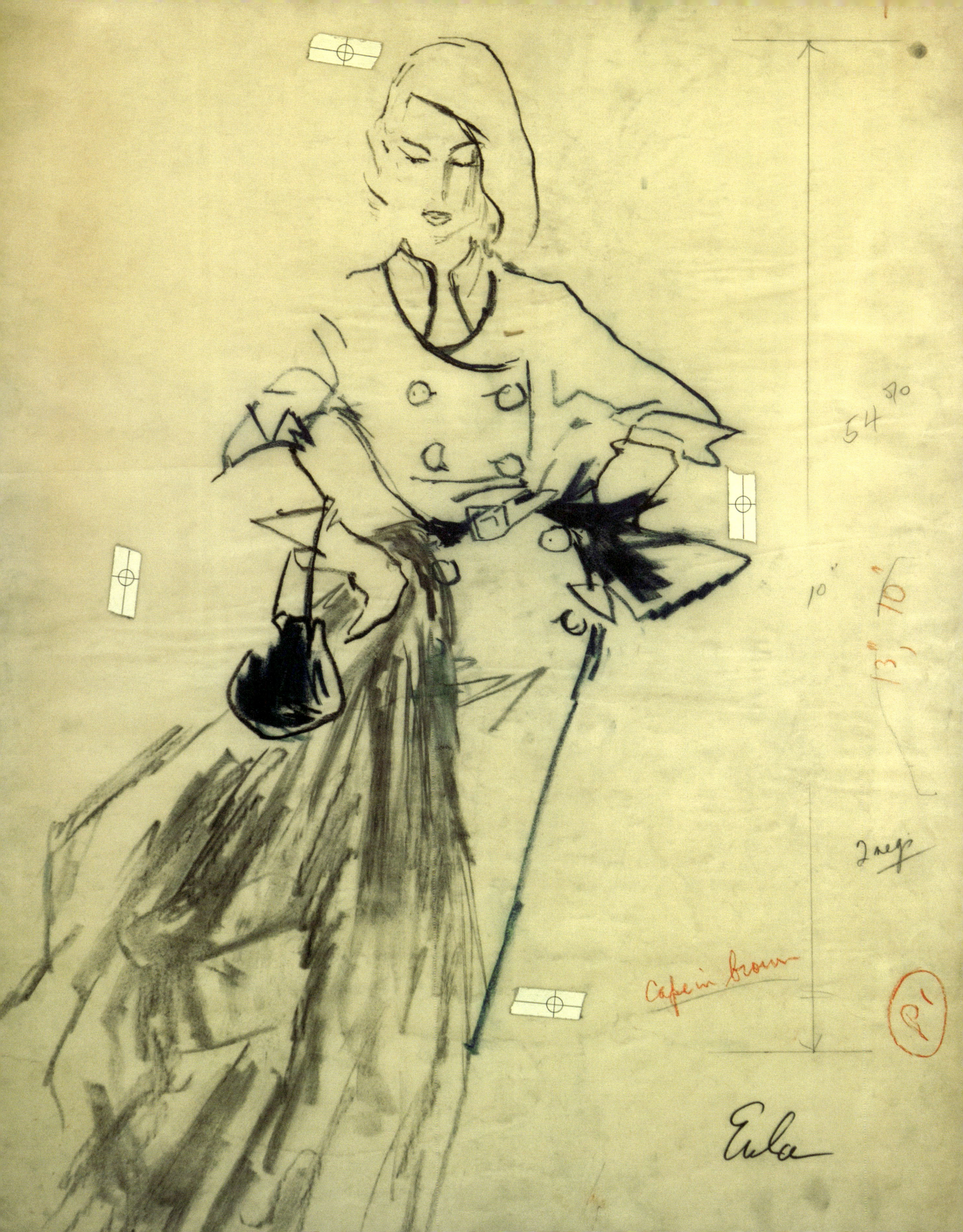

54⁸⁰
10"
13" 70"
2 neg
cape in brown
Eula

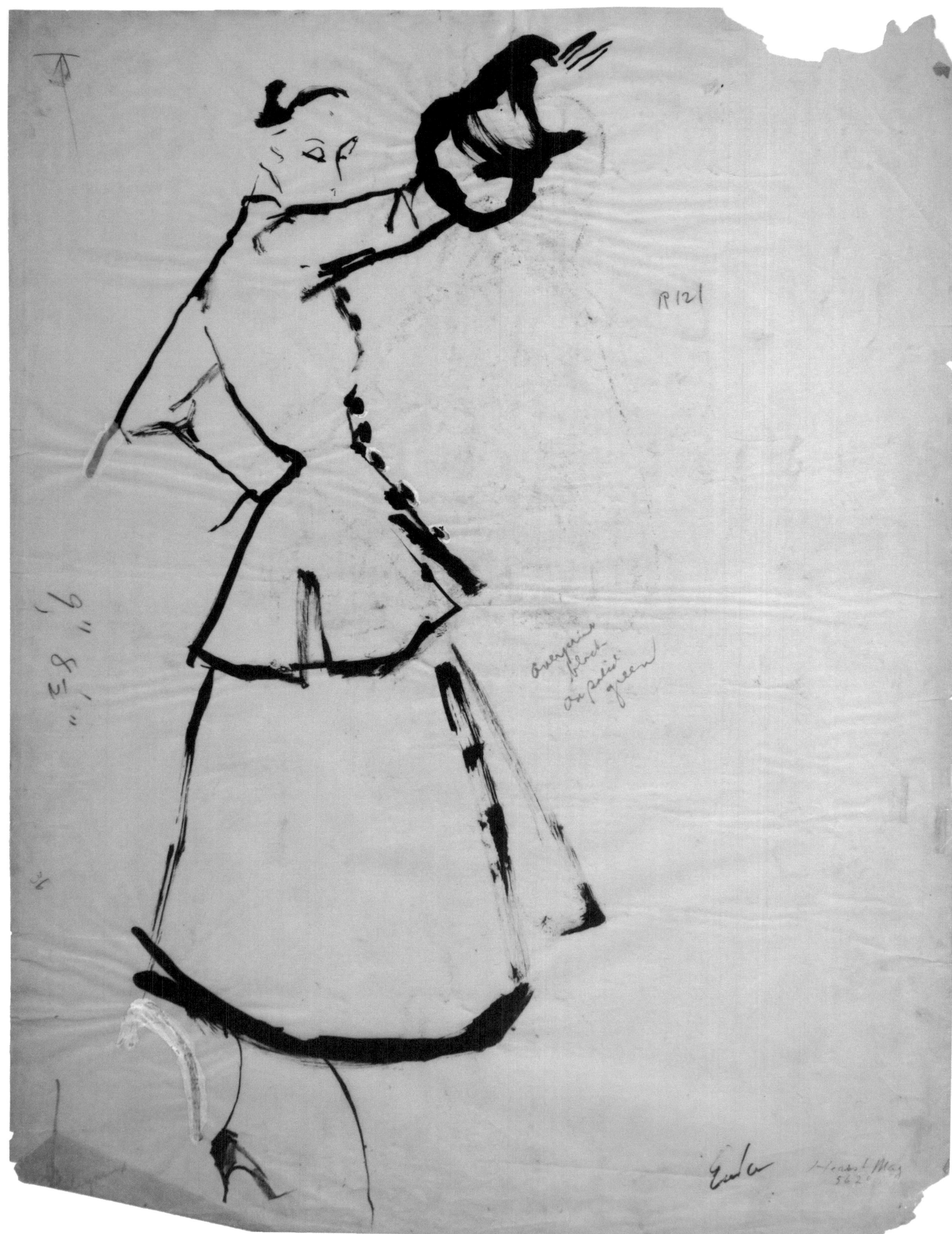

R121
overgaine
black
ox palice green

But as his wartime letters to Lena reveal, Joe was more thoughtful than his glib comments might indicate. Several letters, written from the front, survived. In one, he wrote:

> Sitting here in this old Italian farmhouse by the fire seems all so unreal. Every little noise is magnified to that of a terrific thunderstorm. It's been so long since I've heard a radio or heard any news—for all I know this damn war might be over. Your visions of the front are probably bad—I won't try to soft-soap you. (I never was able to.) You couldn't in your wildest dreams imagine the horrors of it all. I will say everything has its lighter moments, and the days of our present story are just that. . . . You keep asking for pictures. That's out. At least until I can get to Rome or someplace similar. This isn't the U.S., Fatty— altho on days such as we've been having I can almost forget myself. The fire is almost out and frankly Mom so am I—you know Mom, babies aren't the only ones that cry.
>
> —All ways and always, Gig

In another letter, he casually mentioned that he had been awarded the Bronze Star, saying only, "It was a big affair with lots of eyewash and hand shaking." Naturally, Joe might have been eager to avoid adding to his mother's worries. But according to his medal citation, he had "undauntedly ordered" a machine gun to fire on an enemy dugout and had then advanced, firing, until seven Germans surrendered. The fight happened on February 22, 1945, at Mount Belvedere, Italy. Years later, when Eula gave his Bronze Star to Marge's son, Nick, he again sought to downplay his heroics. He told his nephew, "The real truth, sonny boy, is that our guys just walked by them and the Germans gave up." Still, the war must have meant something to him. His life had been spared, after all.

Of course, another explanation is that he didn't want to be encumbered by anything, or anyone. I asked several people about Eula's sexual orientation and whether he'd ever had a significant relationship. On the second point, the answer was emphatically no; he had love affairs and many flings (he once disappeared at the start of the Rome collections after picking someone up), but he never had a live-in relationship. "I don't think he had time for anyone," says James Devens, a friend of thirty years, who maintains that Eula was gay. But others believe that he was bisexual. "Whatever moved his fancy," says Joshua Greene. Kattan concurs: "Yeah, totally. And he didn't hide it. He had that kind of charisma where he could get to the level of everybody." She adds, "I think Joe must have had a crush on Barbara Allen." Many men in the 1970s were probably in love with Allen; she was beautiful and fun to be with, and she and Eula were extremely close. She saw less of him after she married aeronautics tycoon Henryk de Kwiatkowski, but they spoke regularly on the phone until his death.

Most women had no illusions about their adored Joe. Susan Nevelson, an artist and textile designer who has spent much of her life in Italy, met Eula around 1948 in New York. She says they tried sleeping together, "[but] it didn't work." Still, they remained friends. Nevelson, now eighty-eight, told me, "Joe was definitely gay. We had discussions about that." The confusion seems in keeping with Eula's own views about self-determination. He hated the identity politics of gay liberation, comparing its excesses to "Victorian footstools." He was also of a generation that thought one's sex life was nobody else's business. "My sex is obvious," he said. "It's all over my face."

After the war, Eula jumped into the commercial art world. Although photography was dominant at the time, fashion illustration was having a golden period—though it wouldn't last—and there was plenty of work, at magazines as well as department stores. With the enactment of the GI Bill, he was able to continue his education, attending the Art Students League in New York City. There he met Nevelson, who had a small child. She recalls, "One day he called me up, and he wanted to know if I could model for him. He was working for *Town & Country*. I told him I could but that I couldn't leave my daughter, who was then about two. He said, 'Bring the brat with you.'" Nevelson laughs. "So I did, and we worked together a lot after that."

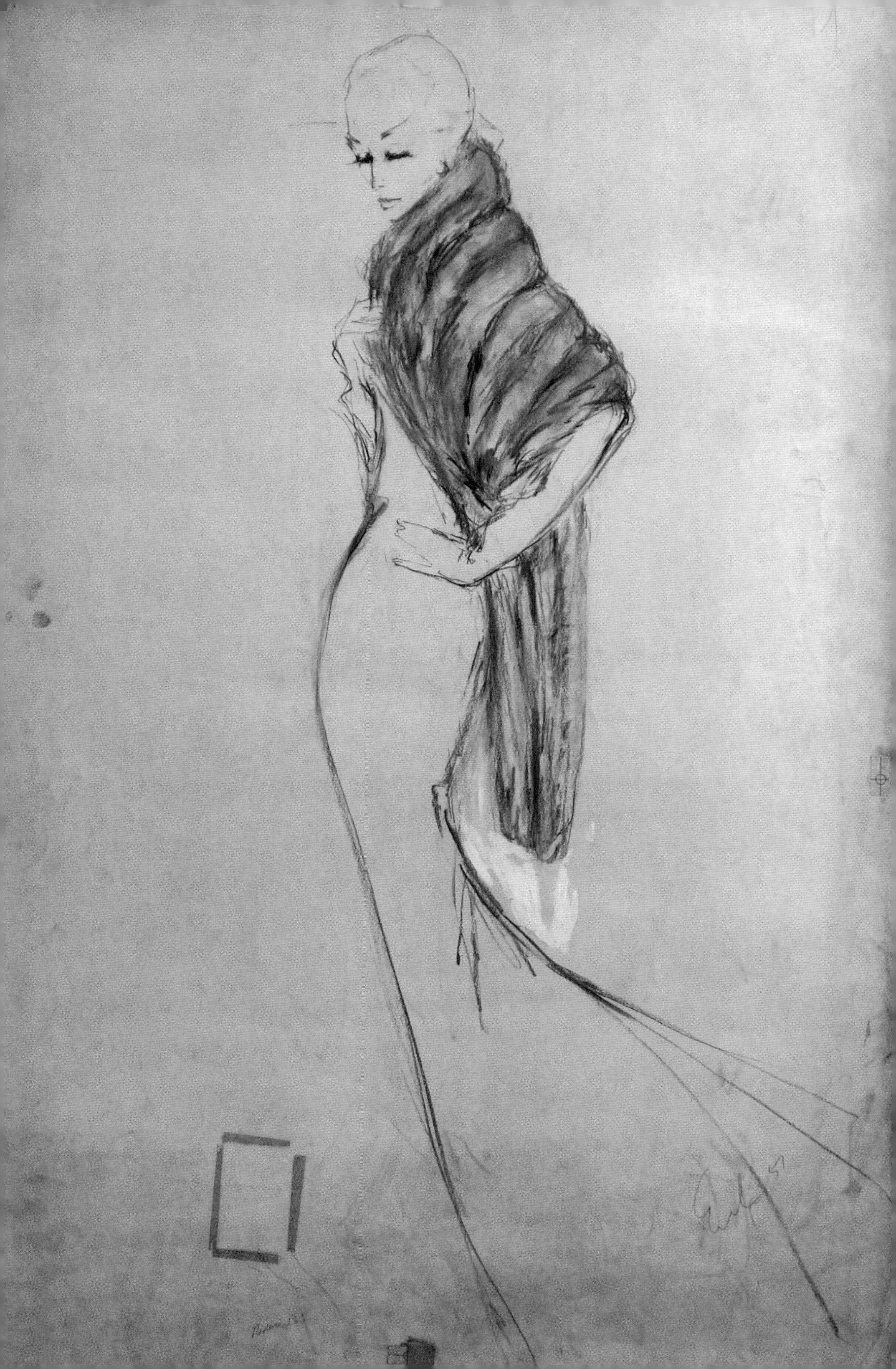

Eula's stock-in-trade was telling people what they were doing wrong, and how he could do it better. For instance, around the same time, he took his sketch pad to Bonwit Teller, then on Fifth Avenue and Fifty-Sixth Street, where the windows featured Dior's new American label, and knocked out some sketches. "Then I went upstairs to the executive offices," Eula recalled in his unpublished memoir. "The art director of Bonwit's was named Ralph Dadieo, a great Dadaist. I said, 'This is the way your ads ought to look.' He said, 'You're right,' and he gave me a job." Eula didn't say what he proposed, but the point of the story was to show that, ever "undaunted," he could act on impulse and get what he wanted.

One person he couldn't fool was Diana Vreeland. In his unpublished memoir, he said, "She has influenced my life to the point where if I talk to that woman on the phone for half an hour, no one can stop me for a week." He found her incredibly inspiring, but her first assignment for him, when she was fashion editor of *Harper's Bazaar*, was a hilarious test—and a classic bit of Vreeland. First she asked Eula to do an illustration using only the color red, but she stressed that it should be a very particular shade of red. "She said, 'You know, it's got to look like red. You know what I mean, *red*. There are ninety reds.' She didn't want any black. She just wanted red on a white background. You know, you can only get so many variations on the breakdown of red.... For two weeks I worked on that job. Finally I went to her and she was all swathed in a marvelous leopard-print chiffon scarf—I could hardly see her eyes. I said, 'I don't know what you are talking about.' And she said, 'Well, isn't that amusing.' They gave the job to a photographer."

No doubt Eula laughed at her response. They became great buddies after that, and in time he followed her to *Vogue* and later helped out with her early costume exhibits at the Metropolitan Museum of Art, beginning with her tribute to Balenciaga in

OPPOSITE: Eula sketching a model in a New York City studio, late 1940s. ABOVE: A sketch of Diana Vreeland entering a Jean Dessès collection presentation in Paris, spring 1968.

1973. It was Eula who came up with the gesture of covering the mannequins' faces with a layer of tinfoil and a ladies' stocking—"anything to get rid of them," he said.

In the late 1940s, *Bazaar* sent him to cover the Paris collections. "That was the true beginning of my Paris experiences," he said.

Filled with new fashion and rivalries, postwar Paris must have been a stimulant for Eula. One wonders if he encountered Keogh or Gruau, who were just emerging. Like Gruau and other classical illustrators, Eula was influenced by Toulouse-Lautrec; an early business card describes his style in that manner. Eula was good at line and movement, but he couldn't capture "the arrogance of fashionable elegance," as the art critic William Packer noted of René Bouët-Willaumez, who caught mondaine Paris to its teeth. But Eula probably couldn't have cared less about that stuff. And with social and political mores changing quickly—and soon to explode in the 1960s—it didn't behoove him to follow anyone or be conventional.

One of Eula's best drawings dates from this period: a Charles James evening dress with a draped shoulder. Published in *Town & Country* in October 1951, the delicate, bare-bones sketch doesn't suggest the complexity of James's craft—nor should it, since people desire clothes mainly for their effect. Minnelli, an expert in these matters, nails the quality, though here she is describing Eula's sketches for Halston: "You saw the dress or the pantsuit and how it moved on the woman. And that was part of the sale, I thought. Because, you know, I move all the time. I would see one of Joe's sketches and it was always true. You'd try that dress on and it did exactly what you saw in the sketch." A similar thing happened when he made the poster for *Liza with a "Z"* after watching a rehearsal. As Minnelli says, "He remembered more than just the costume. He remembered the energy and the intent of the performance."

In later years, Eula's drawings verged on frantic caricature, but underlying everything he did was a faith in the impromptu gesture. And as with the zingers that came out of his mouth, there was equally the certainty that he would get away with it. Costume jeweler Kenneth Jay Lane recalls such a moment, when Eula and Greene were shooting a film of Lane's pieces for the 1966 Coty Awards show:

OPPOSITE: Love from the 1980s: correspondence from Yves Saint Laurent, Hubert de Givenchy, Diana Vreeland, and Yves Saint Laurent and Pierre Bergé.

TELEX FROM FRANCE

SEPTEMBER 5, 1983

DEAR JOE,

I FIND YOUR DRAWINGS IN HARPER'S BAZAAR TO BE MARVELOUS AND CONTINUE
TO TELL YOU OF ALL MY ADMIRATION FOR THE WAY THAT YOU KNEW HOW TO
EXPRESS THE VERY ESSENCE OF MY COLLECTION.

WITH ALL MY LOVE,

YVES

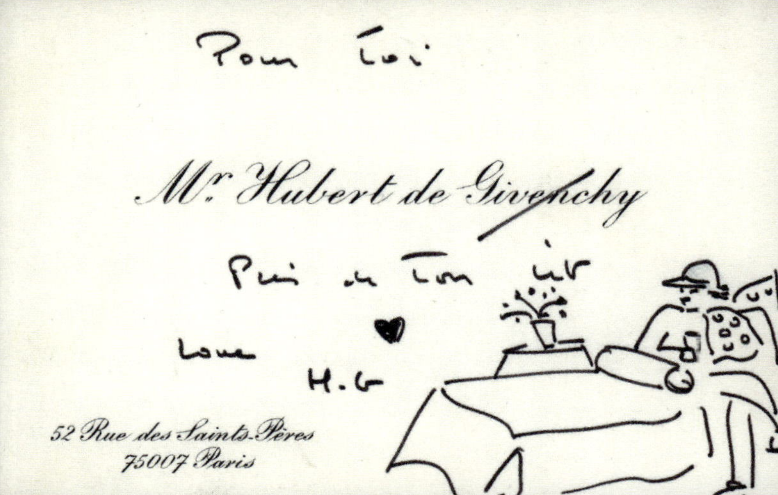

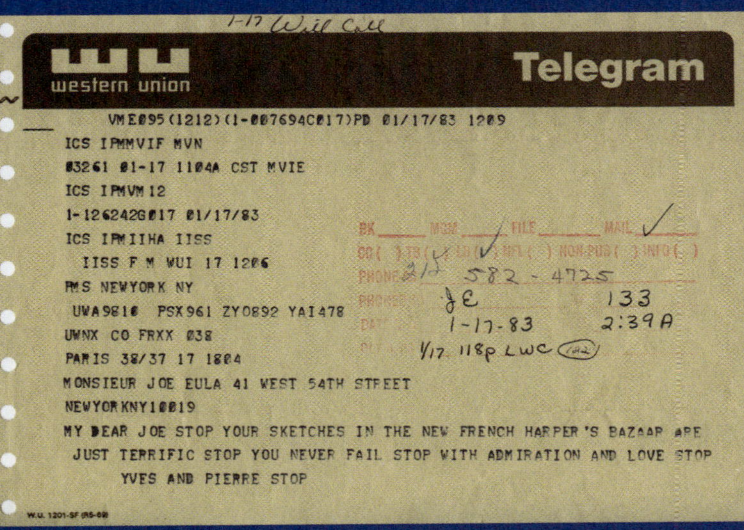

Western Union

Telegram

VME095(1212)(1-007694C017)PD 01/17/83 1209
ICS IPMMVIF MVN
83261 01-17 1104A CST MVIE
ICS IPMVM12
1-126242G017 01/17/83
ICS IPMIIHA IISS
   IISS F M WUI 17 1206
PMS NEWYORK NY
  UWA9810 PSX961 ZYO892 YAI478
UWNX CO FRXX 038
PARIS 38/37 17 1804
MONSIEUR JOE EULA 41 WEST 54TH STREET
NEWYORKNY10019
MY DEAR JOE STOP YOUR SKETCHES IN THE NEW FRENCH HARPER'S BAZAAR ARE
 JUST TERRIFIC STOP YOU NEVER FAIL STOP WITH ADMIRATION AND LOVE STOP
       YVES AND PIERRE STOP

The Metropolitan Museum of Art

SPECIAL CONSULTANT

April 10, 1981

Dearest Joe,

    Thank you so very much for seeing about the
Italian "Harper's Bazaar." It is a perfectly
wonderful resumé of our exhibition - the photographs
are fantastic - the very best we have seen.

    I adore the sketch! There is no one in the
world who wouldn't envy that nose, throat and the
turn of the hair!!

    You are a great, great artist with a sense of
dash and the ridiculous which is, of course, the
only thing!

                    Very sincerely yours,

                    Diana Vreeland

Joe Eula
41 West 54th Street
New York, New York

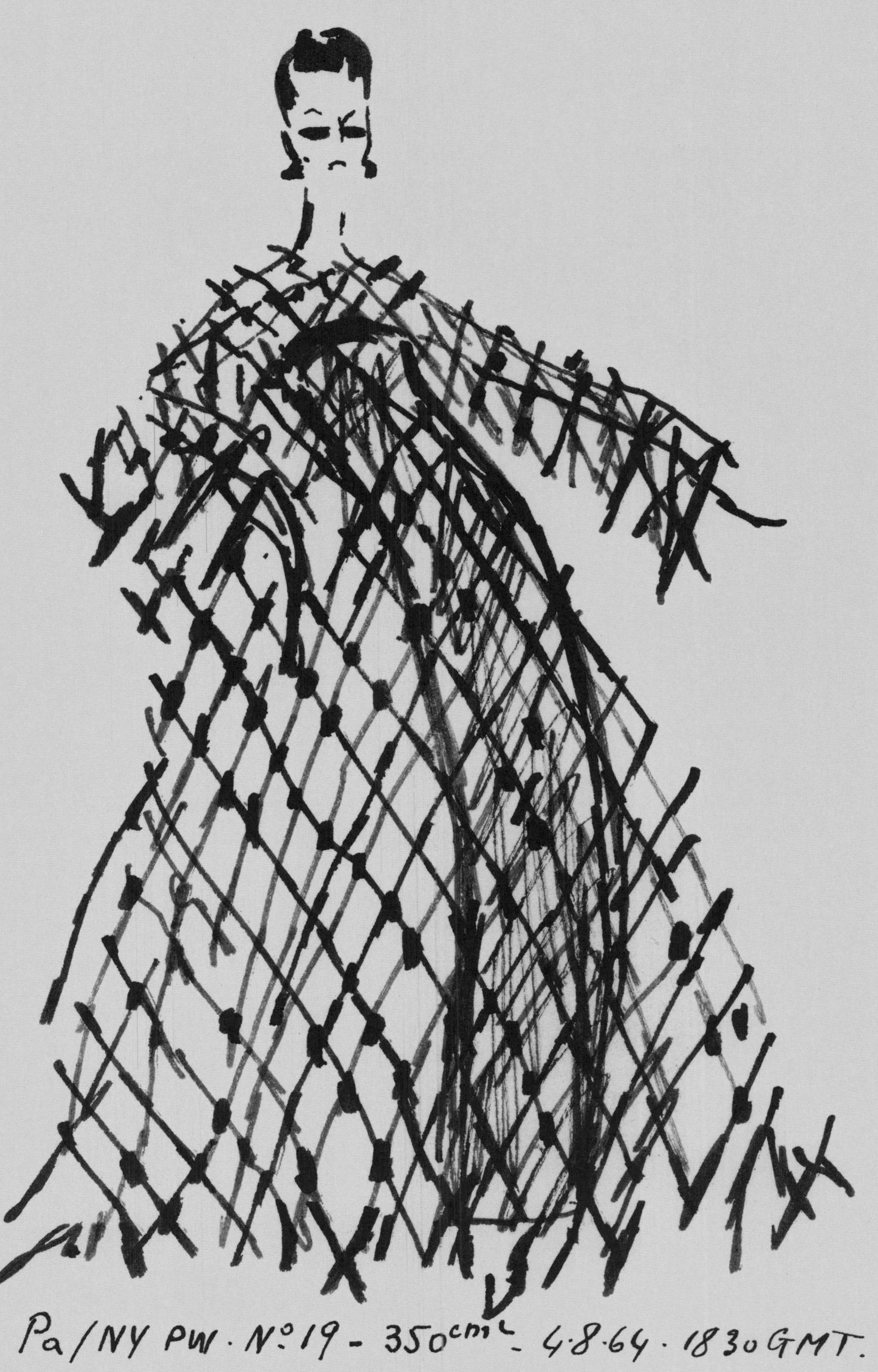
HERTRIB NYK VIA PREWI
Pa/NY PW · N°19 - 350cm² - 4.8.64 · 1830 GMT.

"Milton had a lot of models dancing around with these long earrings of mine, great big long earrings. They were dancing like crazy and occasionally an earring would fall off. And what Joe did to save the day, he'd just throw them back into the film. It made the action even a little more crazy, like the earrings were flying."

Eula initially worked on a freelance basis for Greene, whose studio was above Grand Central Terminal. He helped coordinate clothes for portraits and fashion shoots for Greene's clients, mainly *Look* and *Life* magazines, for which Greene produced dozens of covers. Actress Tammy Grimes, who met Eula and Greene around the time she appeared in the 1964 Broadway musical *High Spirits*, says, "Joe would pick out the outfit. He would see that it looked good. He would arrange the furniture. The hair as well." Grimes, who saw a lot of Eula, adds, "He was a very vital, passionate, funny, talented human being." Greene was good-looking, knowledgeable, and charming. Richard Avedon called him "the best photographer of women I ever knew." Aside from being a master of color, Greene knew how to do a lot with a little: minimal lighting, few effects. This antiglamour approach nonetheless produced heart-stopping images of beauty. Of course, that style also appealed to Eula.

But while he and Greene worked well together, they were even better friends. Joshua Greene says that Eula and his father met in 1947. Milton and his first wife, Evelyn (who later married Avedon), had bought a farmhouse in Weston, Connecticut. The Greenes and Eula redid it, creating "a cross between a stage set and a minimalist gallery space," as Joshua wrote in *But That's Another Story: A Photographic Retrospective of Milton H. Greene*, which he cowrote with his mother, Amy Greene. The barn-style living room featured an ottoman, a table, and a sofa designed specially by Isamu Noguchi. "The environment became a playground for musicians, actors, actresses, writers, and, most of all, fashion models," Joshua wrote.

In 1960, Eula and Greene officially became partners, though they continued to work on separate projects, such as Eula's illustrations for Sheppard at the *New York Herald Tribune*. In 1965 they traveled to Paris to meet their mutual idol, Alberto

Giacometti; Greene had been assigned by the *Saturday Evening Post* to do a portrait of the artist. "Joe was like a little kid, beside himself," said Joshua Greene, who heard the story. "Cartier-Bresson met them for lunch and took them to Giacometti's studio. It was a great day. They both talked about it for years."

Another person they met early on was Andy Warhol. In his *Diaries*, Warhol wrote that Greene and Eula "were the nicest to me on the first day I came to New York," in the summer of 1949. Someone had given him their names to look up. "They told me I could use their phone and everything," he wrote, "but I never took them up on it, because [*laughs*] they were so nice it scared me." One wonders what Eula and Greene made of Warhol, who struck many in the art and advertising worlds in the 1950s as nerdish—he was called "Andy Paperbag" because he carried his drawings in a sack. Within a few years, though, Warhol had become a top illustrator for magazines, as well as for clients such as the shoe store I. Miller and Columbia Records. By the early 1960s, he was a world-renowned artist. Talent apart, Eula did not have Warhol's single-minded drive to become a fine artist, making the question of envy somewhat moot. Barbara de Kwiatkowski, who thinks she met Eula through either Warhol or Halston, believes he harbored some of that feeling: "I think Joe wanted to be an artist—that was always at the core, and he never made it. I do think he was envious of Andy. He never said anything, but I just put the pieces together." She adds, "It makes me mad. Joe wasn't pushy enough for himself. Or he wasn't greedy enough—he certainly wasn't greedy."

What really stands out about Eula's career in the 1960s and 1970s is how varied it was. Although there was a clear financial reason to seek work outside of fashion magazines, which by the mid-1960s were using fewer illustrators, it suited Eula not to be tied down to one thing. And as Warhol said of him, he knew everyone. In working on this book, I came across a 1970 photo of Eula squiring Barbra Streisand into a party in New York given by Valentino. Who knew? He also saw a lot of Lauren Bacall, who was a frequent guest at the parties in his apartment on West Fifty-Fourth Street.

"It was a really good meeting place," recalls Barbara de Kwiatkowski. There was a large parlor at the front, with a beautiful wooden floor, white upholstered sofas

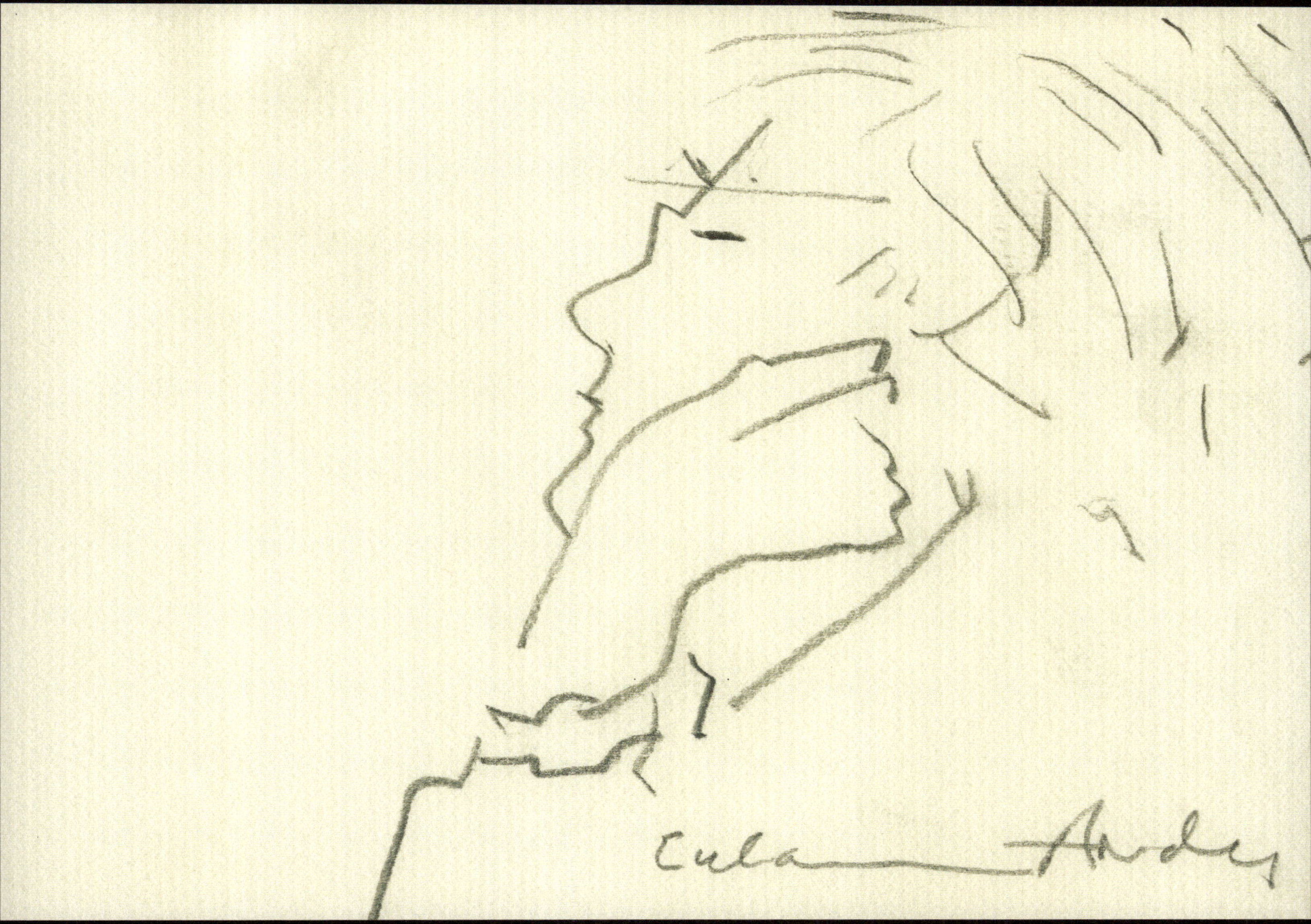

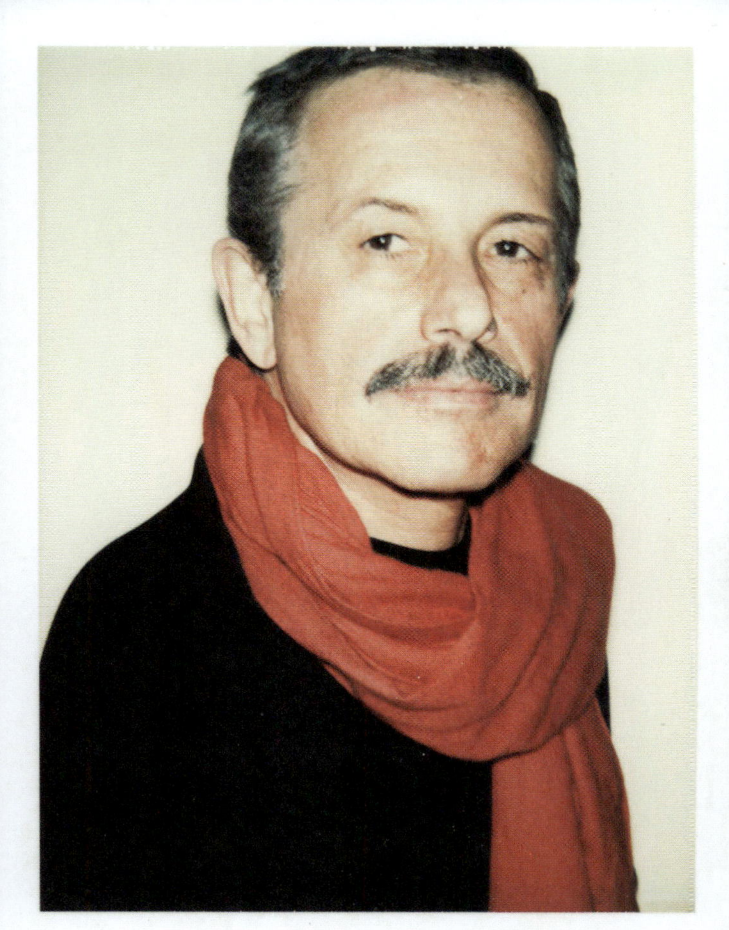
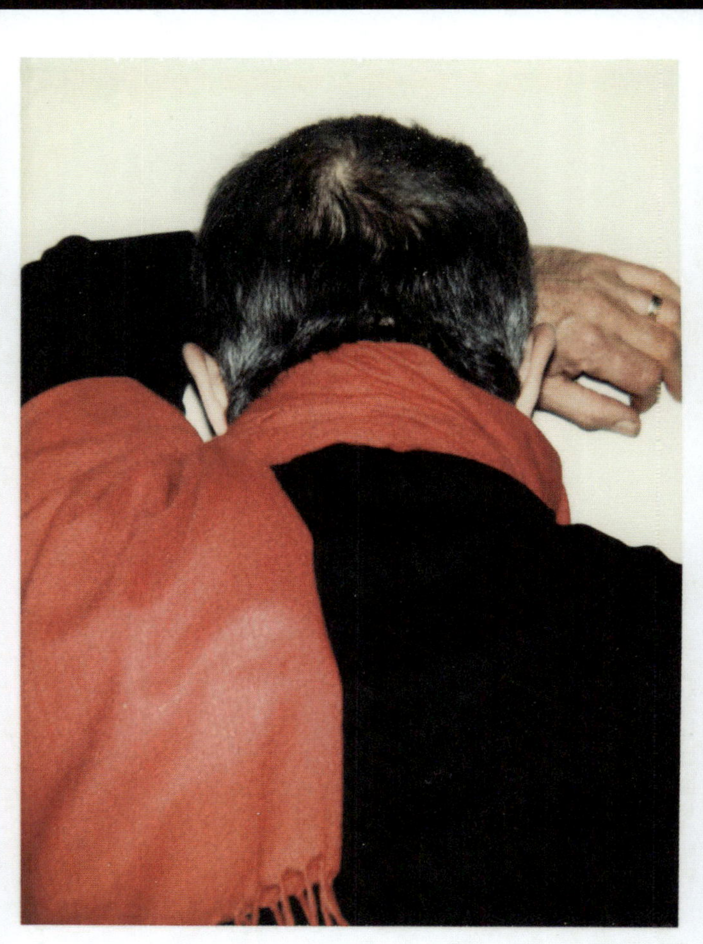

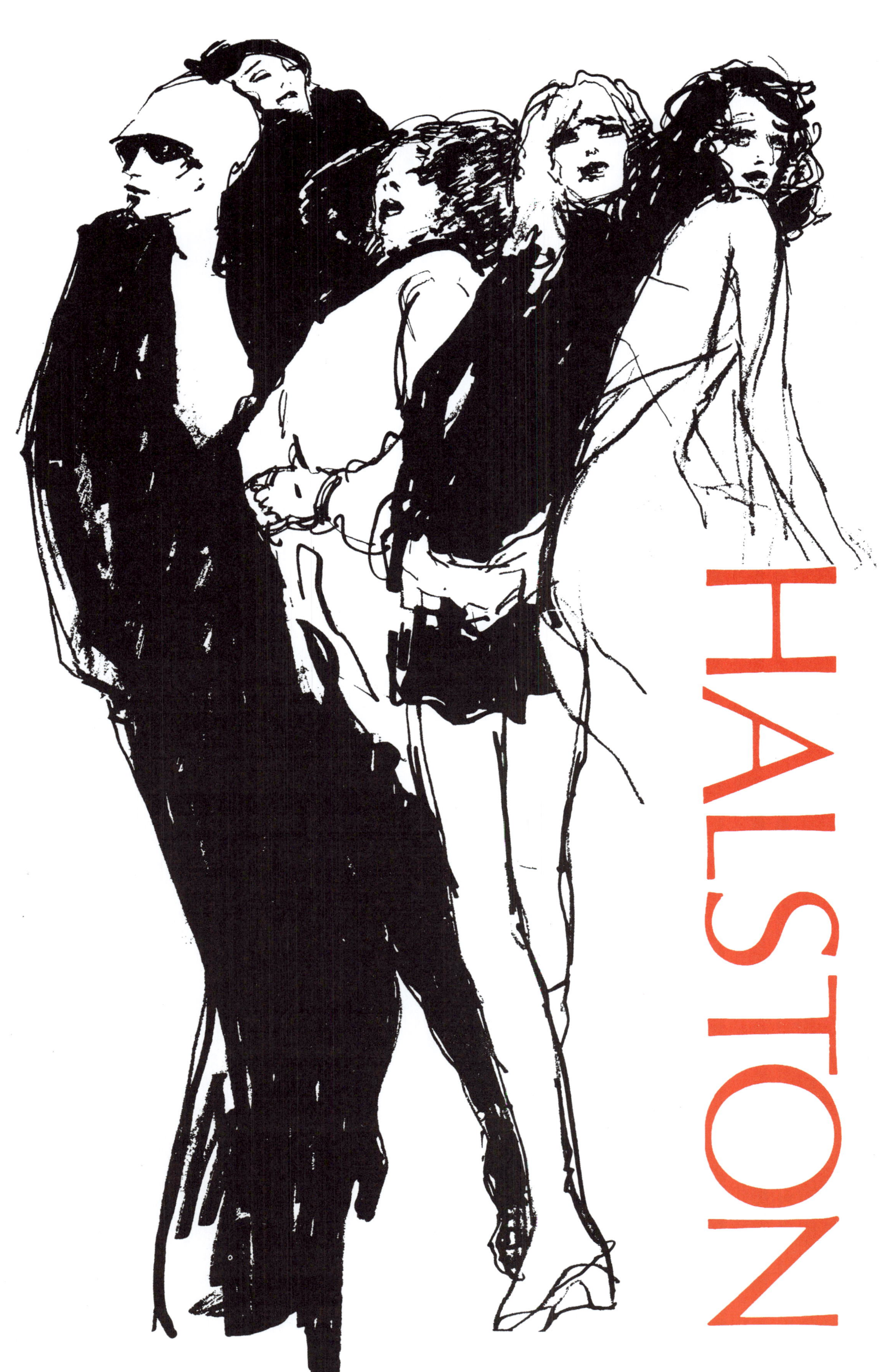

HALSTON

and chairs, and clay-potted orchids set on what were probably orange crates. As Bob Colacello later wrote in his memoir *Holy Terror: Andy Warhol Close Up*, it was the first time he saw "the decorating look that would go from the height of chic to Bloomingdale's basement in the course of the 1970s." Between the parlor and a large back room was a small pass-through kitchen stocked with a few Italian basics and presided over by his maid, Billie, who spoke her mind as freely as Eula did. Everything about the place felt ad hoc—from the drawings tacked on the walls to the shower curtain rigged around the toilet in the open bathroom ("You'd see two little knees bumping out when you passed by," recalls Devens), to the chalkboard that served as his calendar. "It was just cool," says Kwiatkowski of his home.

By 1969, Eula had ended the partnership with Greene and gone to work for H, as Eula and others called Halston. Although Eula was coy about the circumstances, Joshua Greene says the breakup wasn't dramatic. "Milton was getting ill and he wasn't making that much money with *Life*," he says. "*Life* was paying the rent for the studio and then *Life* dropped the studio." One of the last projects Greene and Eula did together for the magazine was a cover shoot with Faye Dunaway dressed in fashion inspired by the movie *Bonnie and Clyde*, taken against a backdrop of gangster silhouettes painted by Eula. Greene spent his last years in California, and, according to his son, the two men spoke occasionally. Greene died in 1985.

Apart from World War II, the decade Eula spent with Halston was the most significant experience of his life. The quality of the work was equaled, and in some quarters surpassed, by the excitement of the scene—the attractive people, the parties, and the drugs. Eula was a regular user throughout his adult life; several old friends thought he was an addict. His consumption of cocaine in the 1970s and early 1980s was probably a factor in one or two poor business decisions he made, notably his involvement in *Got Tu Go Disco*, a Broadway musical about the disco era; the $2 million production bombed, closing after seven performances. The cocaine may also have contributed to some uncharacteristic boorishness. In the mid-1980s, when Halston was no longer in control of his company or his name and was fast losing a grip on his life, Eula would sometimes boast, "You know who was Halston? I was

Halston." But in the main, friends say, he kept his head. "Joe was wild but not self-degrading, as Halston became," says Kenneth Jay Lane. Kwiatkowski says, "Joe was very wise in many ways. You don't really see pictures of him at Studio 54."

Considering that Halston's fashions did take over the world for a moment, it's surprising that Eula's involvement has received scant critical attention. To be sure, Halston had very good taste and a devoted following among the society ladies and fashion editors. He was also ambitious. "He kind of lived and breathed

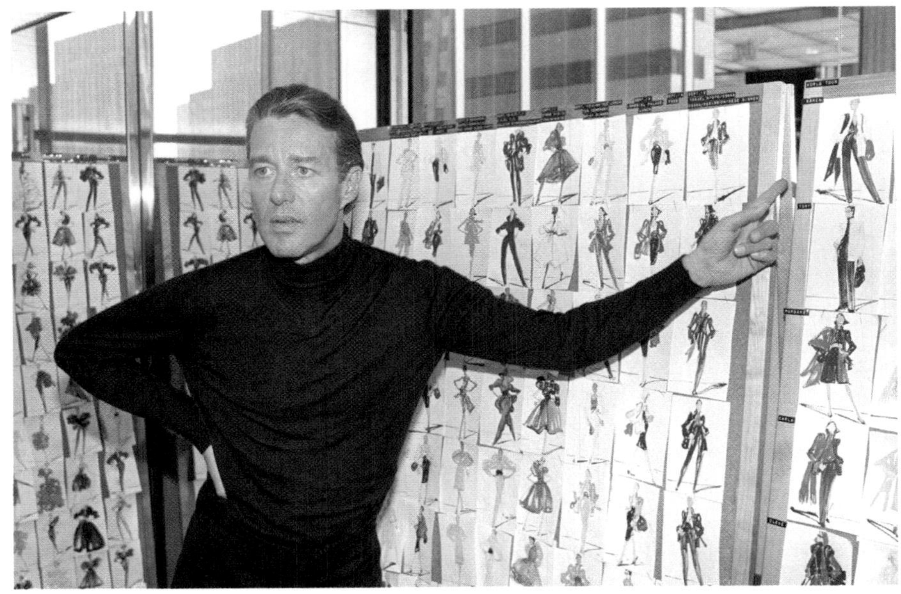

fashion," recalls Nancy North, whose late husband, Bill Dugan, was the designer's executive assistant from 1972 to 1984. Although Halston showed his first fashion collection in 1966, with backing from Bergdorf Goodman, his progress was slow; at the start of 1968, the *New York Times* still referred to him as a hat designer. China Machado, who remembers the early clothes as ladylike,

believes Eula gave Halston an edge. "Here was Halston, with all his ladies, being comme il faut," she says. "And Joe came in and was, like, 'What the fuck?' He was the most outrageous person. I think it loosened Halston up. Maybe he helped Halston be a more fluid designer."

But others say the relationship was more complex and mysterious than that. As Minnelli says, "Halston was loose enough. He always knew what he wanted. No, I think Halston found Joe for his line." Both Eula and his friend Elsa Peretti were obsessed with line. In 1969 Peretti designed her first piece of jewelry, a tiny silver bud vase worn around the neck on a leather cord. That year, the designer Giorgio di Sant'Angelo showed the necklace with his chic hippie dresses. "Once I draw the line," Peretti said of her methods, "it's there. I don't touch it. It becomes my theme." The natural shapes of bones, pebbles, and shells inspired her, and they became the essence of her early work for Tiffany. It was Halston who accompanied Peretti to

ABOVE: Halston in his studio. OPPOSITE: Halston and Martha Graham, 1979, probably for an event invitation. PAGES 54–55: Eula would sketch entire collections in progress for Halston and other designers, filling in with color later.

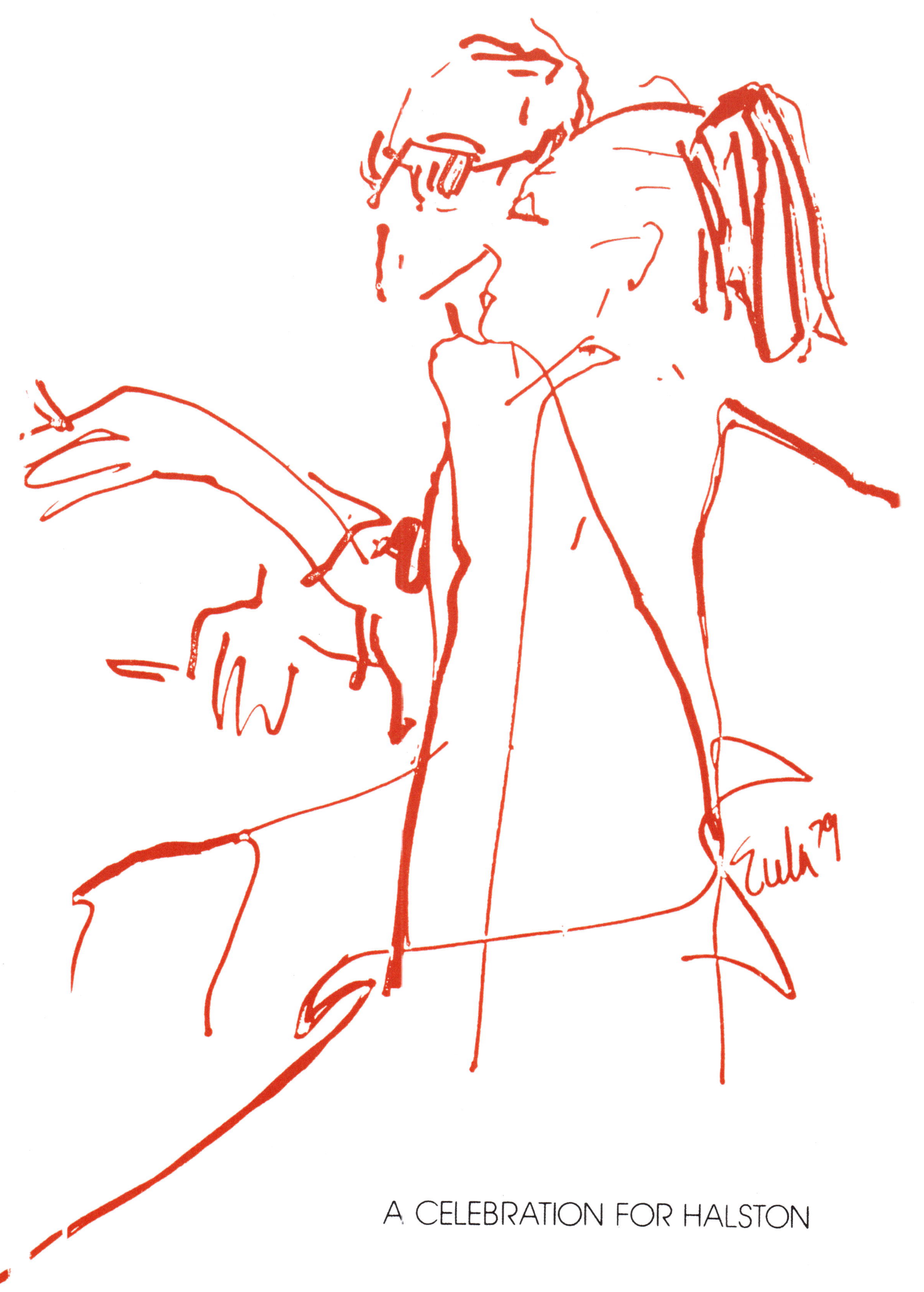

A CELEBRATION FOR HALSTON

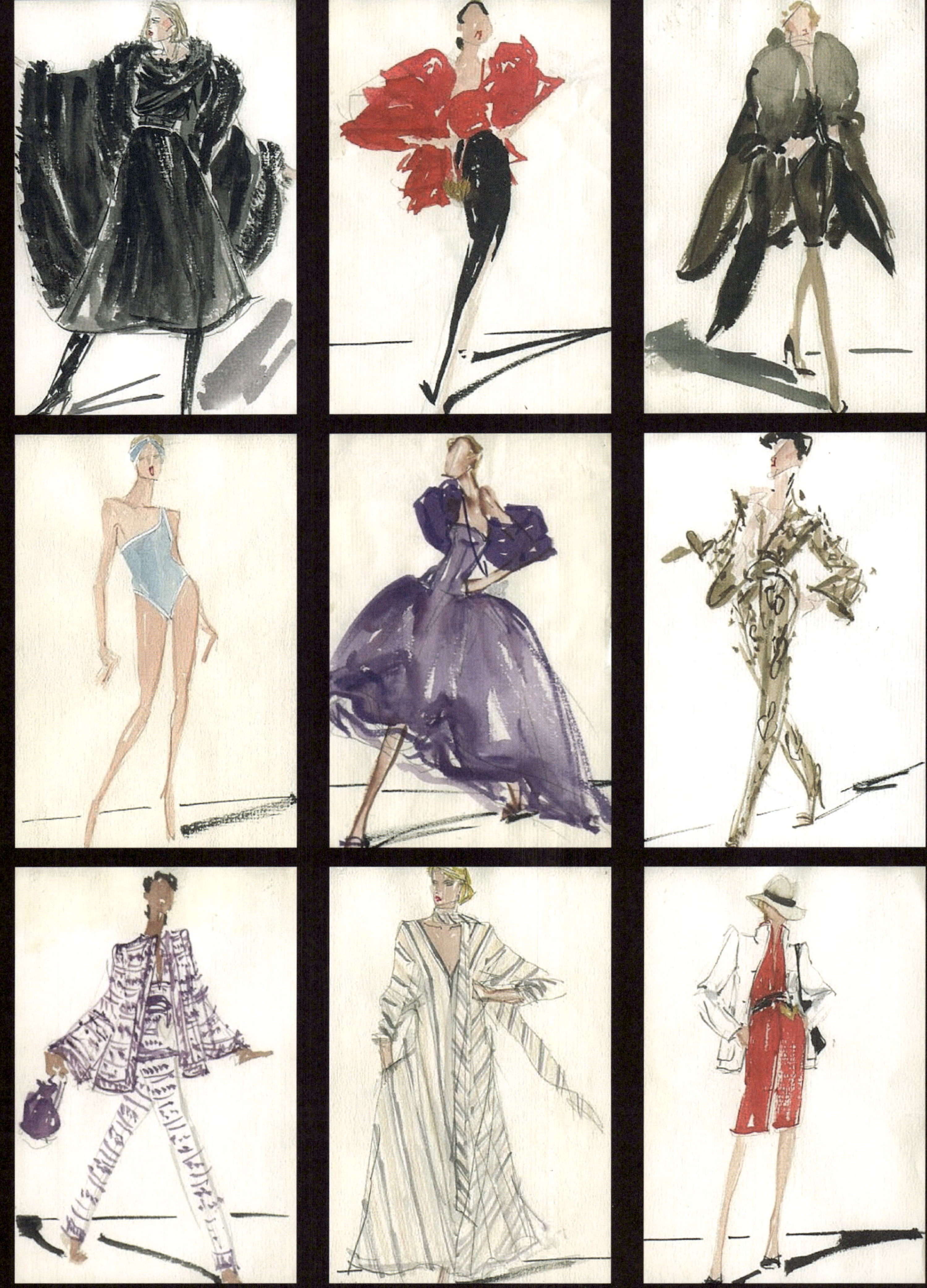

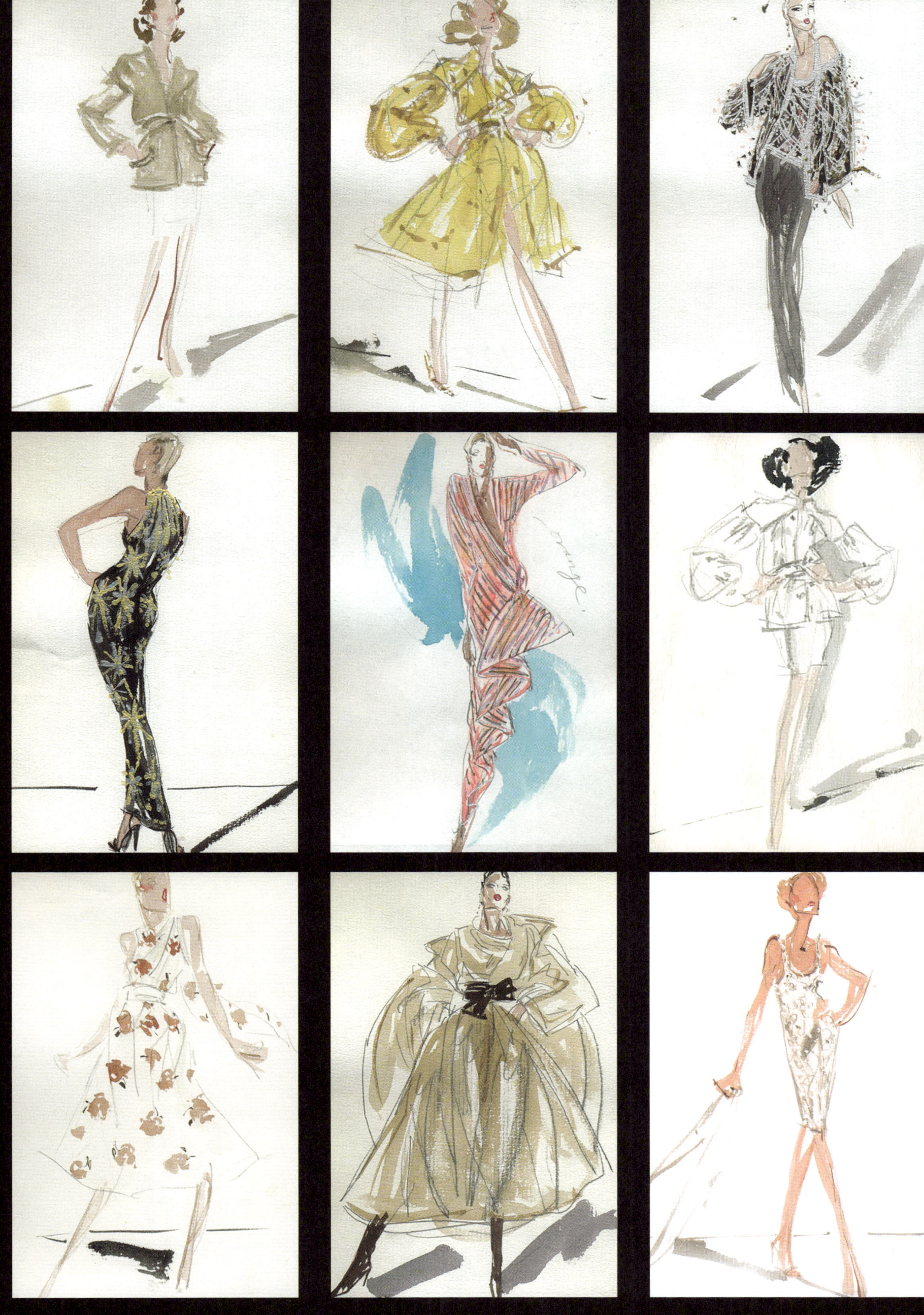

Tiffany in 1974 to meet its chairman, Walter Hoving, and to present her designs, and it was Halston who did most of the talking.

In Eula, Peretti found a true kindred spirit. They were two worldly people with volcanic personalities who could take pleasure in the most ordinary things. Both were wise, in their way. Eula visited her often at her home in San Martí Vell, a village in Spain north of Barcelona, where in 1969 she bought several run-down houses for $2,000 each. There is a wonderful photograph (opposite, bottom) of Eula and Peretti taken with the Spanish sculptors Xavier Corberó and Jaume Cubells and the designer Fernando Sánchez. They are sitting on the ground around a campfire, eating a stew or paella that is cooking in a large pan placed directly on the rocks. Carafes of red wine rest at their feet. The photo says a lot.

"I think they [Eula, Halston, and Peretti] all inspired each other," says the model Karen Bjornson, who went to work for Halston in 1970, initially in his townhouse at East Sixty-Eighth Street and Madison Avenue. She, too, remembers the importance of line to Eula when he sketched a dress: "He wanted it down to the line—he'd say, 'Let's get the line right.'" Instead of doing Polaroids of models, Eula sketched each look. Bjornson adds, "I think he was a sounding board for Halston, as were the former editor D.D. Ryan and Bill Dugan. They were all around the desk, discussing what was to be shown." Also in the studio, at least in the early days, was the legendary couturier Charles James. "He had a huge influence," North says. "He could translate his fashions from the 1950s into the simplest clothes without zippers, which Halston then did." Working closely with Halston and Dugan were the assistants Stephen Sprouse and Enrique Maza.

North recalls, "Halston would say, 'All right, everybody, show me your sketches,' and they'd put their sketches on the table, and he'd say, 'Oh, these are terrible,' and he'd throw them in the wastebasket. Then, two days later, he would have a whole line of new sketches, and they'd know where these ideas came from. They'd look very familiar."

There was great camaraderie, but to North and others, Eula didn't have a defined role beyond sketching the clothes. "I think he was a peer for Halston," she says.

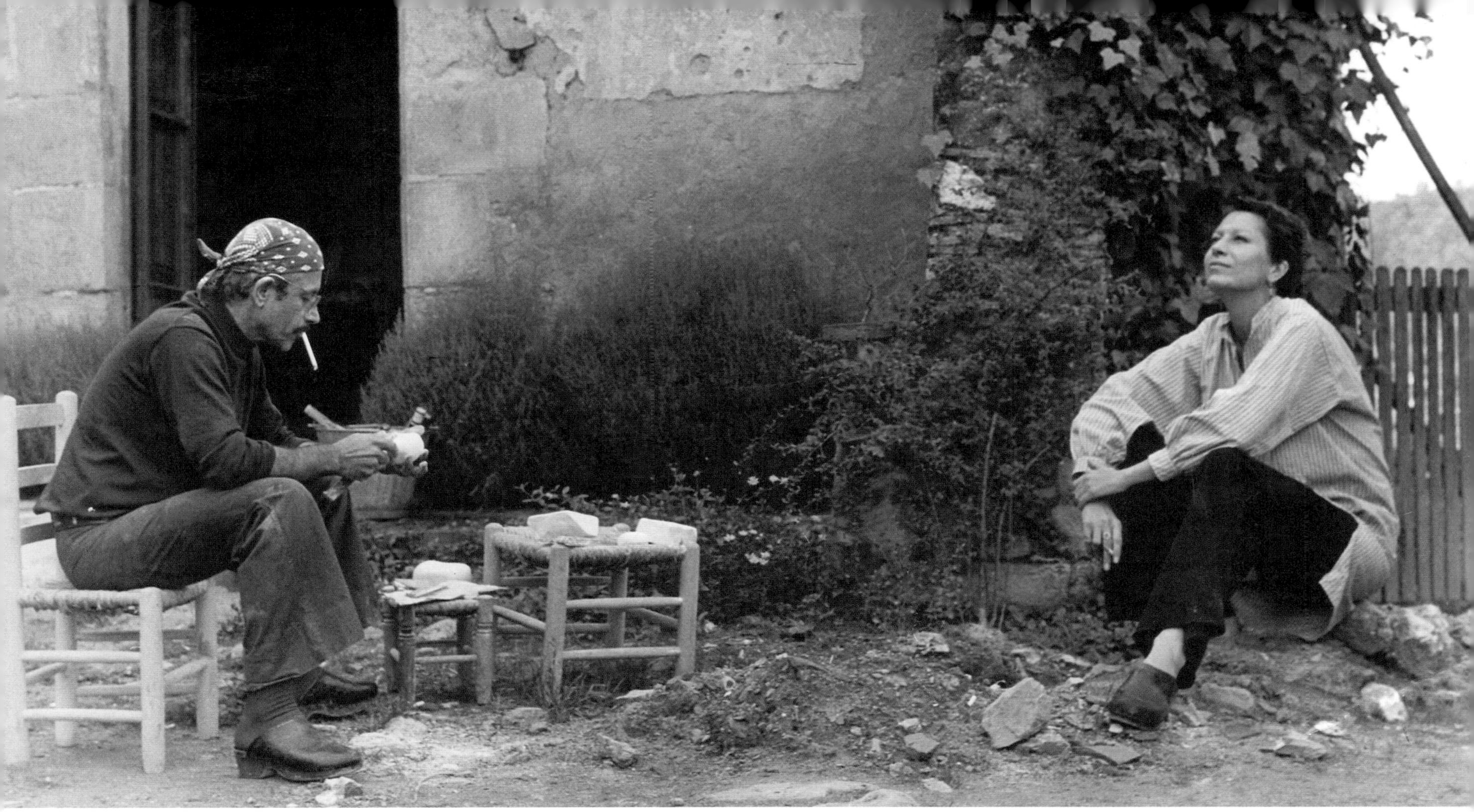

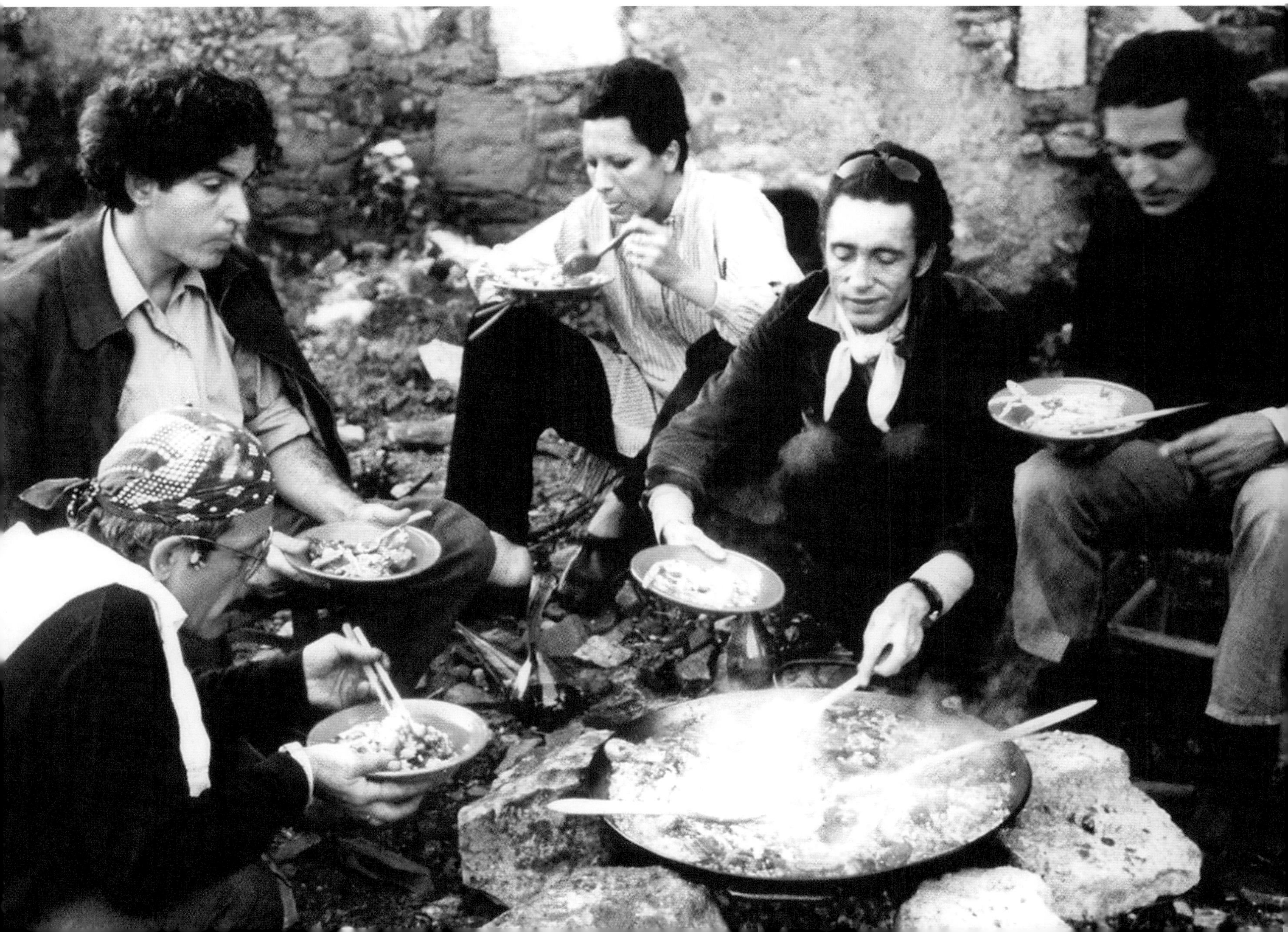

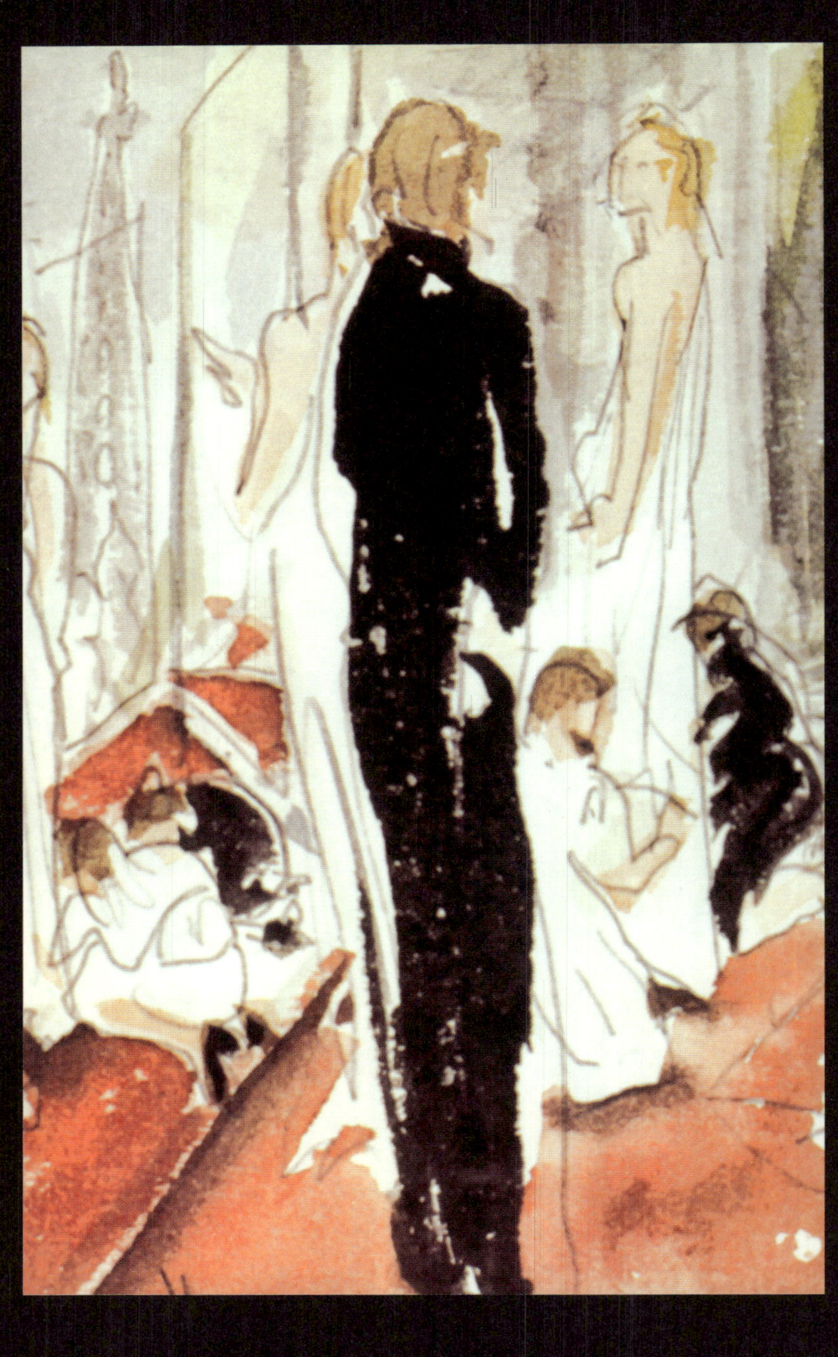

"I don't think Halston had much success getting his peers to like him. He was off-putting, controlling, and manipulative. He was pretentious. And Joe was also controlling and manipulative. I think that was the crux of their relationship, because I don't remember a specific role for Joe."

Maza, who was nineteen when he joined the studio, admits he didn't care for Eula. No doubt the age difference was a factor, and Maza and Sprouse were also competing for Halston's attention. He says, "Stephen and I sort of resented Joe, because he would show up in the middle of the day when we were busy sketching or with the collection. Joe would come in with his unbounded energy and disrupt everything. Halston, of course, was delighted. Joe had the energy of a person in his twenties. He would say, 'H, I've got this great idea. H, I've got this great idea.' And Halston would say to Stephen and me, 'Isn't that a fabulous idea of Joe's?' And we were, like, oh, God."

Maza goes on, "We would show up in the morning and Halston would have all these sketches pinned up on the wall, and Joe had been there in the evening. Joe had a big hold over Halston." Inevitably, there were blowups. Maza remembers one time when Eula was persona non grata in the office: "It lasted maybe two months, and then he was back, with his projects and his energy." Maza found something sad in all this and wondered if Eula was living his own aspirations vicariously through Halston, causing tension. He says, "Joe had some great ideas and he was wonderful at sketching in the moment. He would throw himself on the floor, take out his watercolors, and start sketching Betty Bacall in the fitting room. Or Babe Paley talking to Halston. He would scribble these things, and with a few lines he would capture the moment. Stephen and I could not do that. Joe was his own best invention, I think. And he made himself indispensable to Halston."

In 1973, Halston and his entourage flew to Paris to participate in the now-famous Battle of Versailles. The fashion show was organized by Eleanor Lambert, the doyenne of publicists who organized the first New York fashion shows and controlled the International Best-Dressed List, and Gerald Van der Kemp, Versailles's curator, to raise money to restore the palace. With more than seven hundred guests, from royals to celebrities, in attendance, the show set five American designers (Oscar

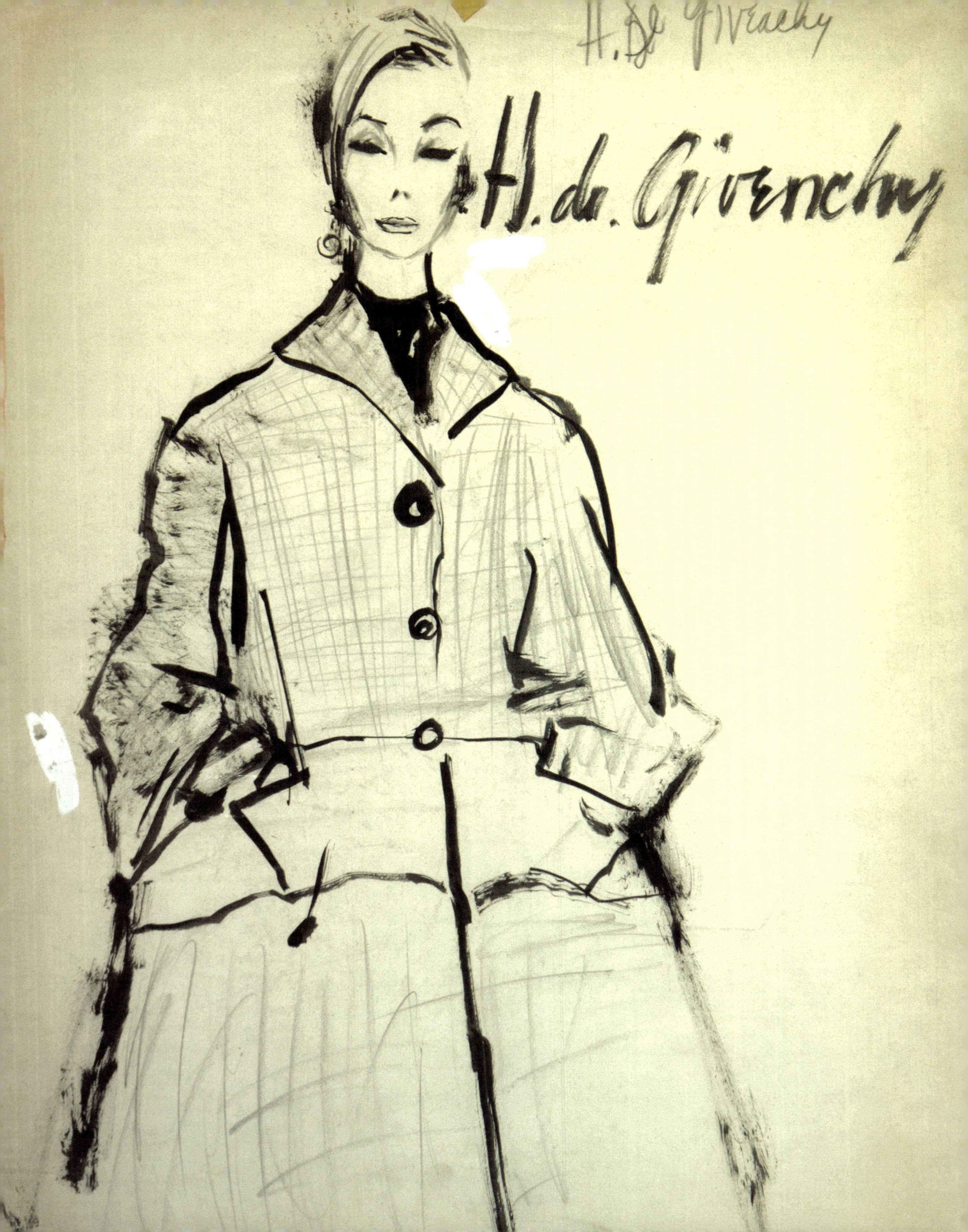

H. de Givenchy
H. de Givenchy

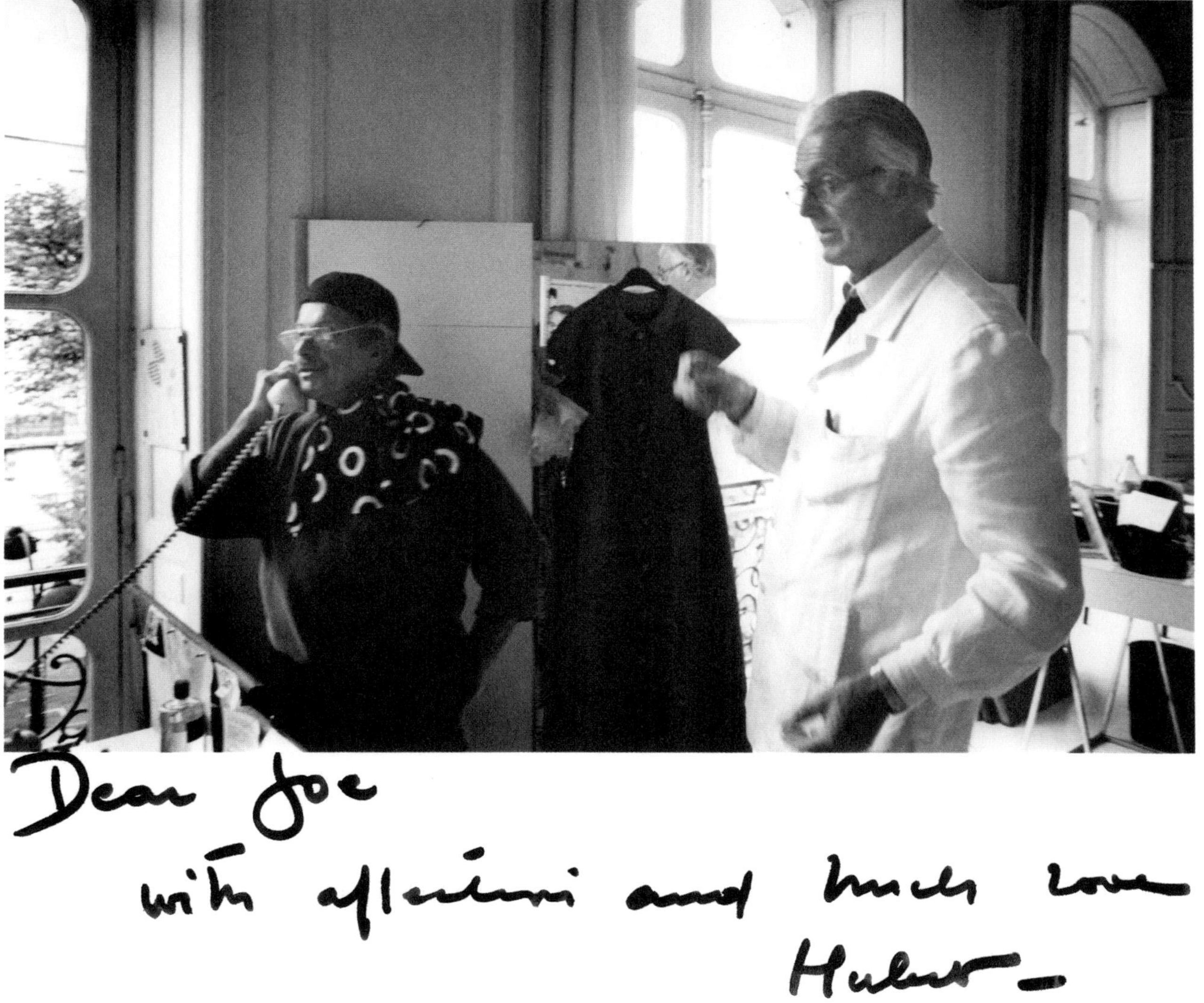

de la Renta, Bill Blass, Stephen Burrows, Halston, and Anne Klein) against five Paris couturiers (Pierre Cardin, Marc Bohan of Christian Dior, Hubert de Givenchy, Yves Saint Laurent, and Emanuel Ungaro). Supremacy in fashion belonged by rights to the French, and they let the Americans know that by mounting a spectacle with lavish sets and performers such as Rudolf Nureyev and Josephine Baker. While the Americans at least had Liza Minnelli to their advantage, their sets were lacking. Eula, serving as set designer for the Americans, had to scrub his original plan to use drapery in the background when he realized that he had made measurements in yards instead of meters. At the last minute, he scrounged up a white seamless photography backdrop and drew a sketch of the Eiffel Tower with a broom and black paint. That sketch was the Americans' sole prop on an otherwise black stage, and it telegraphed that simplicity and a sense of spontaneity were the great virtues

OPPOSITE: A sketch of a Givenchy coat, date unknown. ABOVE: Eula in Paris with his friend Hubert de Givenchy, 1980s. PAGES 62–63: A watercolor of a later collection by Givenchy, 1987–88.

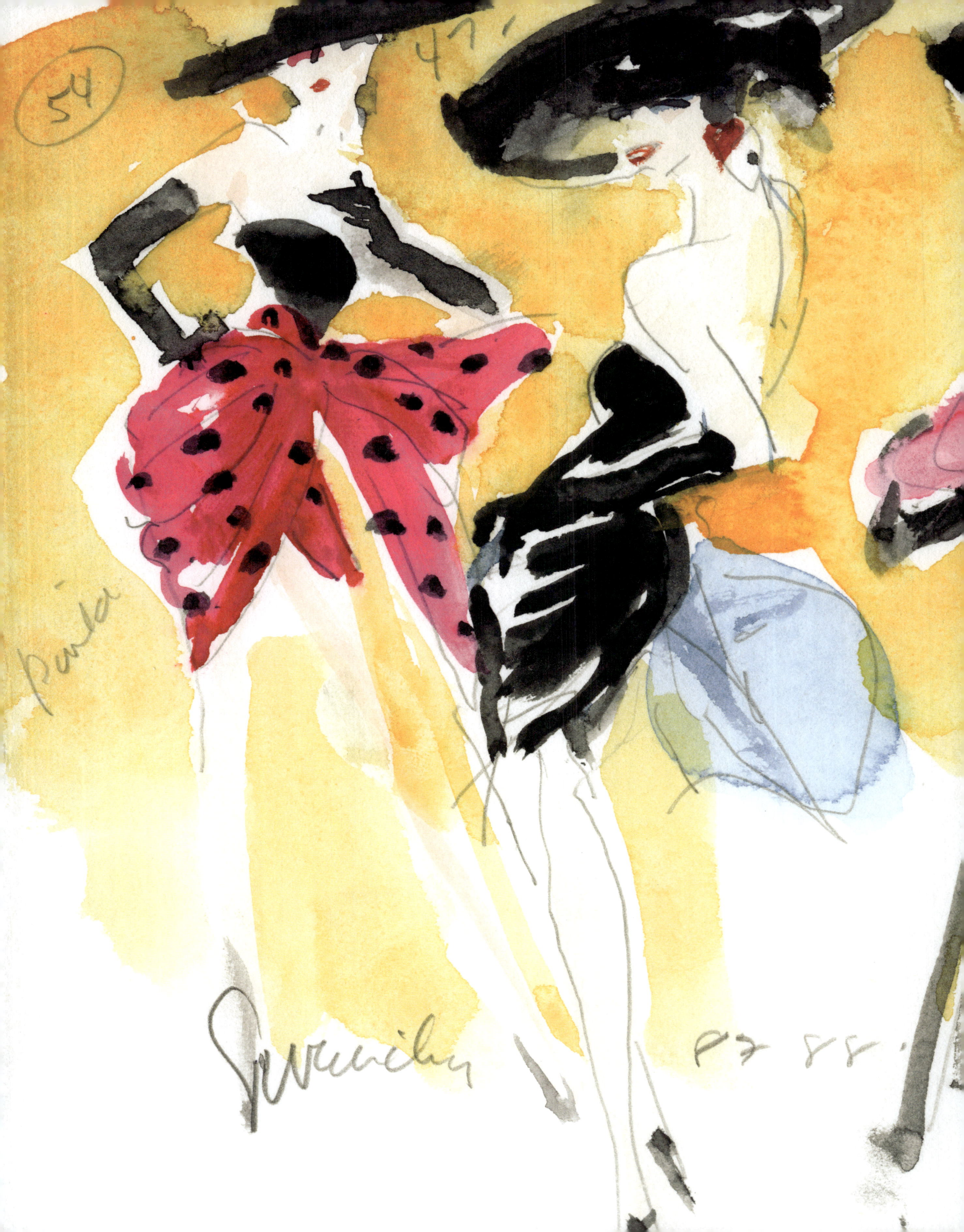
54
Paula
Sevenely

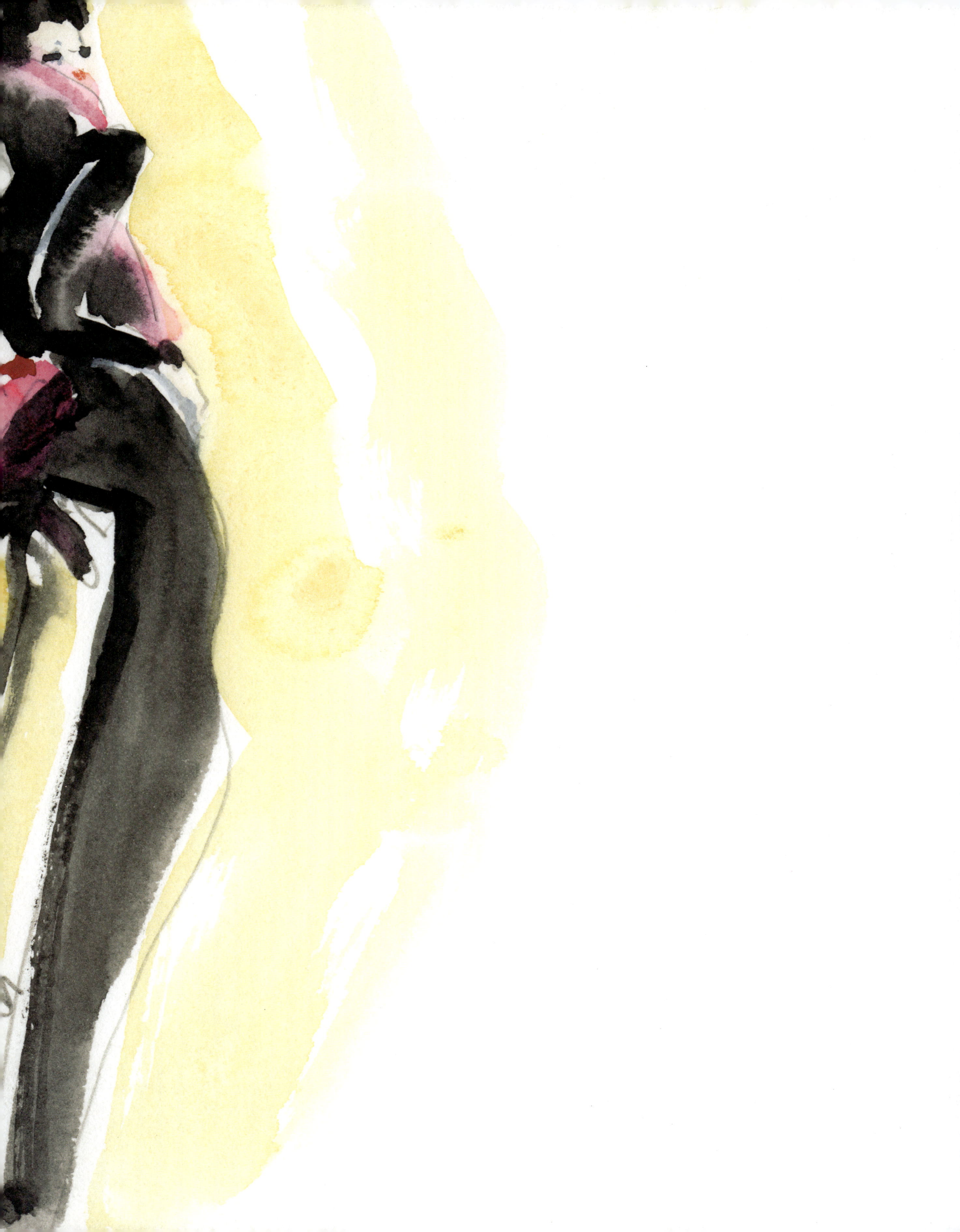

of American fashion. Suddenly the French clothes looked passé. What's more, the American designers used black models in their presentation—in what is now hailed as the breakthrough moment in fashion for black women—and so, in still another way, their fashion looked new and modern to the predominantly French audience.

Eula remained with Halston through the company's move from the Upper East Side to the Olympic Tower in midtown Manhattan in 1978, following Norton Simon's purchase of Halston's company. Although the group seemed literally on top of the world in its new digs overlooking St. Patrick's Cathedral, and Halston and his entourage were out at Studio 54 almost every night, Eula groused that Halston was getting too grand. "Listen," he told him, "you're not God yet." He also complained to his friends that Halston was working him to the bone. Ron Ferri says, "Joe didn't want to work with him anymore, and he didn't." It's unclear what caused the rupture, but one factor was Eula's decision to get involved in *Got Tu Go Disco*. "It was a terrible show," remembers Charles Tracy with a laugh, adding, "Halston had told him not to do it. I think that was the beginning of their breakup. It wasn't a real falling out. They just stopped." Minnelli concurs: "Halston never said a bad word about Joe. Never."

What few of his friends knew was that Eula was seriously overcommitted financially. He had agreed to help a new modeling agency, Xtazy, based in New York, round up girls for the Paris shows. He apparently assured Xtazy's owners that he could get Valentino, whom he knew, to use some of the models, and he demanded that his $50,000 fee be paid in twenty-dollar bills and delivered in a shopping bag. It was. But when Eula didn't follow through—he actually went AWOL, according to an account in *New York* magazine—the agency sued him.

Still, it's hard to believe that these distractions alone were to blame for the breakup with Halston. Ferri says, "I think it was all to do with coke. Everybody gets nasty on coke, after all. And they did enough to blanket all of Central Park."

As the 1980s began, Eula continued to go at full tilt. He worked for Valentino (whose partner, Giancarlo Giammetti, said he knew nothing of the Xtazy affair) and, in 1983, spent two weeks in Japan with Givenchy for a thirty-year retrospective.

OPPOSITE: Reflected glory: drawing in the Halston studio, probably for an advertisement, 1979. PAGES 66–67: Eula's drawings especially evoked how Halston's clothes were meant to be seen.

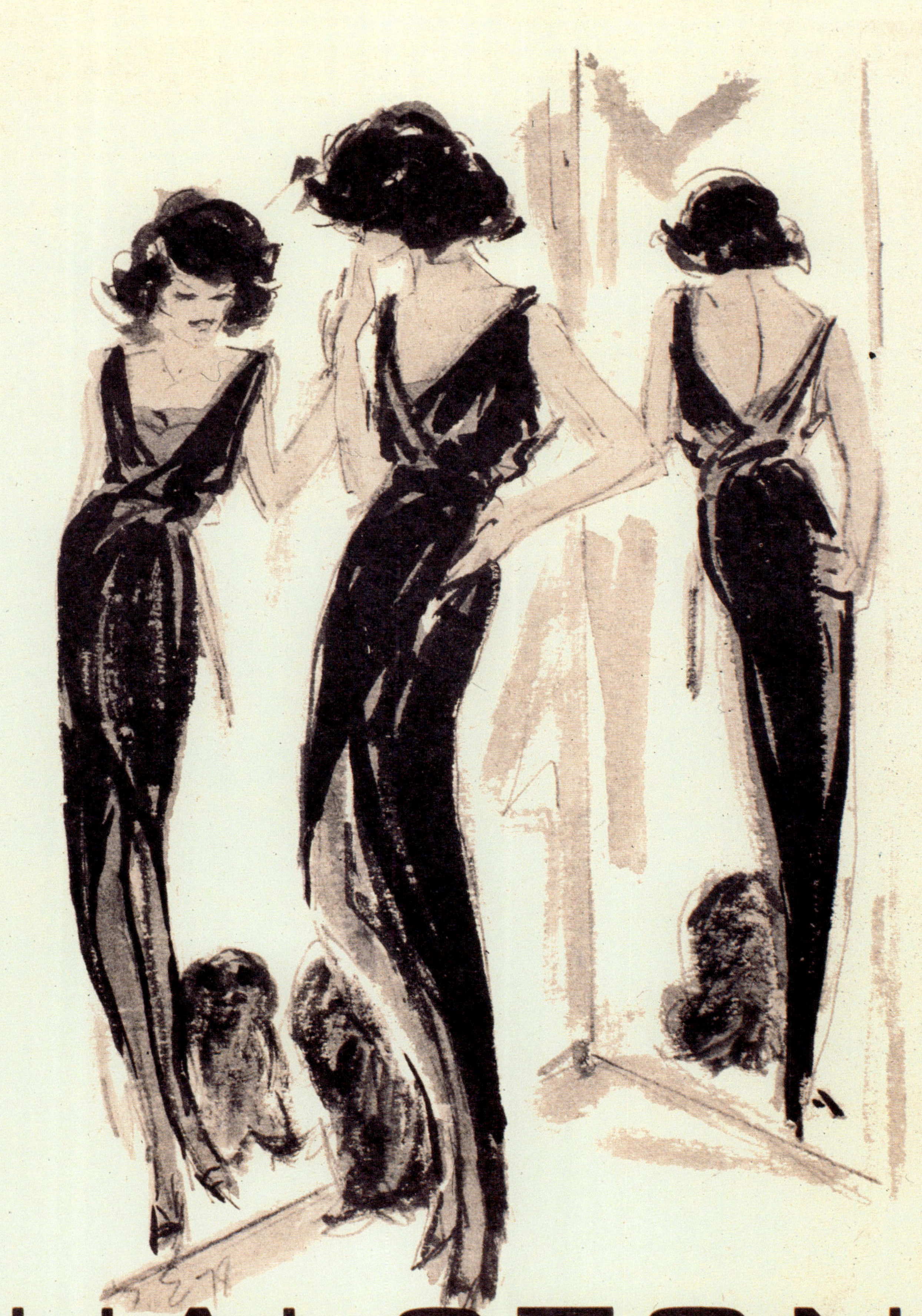

HALSTON

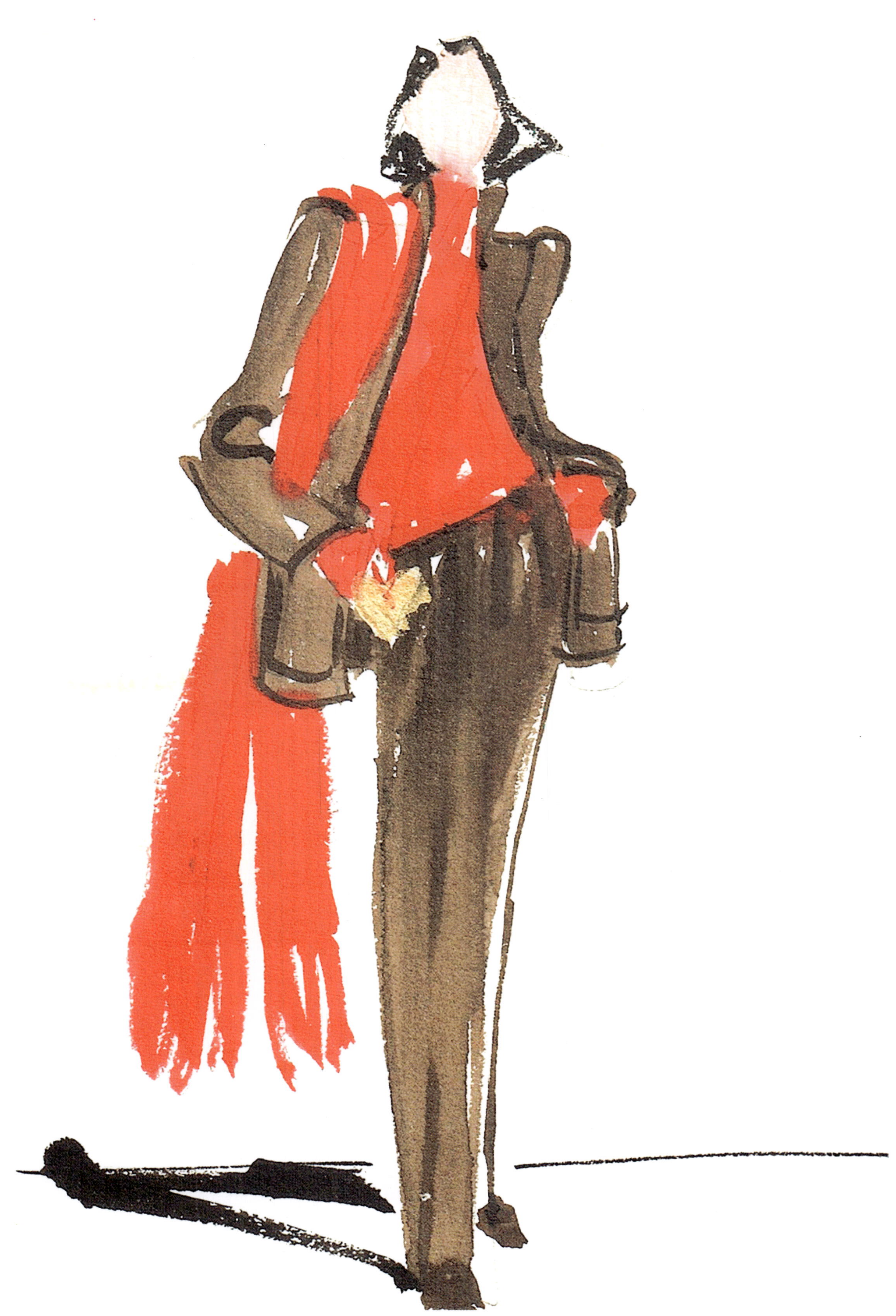

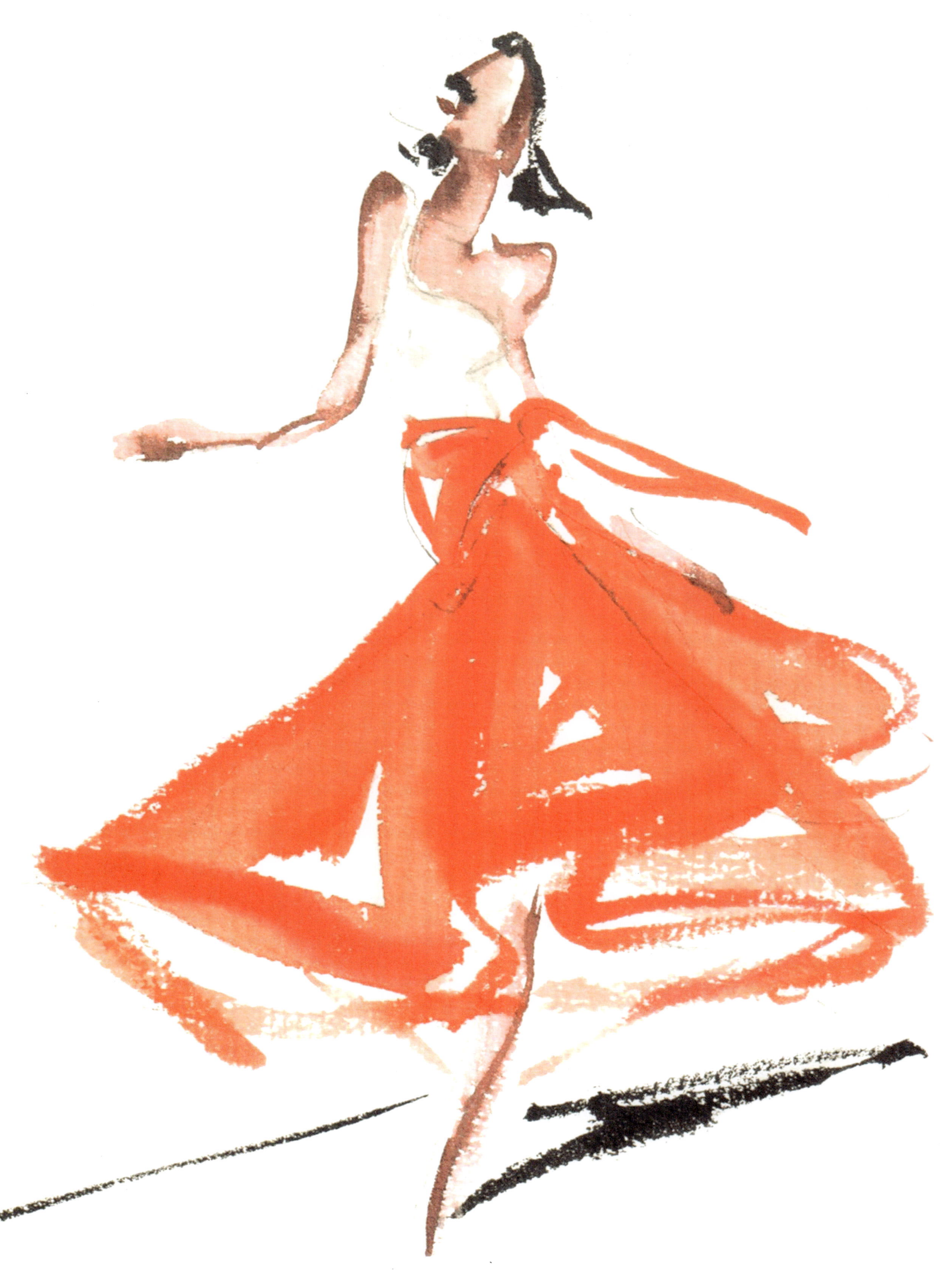

But the decade was really marked by Eula's long sojourn in Italy, though he still spent time in Hurley. He returned to sketching the collections for Italian *Harper's Bazaar* as well. Kattan wanted Eula to work at her magazine, and when she called him, he invited her to dinner at his apartment. She says, "I remember walking up the stairs, and he opened the door. I had brought him a truffle from Italy. He was very impressed that I did that. We sat on the floor and had dinner. It was sort of like love at first sight." But when Kattan raised the matter of a contract, Eula barked, "A contract? Forget it! I don't need a contract, or we'll talk about it later." Perhaps he was playing hard to get. In the end, *Bazaar*'s publisher, Giuseppe Della Schiava, made him sign a contract. To sketch the European collections he was paid $100,000 a year, a large sum at the time. Eula's dealings with money seemed quite offhand, even funny; he had money stashed in the backyard of his house in Hurley. But he'd had tax troubles, and at one point, according to Kattan, who worked with Eula for fourteen years at *Bazaar*, Della Schiava bailed him out. "Joe didn't care," she said. People couldn't say no to Eula, because his entire being was to say yes. "He was a joy, a very positive person," says Kattan.

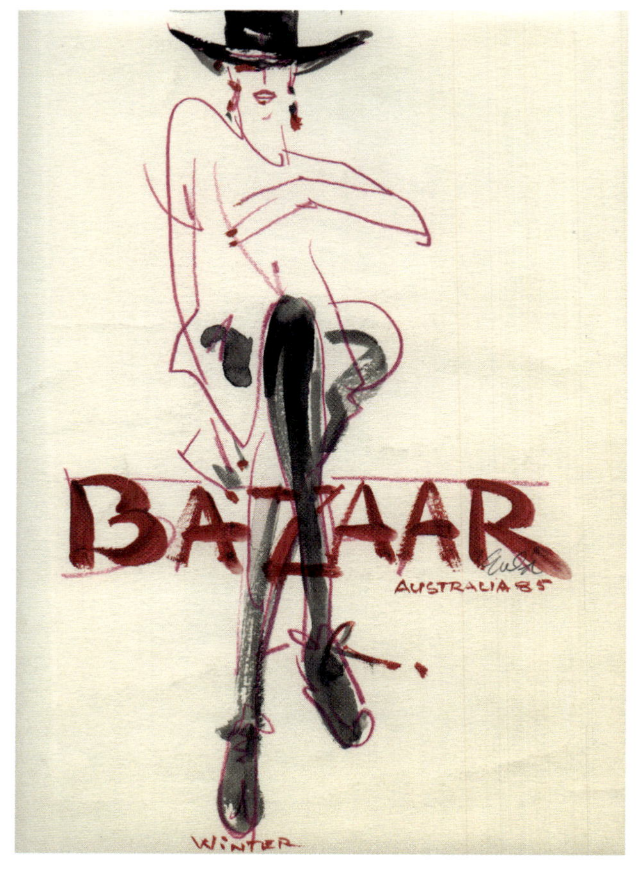

During the 1990s, Eula continued to work, mostly for Geoffrey Beene, Josie Natori, and Tiffany, doing illustrations and a line of exuberant place settings featuring roosters and flowers. He still saw a lot of Peretti and his old friends, and he made new ones, such as Amy Spindler, the style editor of the *New York Times Magazine.* In 2002 he covered Saint Laurent's farewell collection in Paris for Spindler, bringing his career almost full circle, since forty years earlier he had witnessed the designer's first show in the company of Eugenia Sheppard. The series of sketches, "Au Revoir, Yves," saw Eula at his best, as they captured both the scene and the emotion of a giant's final triumph (see pages 72–79). Nancy North remembers seeing Eula in his later years: "a much more conscious man, less dismissive." He had begun to wind

ABOVE: A drawing for *Harper's Bazaar*, 1985, possibly for a magazine promotion. OPPOSITE: Eula spent much of the 1980s and early 1990s illustrating for *Harper's Bazaar*.

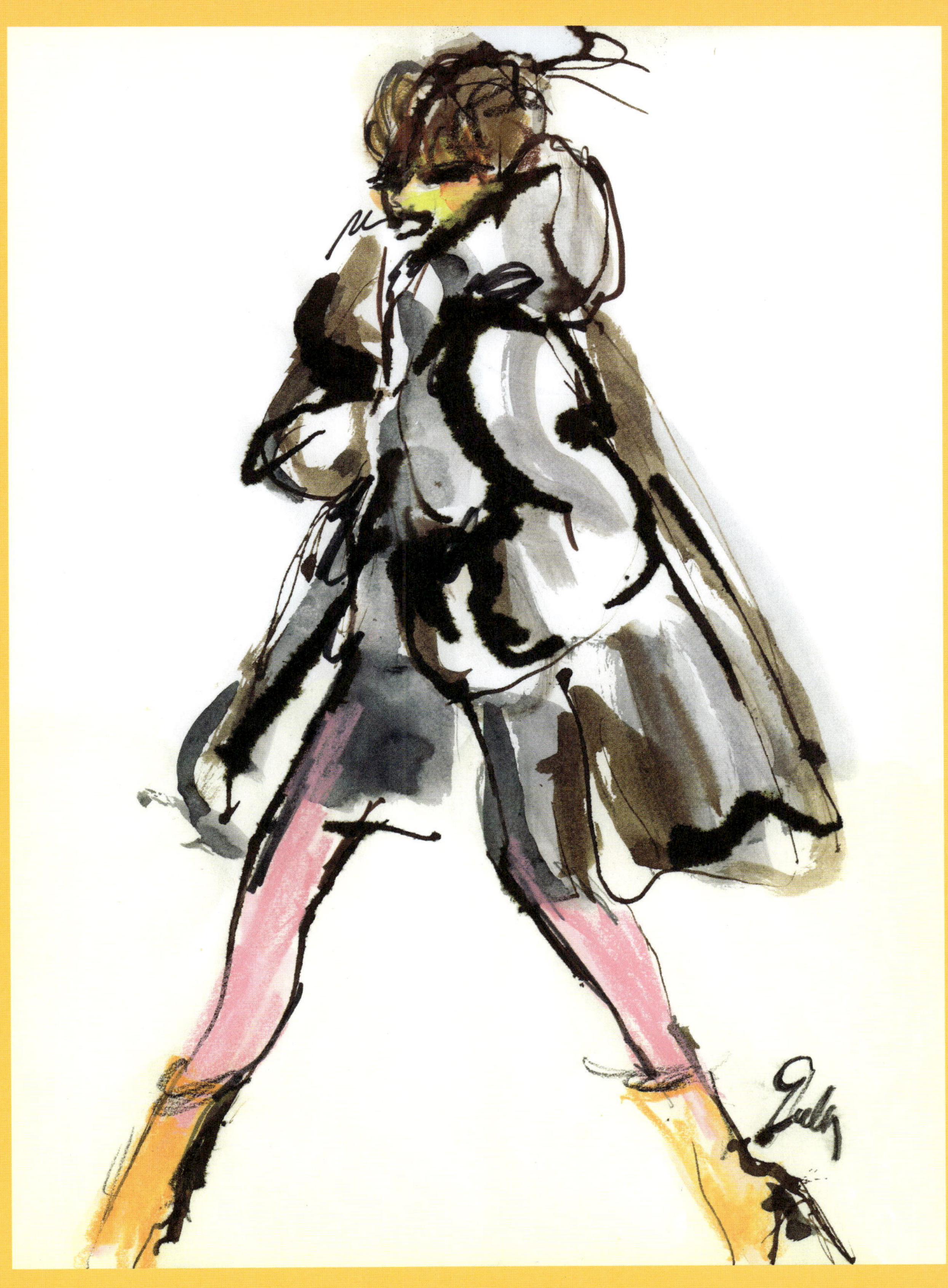

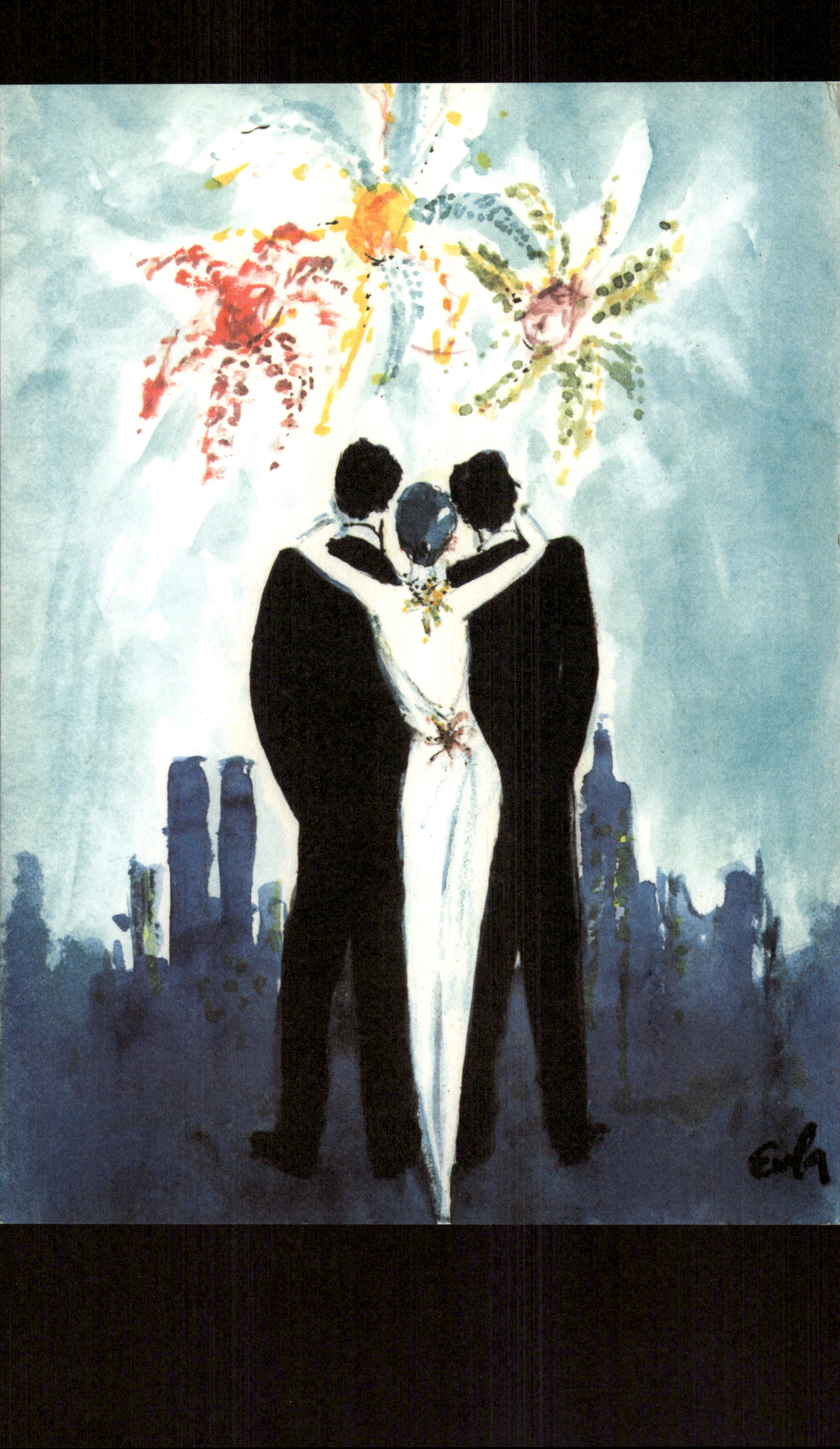

down. When Paul McCartney made him an offer on the West Fifty-Fourth Street apartment—after Eula had rebuffed the former Beatle—he finally let it go and took a smaller place in the Osborne, where I first met him. He really wanted to be in Hurley. "Yes, he wanted to be there, period," says Tracy.

Eula died at age seventy-nine on October 26, 2004, in Benedictine Hospital in Kingston, New York, from lung cancer. It can't be properly said that an era ended with this passionate, stubborn, productive, wily man. Because, in truth, not only did Eula define his era by capturing its movement and frenetic energy in an emphatic line, but he also anticipated the present era of the stylist-designer–taste maker, the all-seeing, now highly paid individual who does it all. Eula was the forerunner. When you look at the wonderful drawings in this book, consider that they are only a small part of an extraordinary legacy.

— Cathy Horyn

my artist friend Ron Ferri. We remade
the room into our atelier.

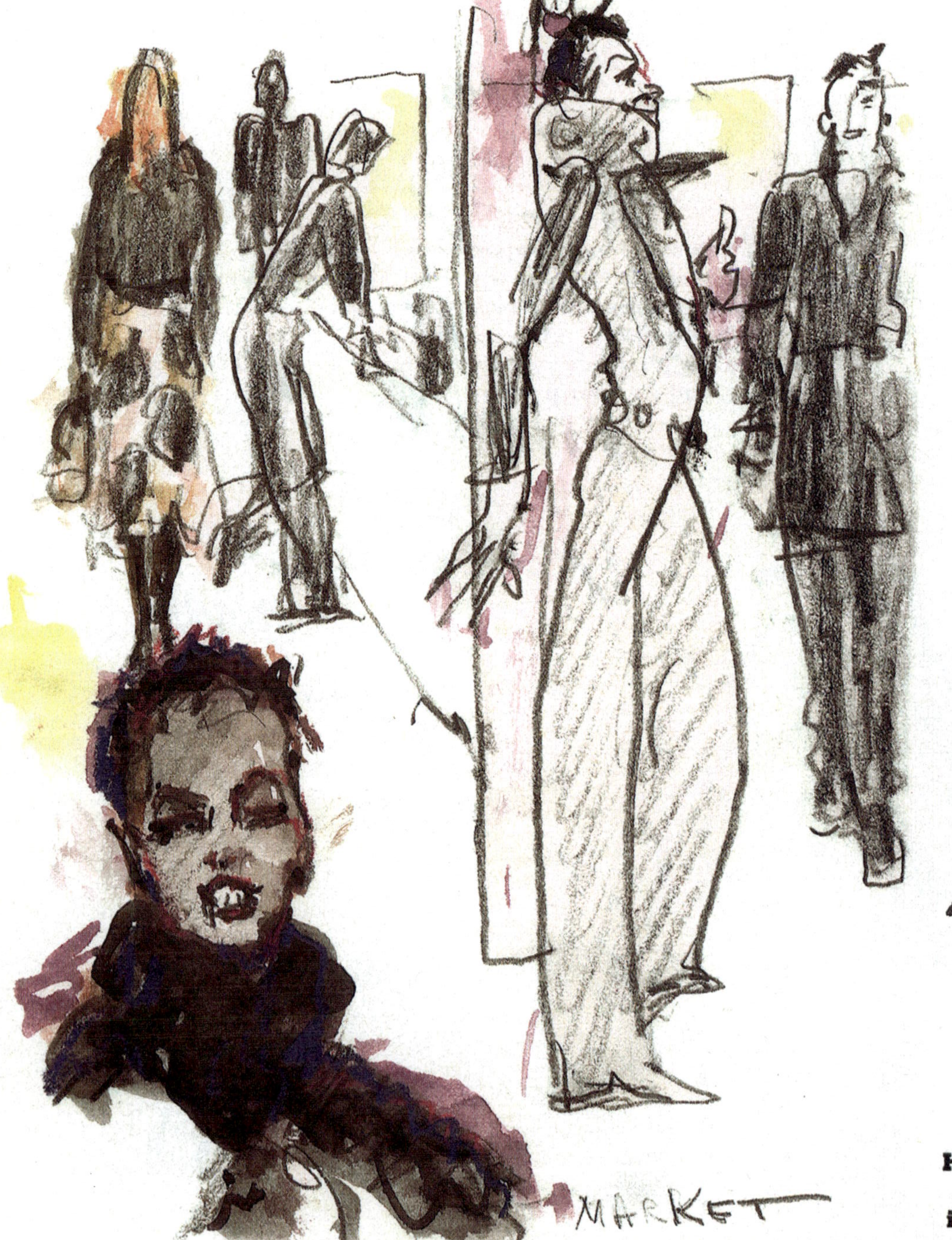

We lunched at Market, the hot new restaurant of Jean-Georges
Vongerichten. At lunch, I started reminiscing — about Yves moving from
Dior to open his new place on Rue Spontini in 1962 (sounds like an
Italian elixir), where he wowed the world with pea jackets, sacks, coolie
clothes and the start of signature silk scarves that took off
for decades. Women were not allowed in restaurants with slacks.
Trousers were out. Yves changed all that.

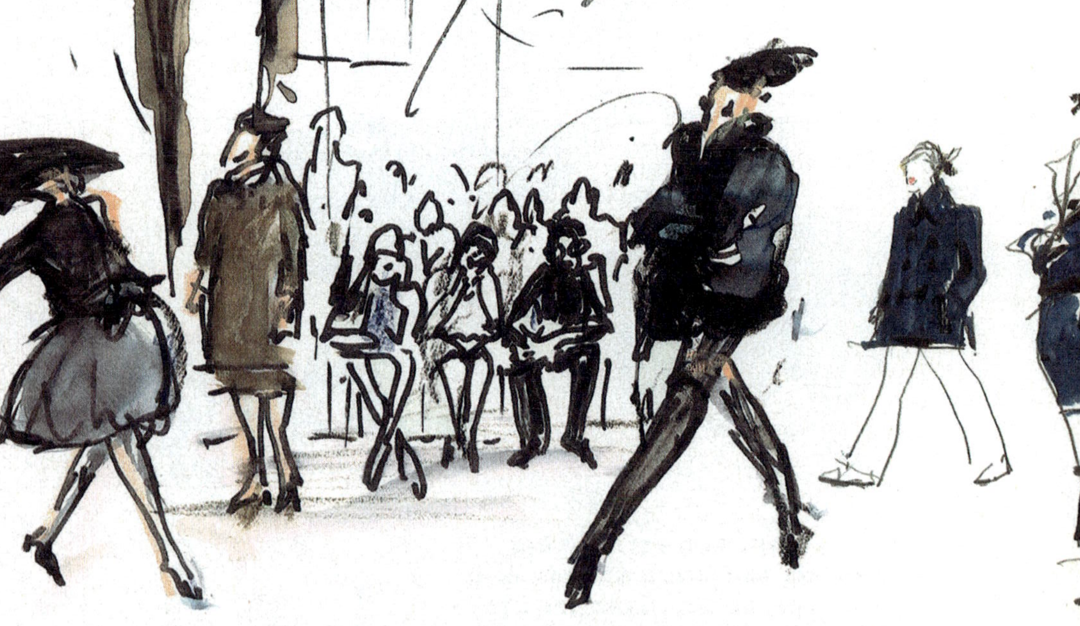

Here's Diana Vreeland arriving
with Françoise [de Langlade],
the American editor and the French
editor of Vogue, with their new haircuts
from Alexandre. Also arriving,
Gloria Guinness smoking. They all
smoked at the shows then.

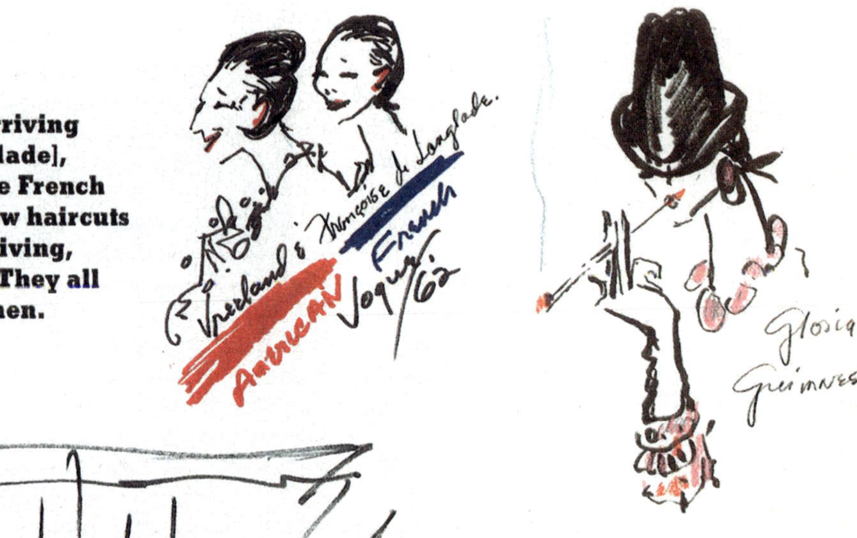

The first Yves show I sketched was his first collection for Dior in 1958 or '59.
He was 21 years old. That was an absolute revolution, a trip to the moon in fashion. Alligator
motorcycle jackets trimmed in fur and bubble lace skirts and oversize sweaters done
in lace. And that was all for cocktail! This is Suzanne Luling, a great friend of Pierre Bergé's
and Yves's, calling out the numbers at the show.

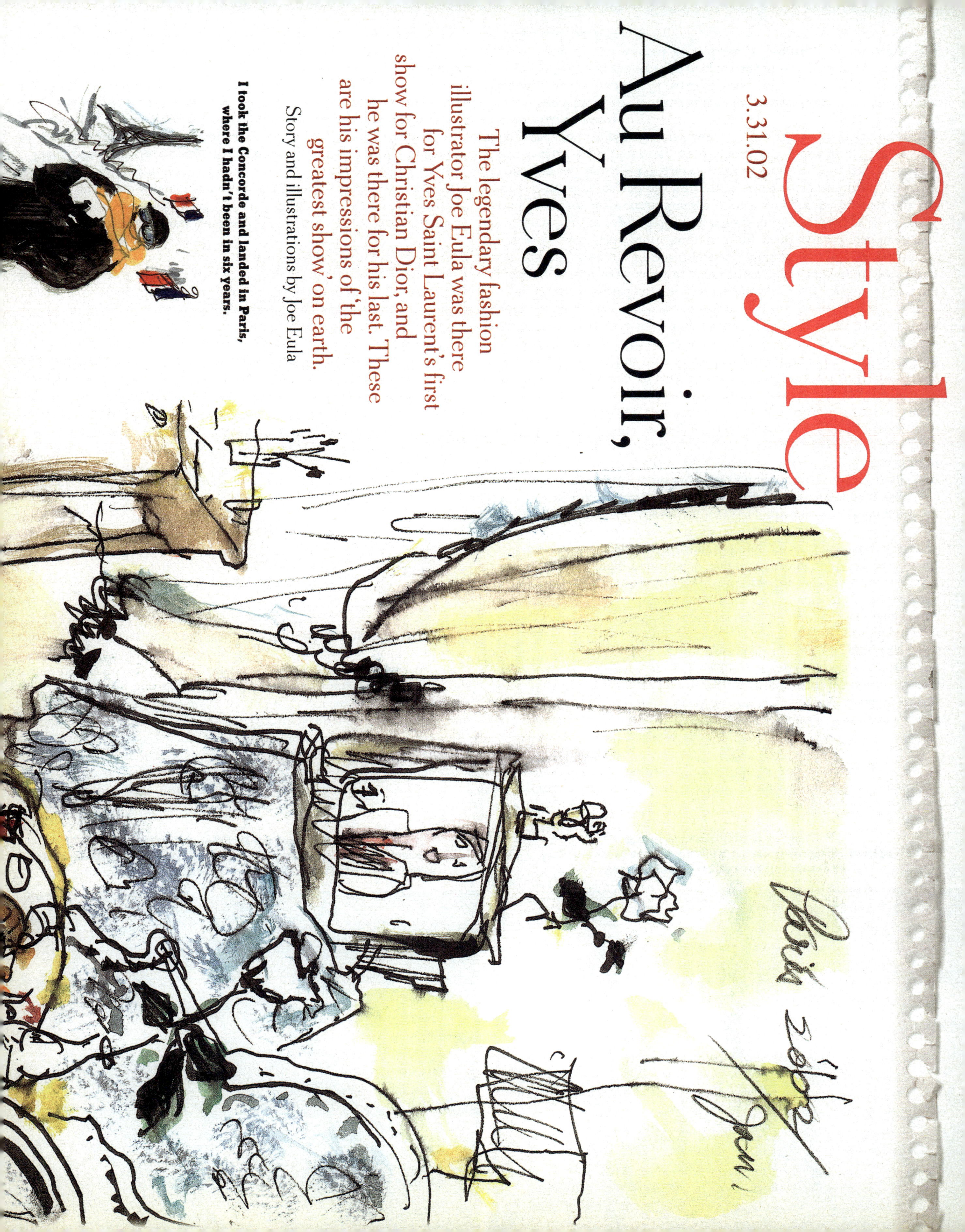

Style

3.31.02

Au Revoir, Yves

The legendary fashion
illustrator Joe Eula was there
for Yves Saint Laurent's first
show for Christian Dior, and
he was there for his last. These
are his impressions of 'the
greatest show on earth.'

Story and illustrations by Joe Eula

I took the Concorde and landed in Paris,
where I hadn't been in six years.

Yves's pug.

Before the show, at a salon de thé. The press,
the black barricade, are clutching their invites, screaming,
"There's never any color in Paris!"

Backstage at the show, Loulou de la Falaise
trying to look nonchalant.

The hush as everyone takes their seats.
Givenchy is still giving his last words of praise. It's a shame the
top designers like Yves and Givenchy didn't train people to
take over as Balenciaga did. With Balenciaga, you had Ungaro,
Courrèges and Givenchy himself. Dior produced Saint
Laurent. But nobody came out of Saint Laurent and Givenchy,
and this is the pity of today's couture.

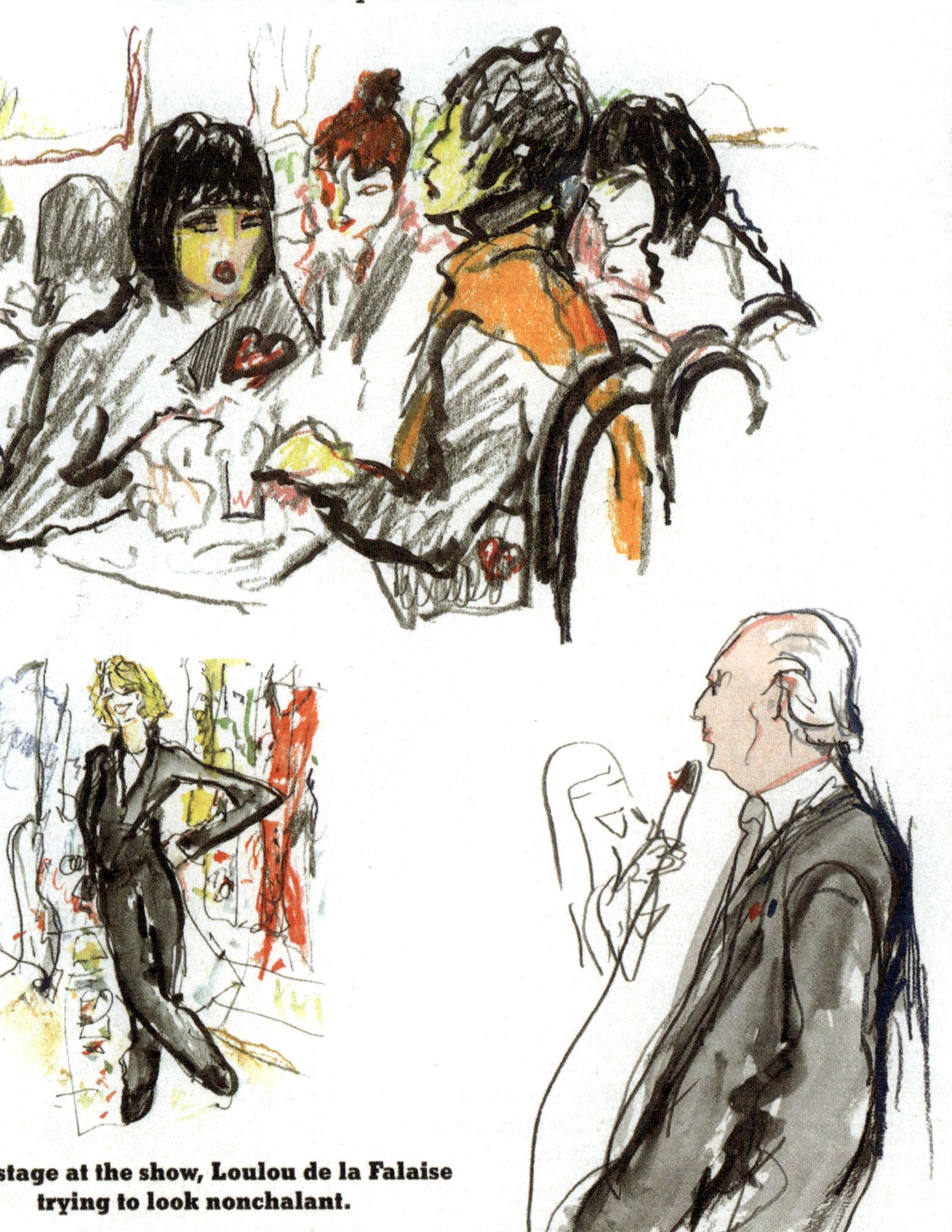

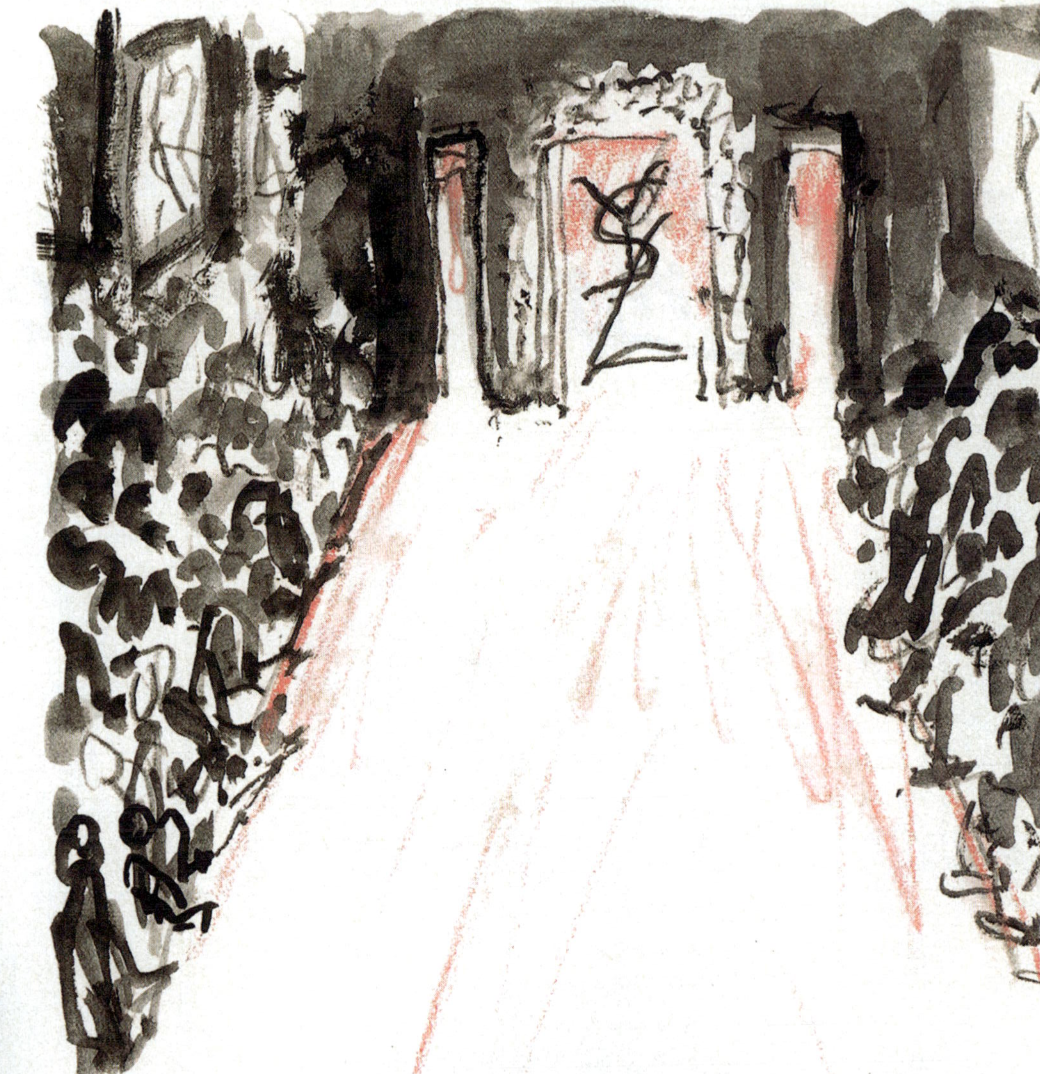

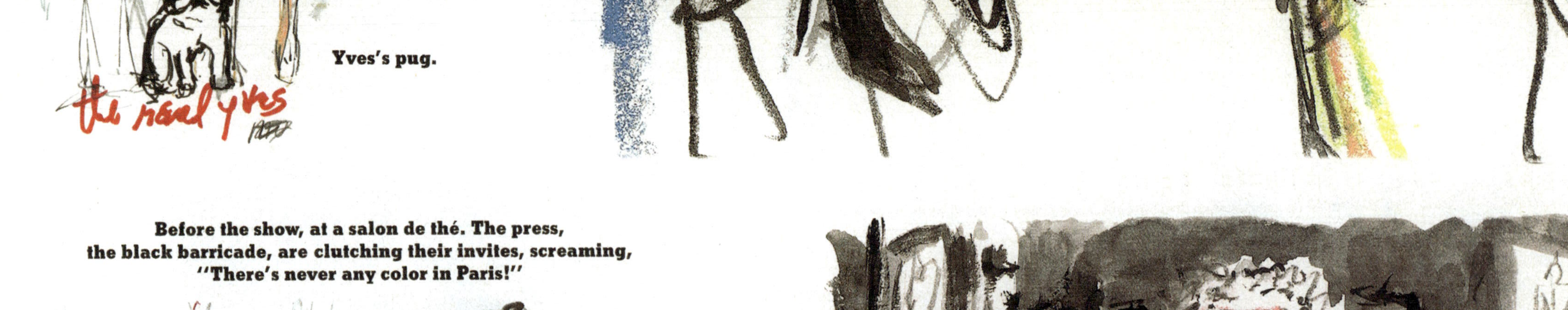

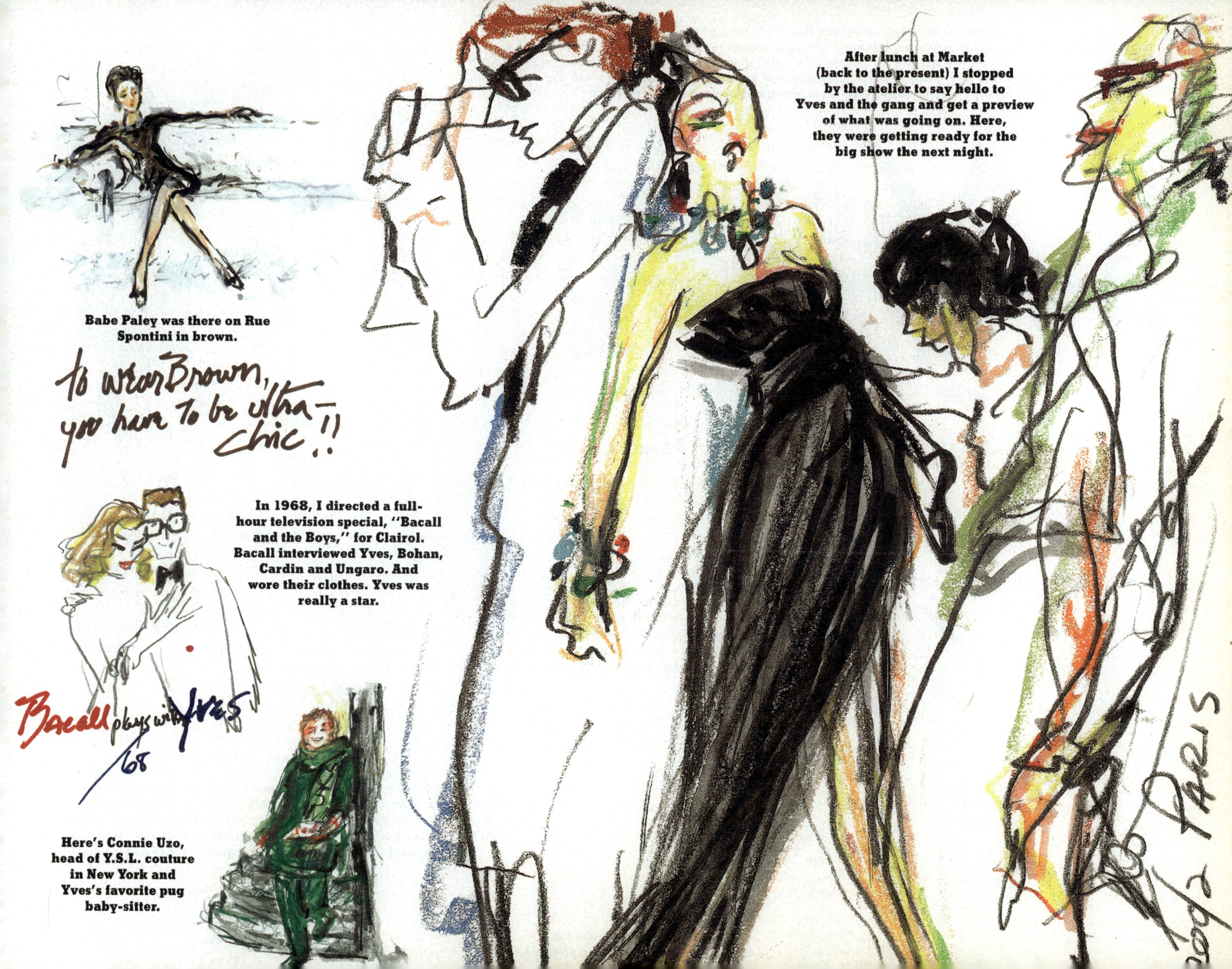

Babe Paley was there on Rue Spontini in brown.

To wear Brown, you have to be ultra — chic !!

In 1968, I directed a full-hour television special, "Bacall and the Boys," for Clairol. Bacall interviewed Yves, Bohan, Cardin and Ungaro. And wore their clothes. Yves was really a star.

Bacall plays with Yves '68

Here's Connie Uzo, head of Y.S.L. couture in New York and Yves's favorite pug baby-sitter.

After lunch at Market (back to the present) I stopped by the atelier to say hello to Yves and the gang and get a preview of what was going on. Here, they were getting ready for the big show the next night.

Paris

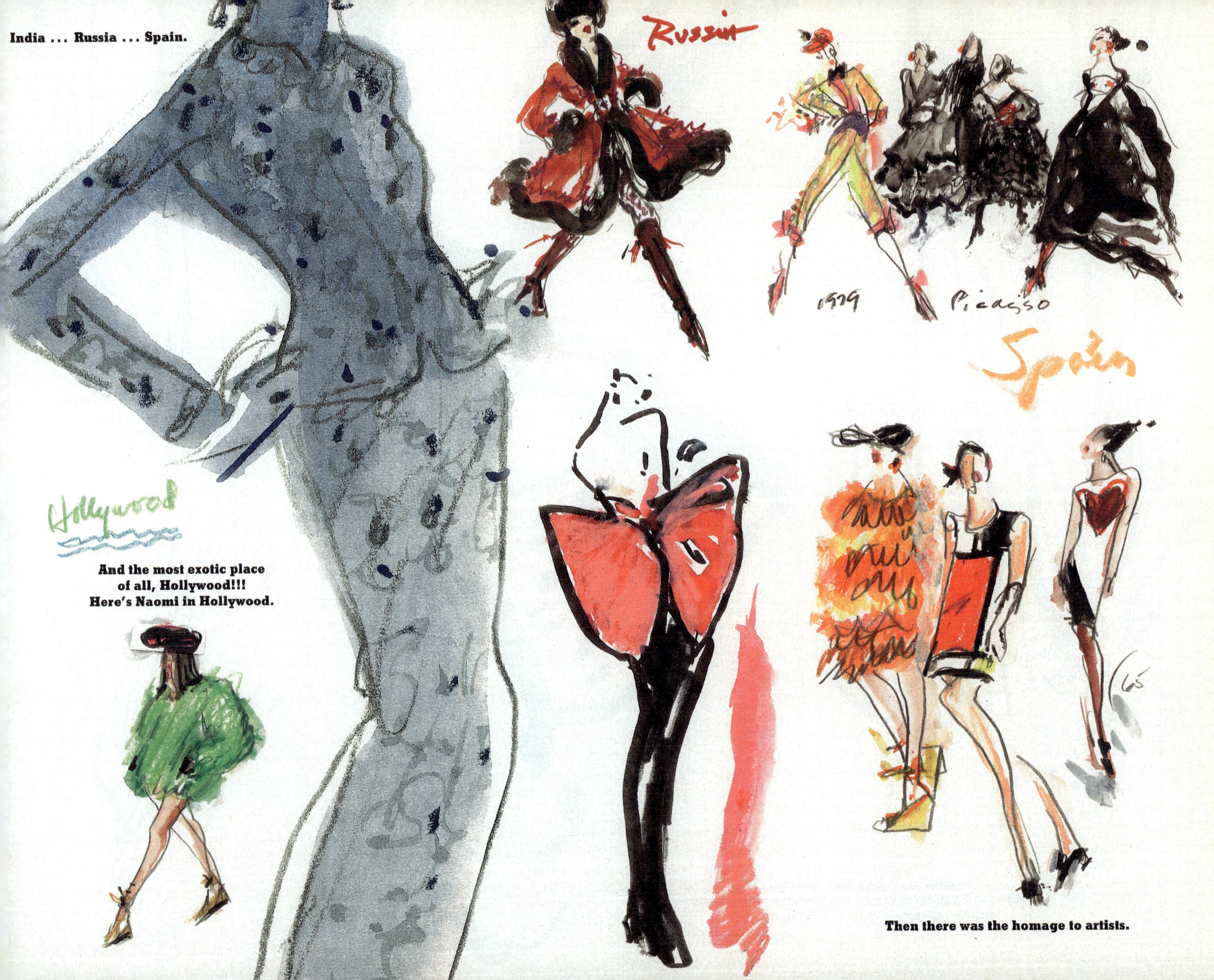
India ... Russia ... Spain.
Russia
1929
Picasso
Spain
Hollywood
And the most exotic place
of all, Hollywood!!!
Here's Naomi in Hollywood.
Then there was the homage to artists.

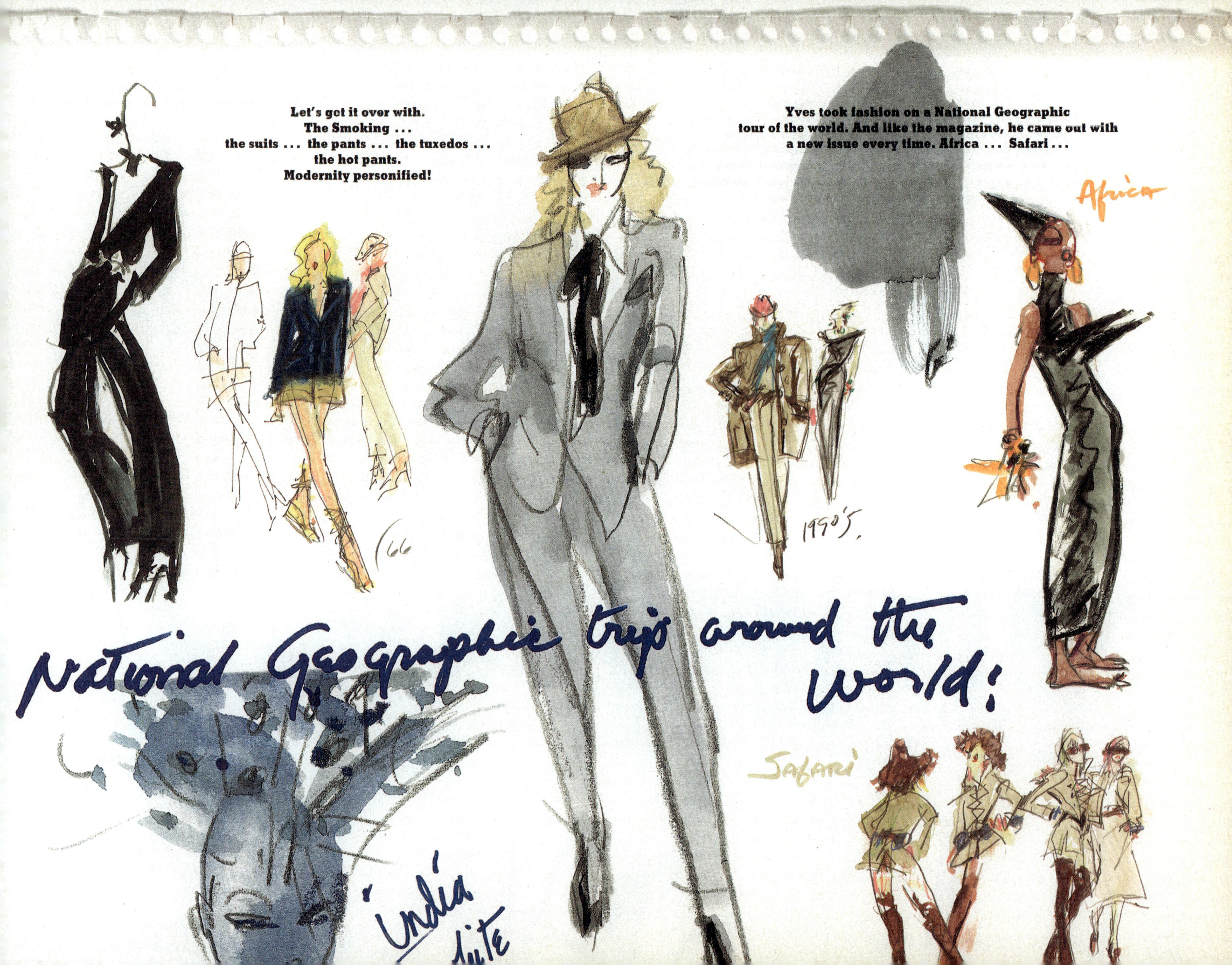

Let's got it over with.
The Smoking …
the suits … the pants … the tuxedos …
the hot pants.
Modernity personified!
Yves took fashion on a National Geographic
tour of the world. And like the magazine, he came out with
a new issue every time. Africa … Safari …
Africa
1990's.
National Geographic trips around the world!
India
Safari

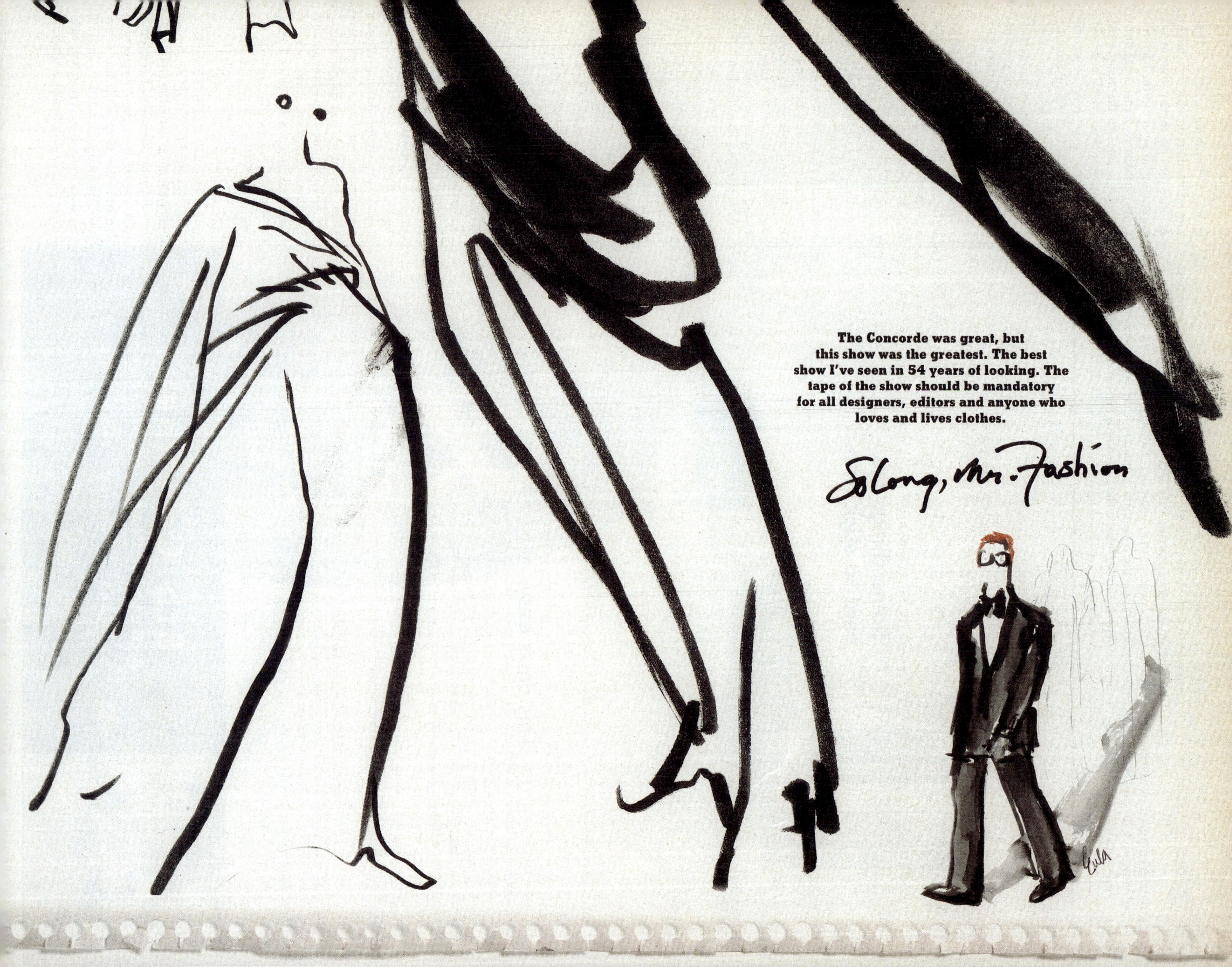

The Concorde was great, but this show was the greatest. The best show I've seen in 54 years of looking. The tape of the show should be mandatory for all designers, editors and anyone who loves and lives clothes.

So long, Mr. Fashion

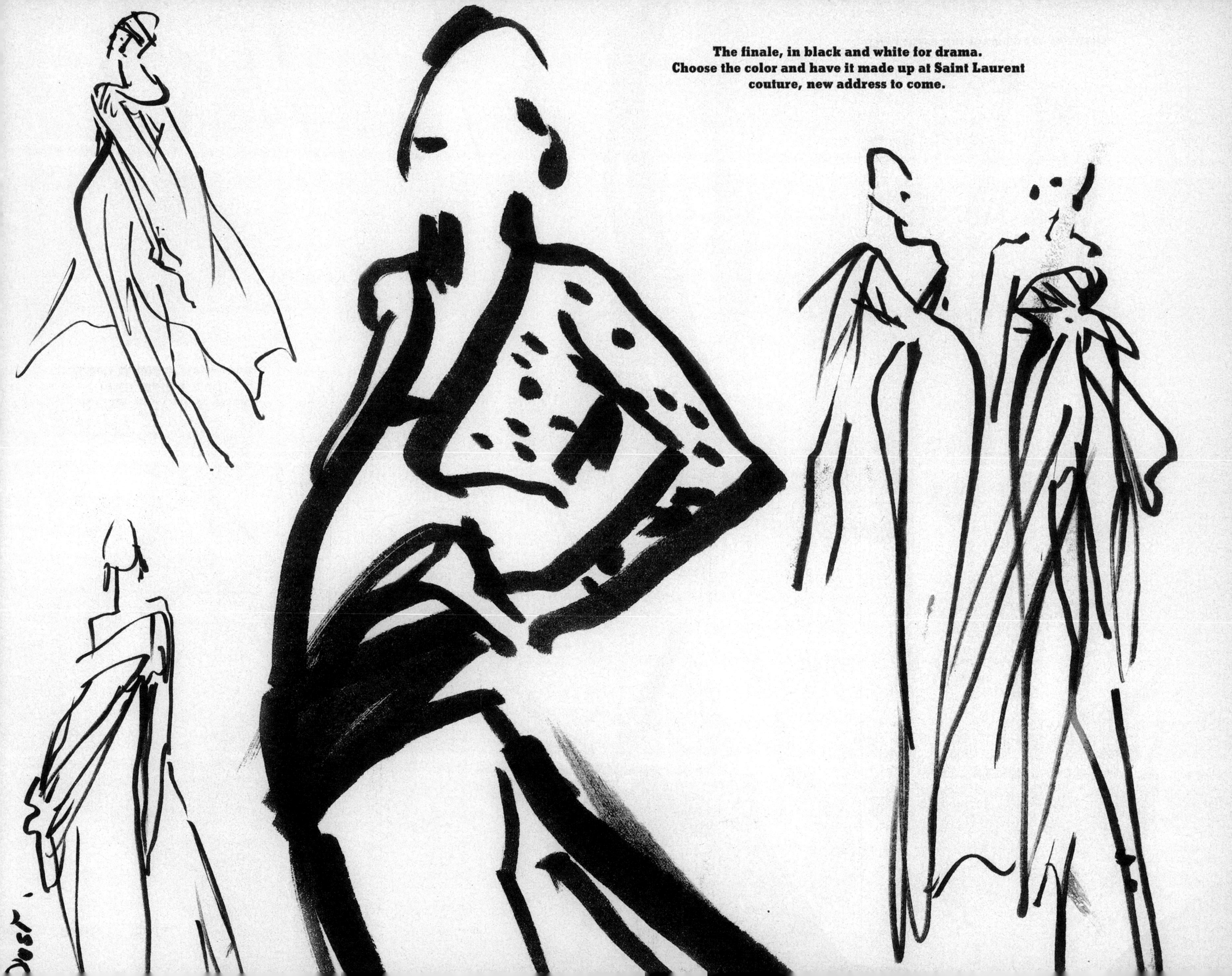

The finale, in black and white for drama. Choose the color and have it made up at Saint Laurent couture, new address to come.

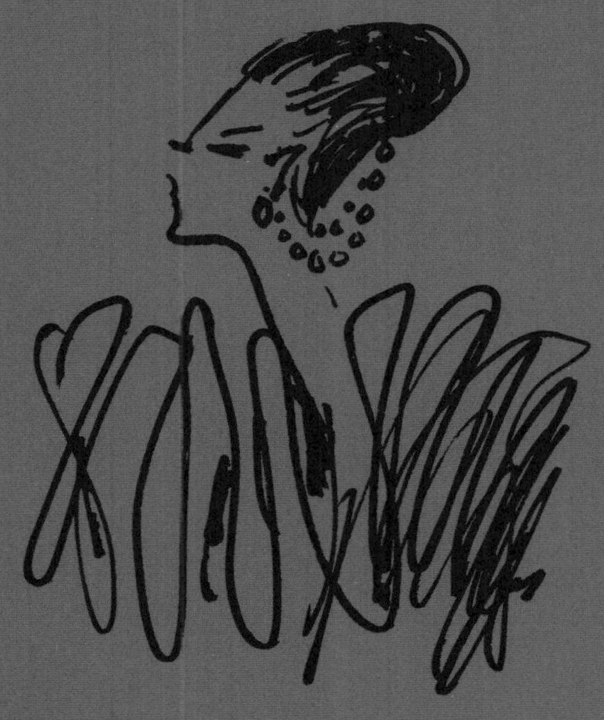

Plates

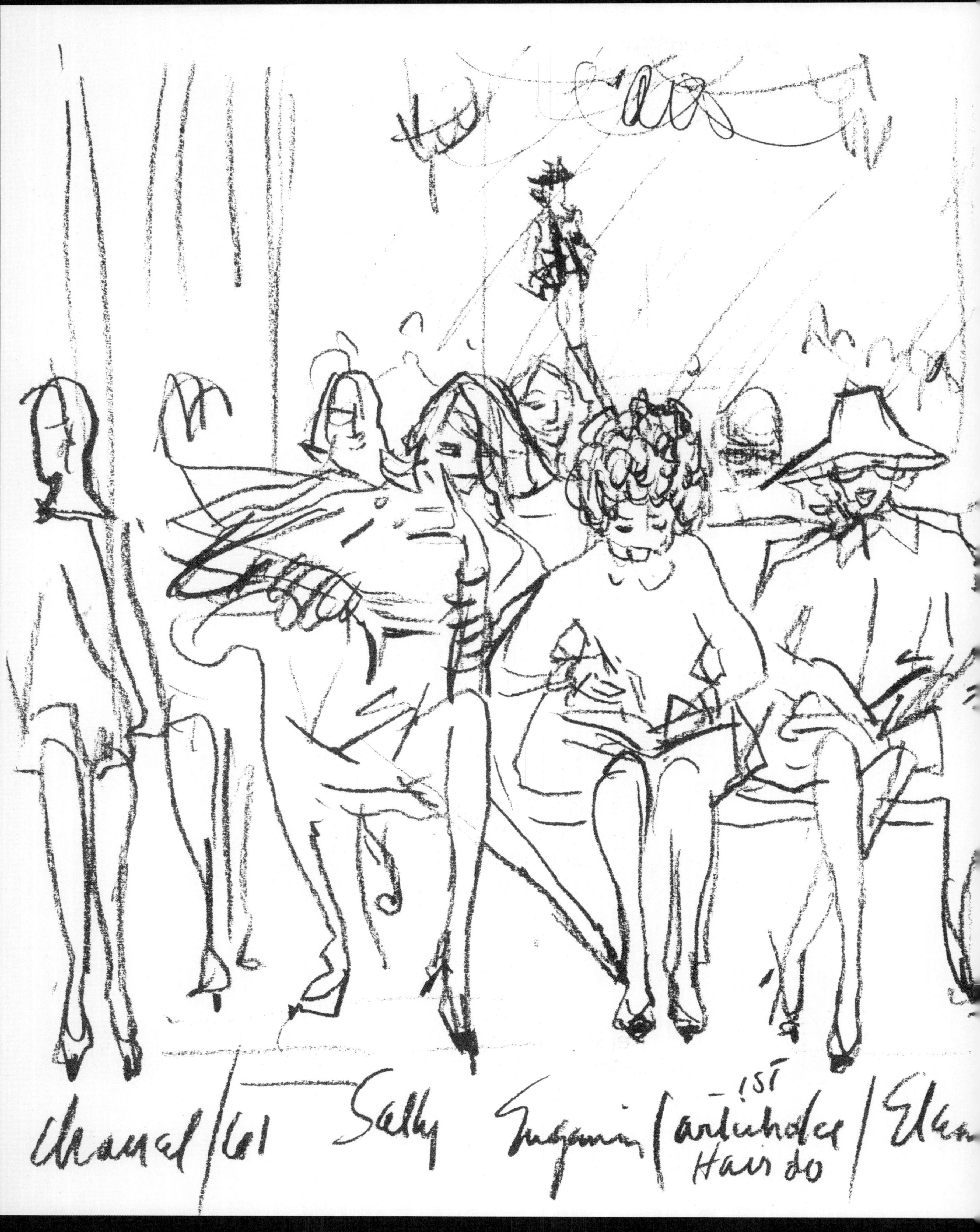

Chanel/61
Sally
Benjamin / artichoke / Elea
1st
Hair do

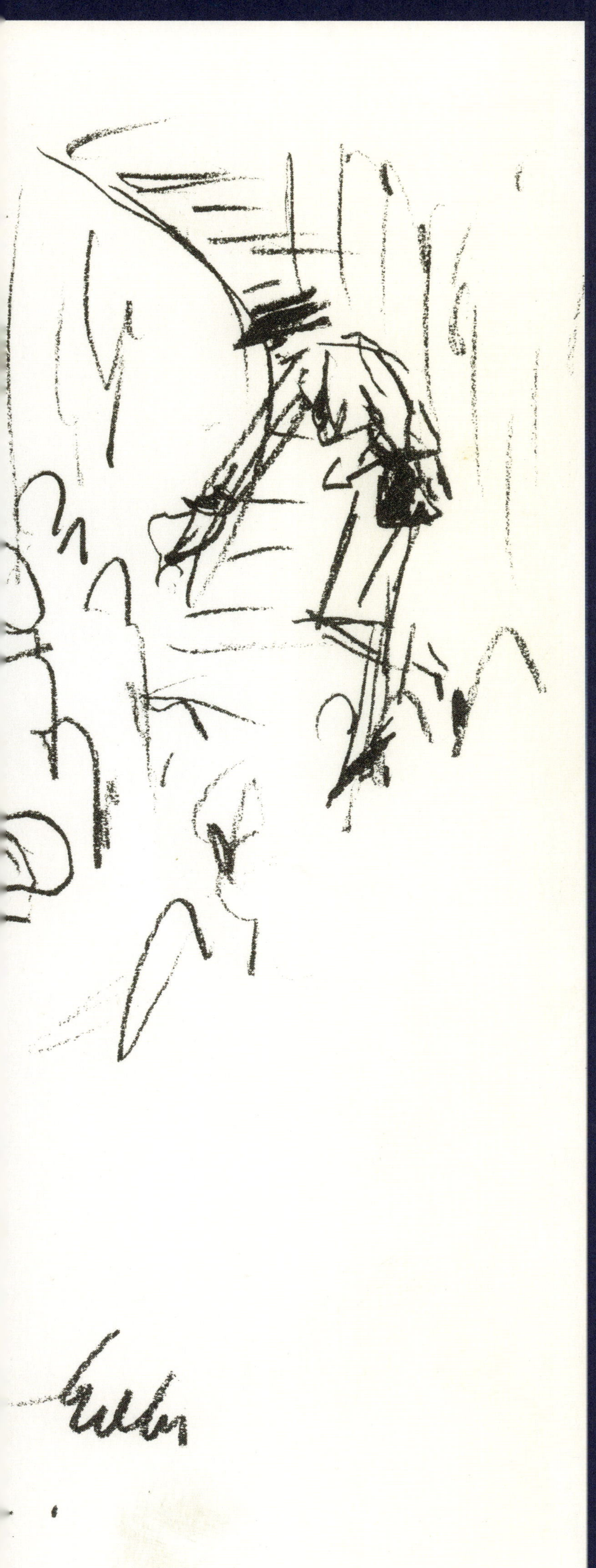

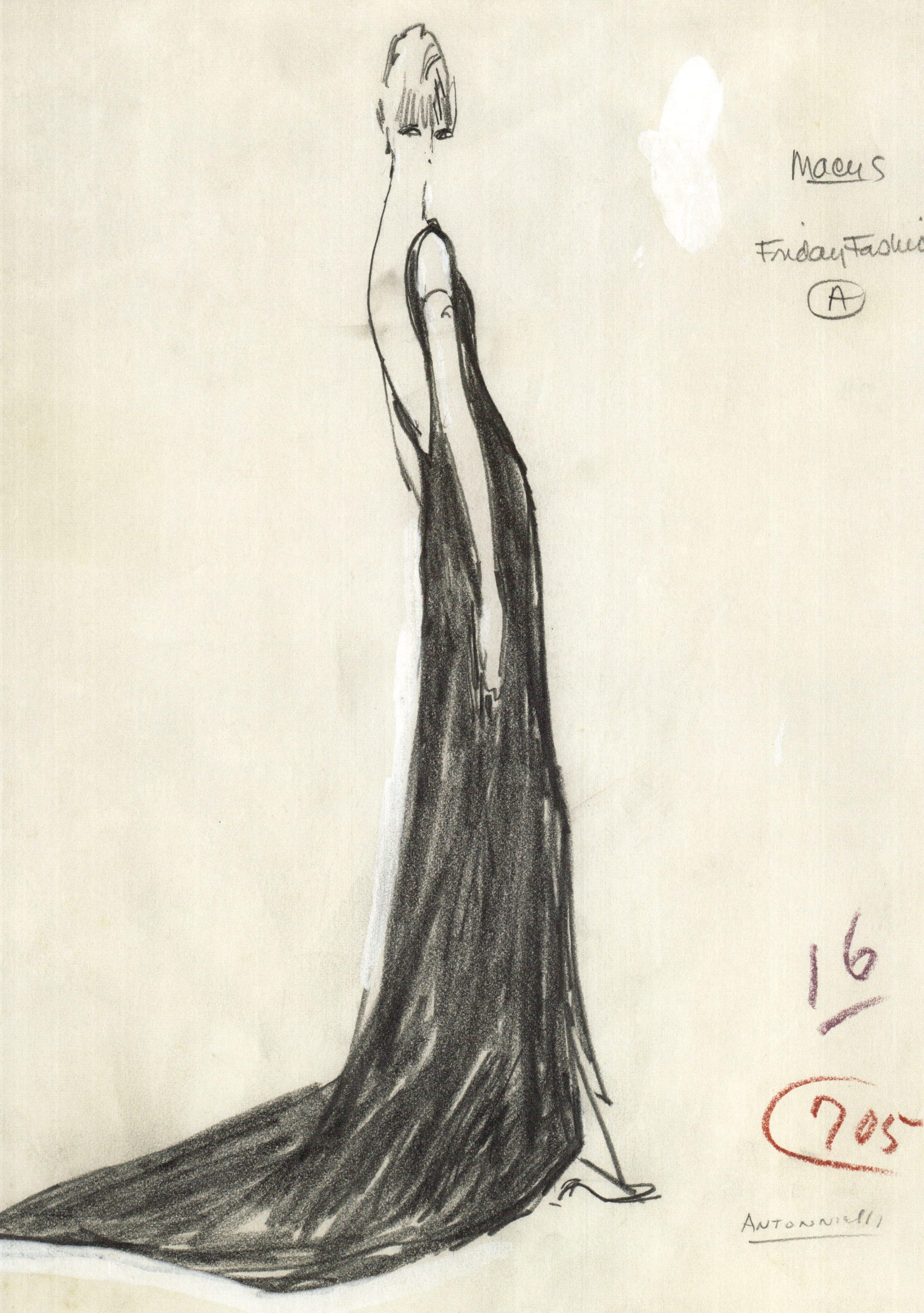

Macys
Friday Fashion
A
16
705
ANTONNIELLI

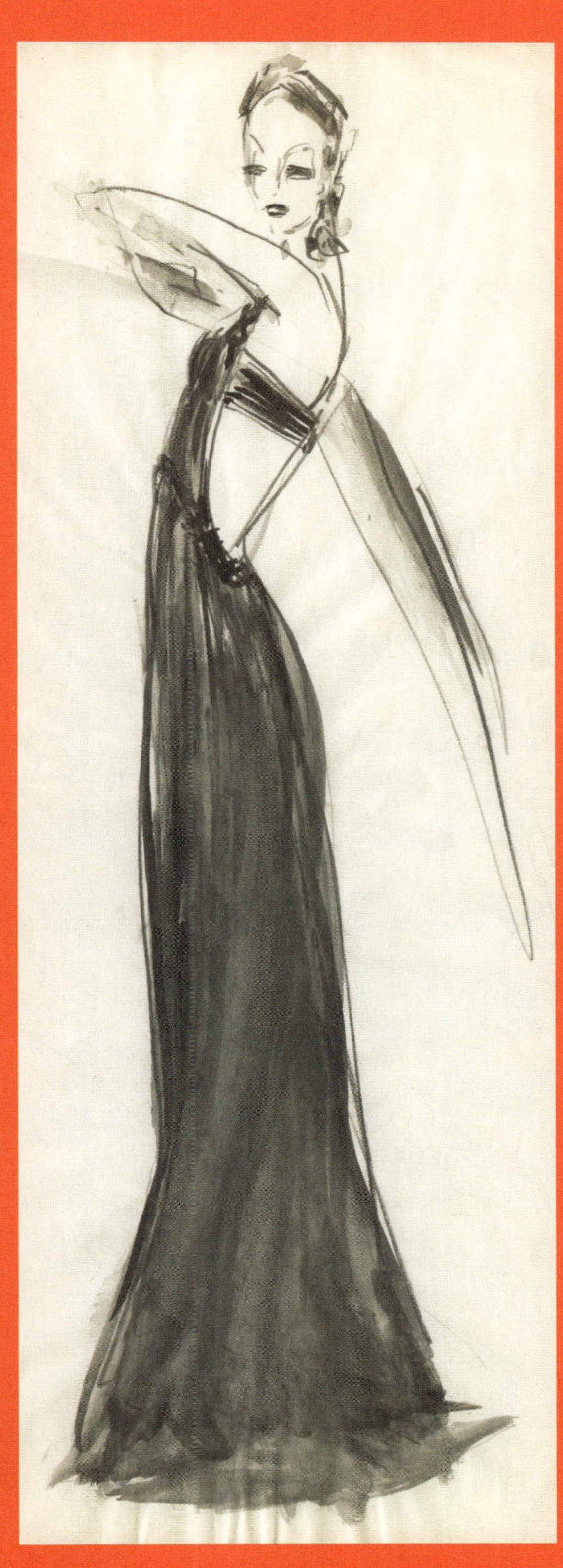

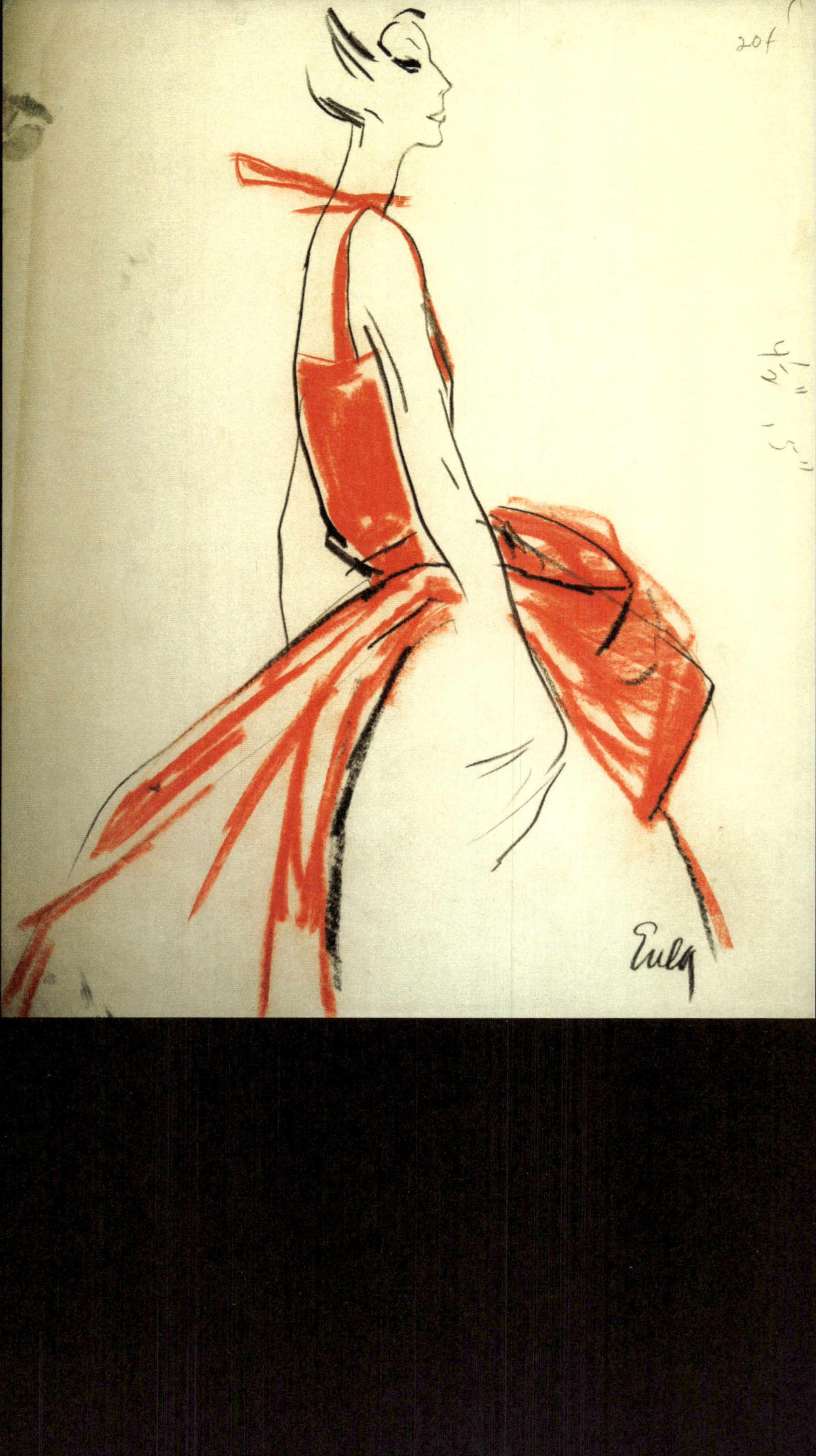

20f
4½"=5"
Eula

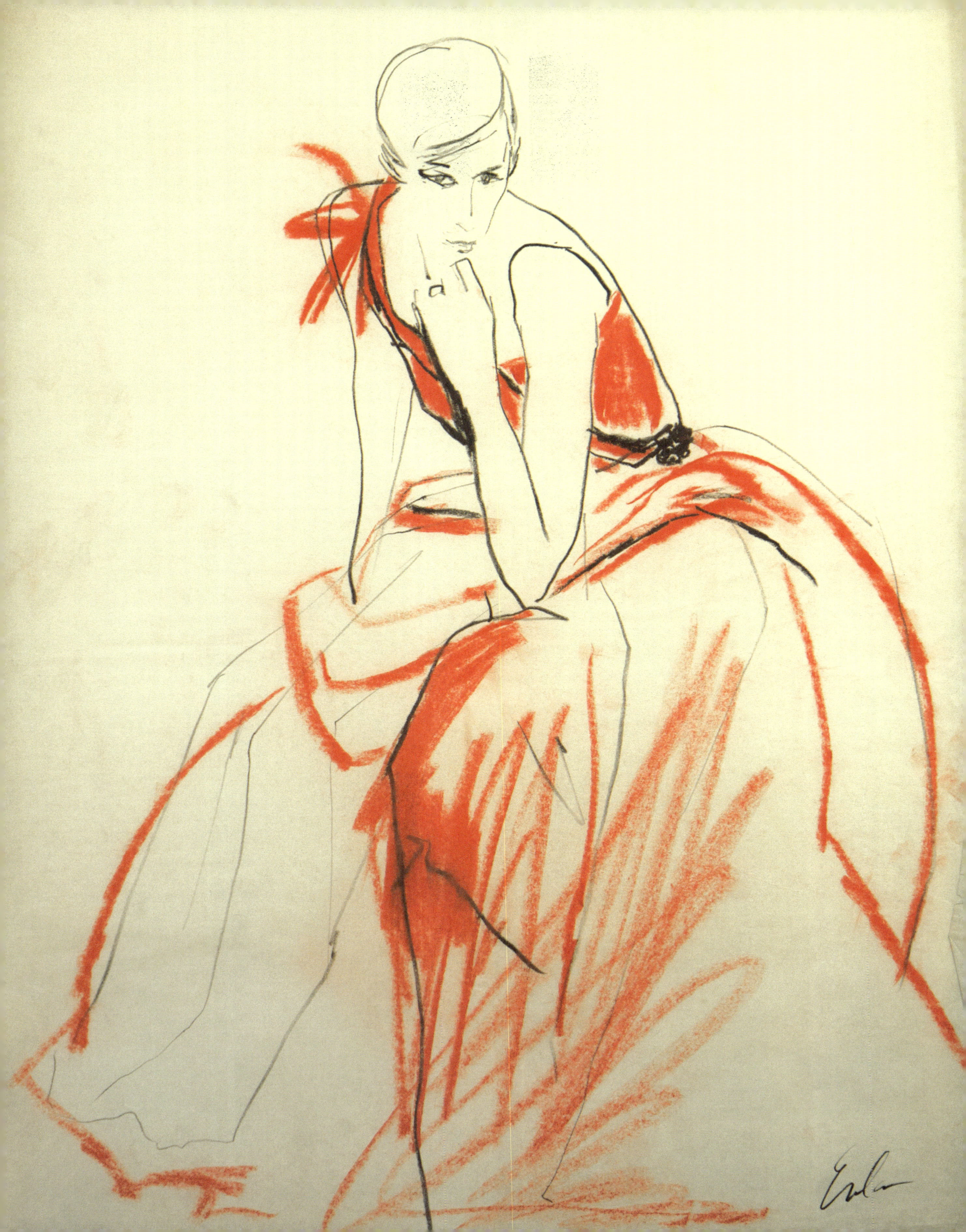

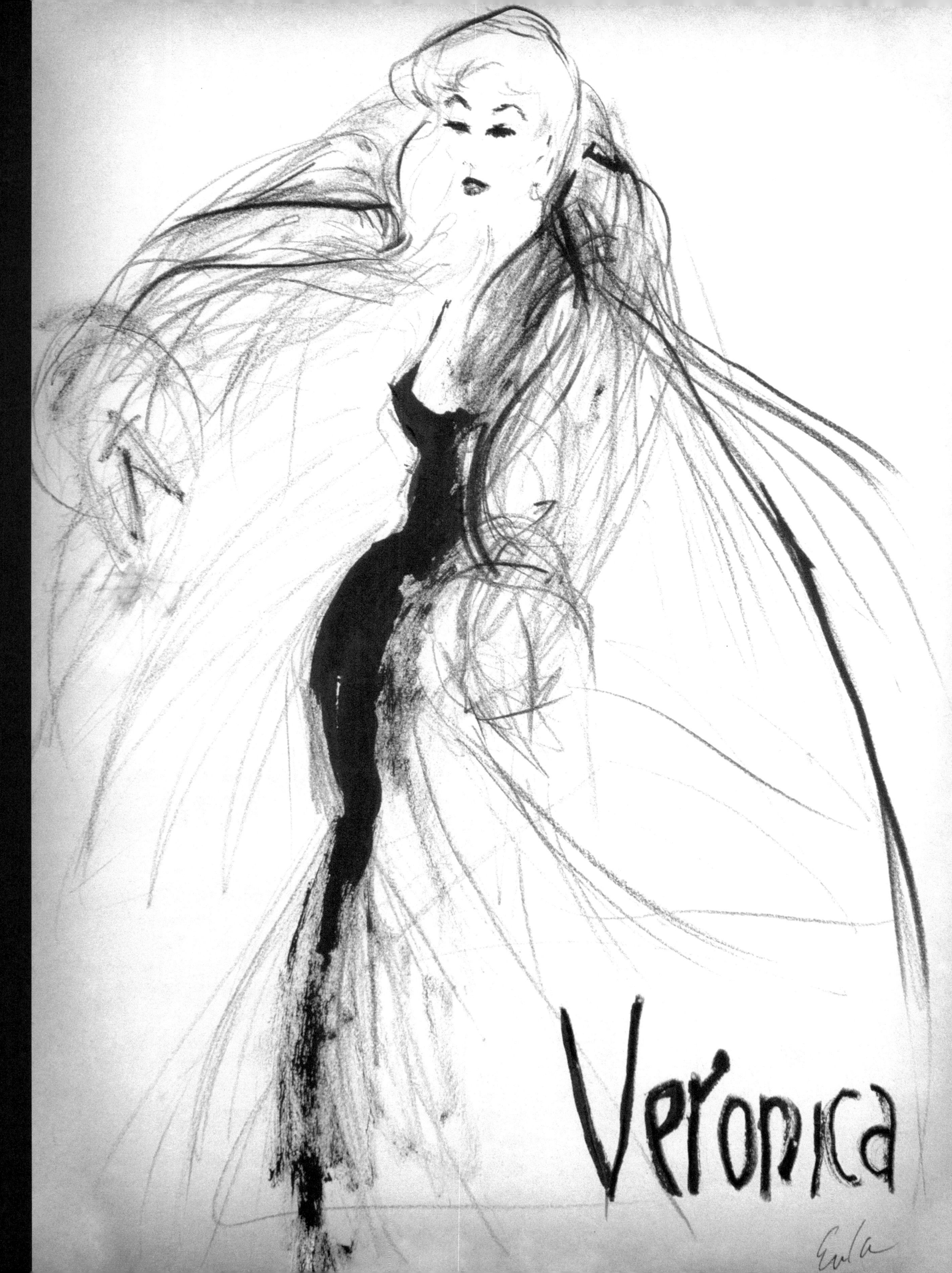

Veronica

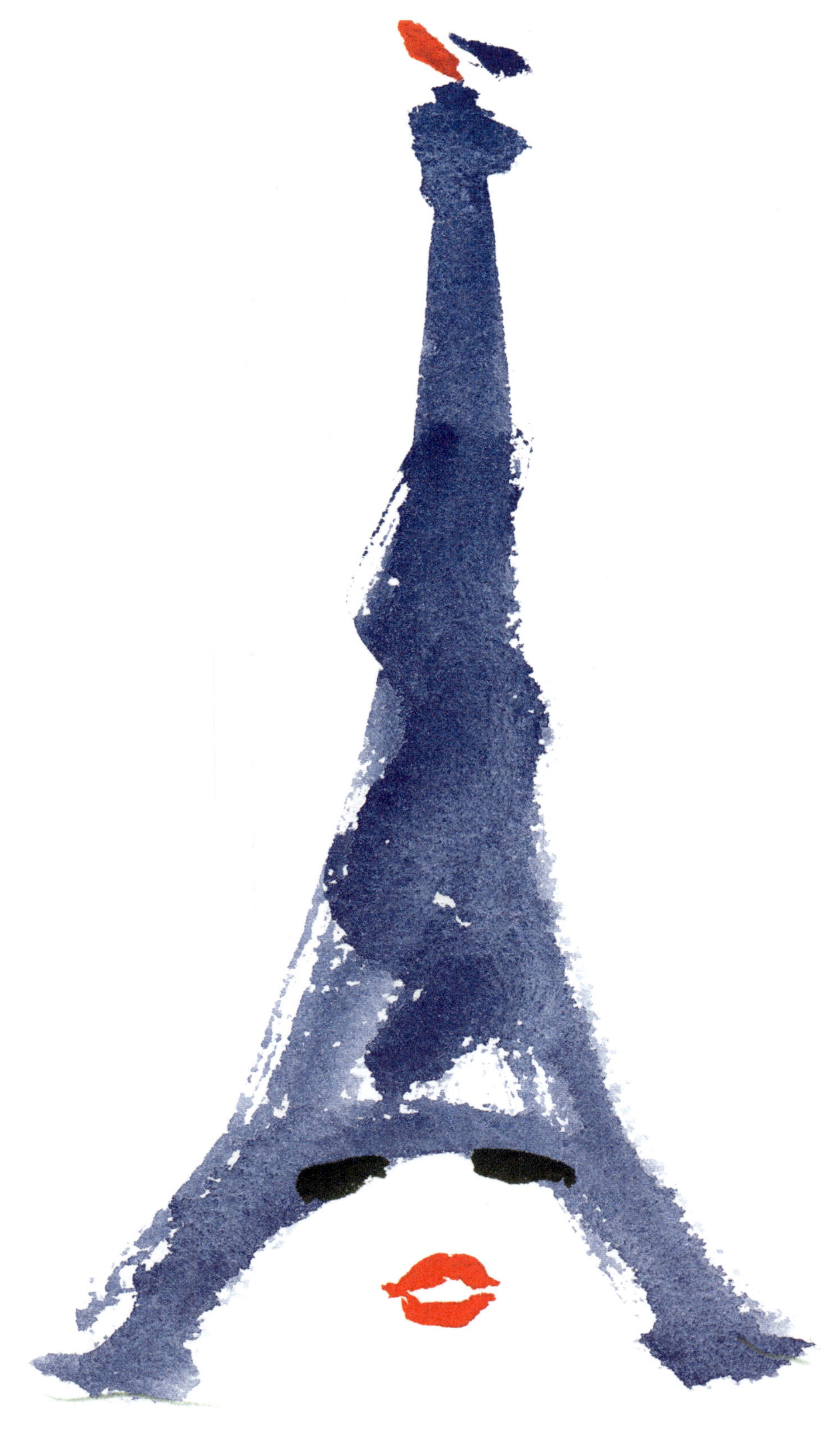

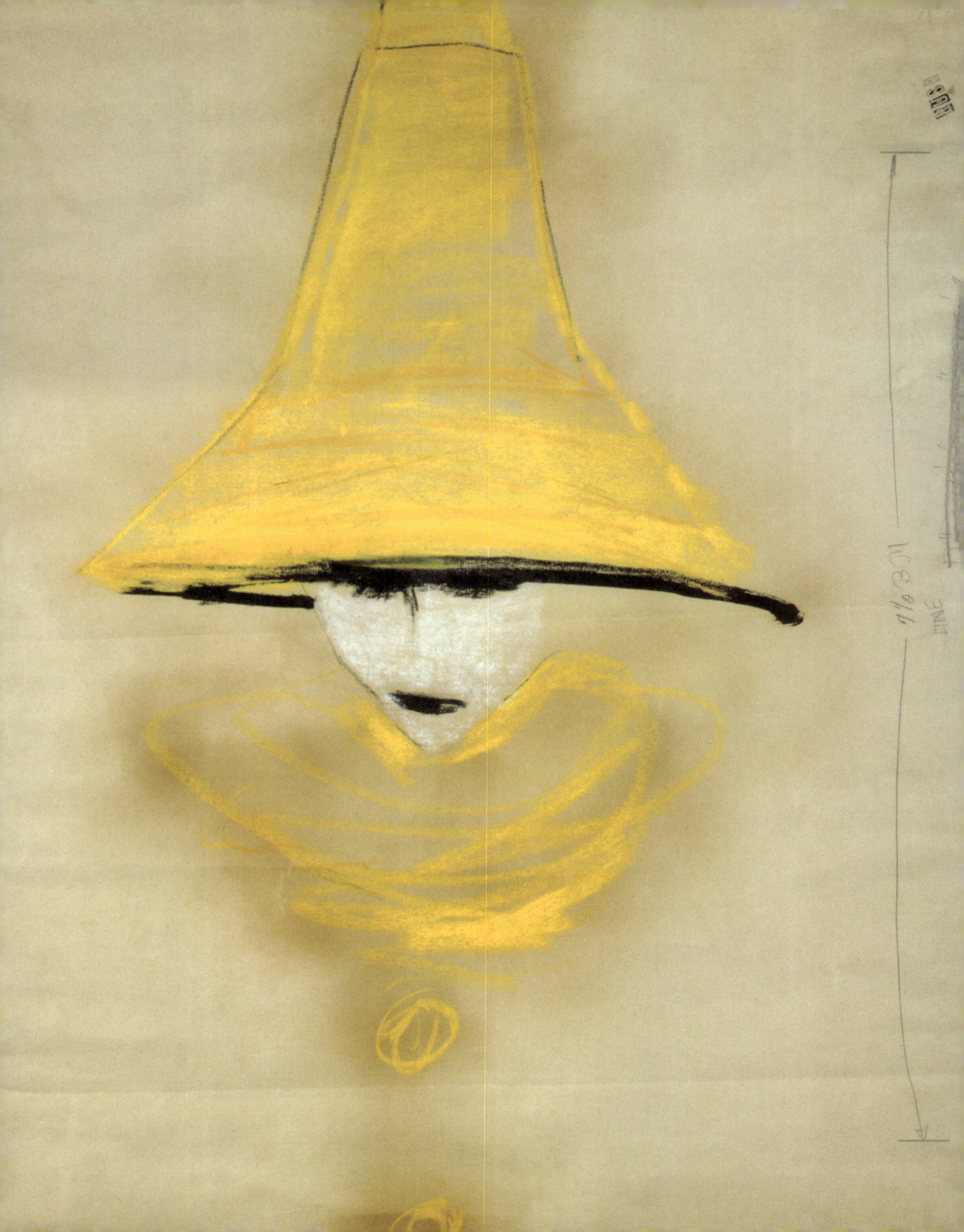

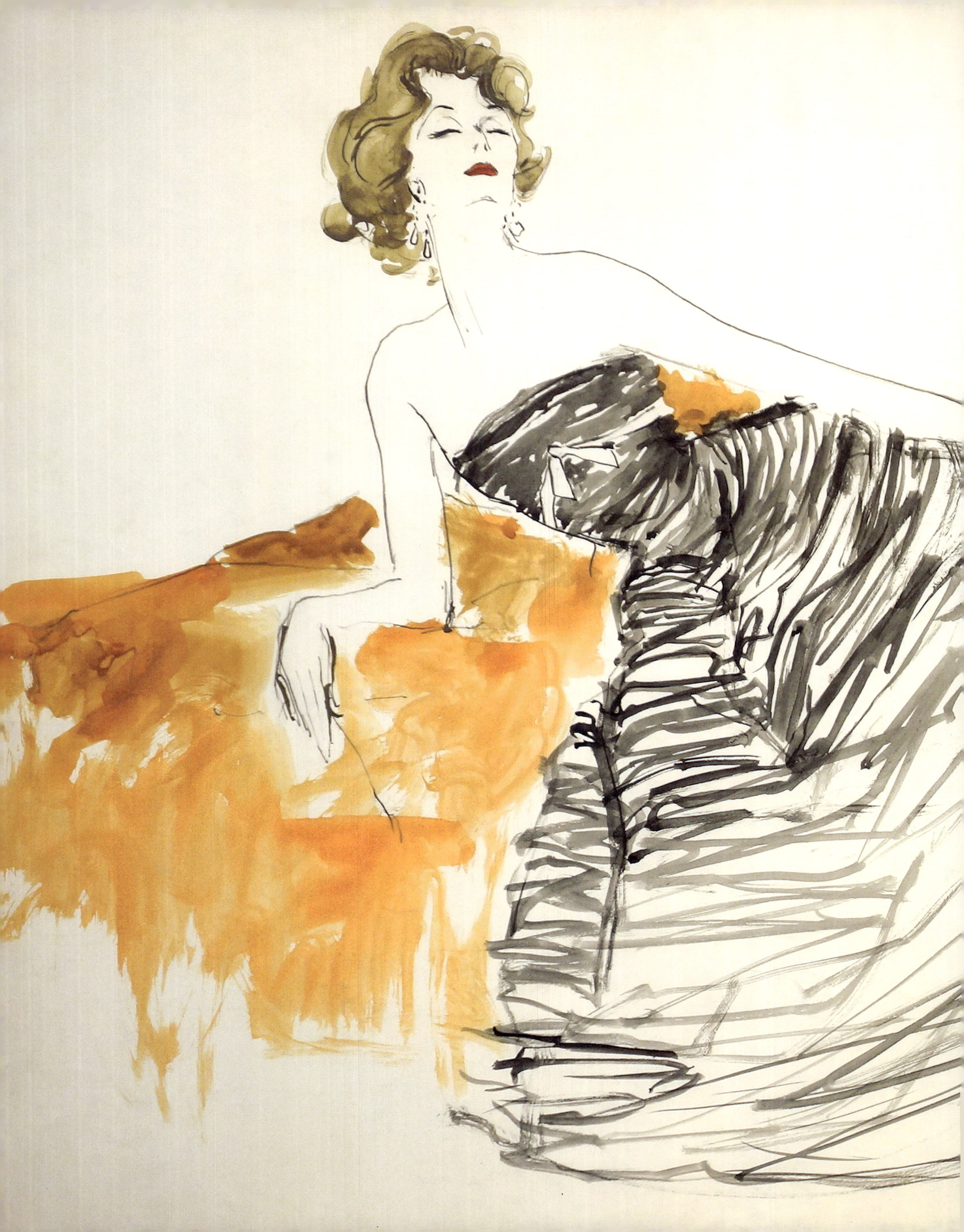

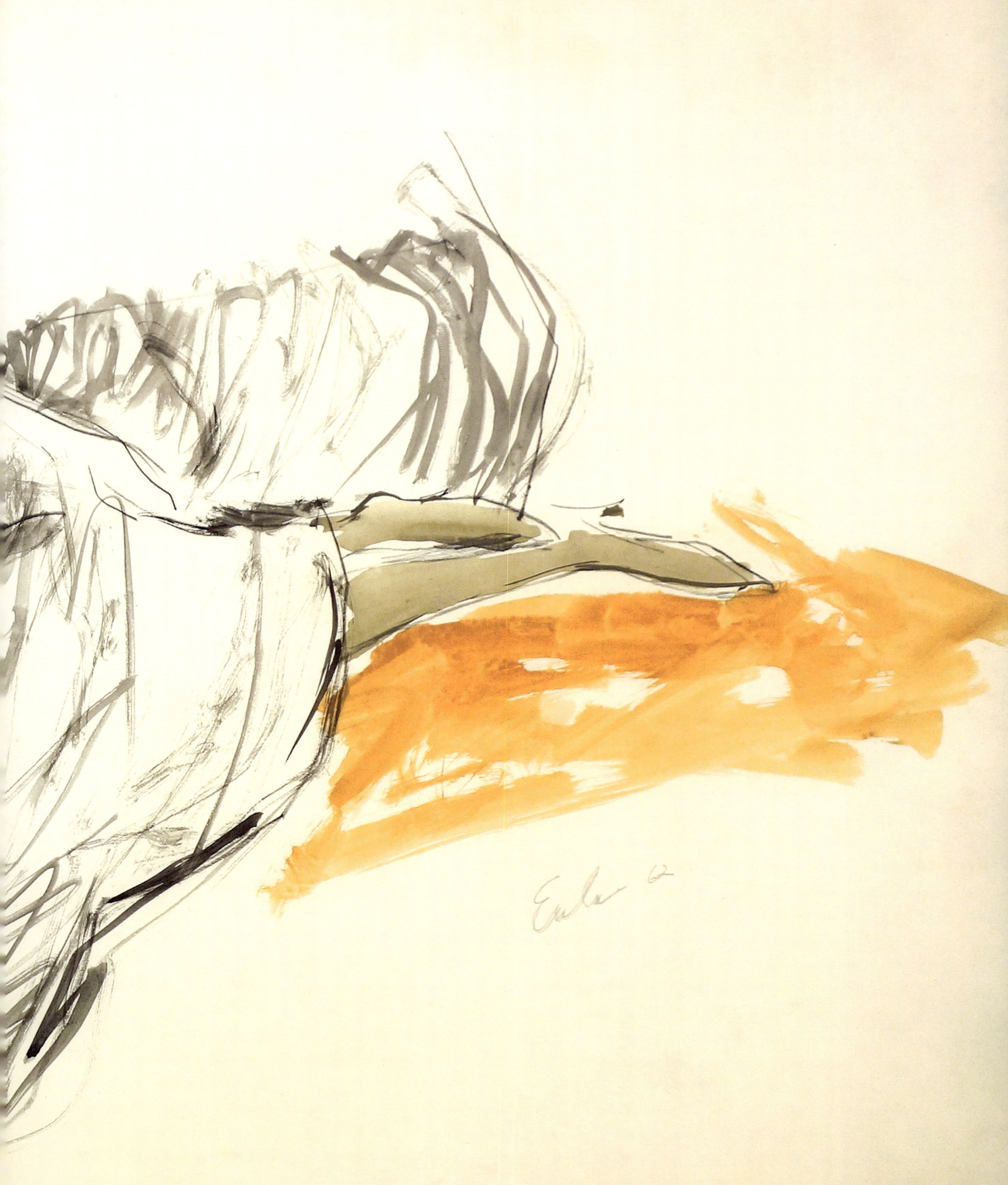

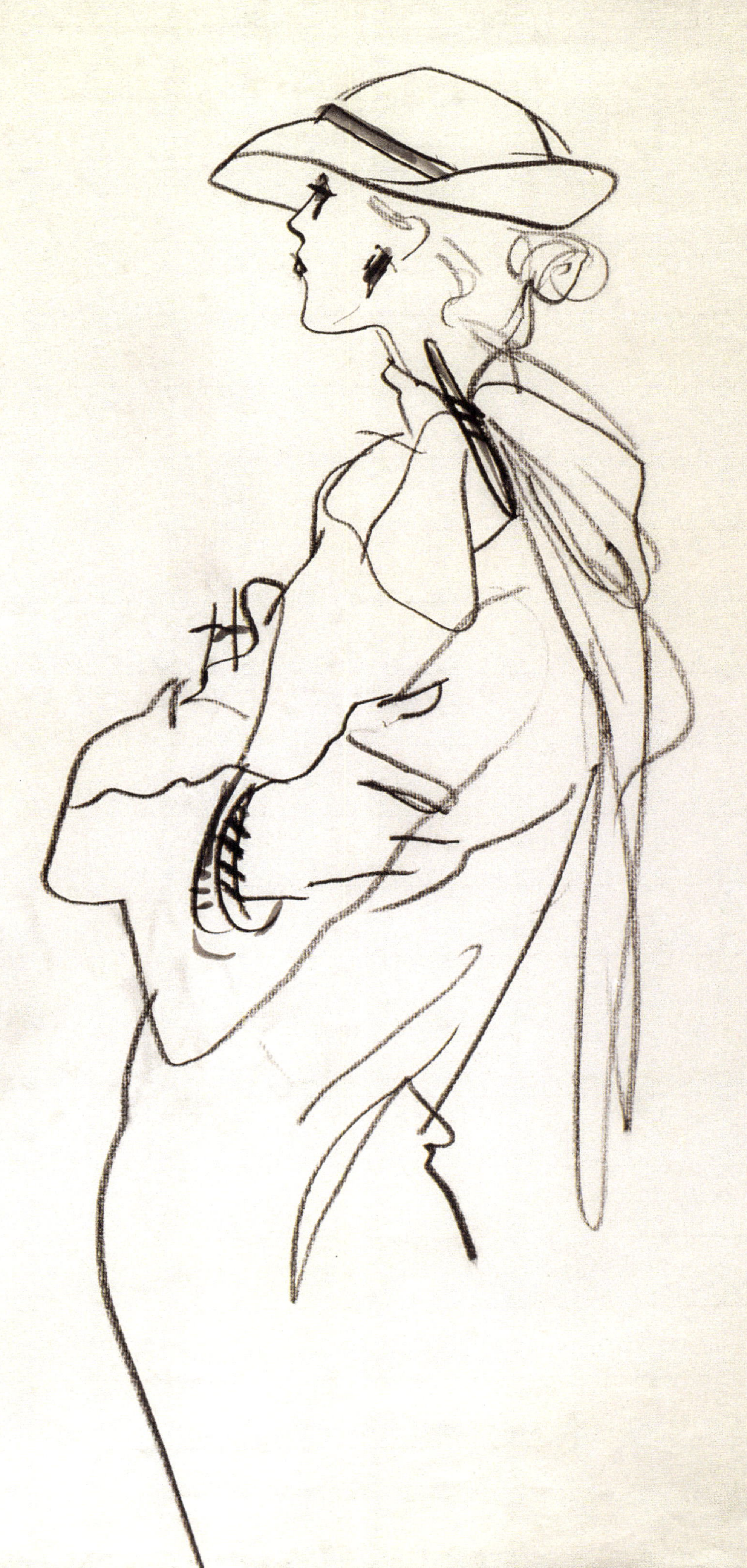

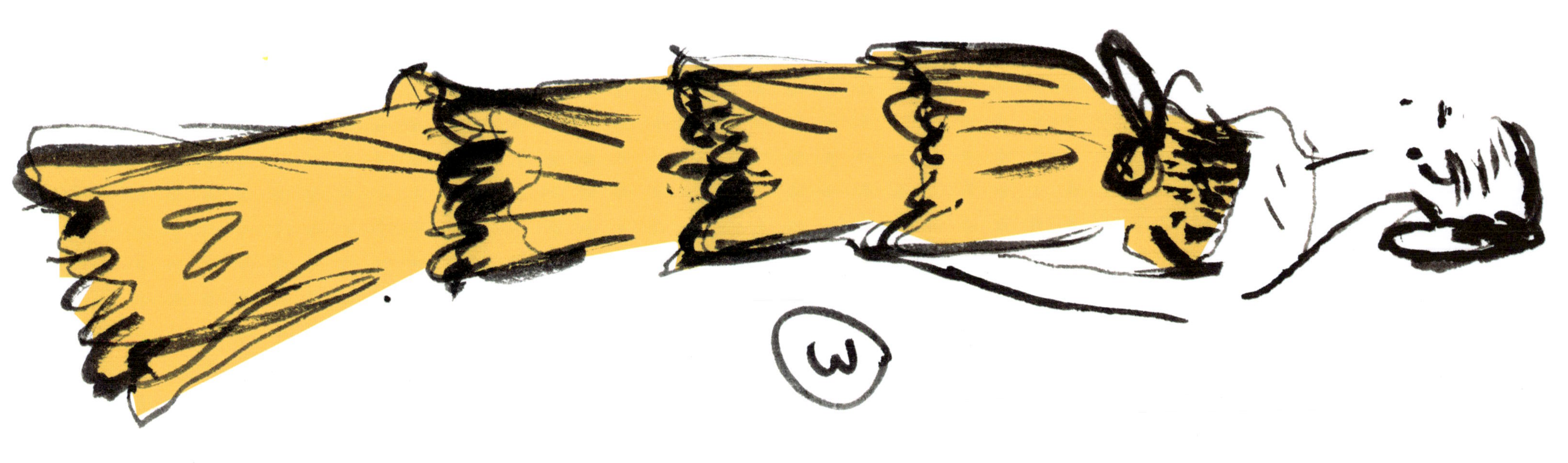
HERTRIB NYK - VIA PREWI
Pa/Bw. N° 11 - 3/8 - 1825G - 150 Sg.
3

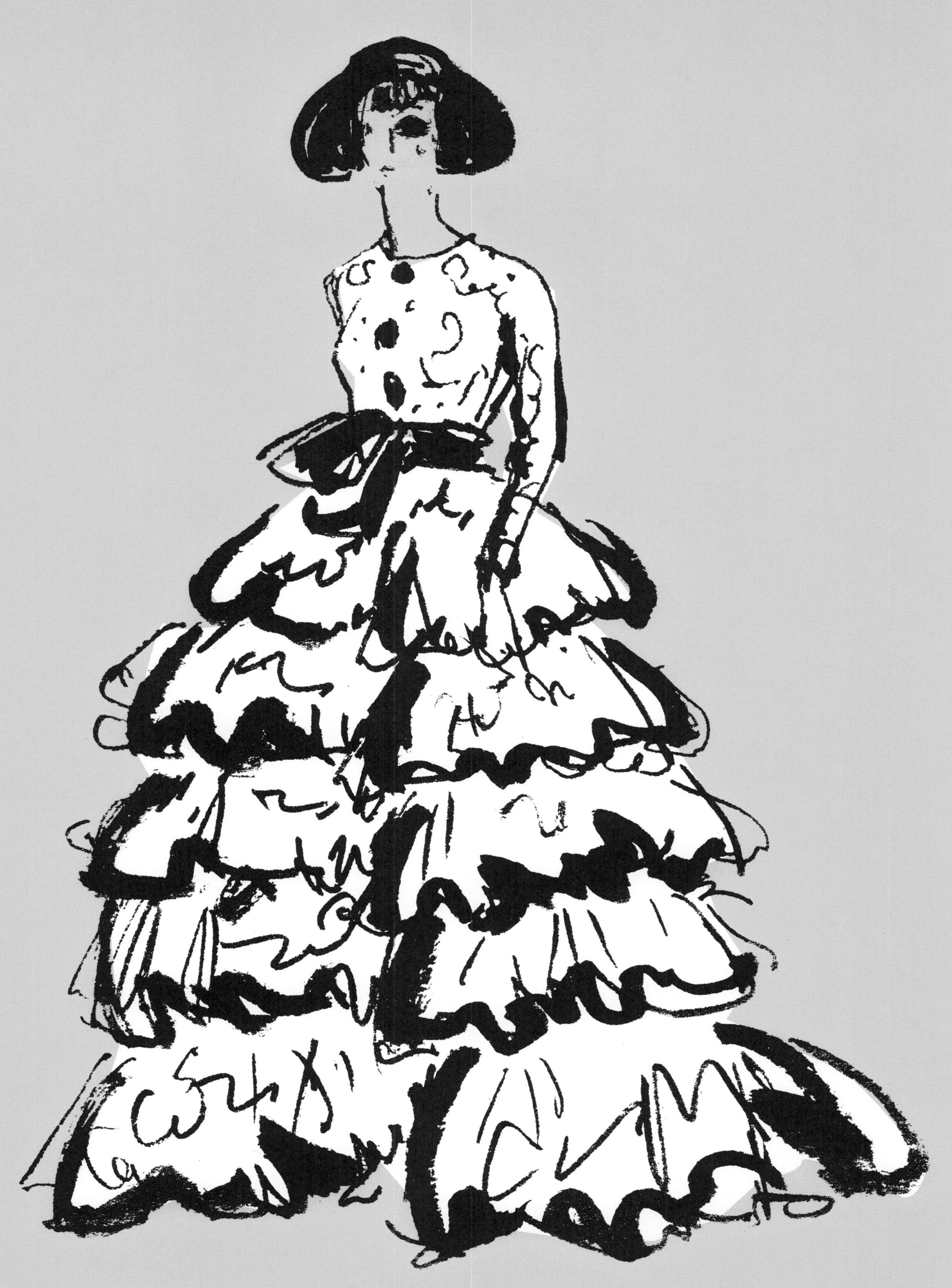

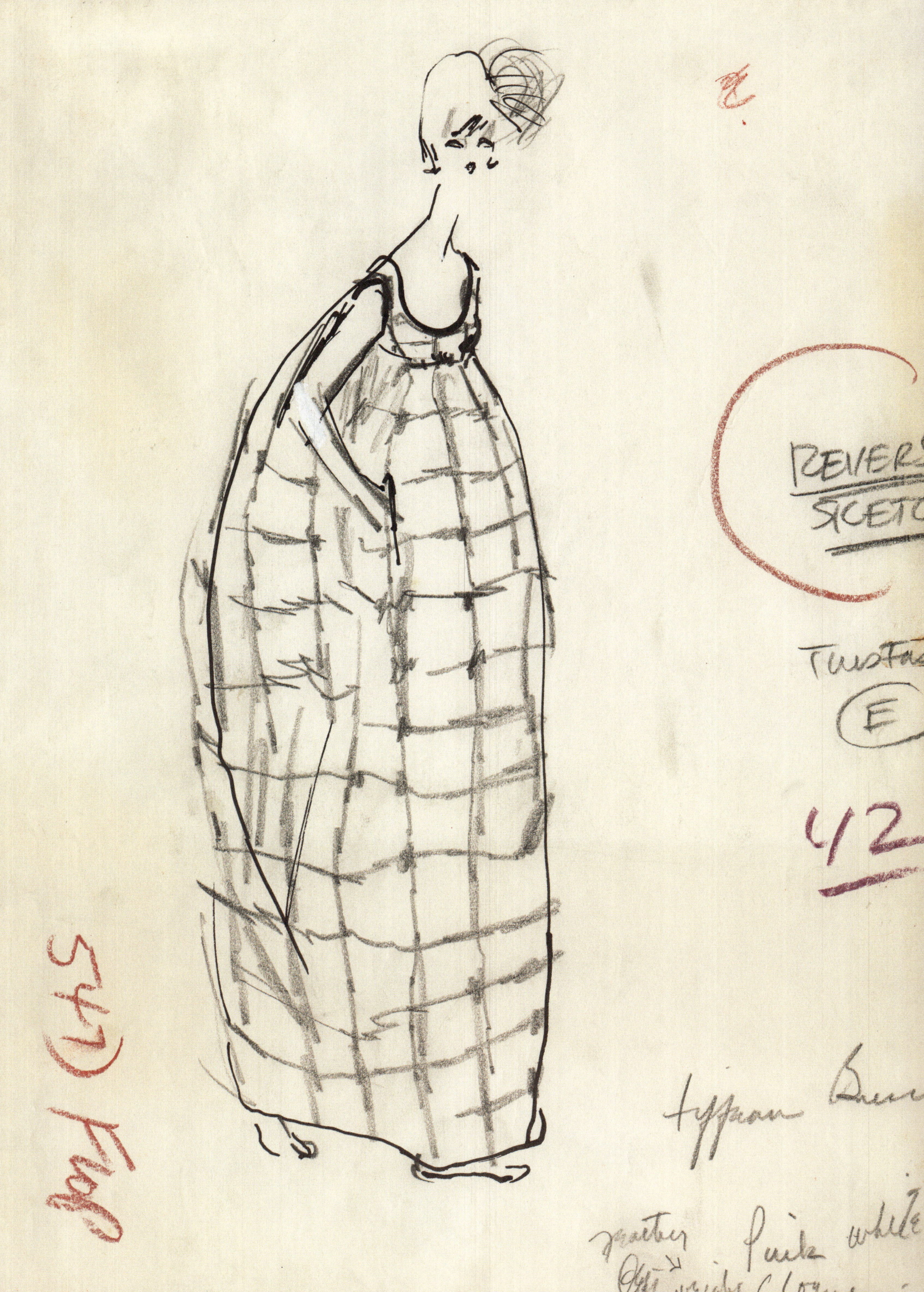
REVERS
SCETC
TwoFac
E
42
tiffman bur
matter   pink white
off weight cloque

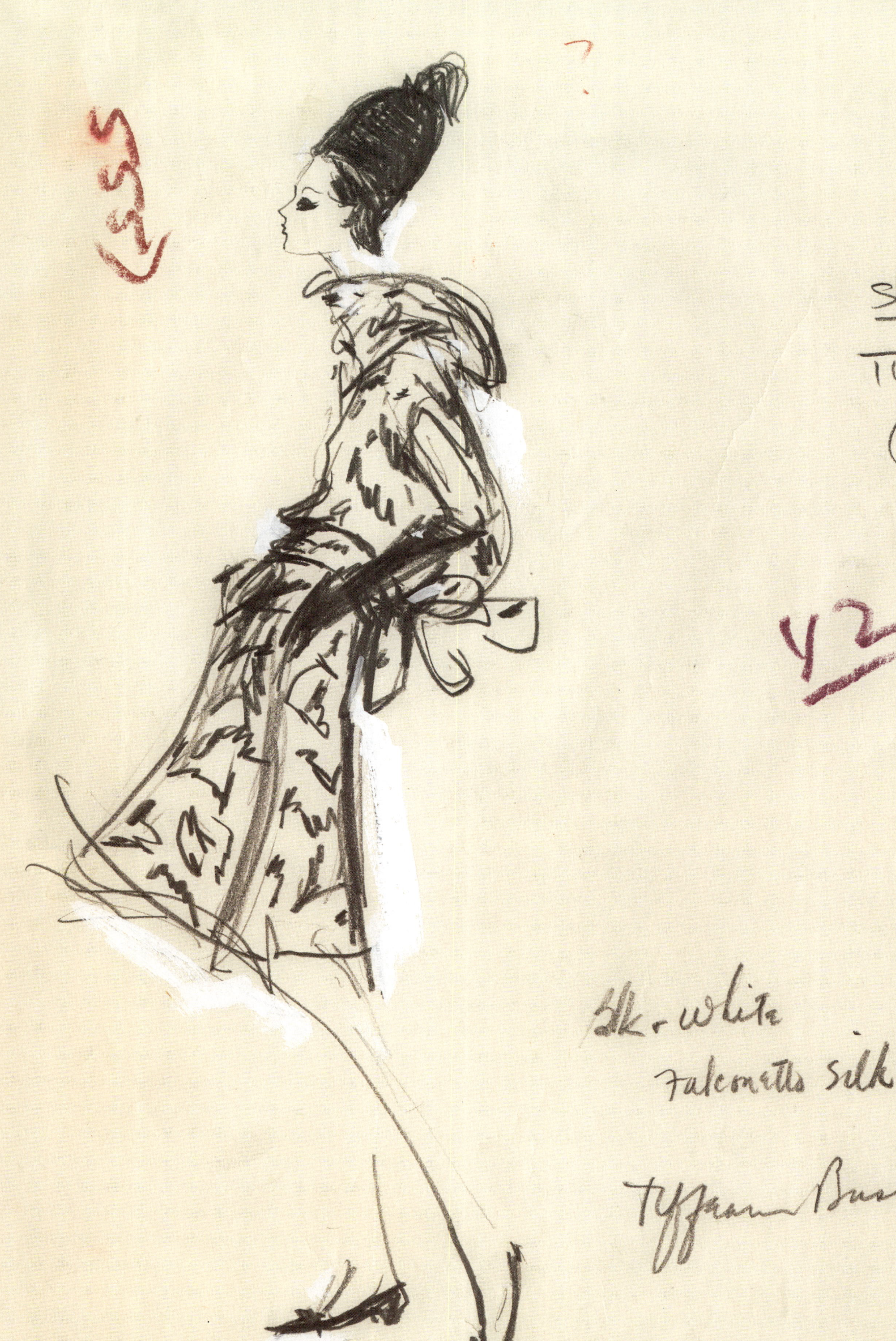

shows
Tues Fac
D
Blk + White
Falconetto silk Print
Tiffany Busch

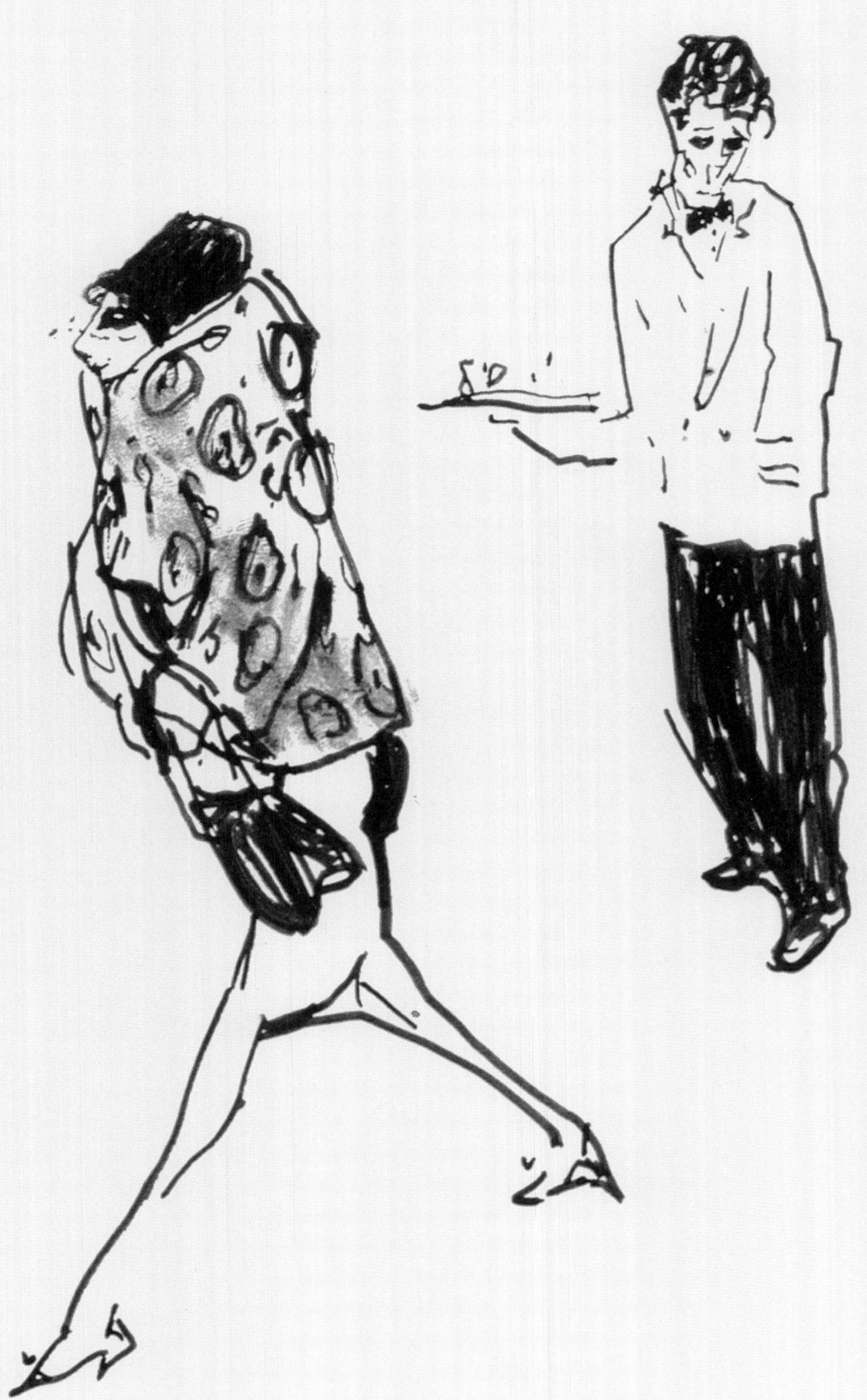

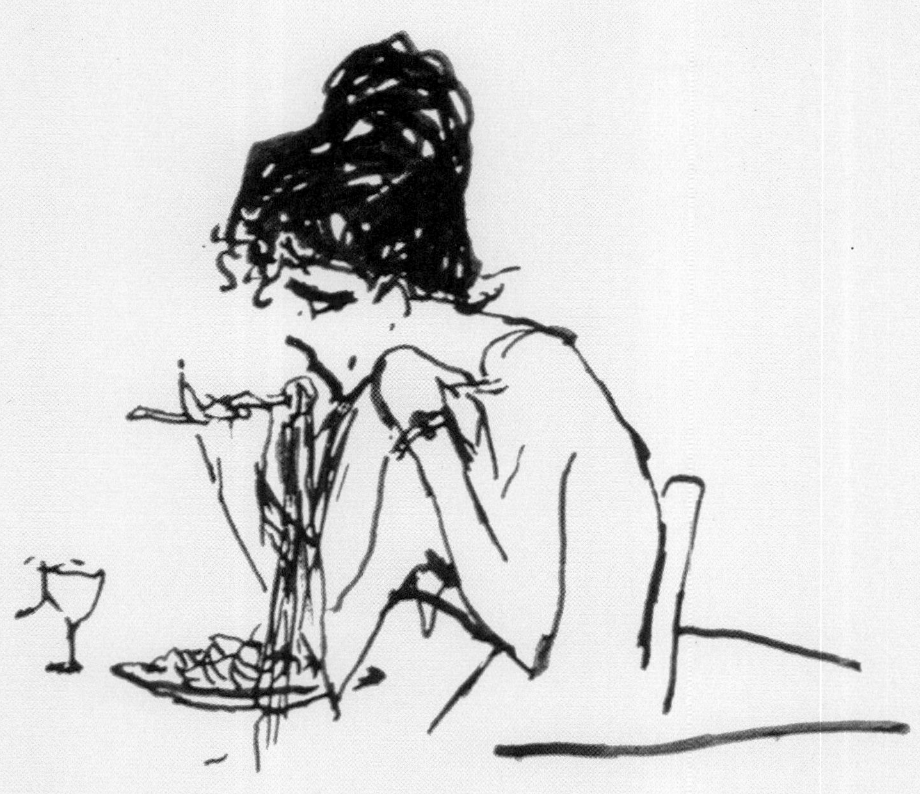

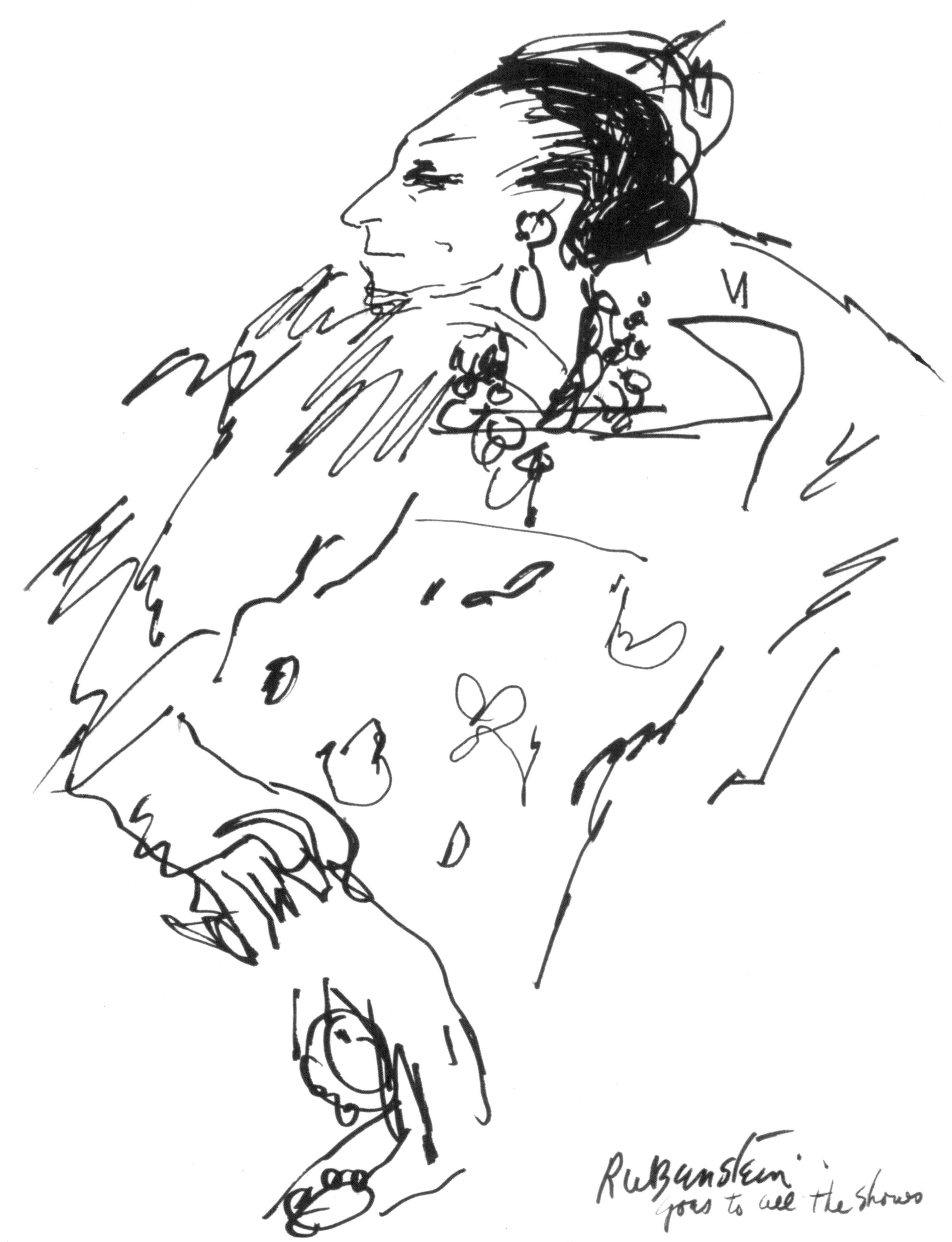

Rubenstein
goes to all the shows

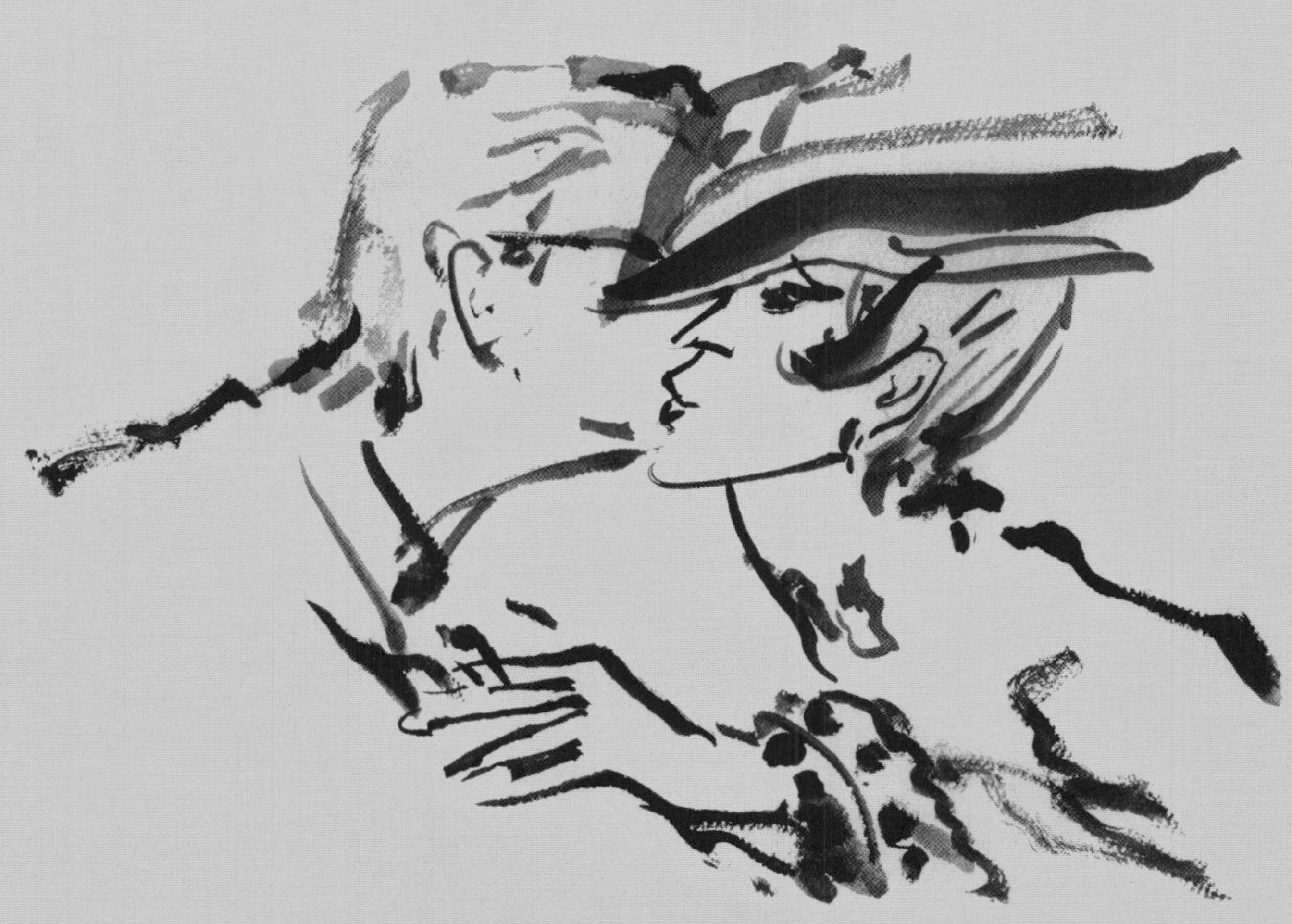

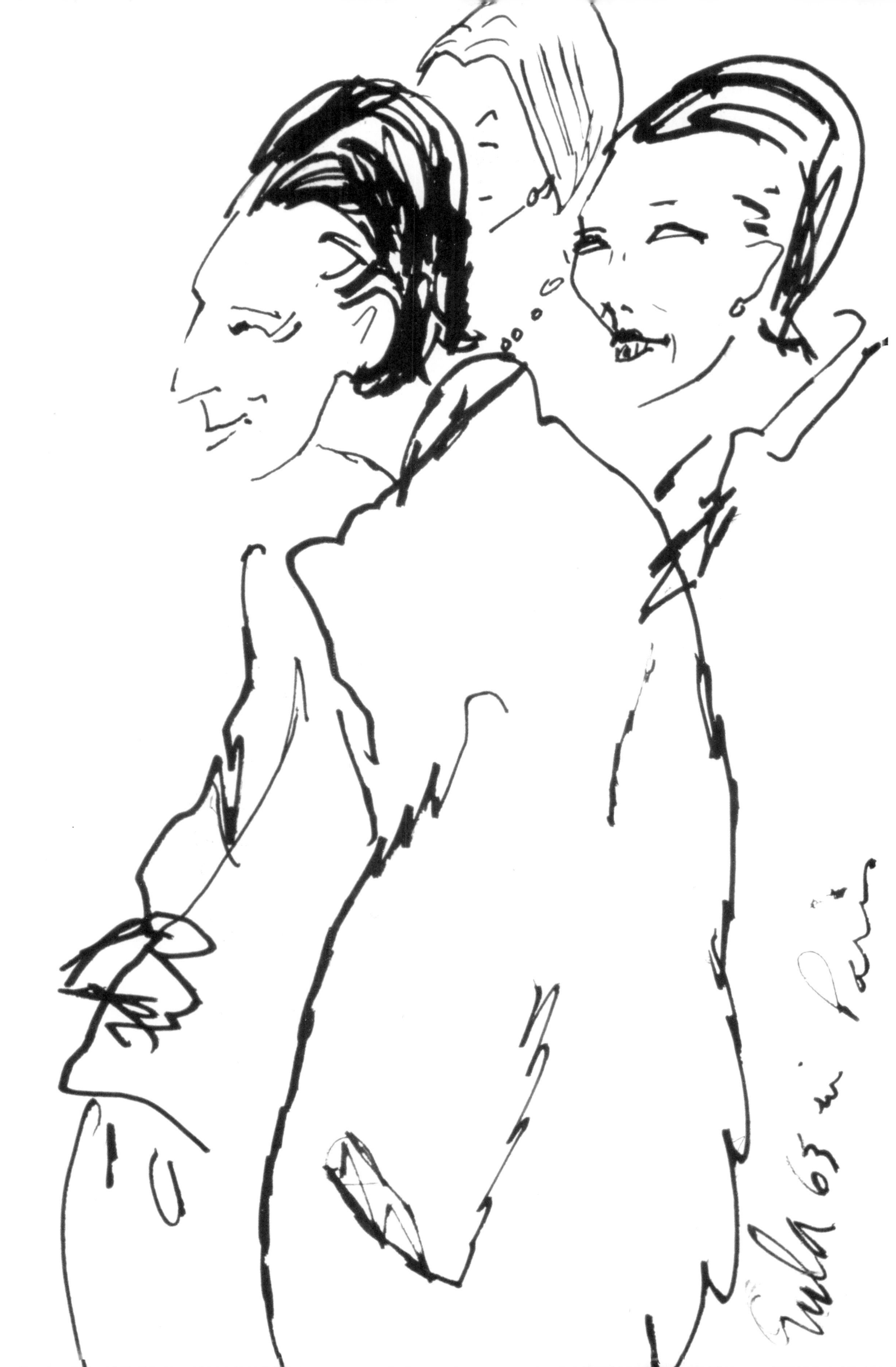

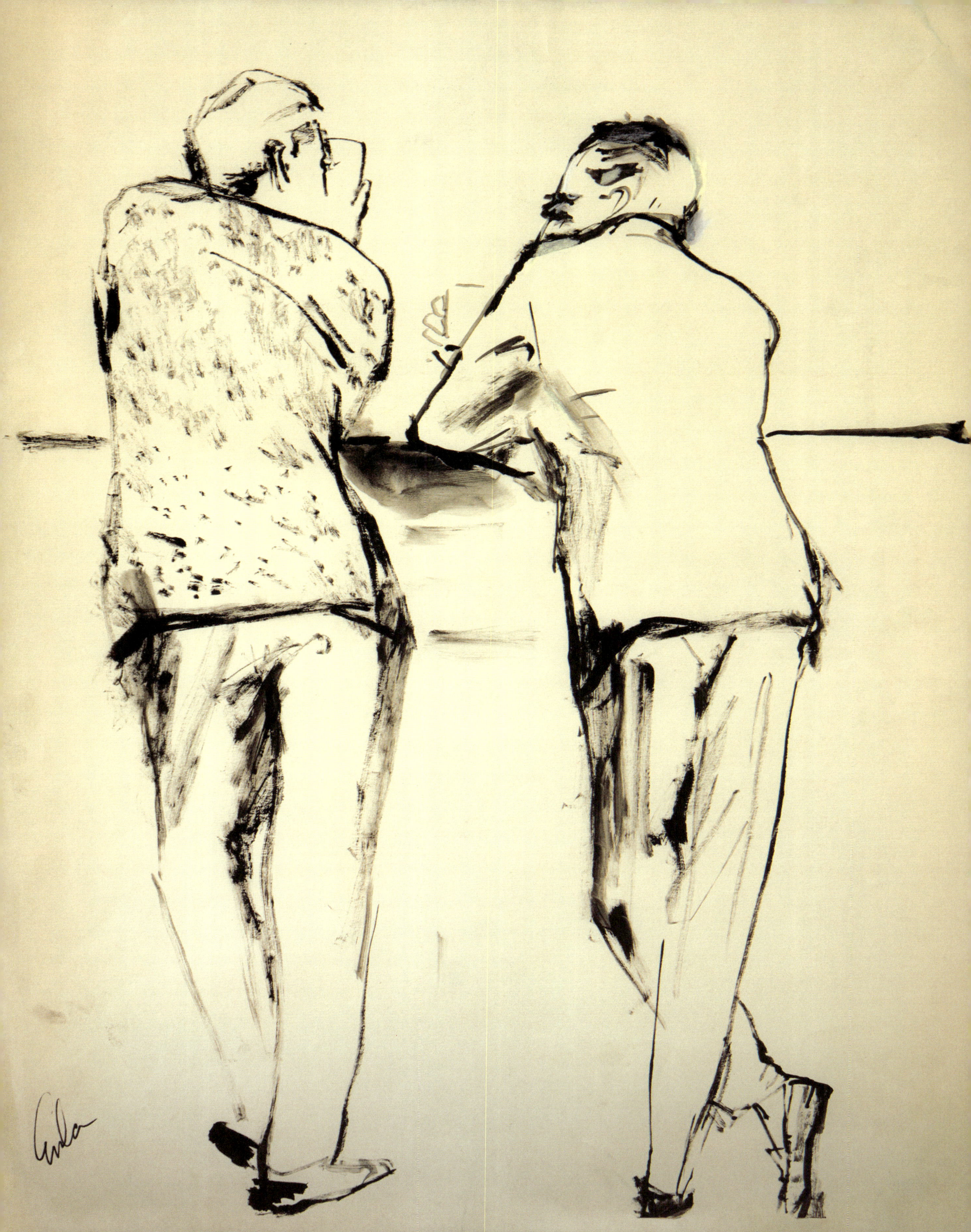

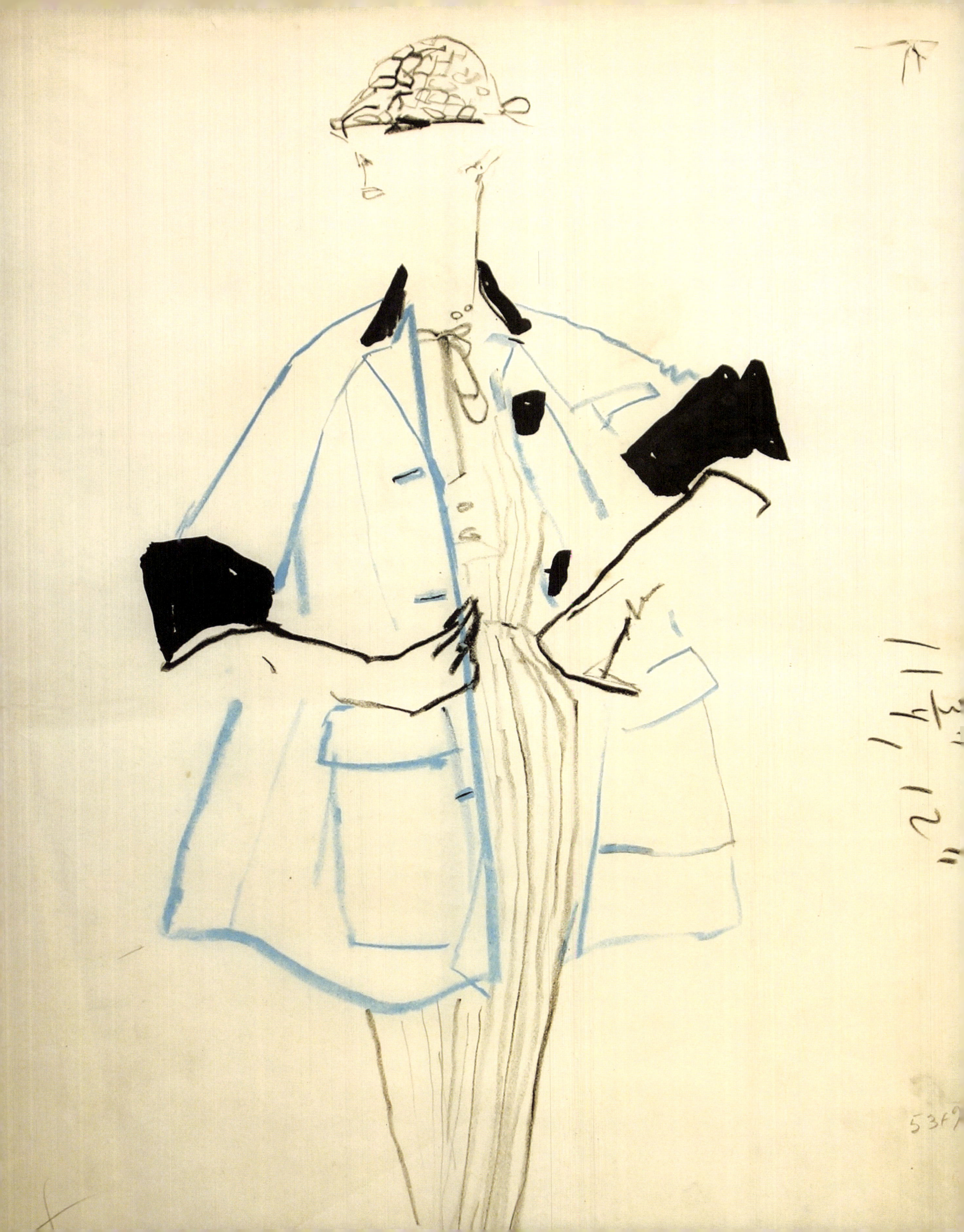

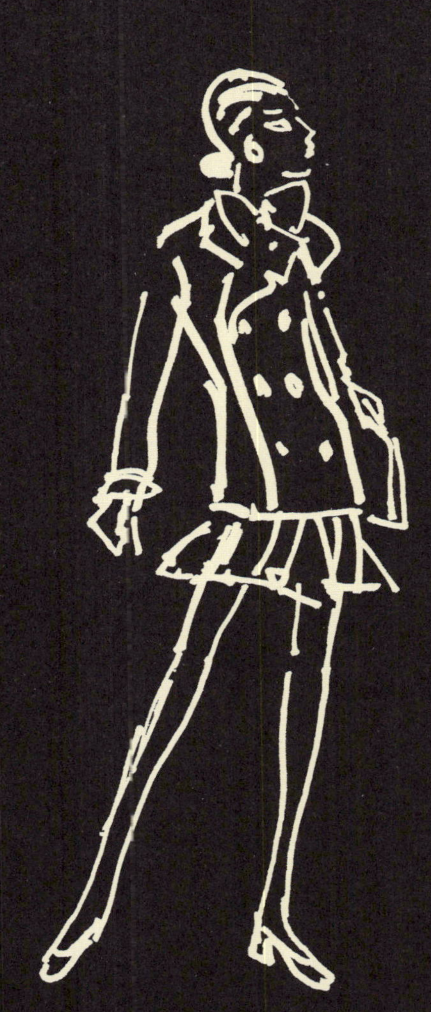

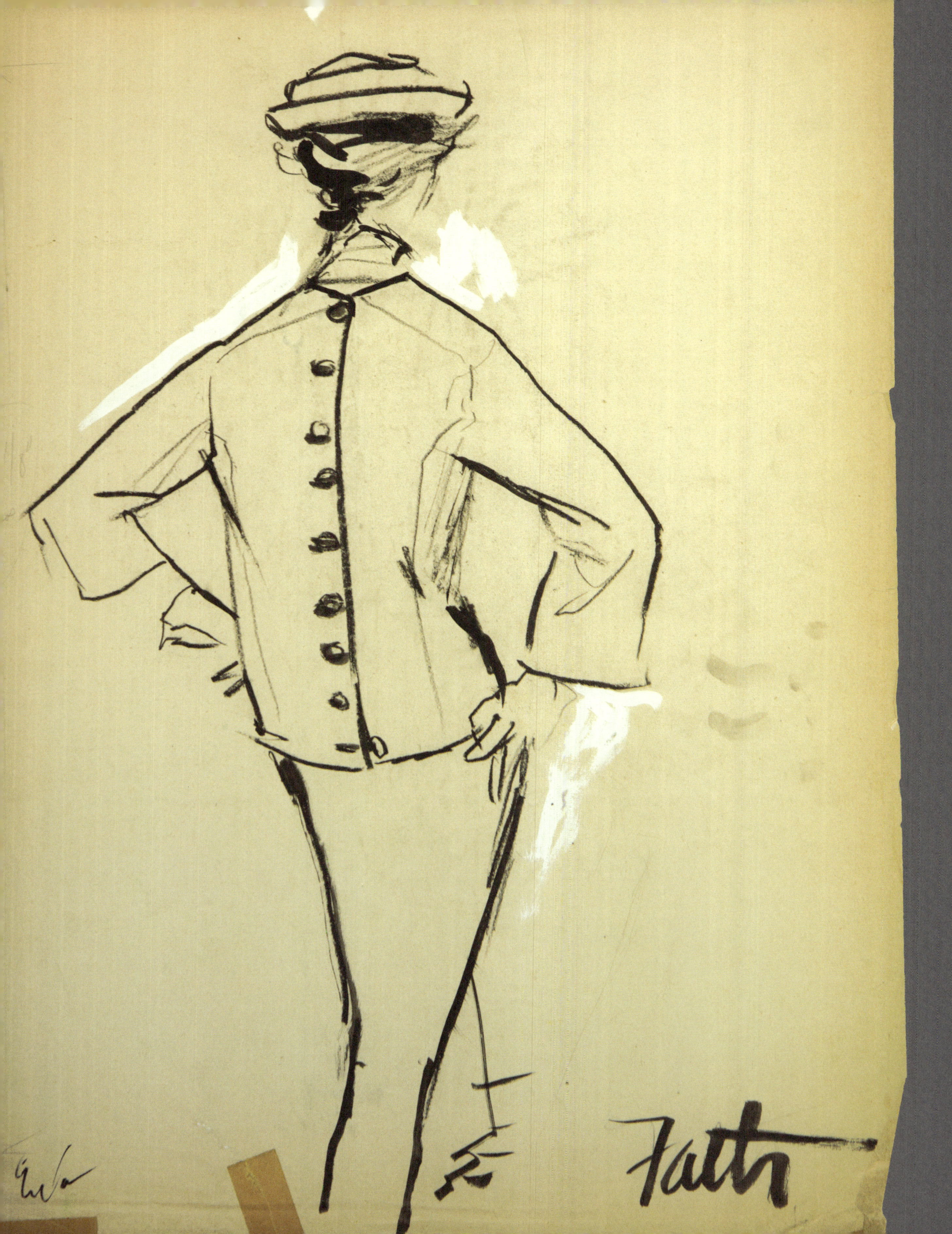
Fath

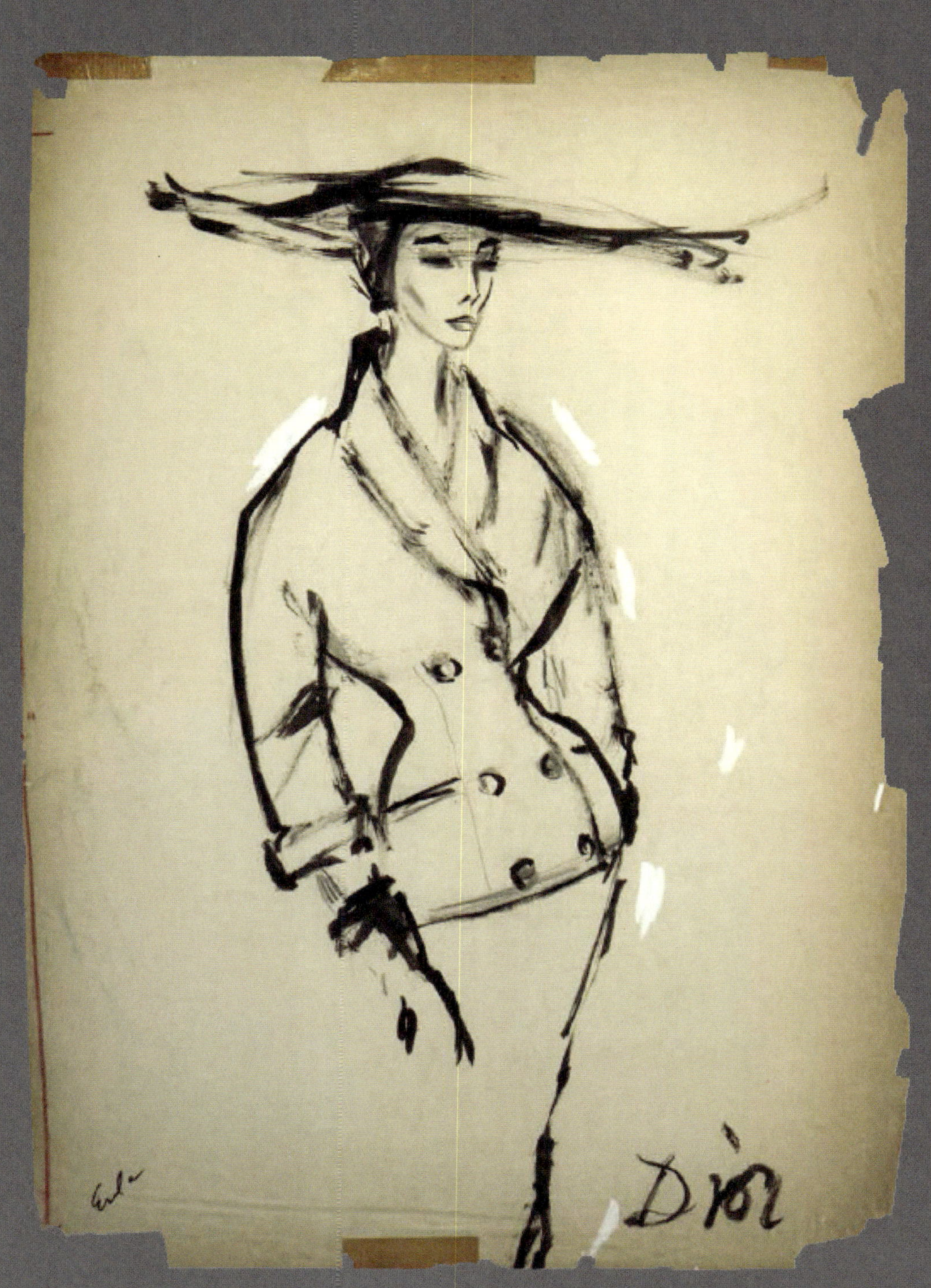
Dior

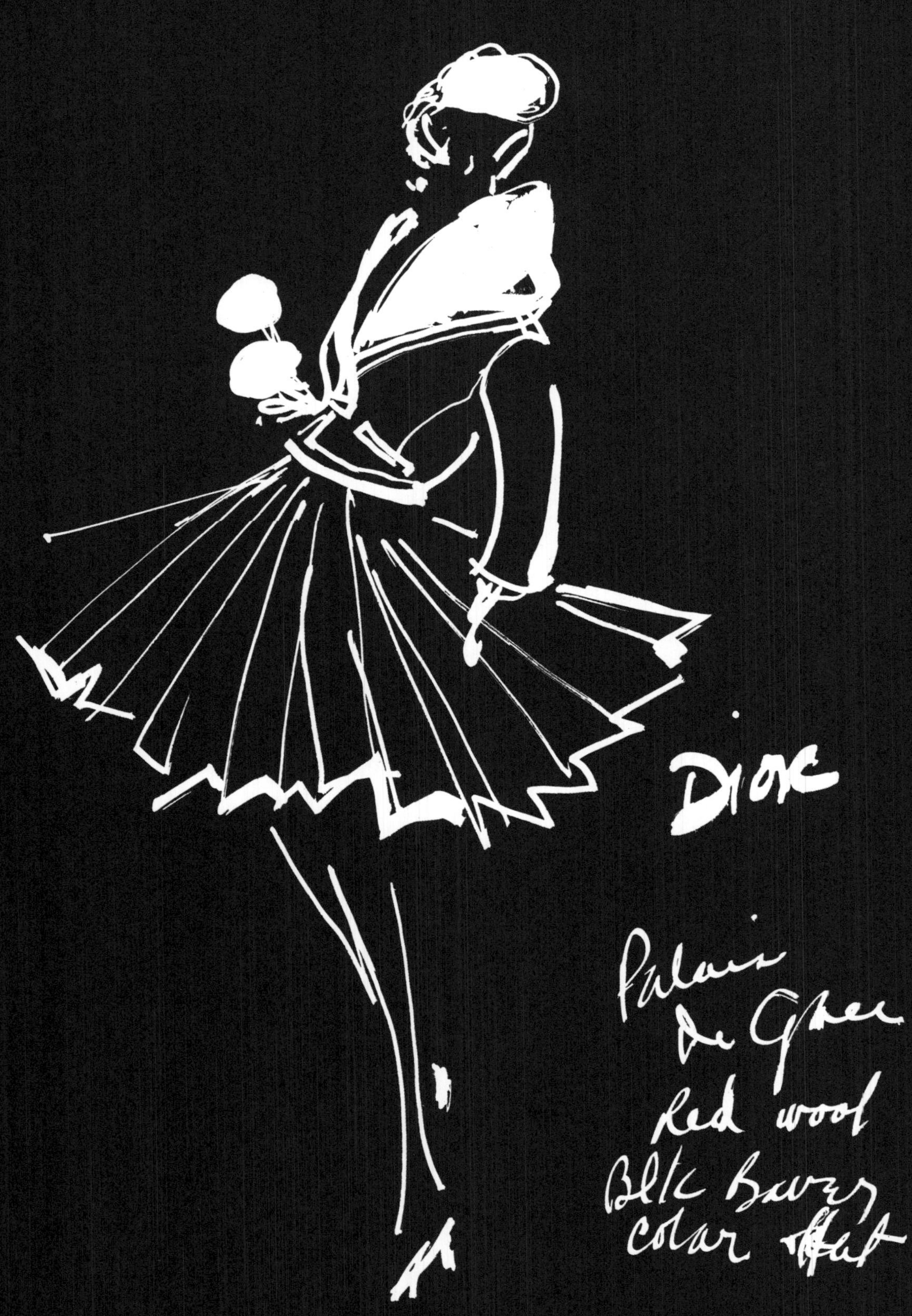
Dior
Palais
De Glace
Red wool
Blk Beaver
colar Hat

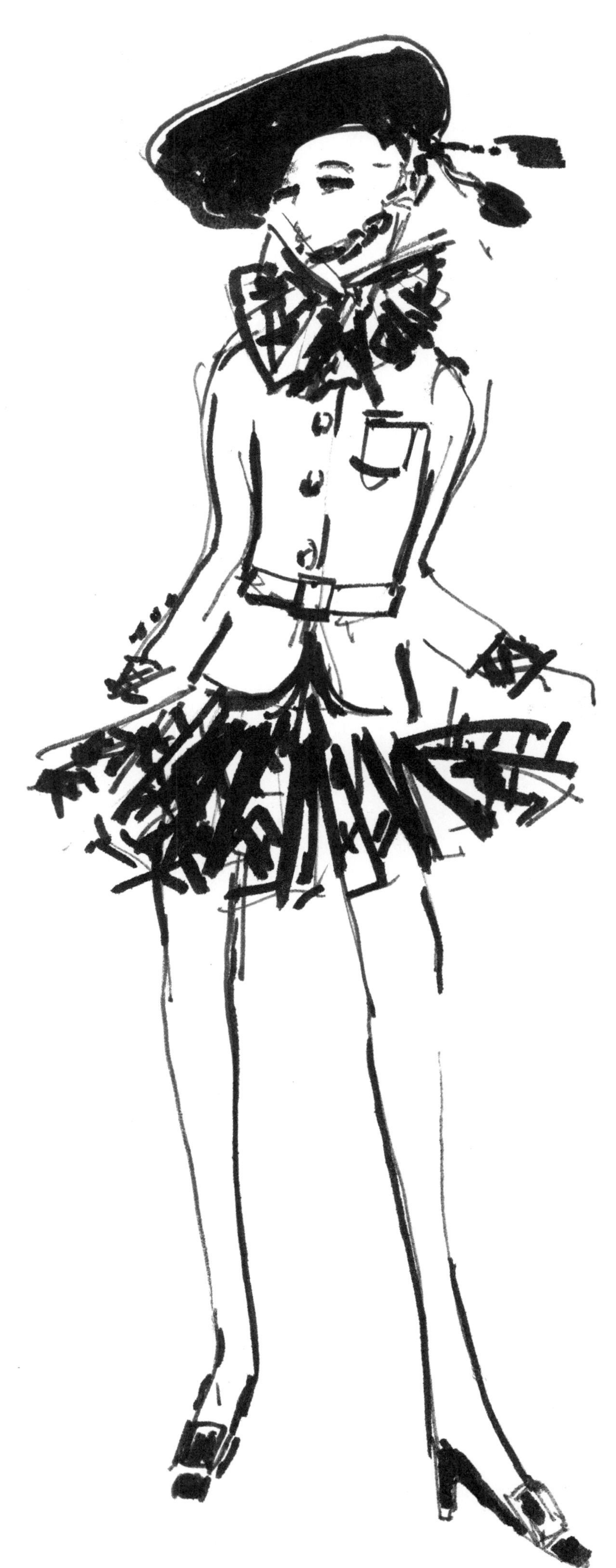

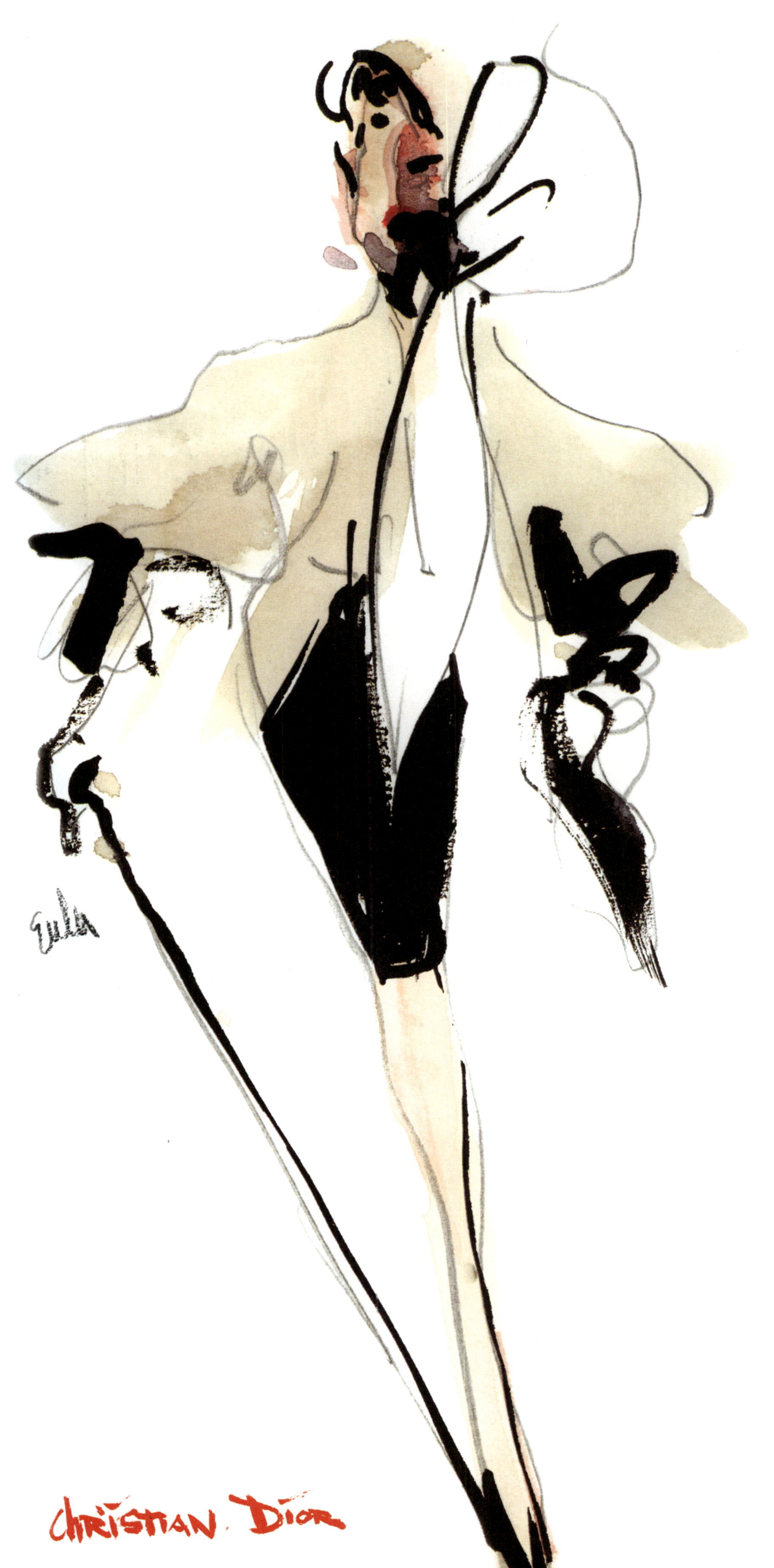

CHRISTIAN DIOR

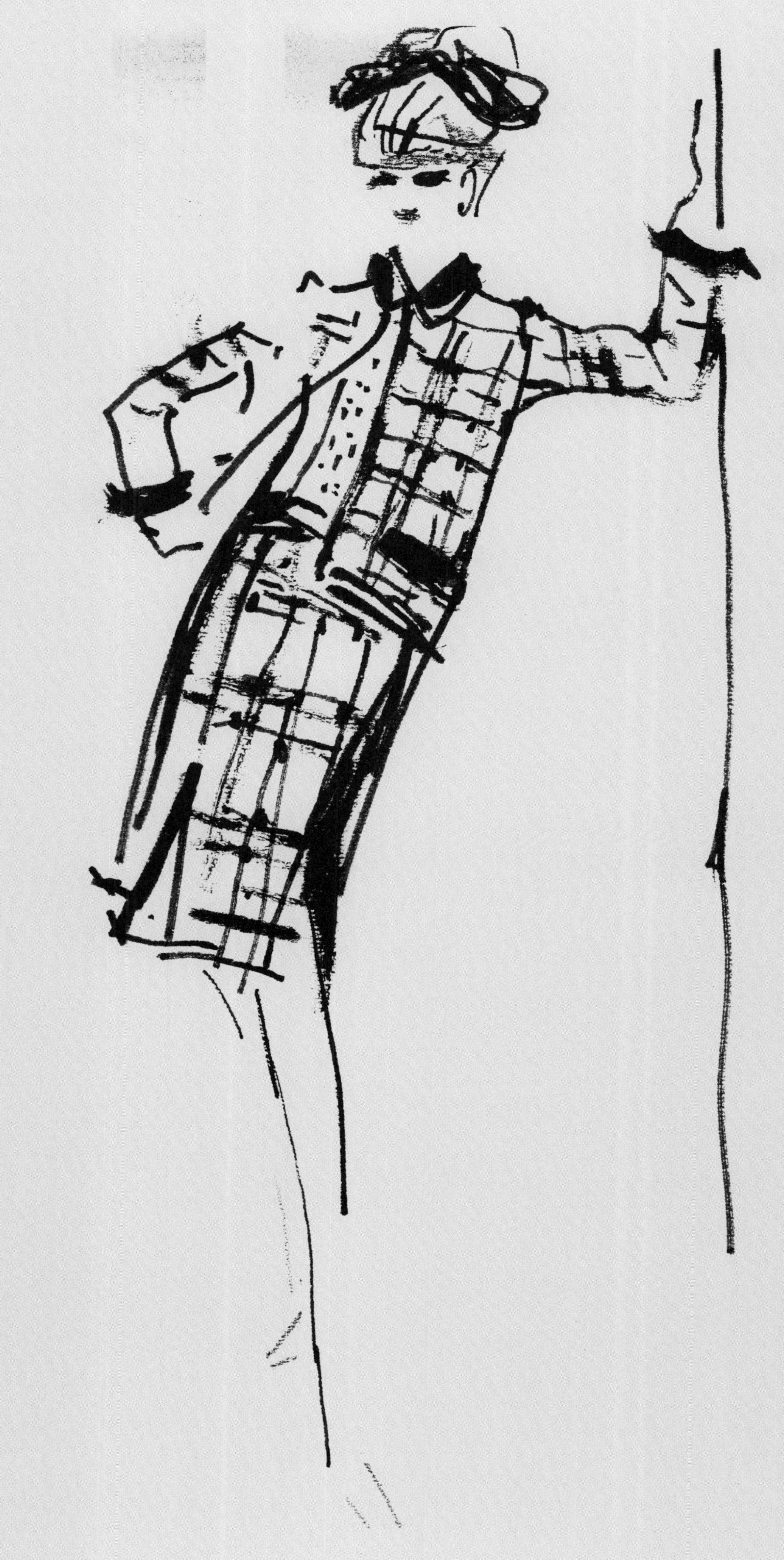

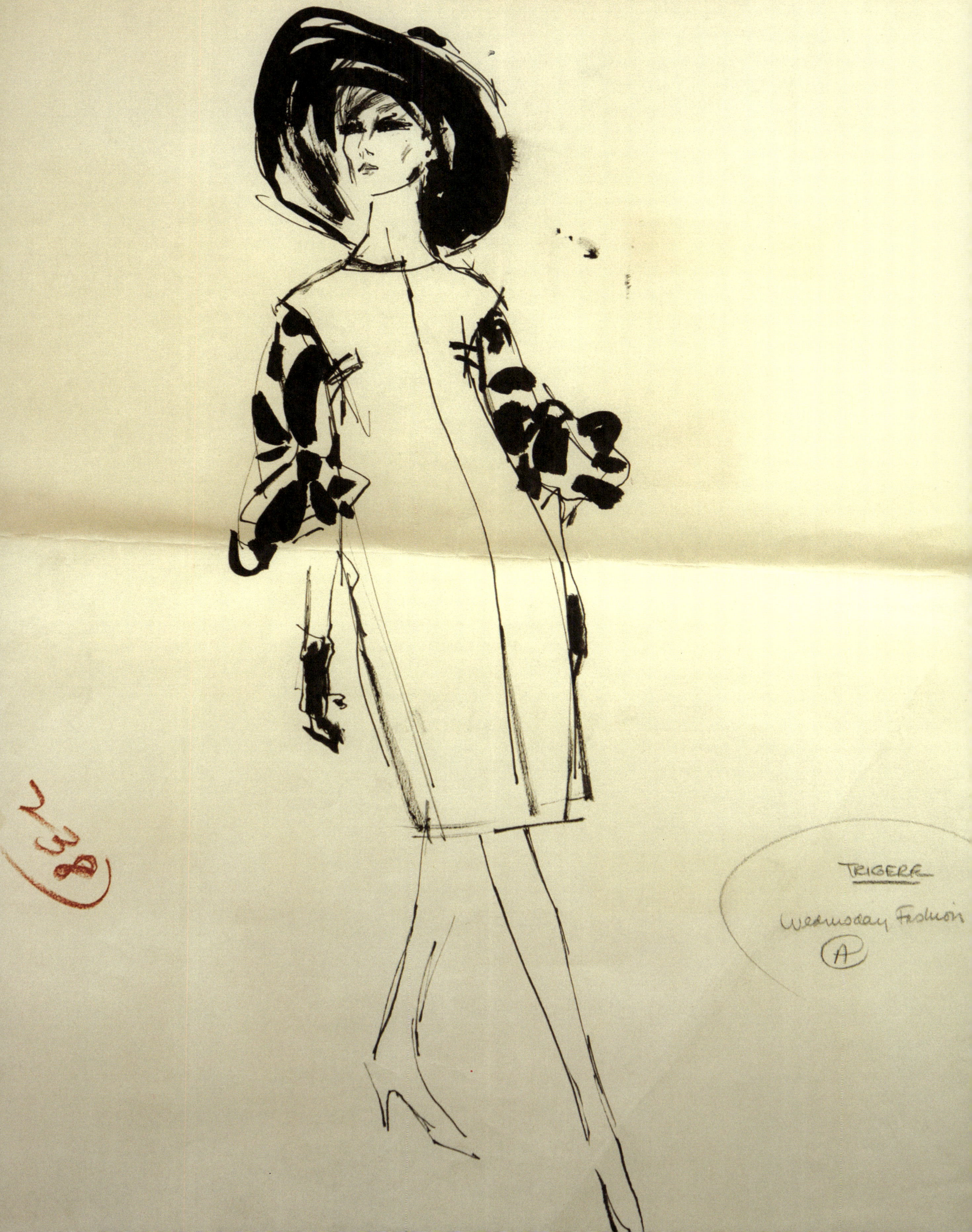

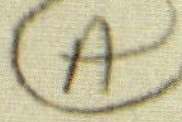
TRIGERE
Wednesday Fashion
A

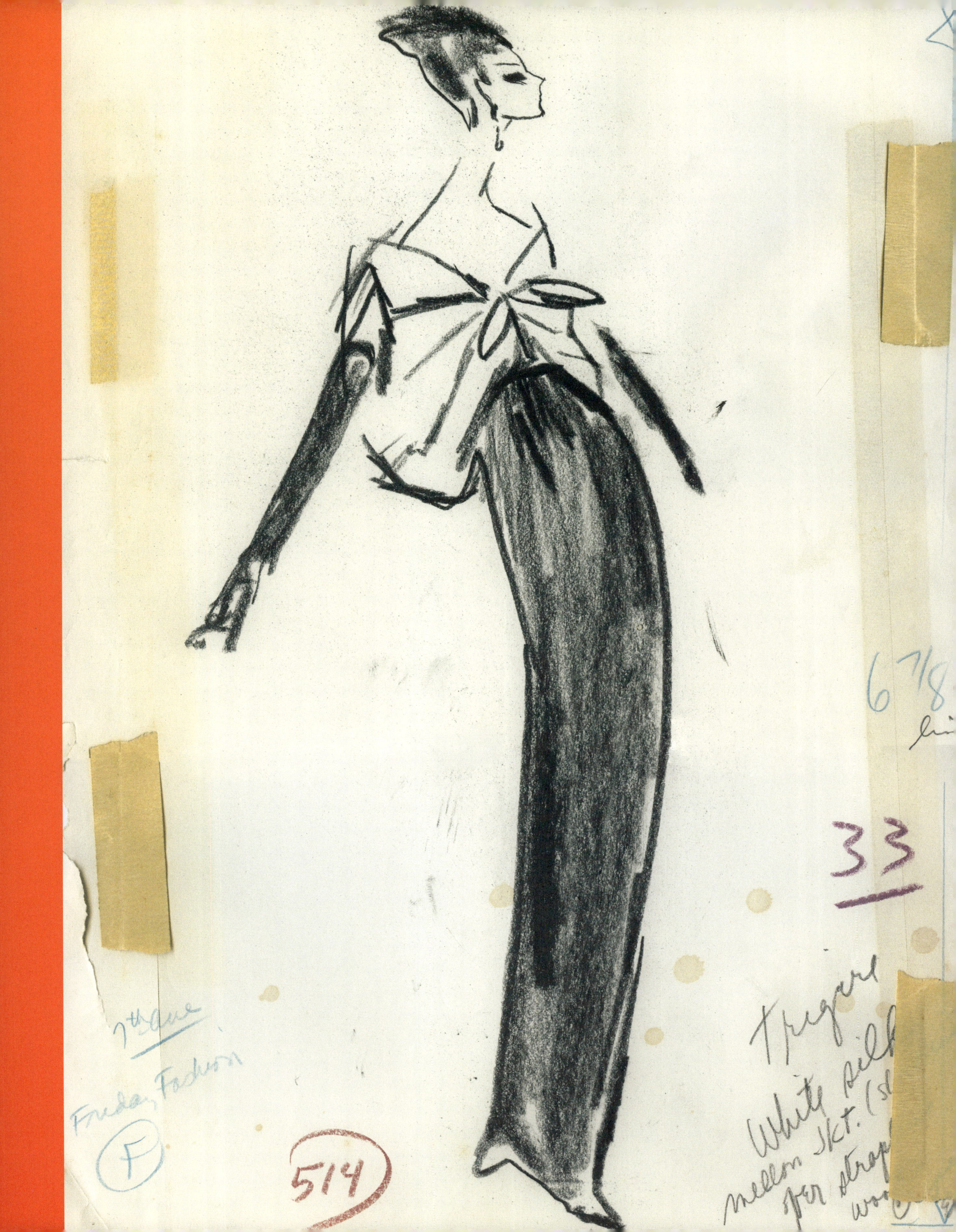

7th Ave
Friday Fashion
F
514
6 7/8
33
Tregare
White silk
mellon skt. (s
per strap
wool

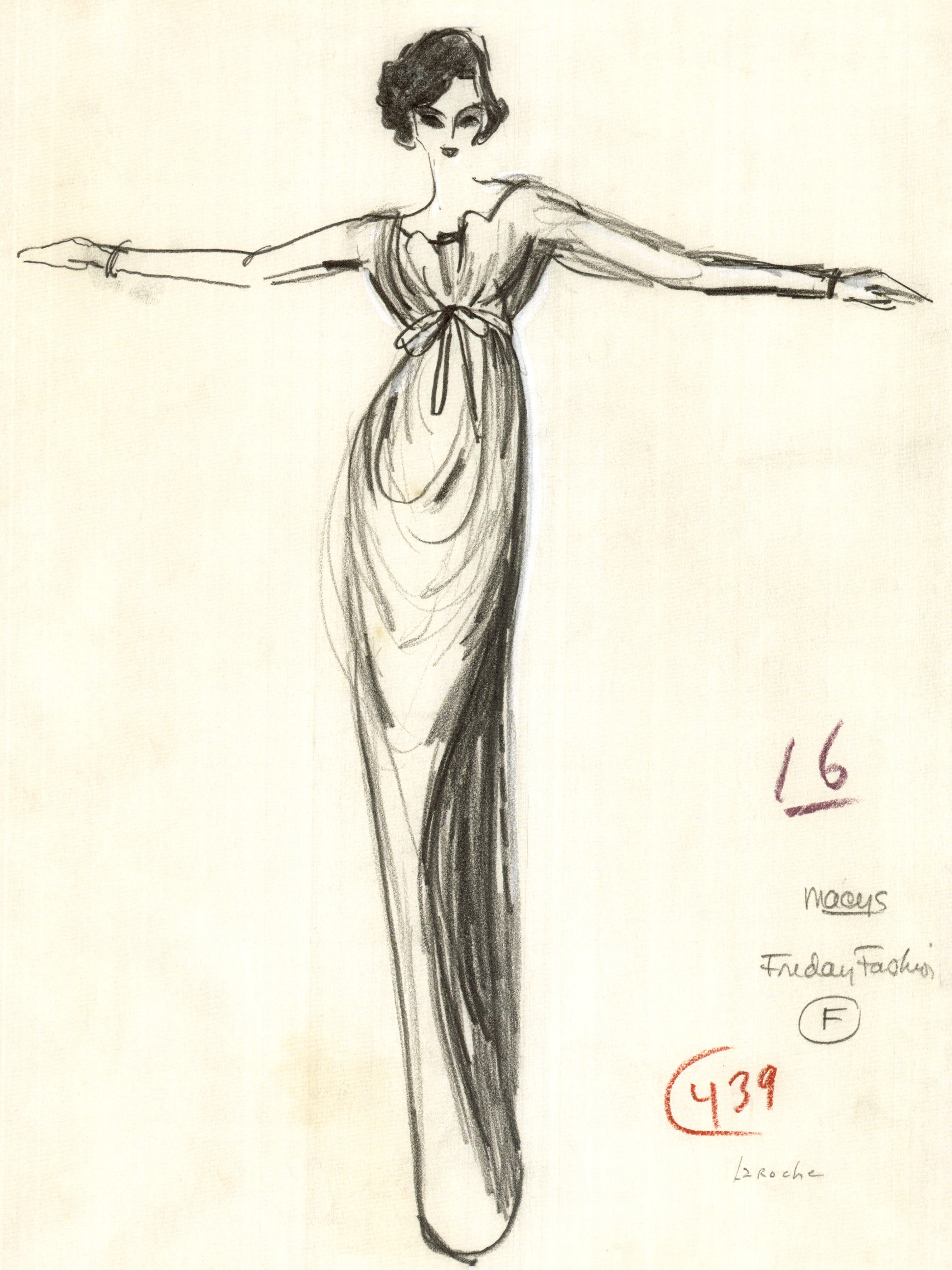

16
macys
Friday Fashion
F
439
Laroche

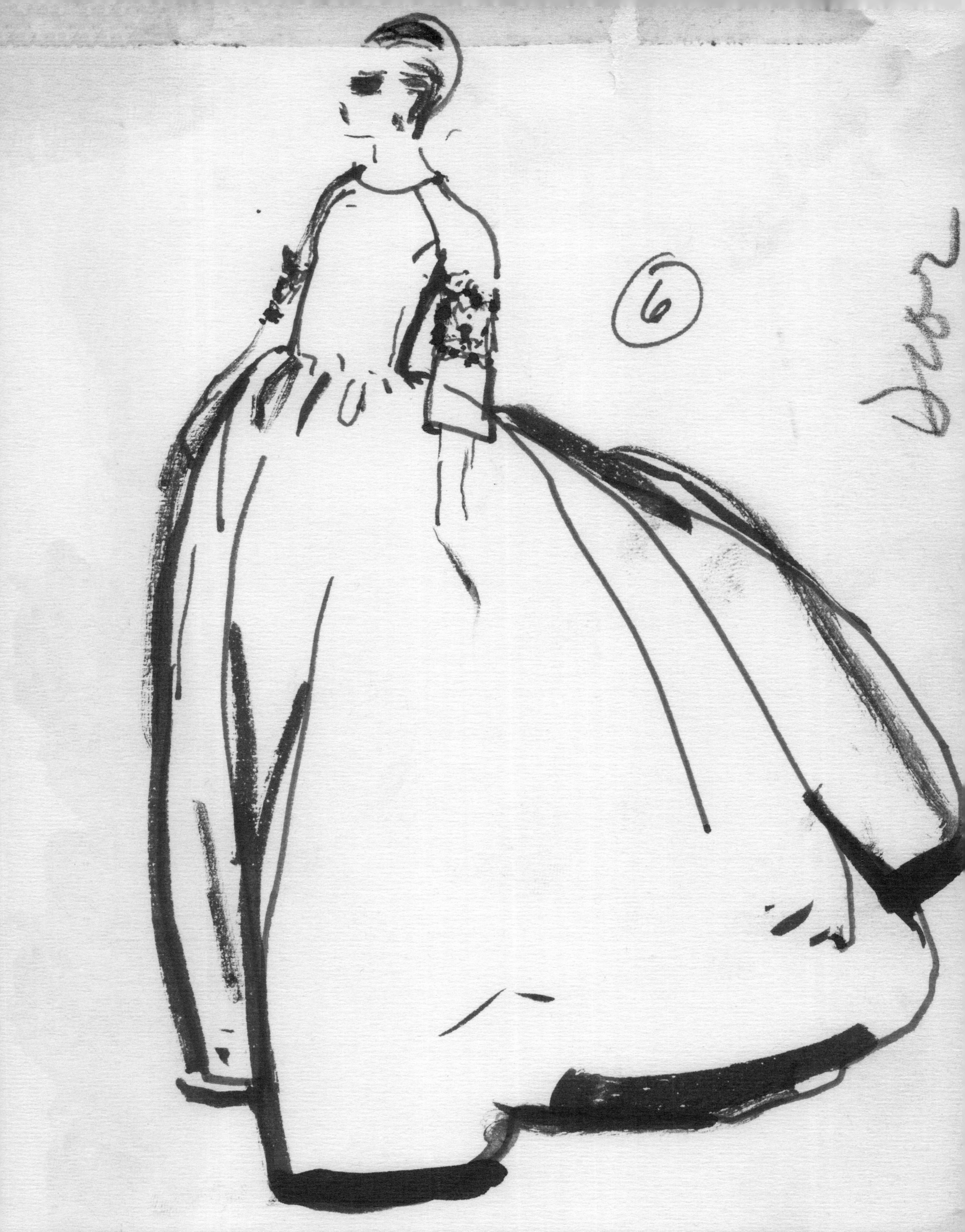

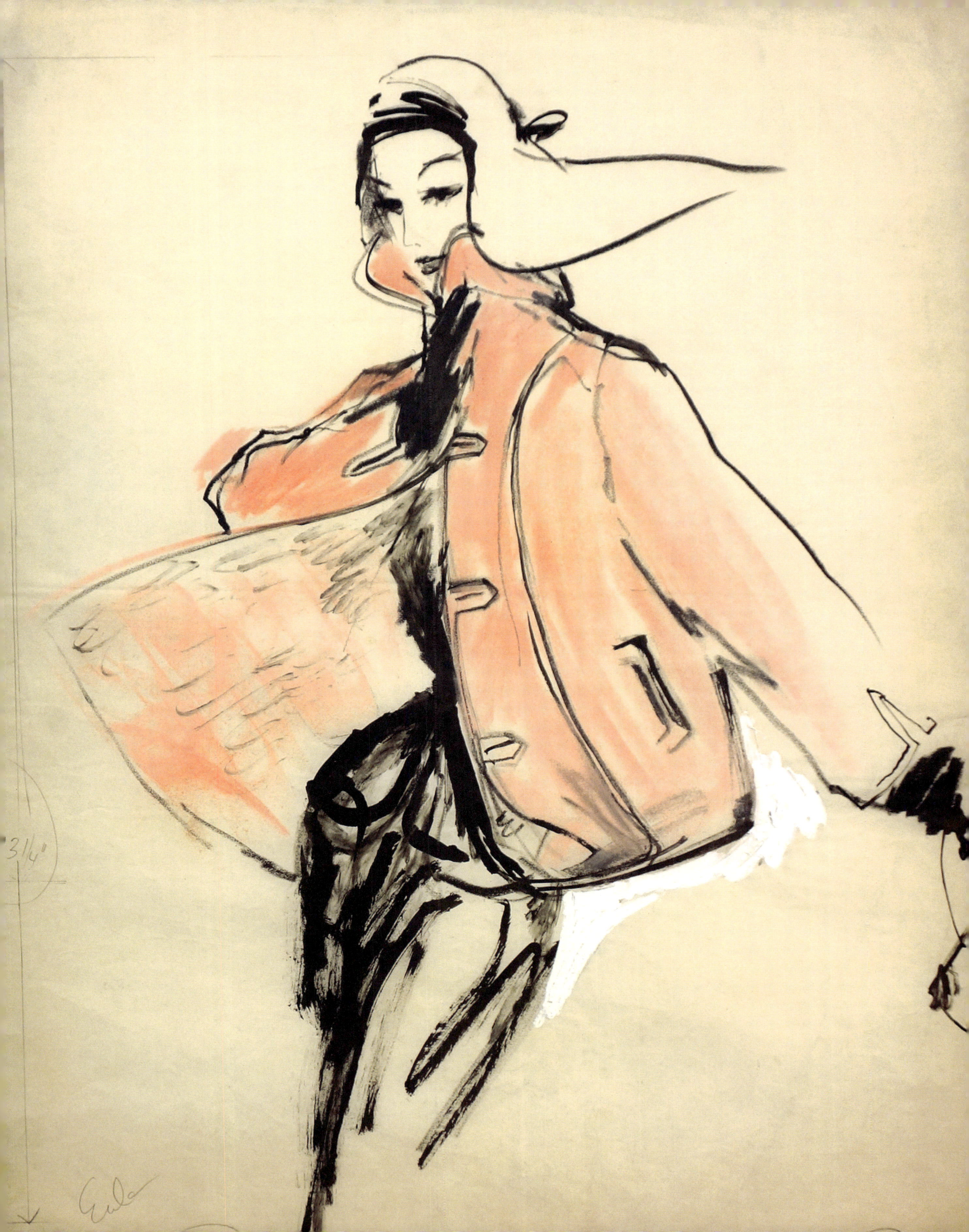
3/4"
Eula

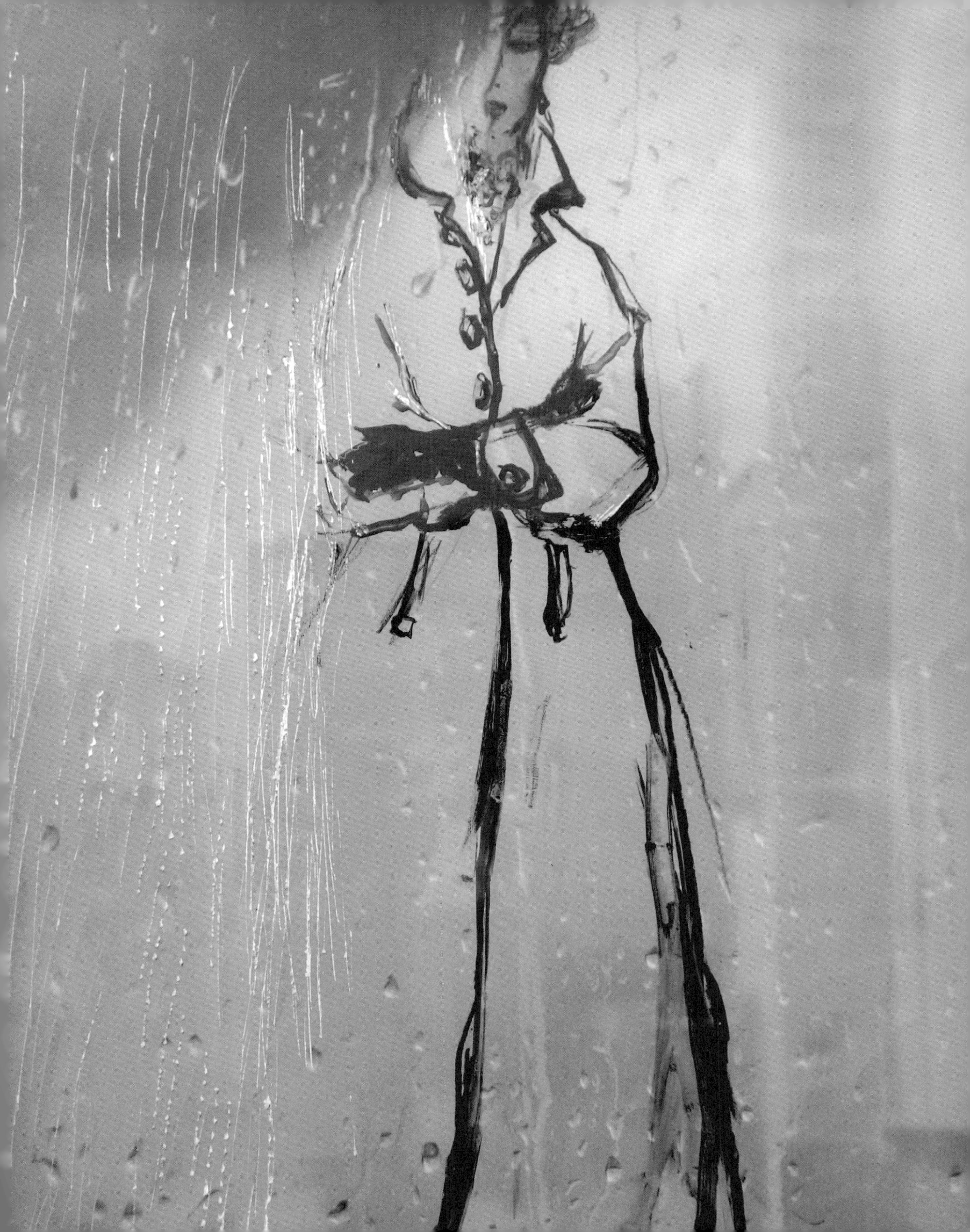

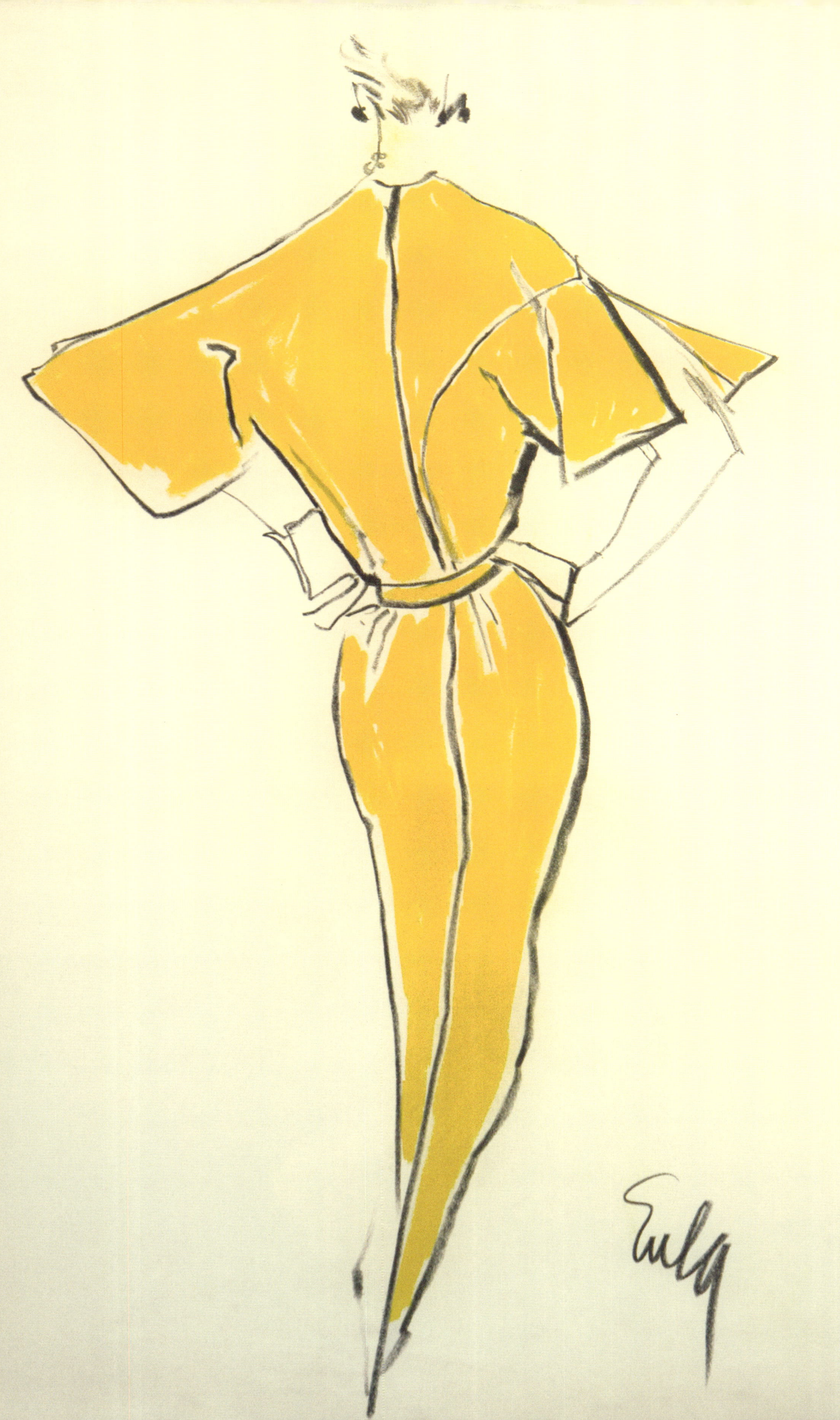

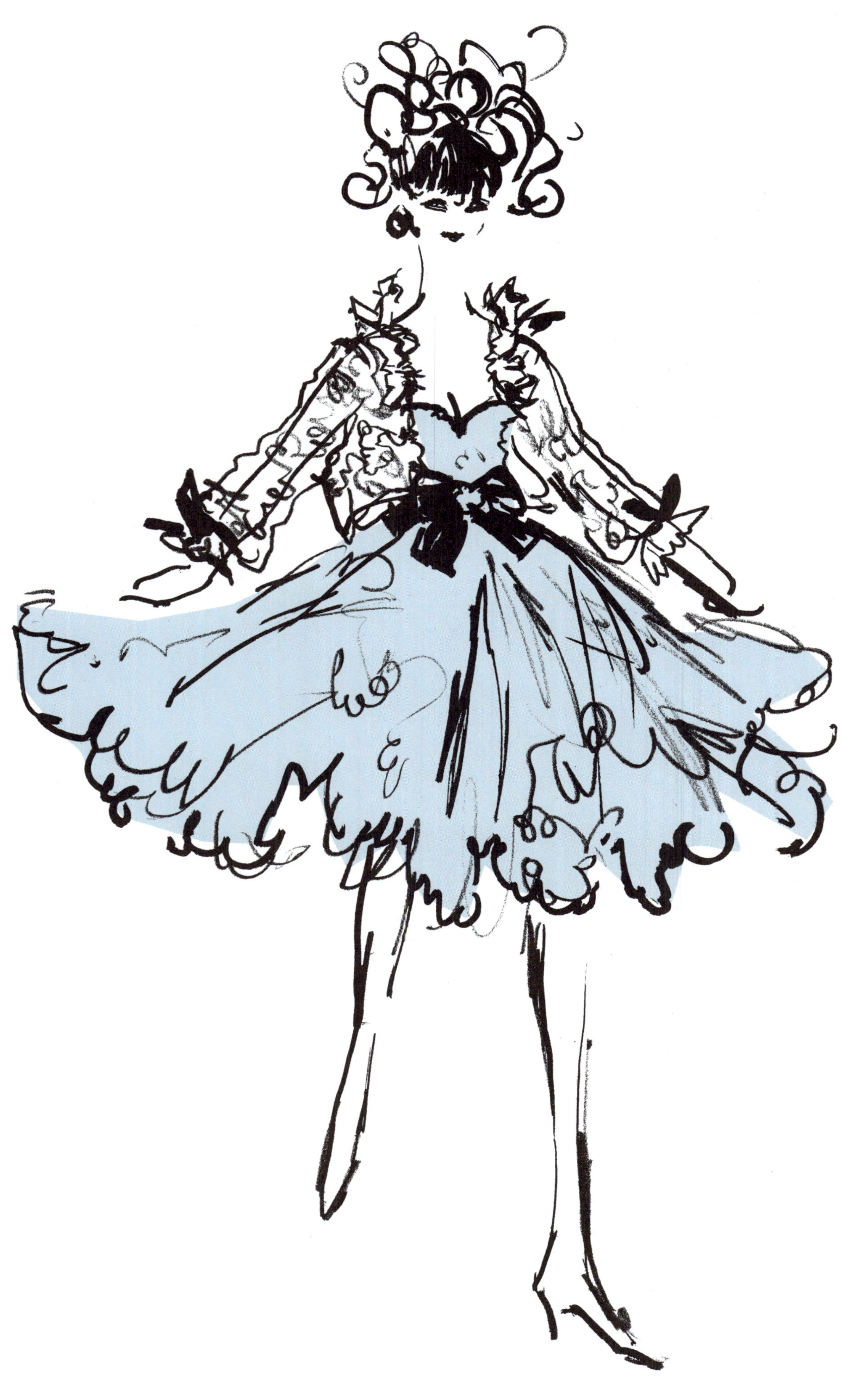

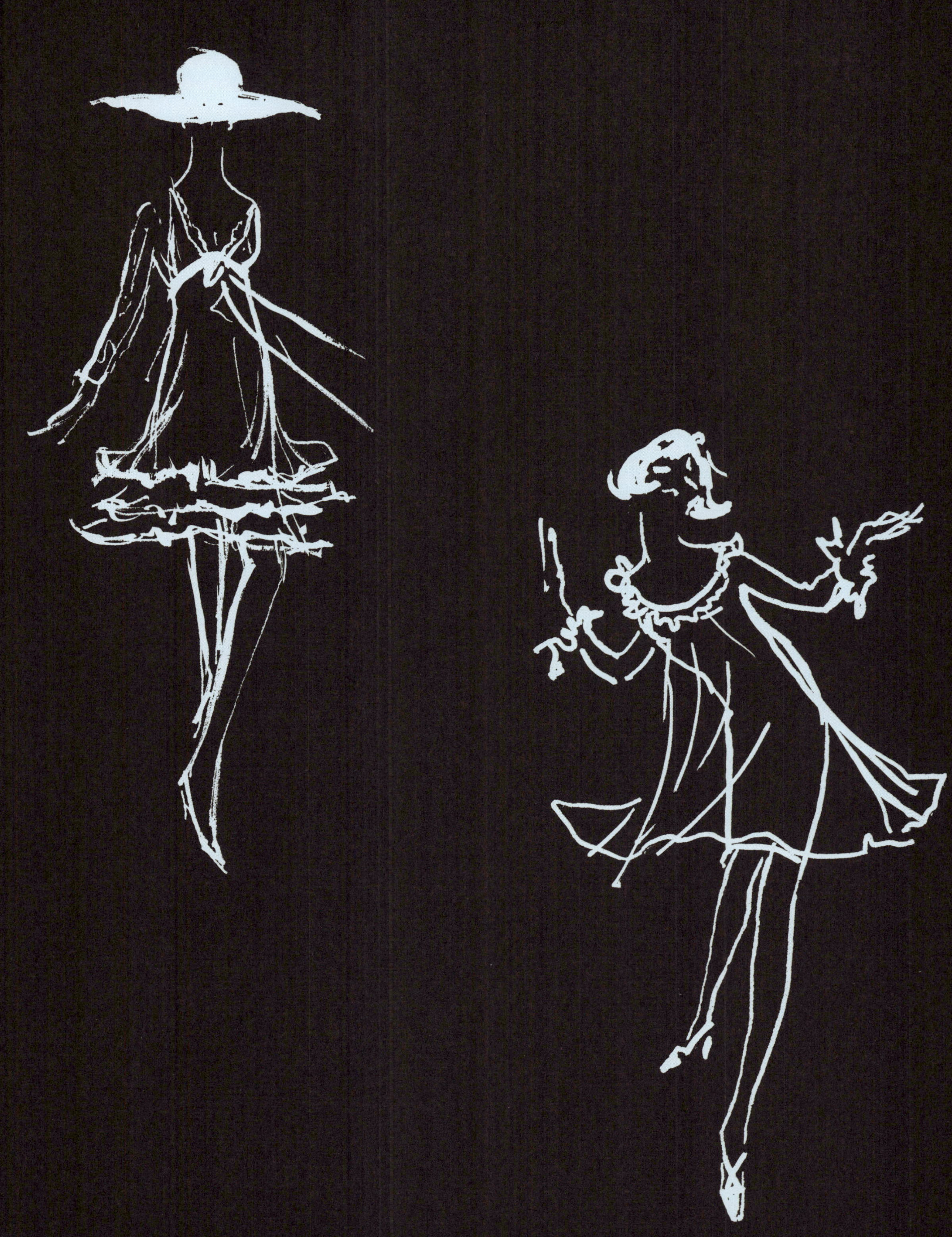

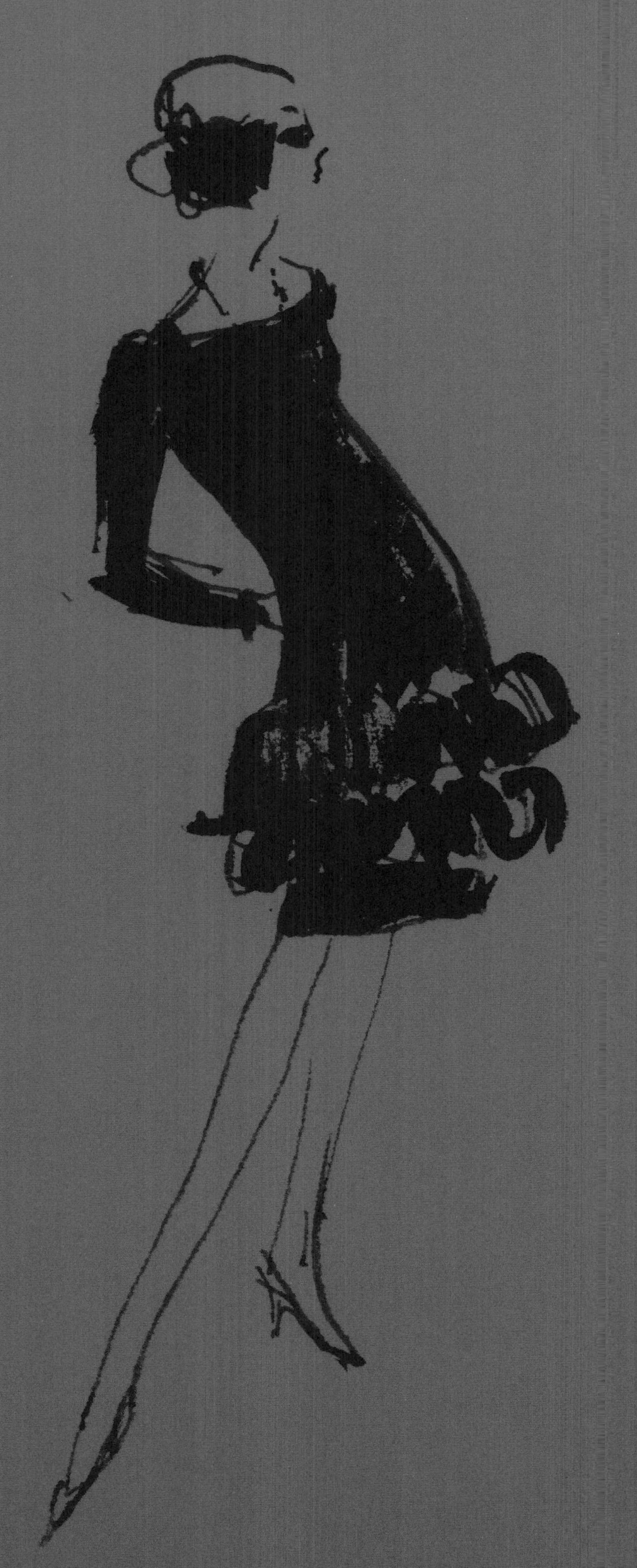

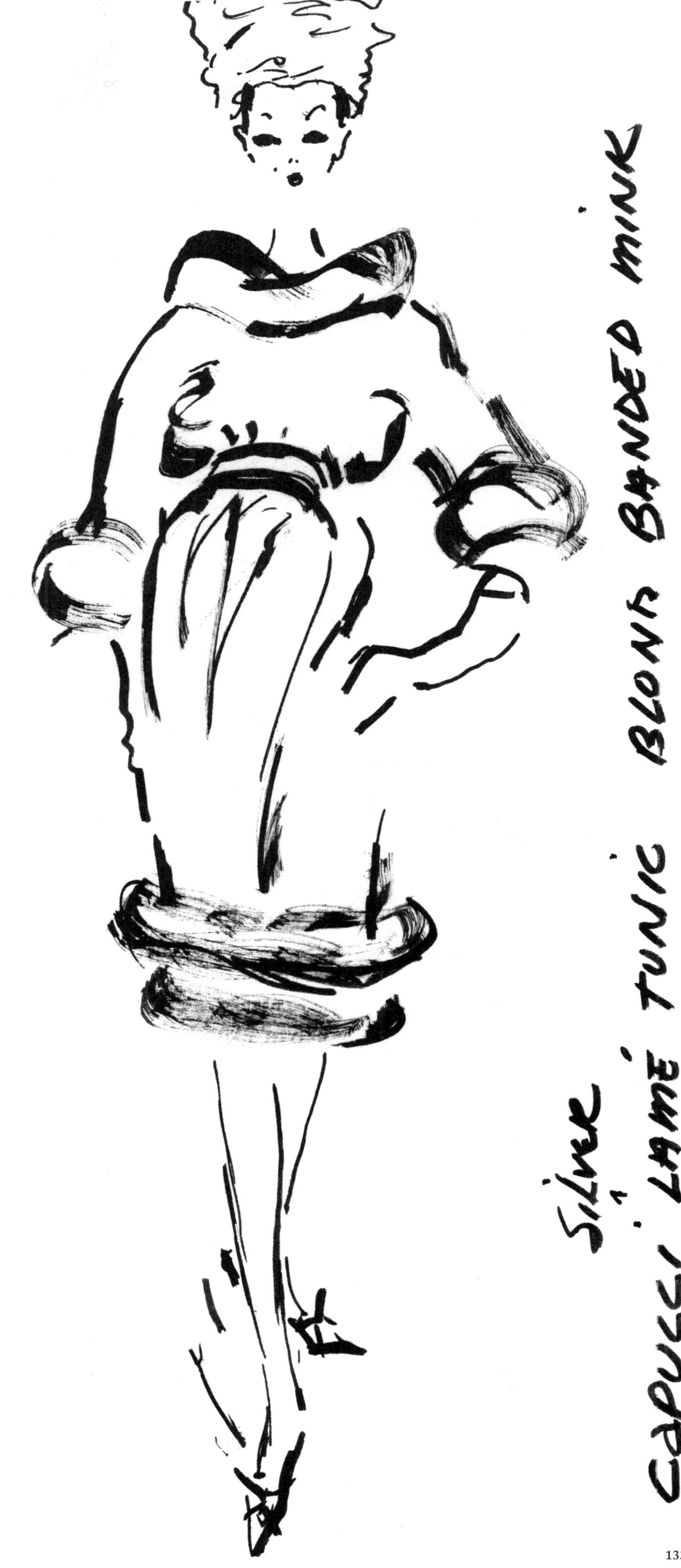

Silver
CAPUCCI LAMÉ TUNIC BLOND BANDED MINK

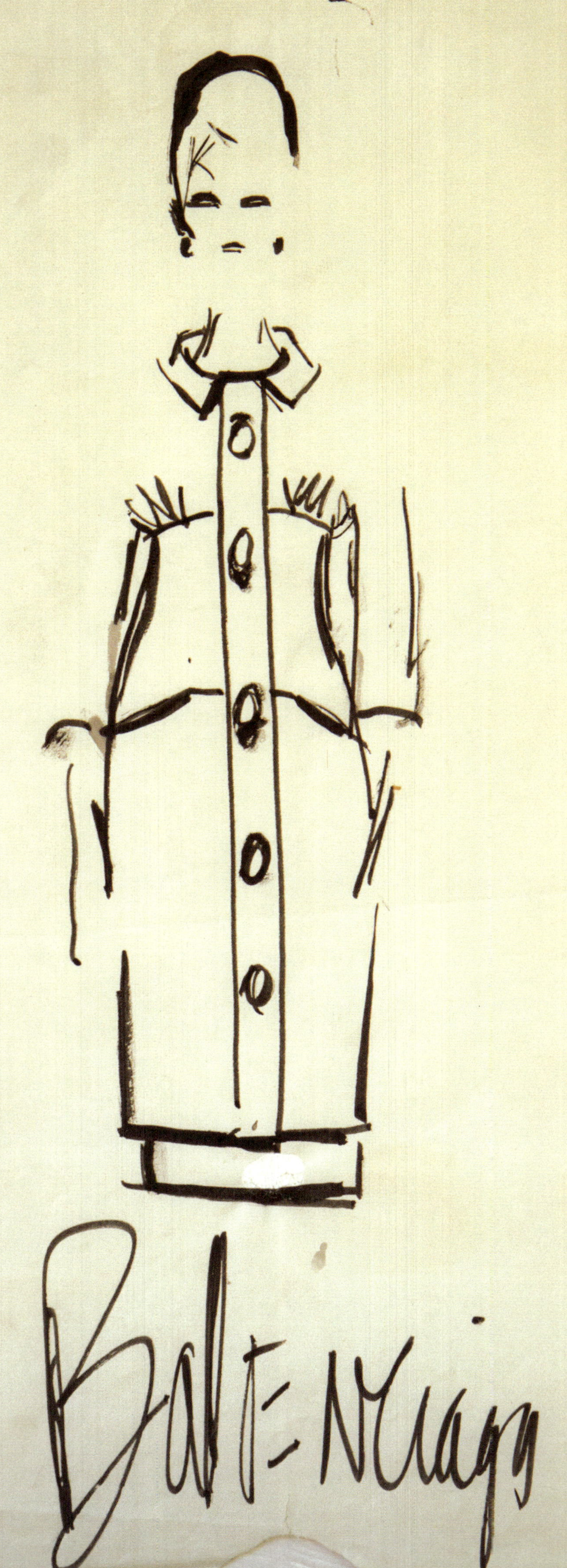

Balenciaga

Macy

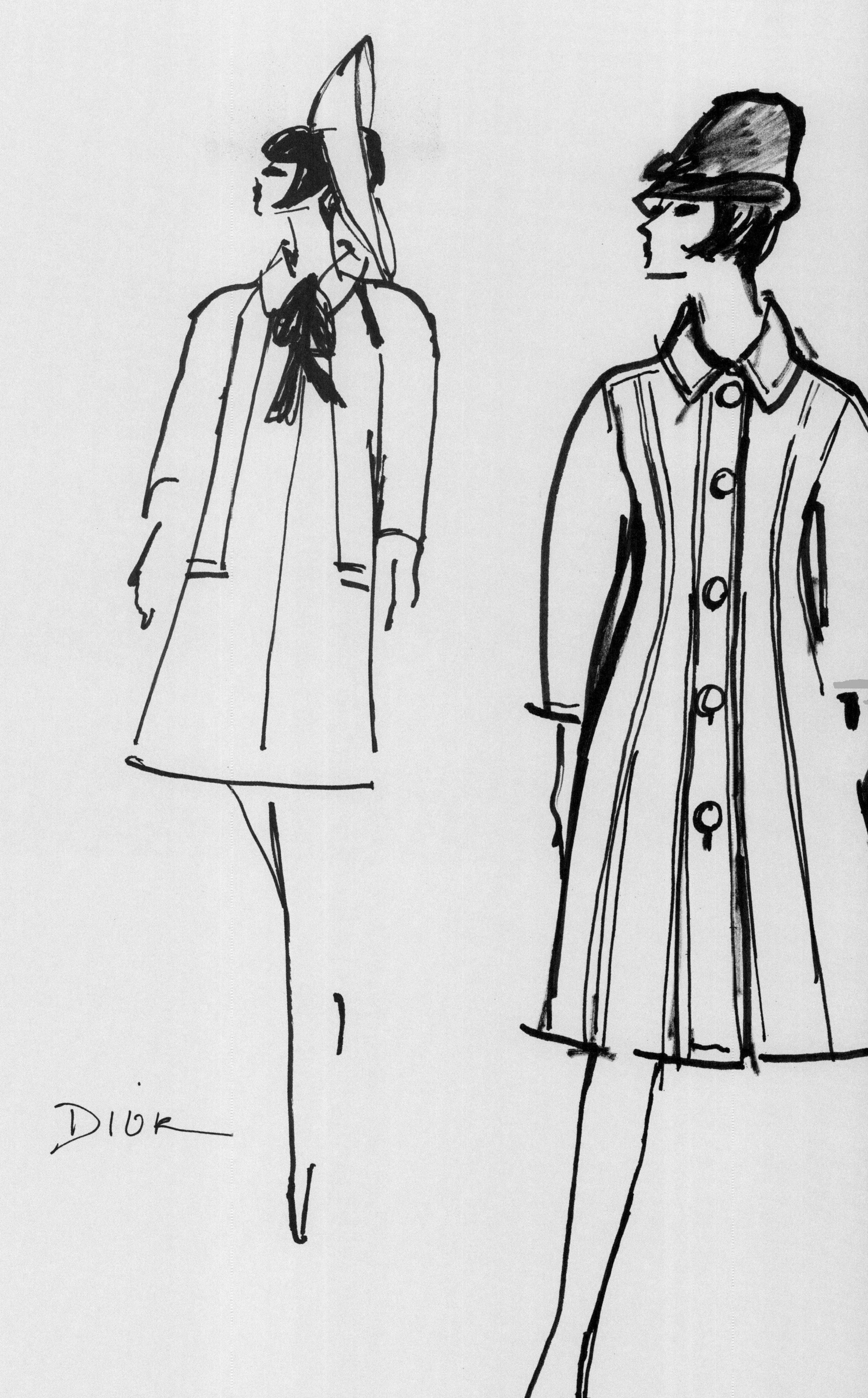

DIOR

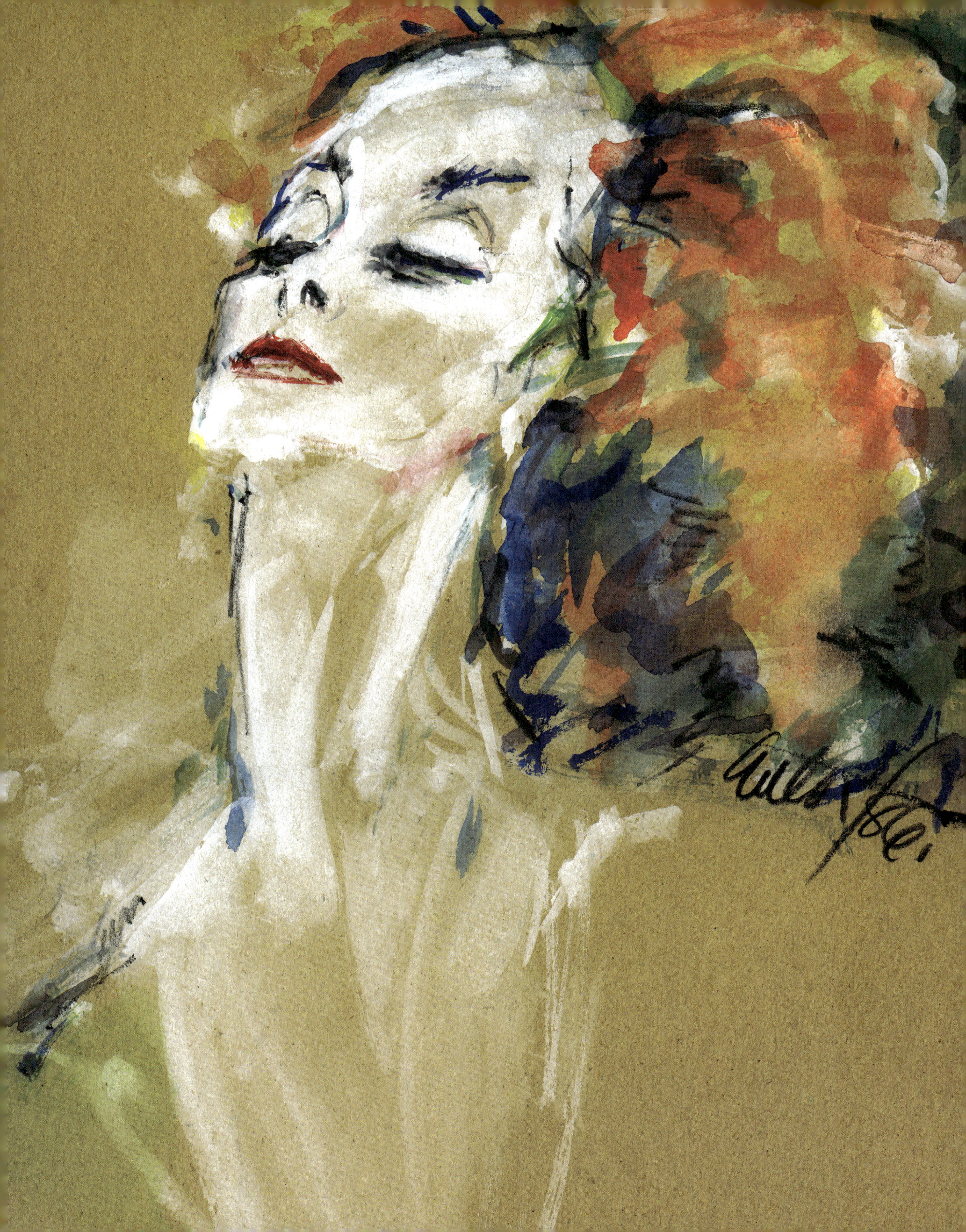

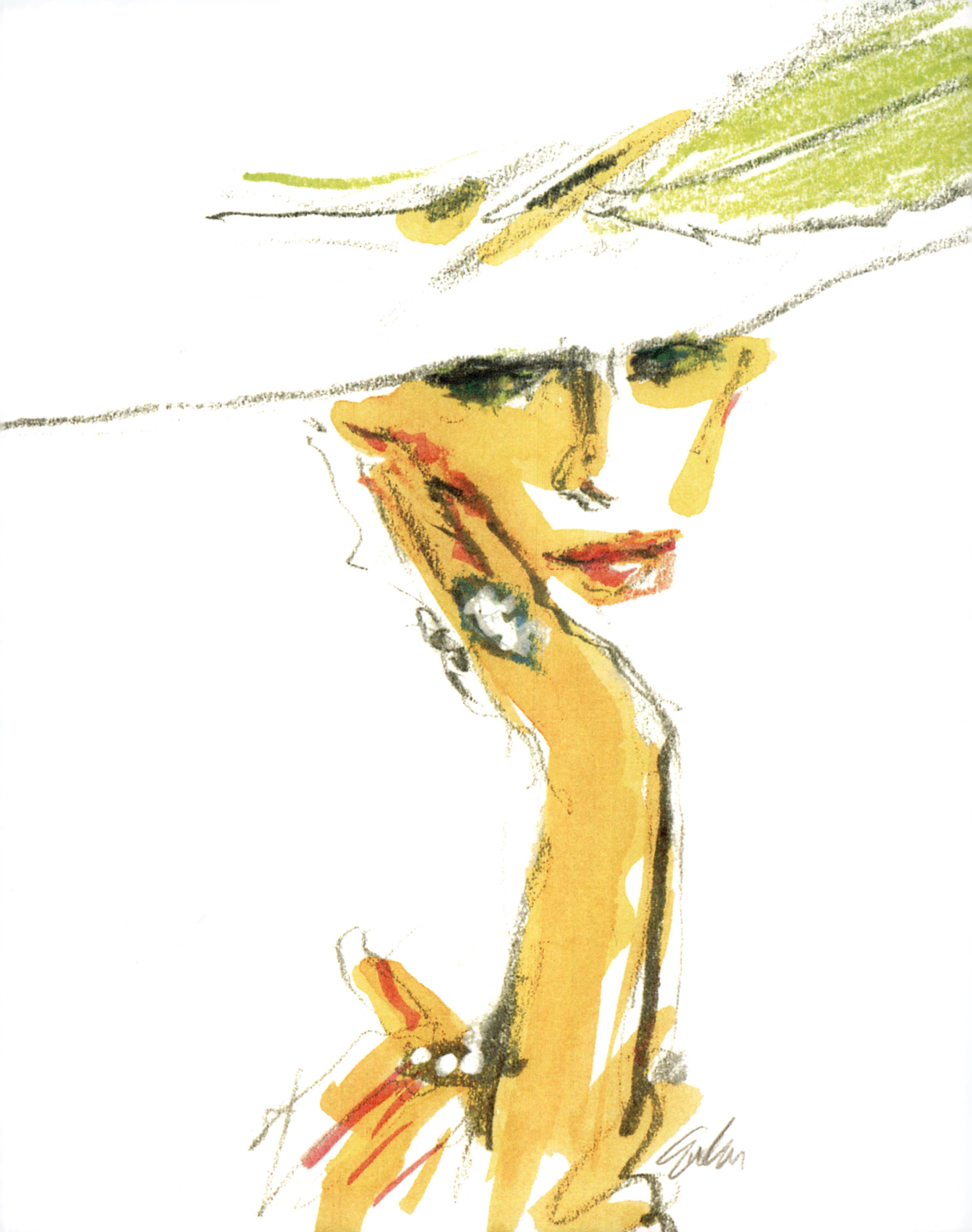

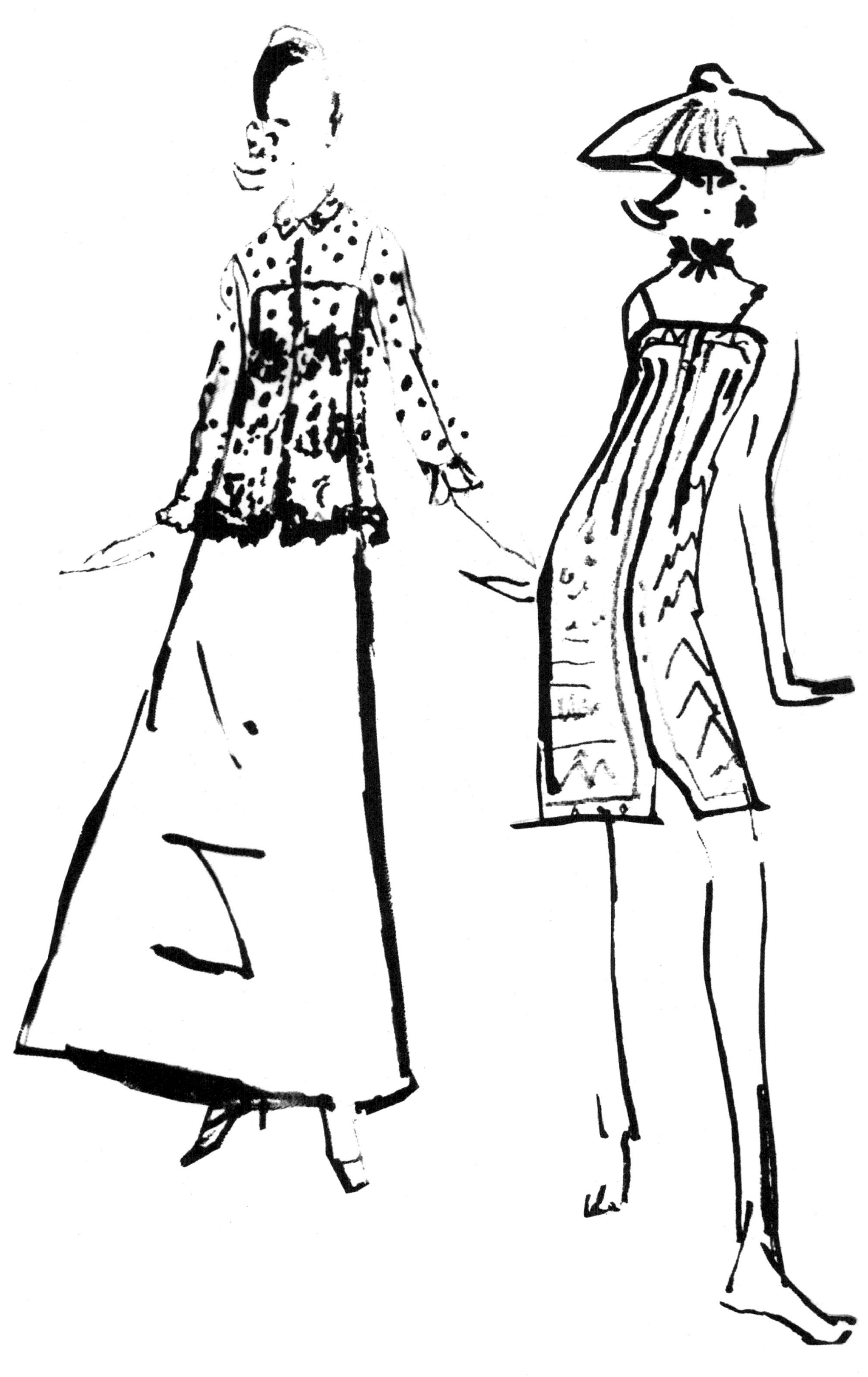

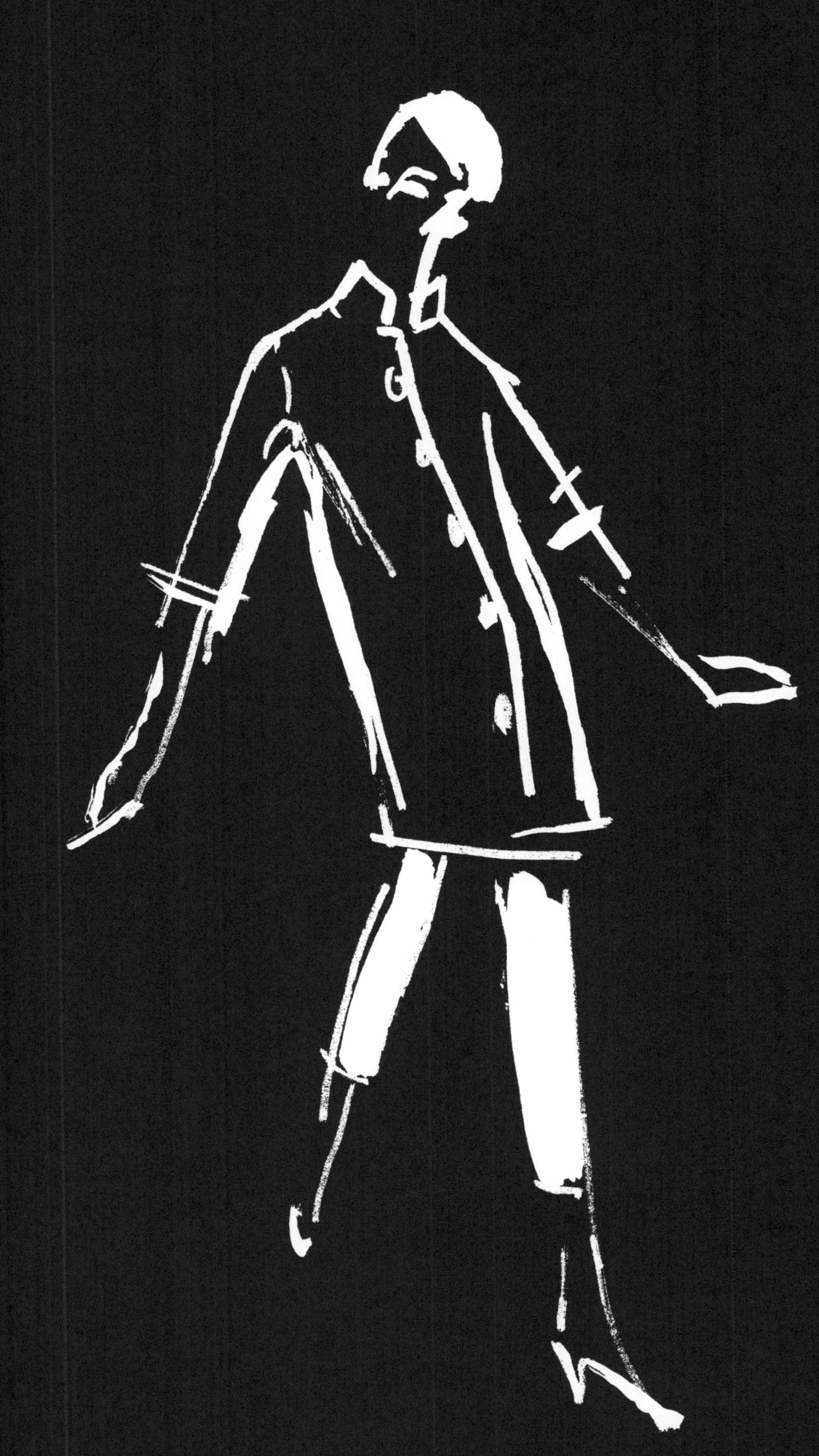

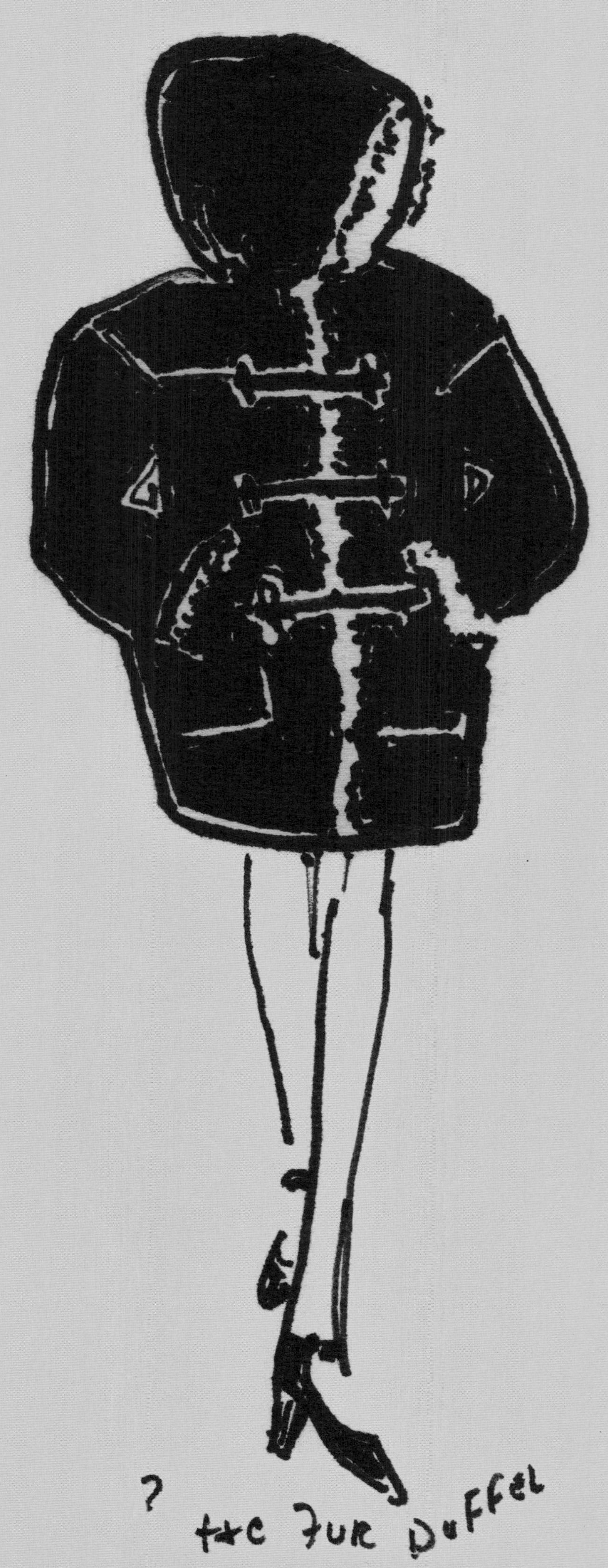

? the Fur Duffel

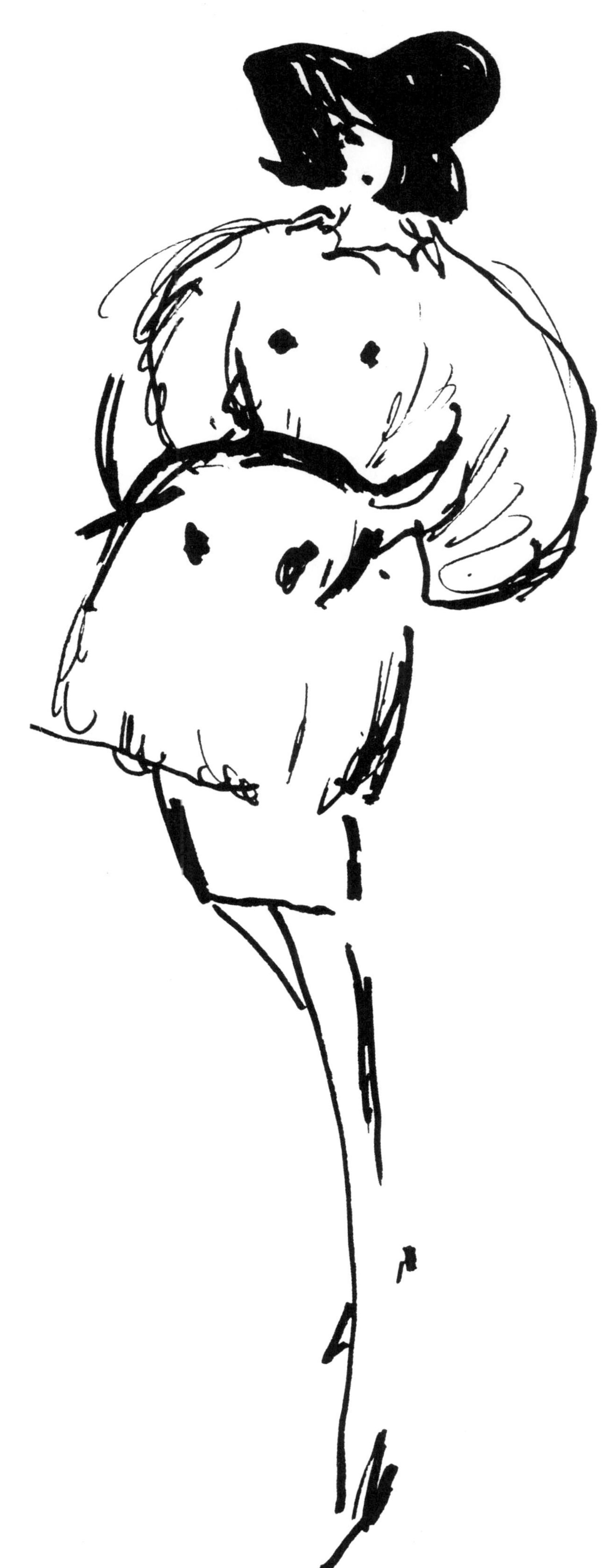

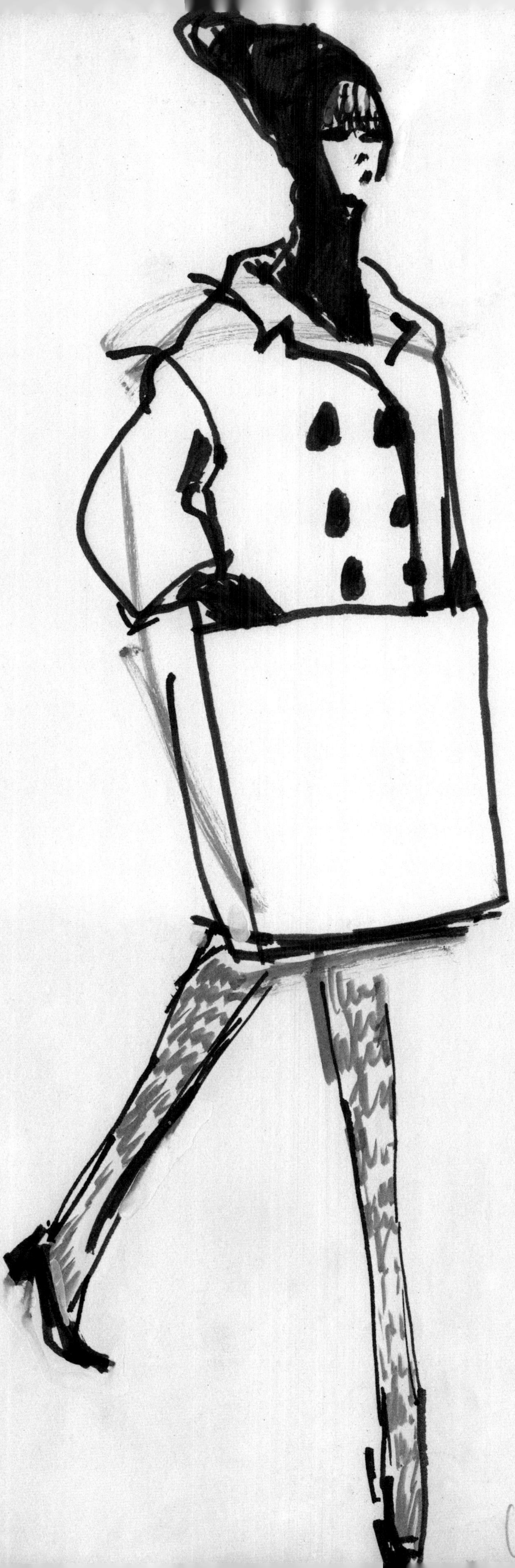

Pull over coat in
mustard
Yellow

60's,
Early

Eugenia

Jacques
said He
was putting
these colored
stockings with
but didn't arrive
from Van Realte

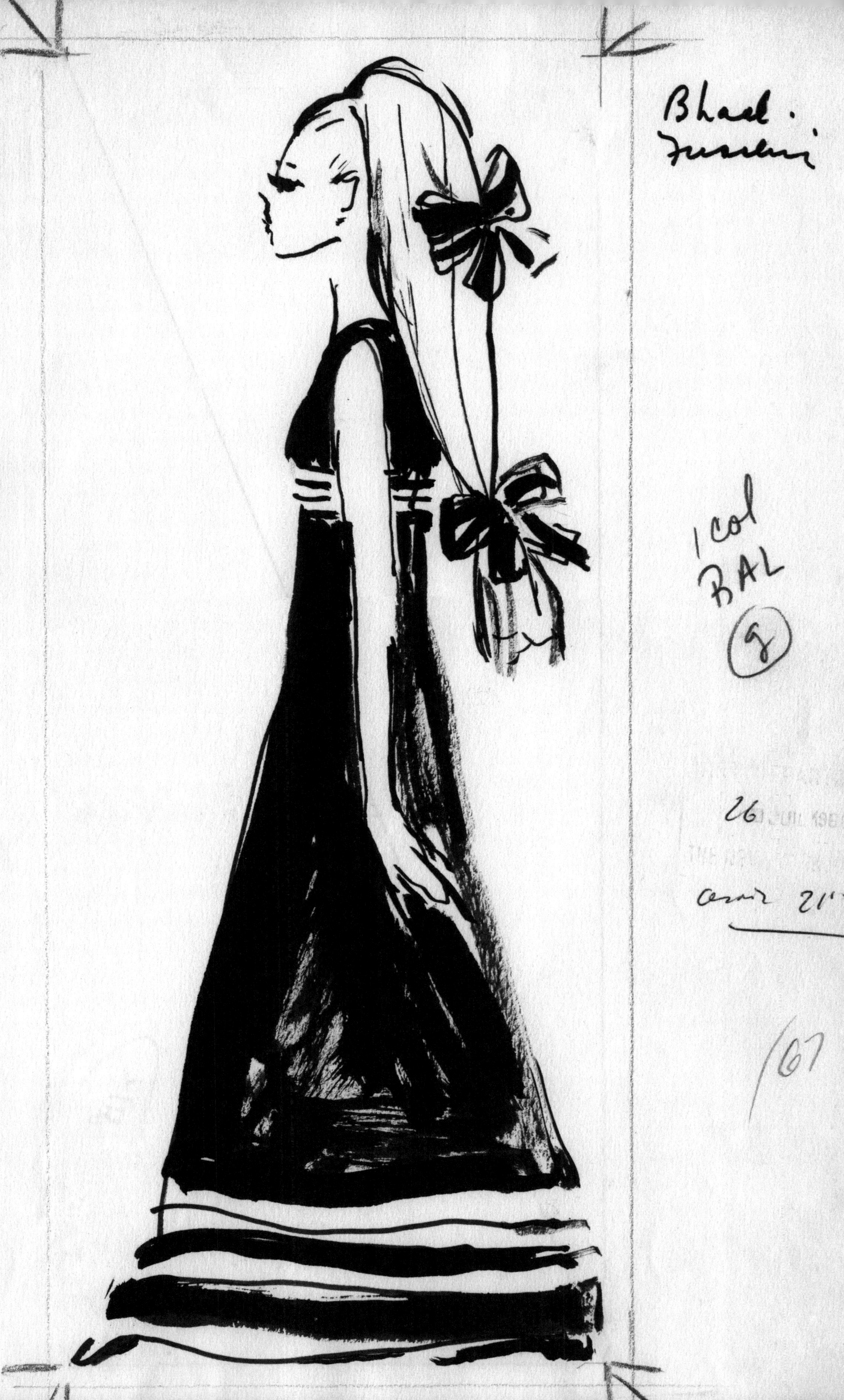

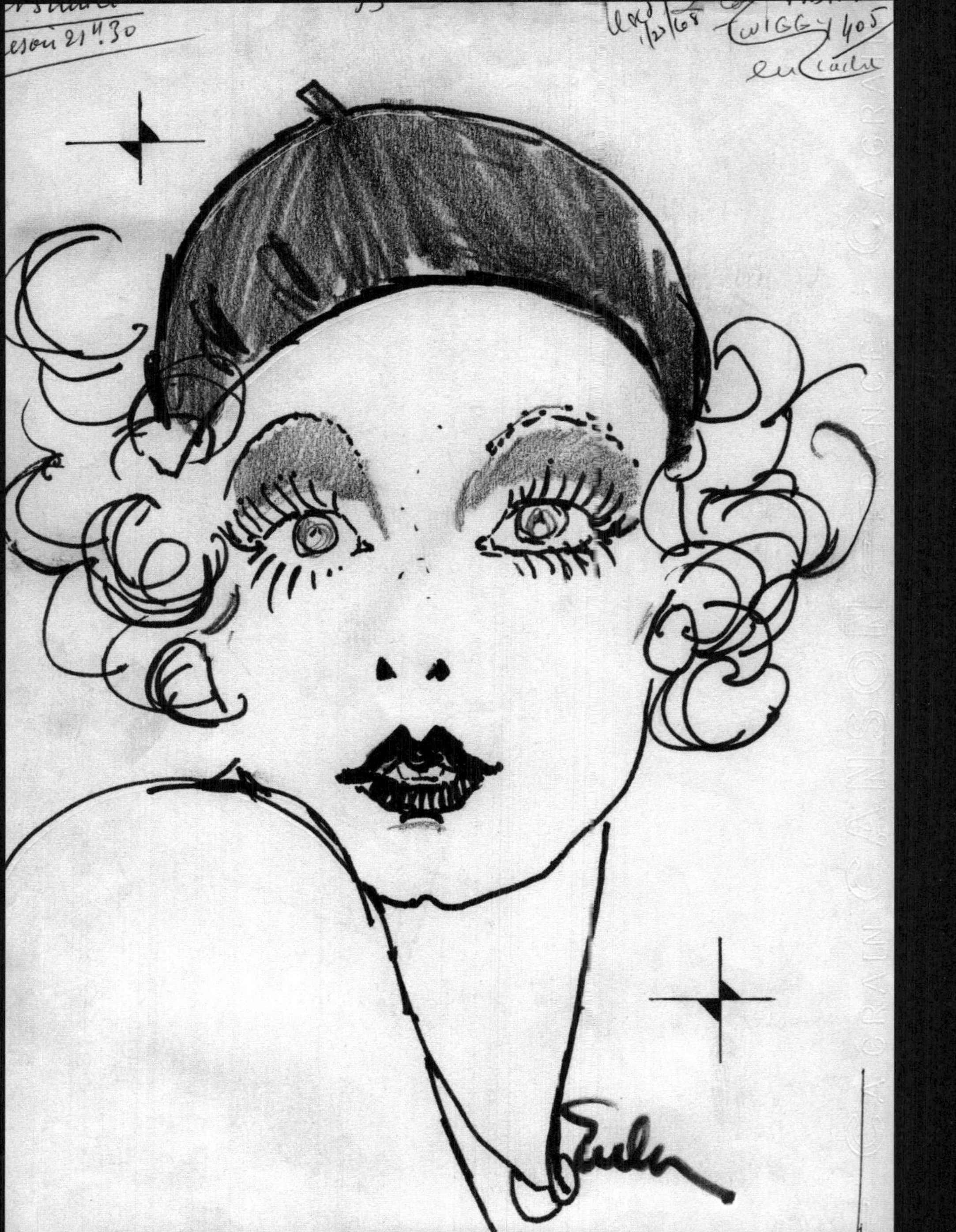

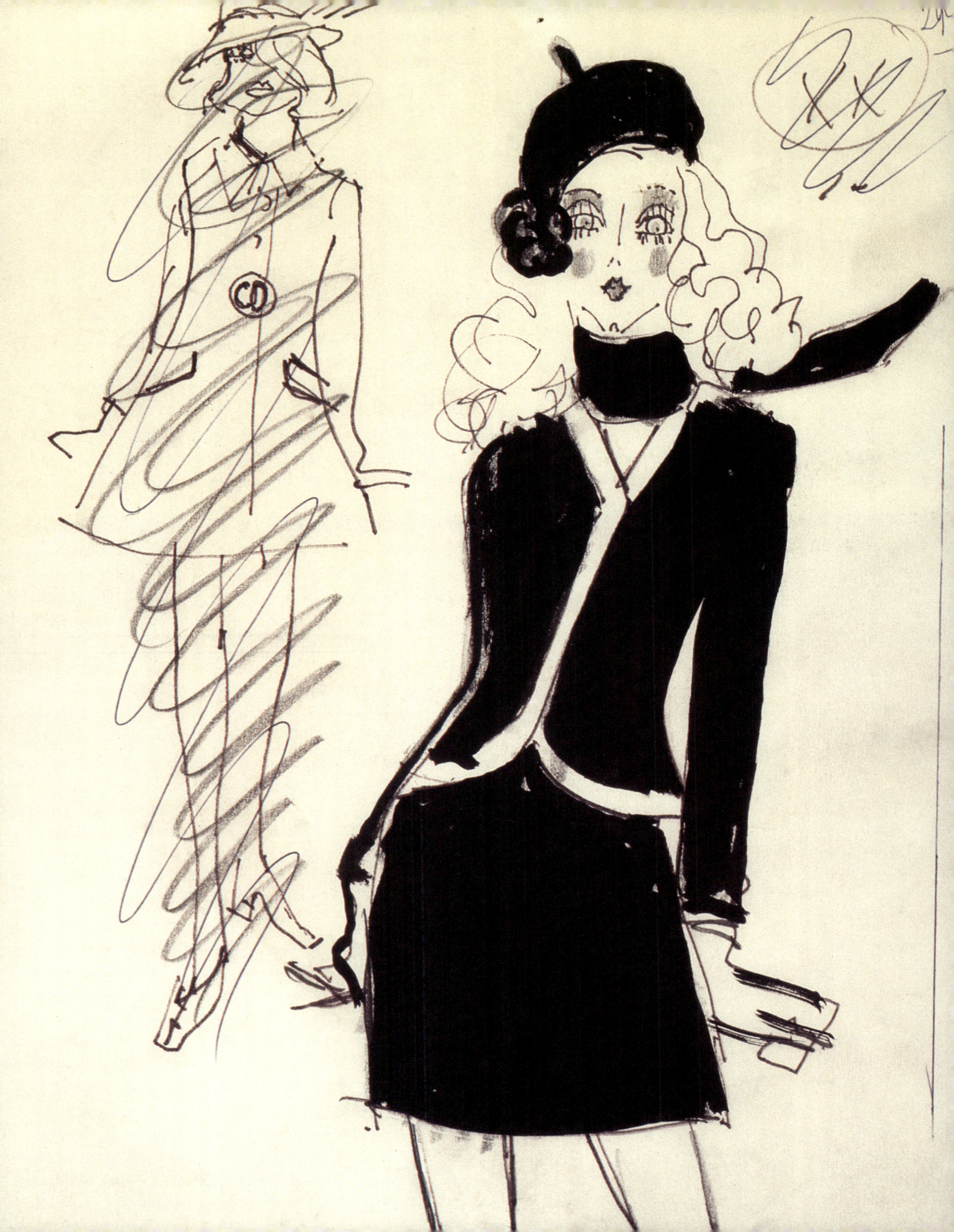

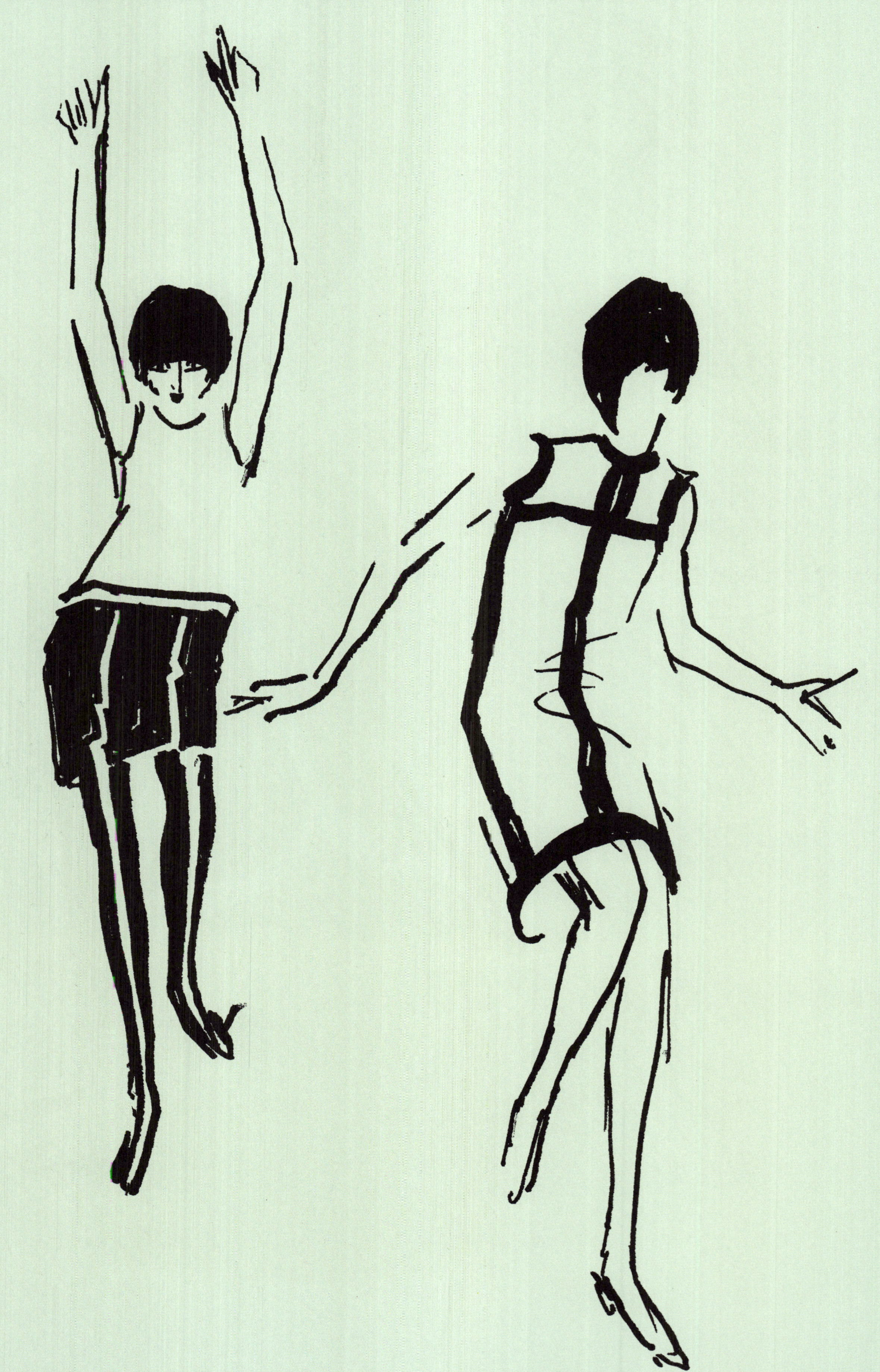

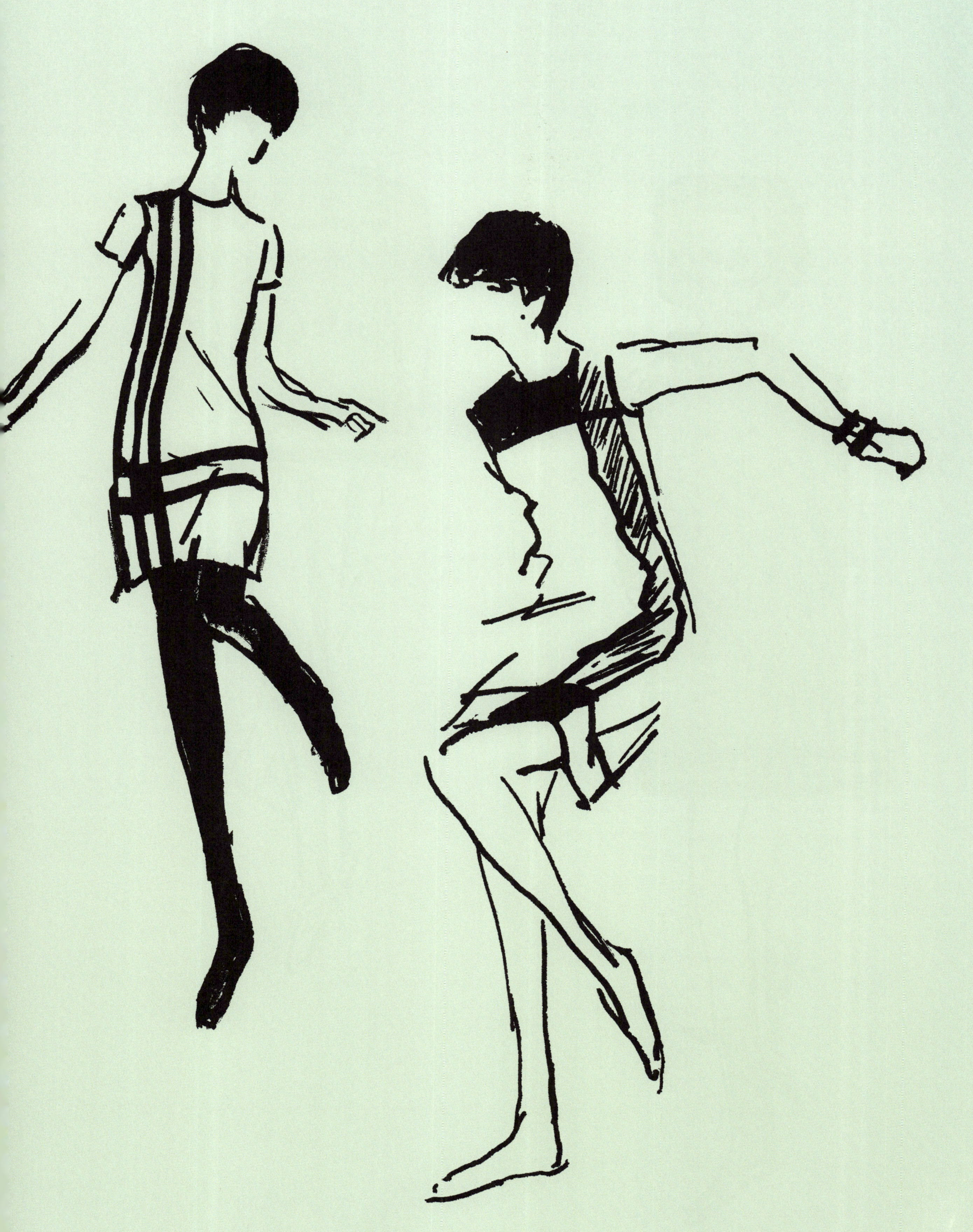

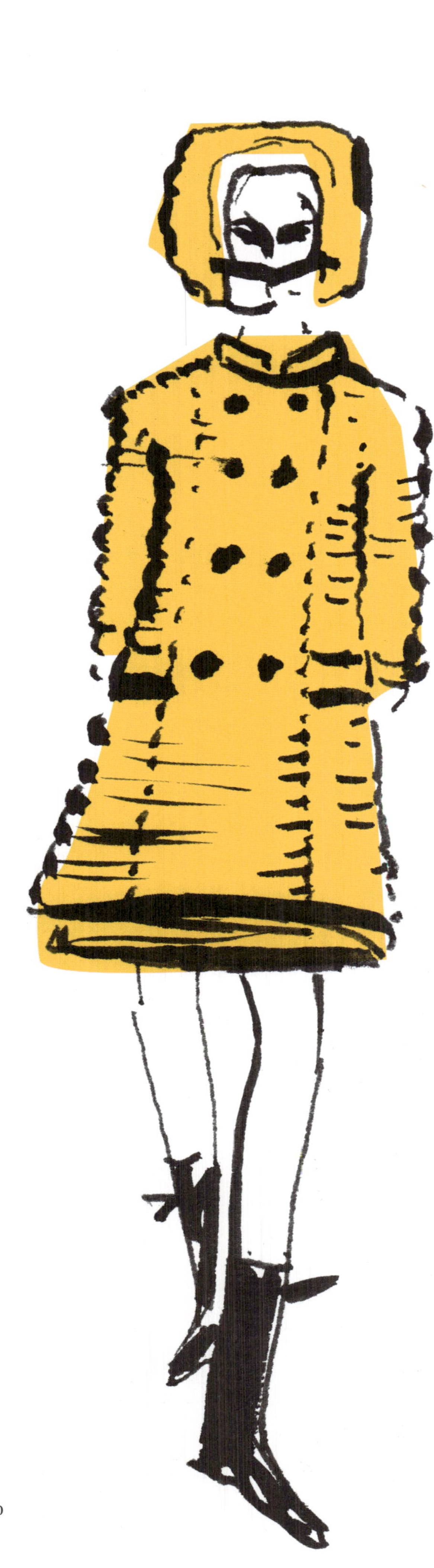
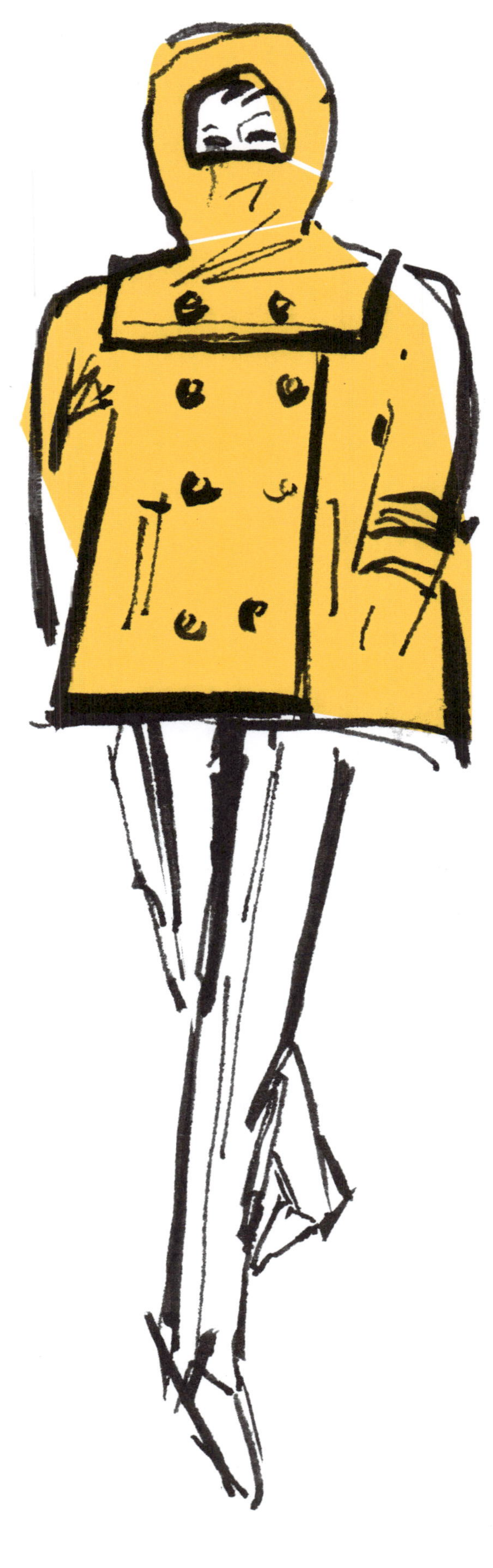

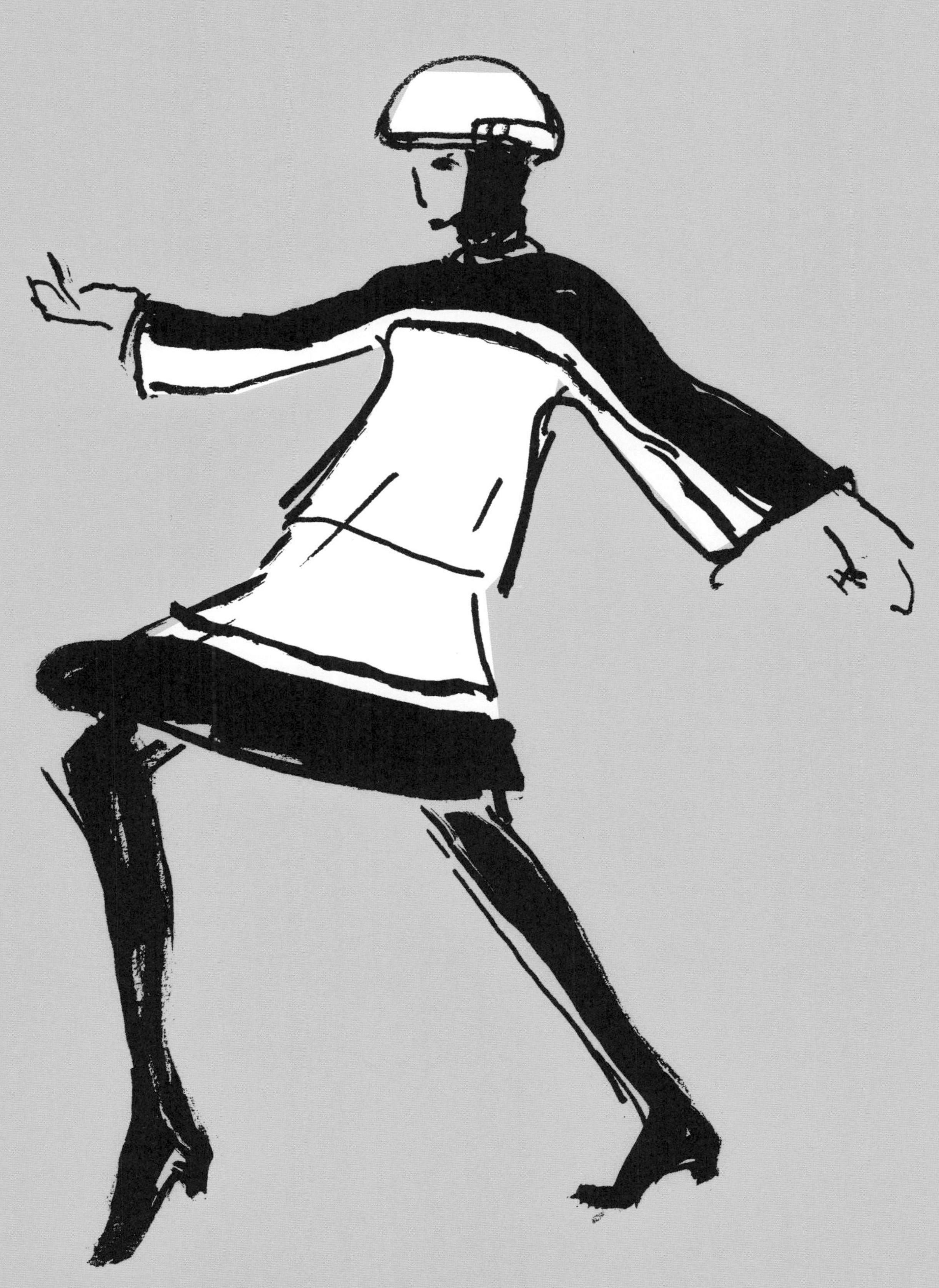

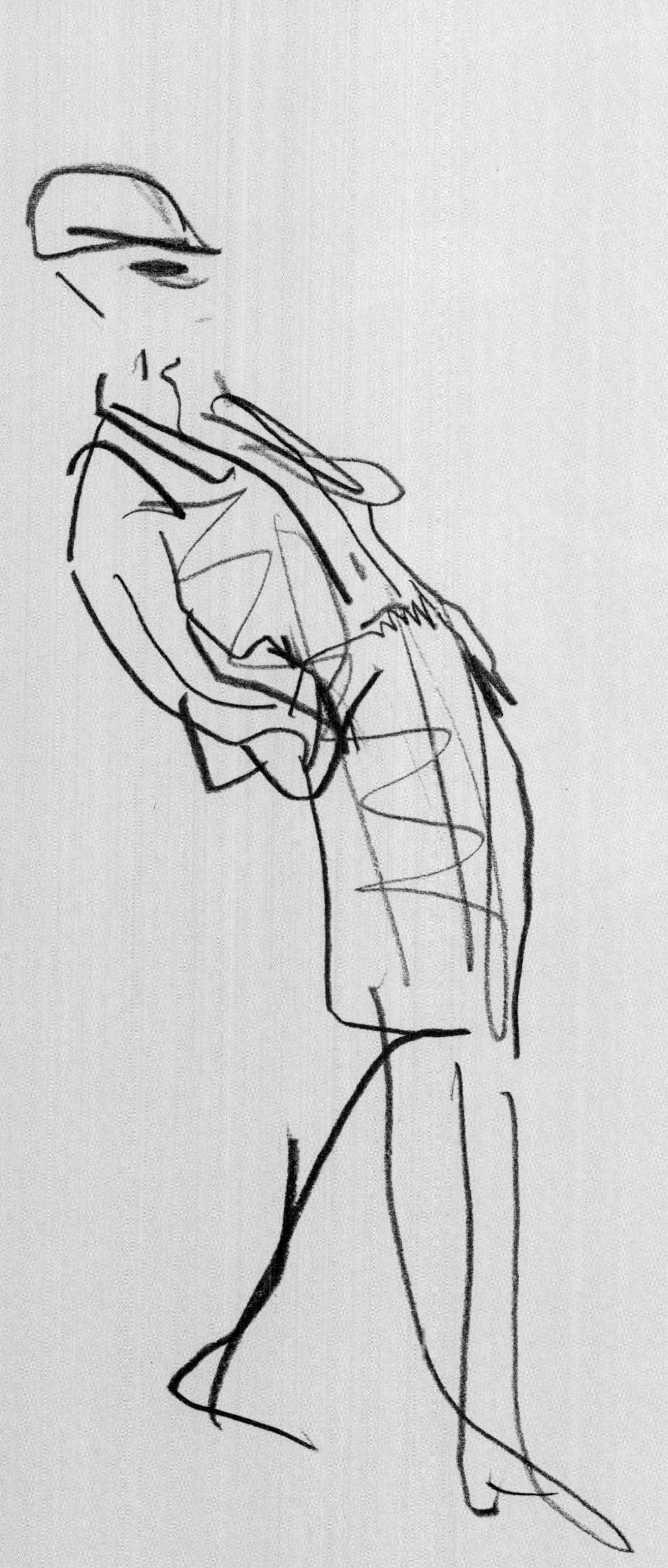
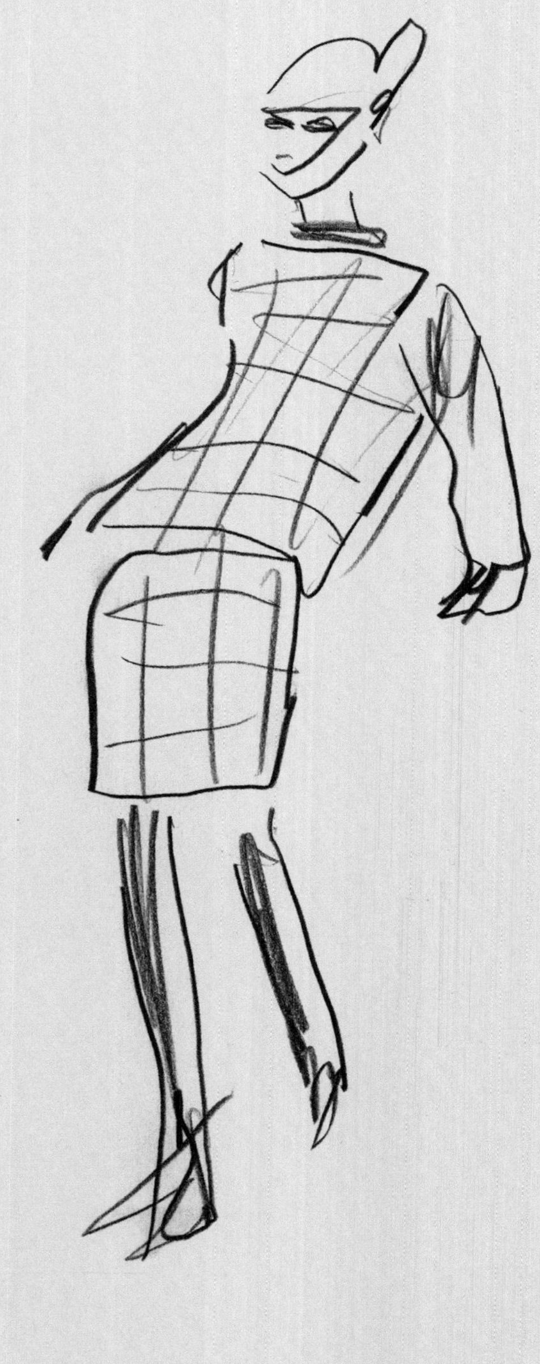

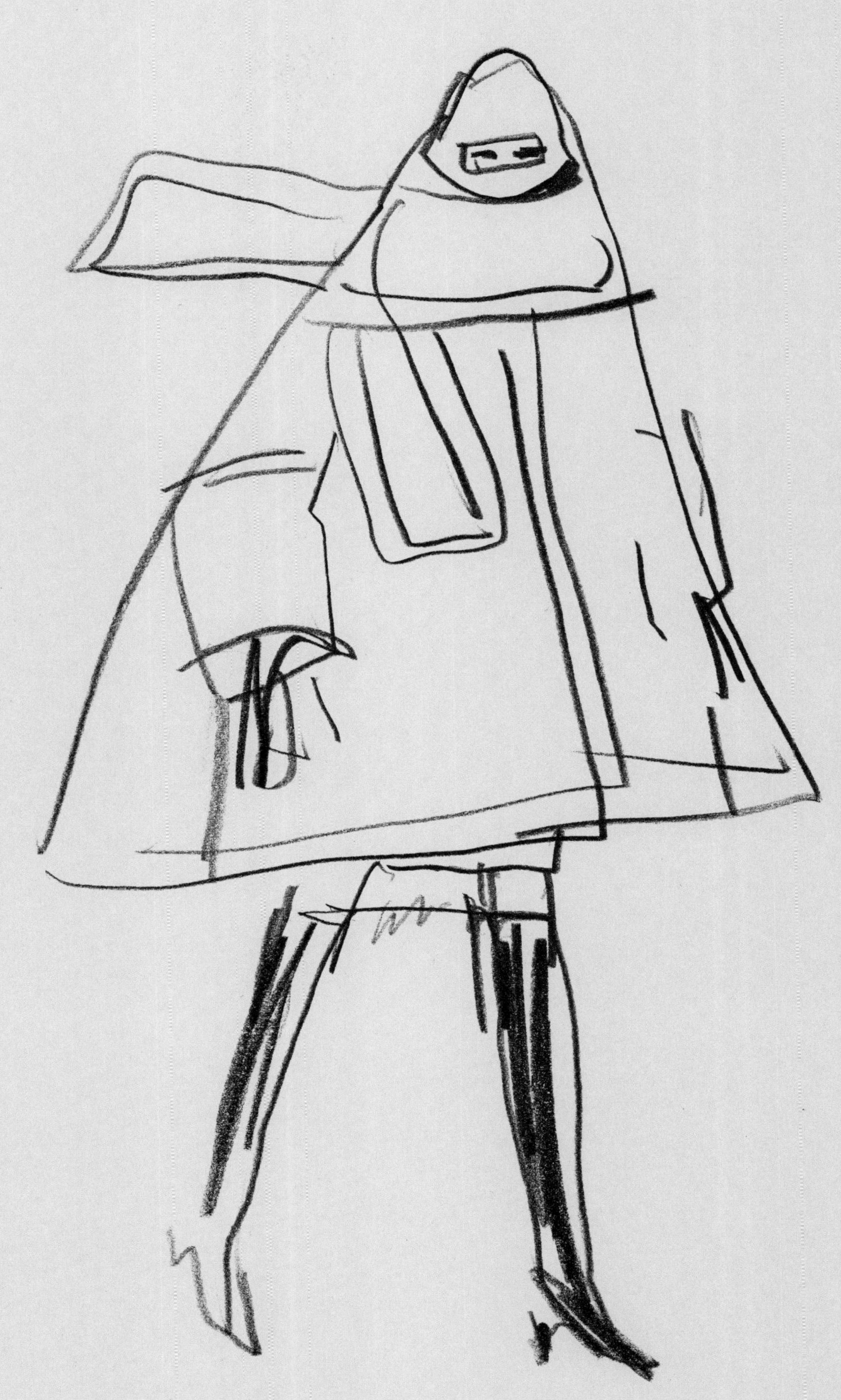

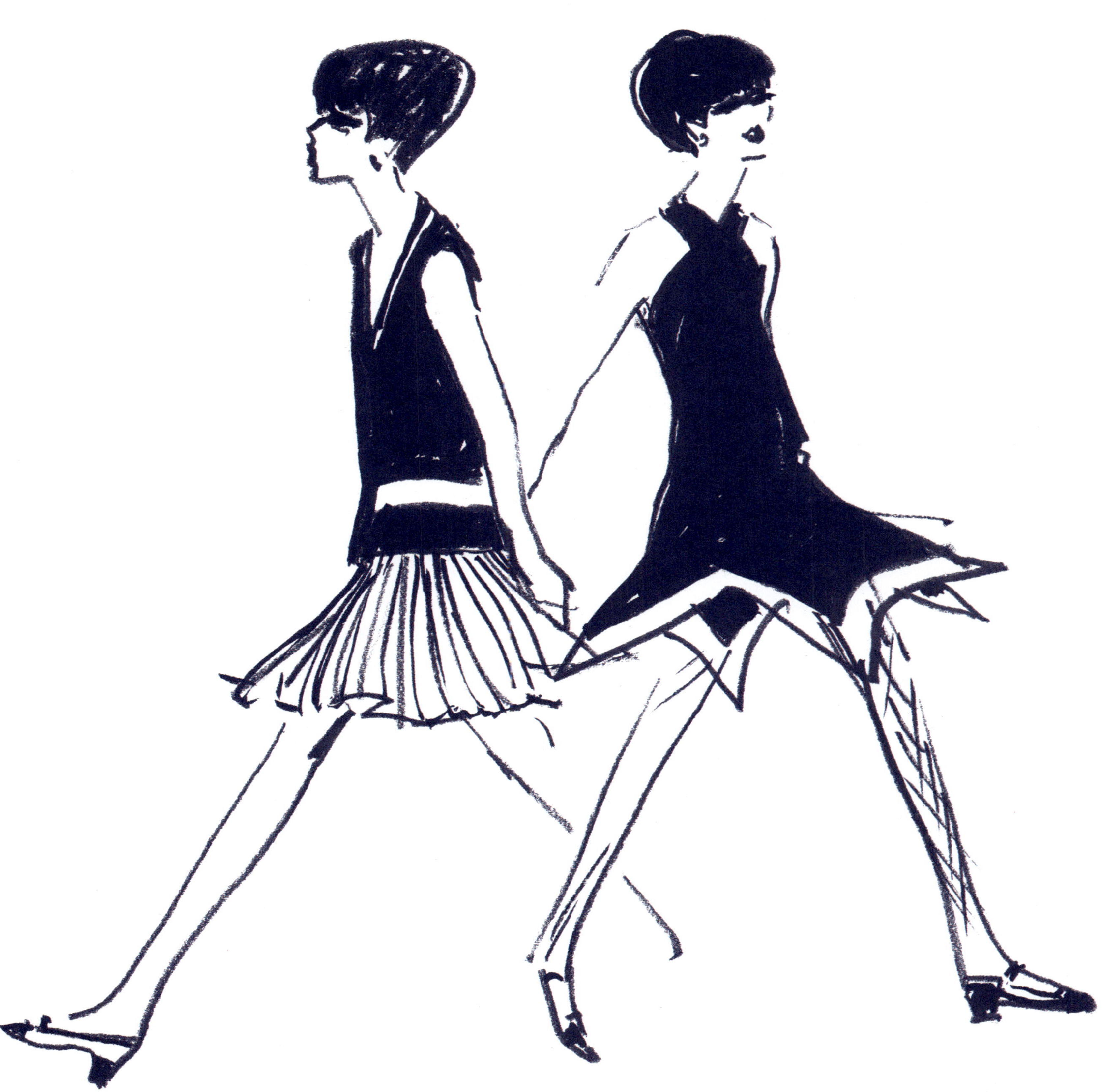

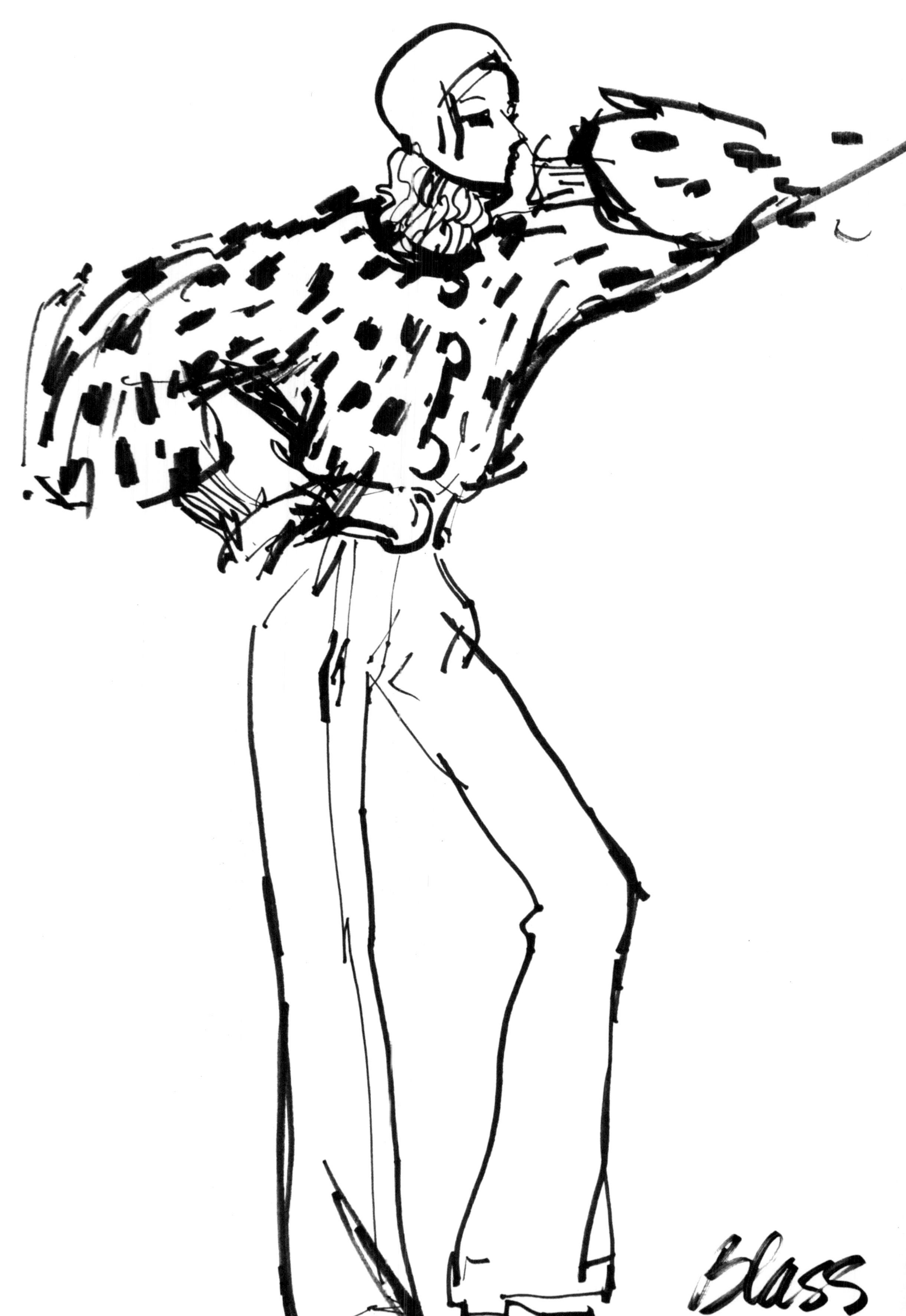

Blass

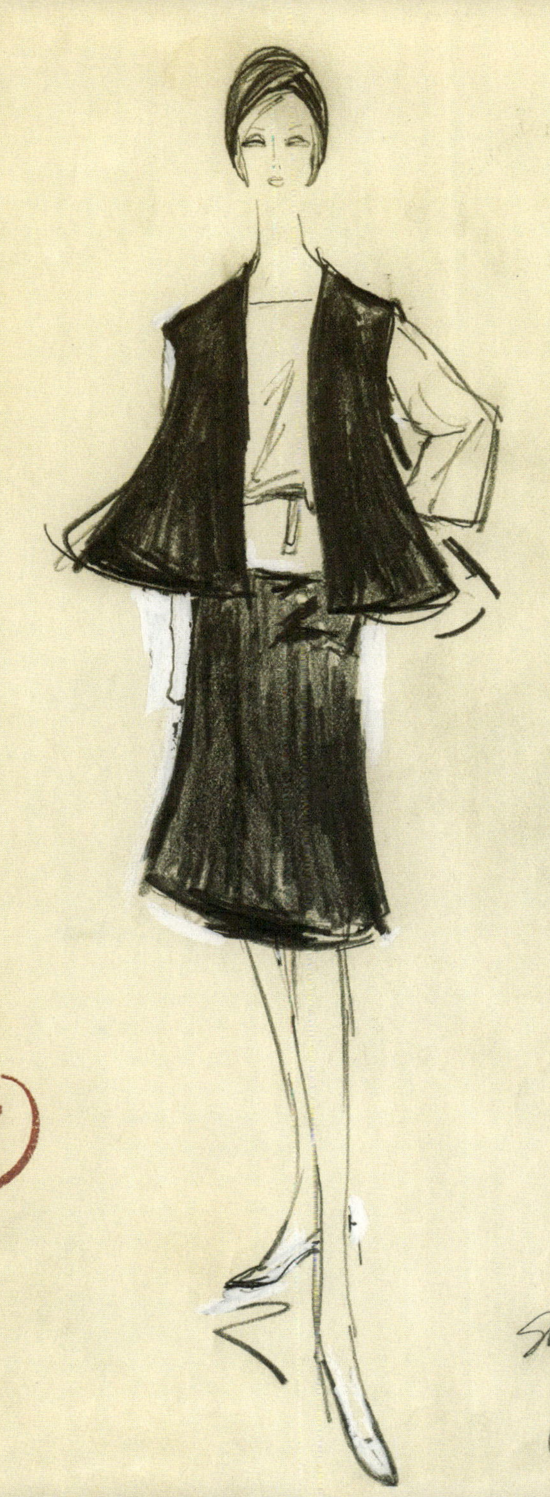

shoes

Tuo Fashion
©

42

759)

Blass
Blk + white
all Bias cut.
Showed collection
with all
White Shoes.

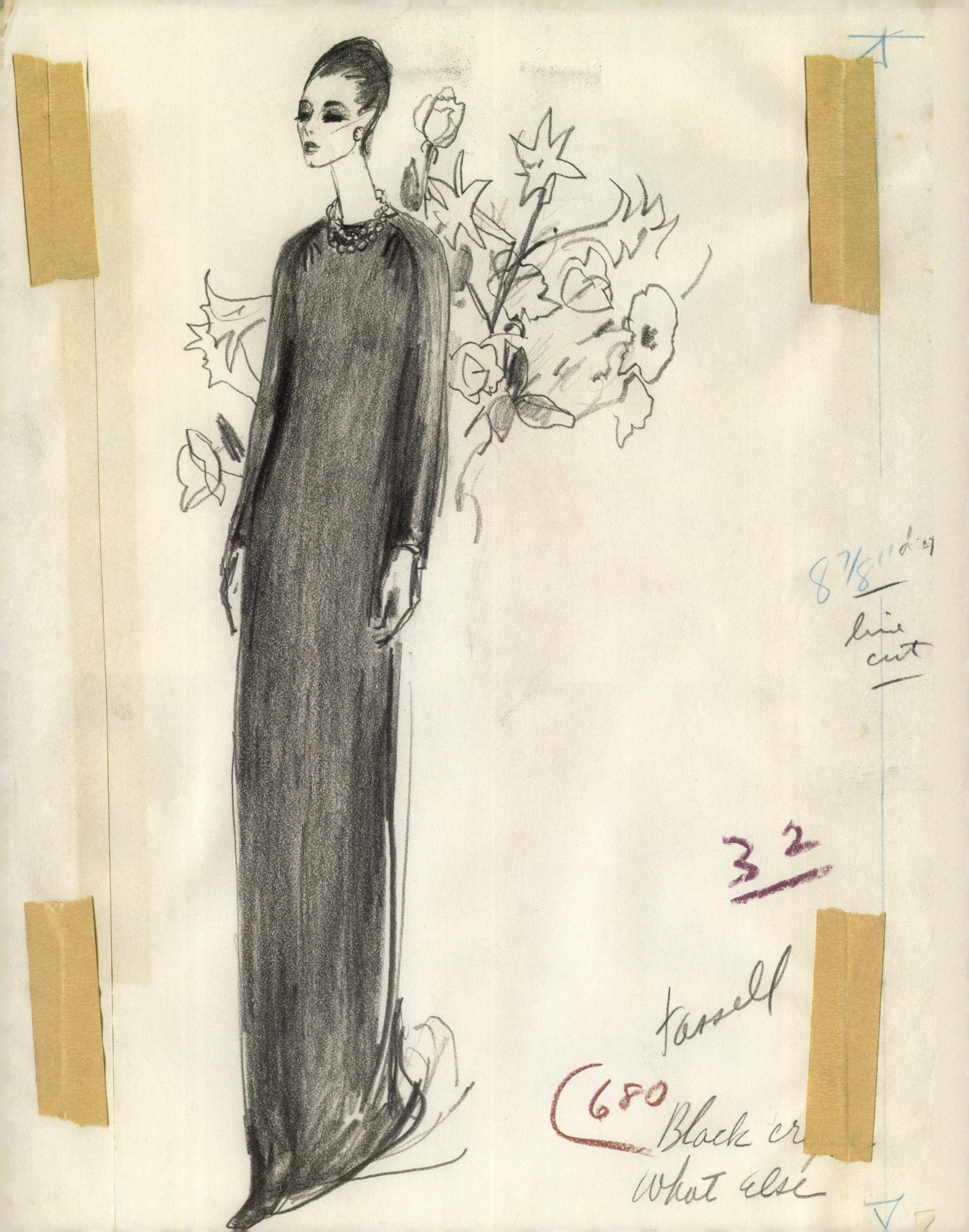

8 7/8" long
line cut
3 2
tassel
680 Black cr
what else

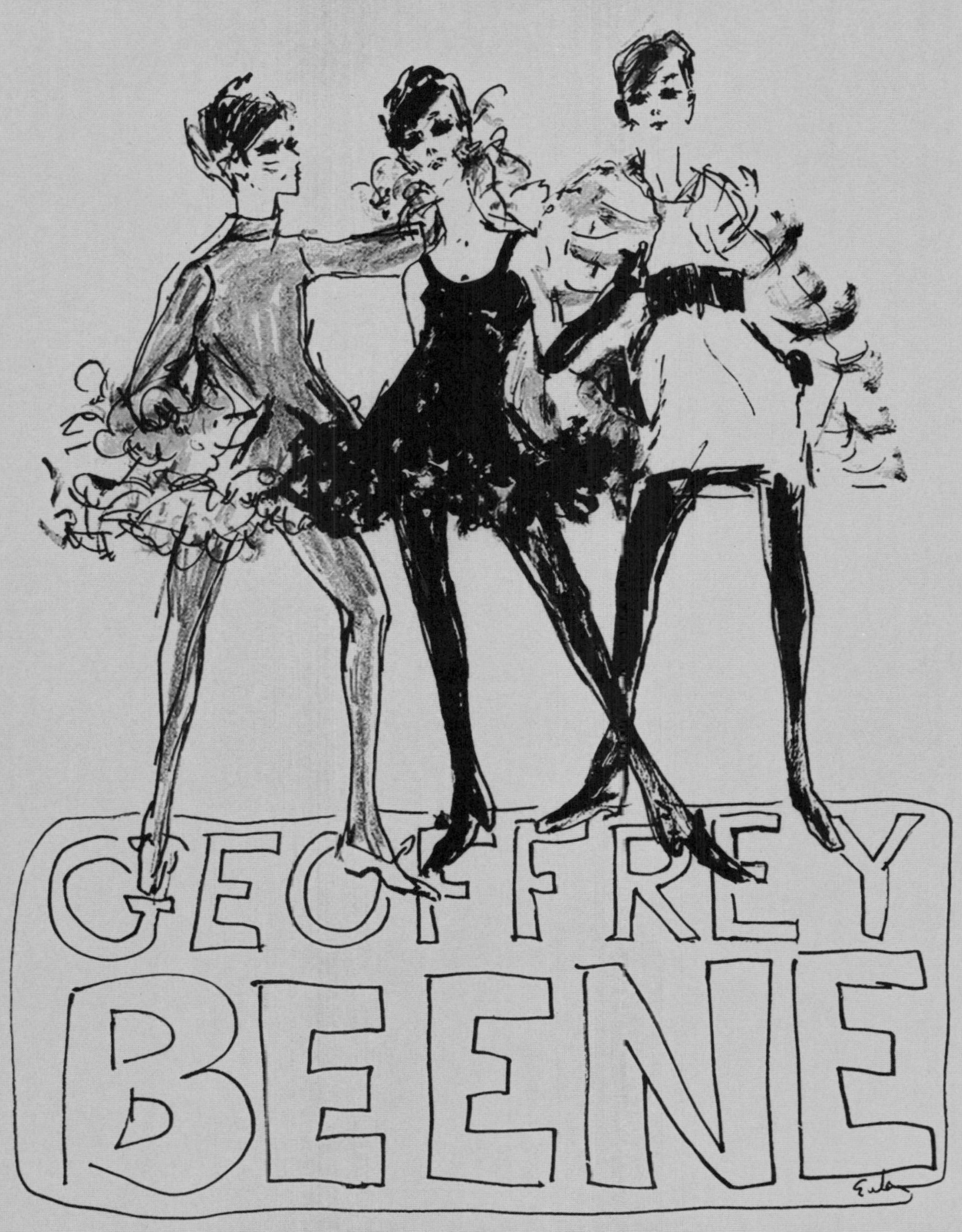
GEOFFREY
BEENE

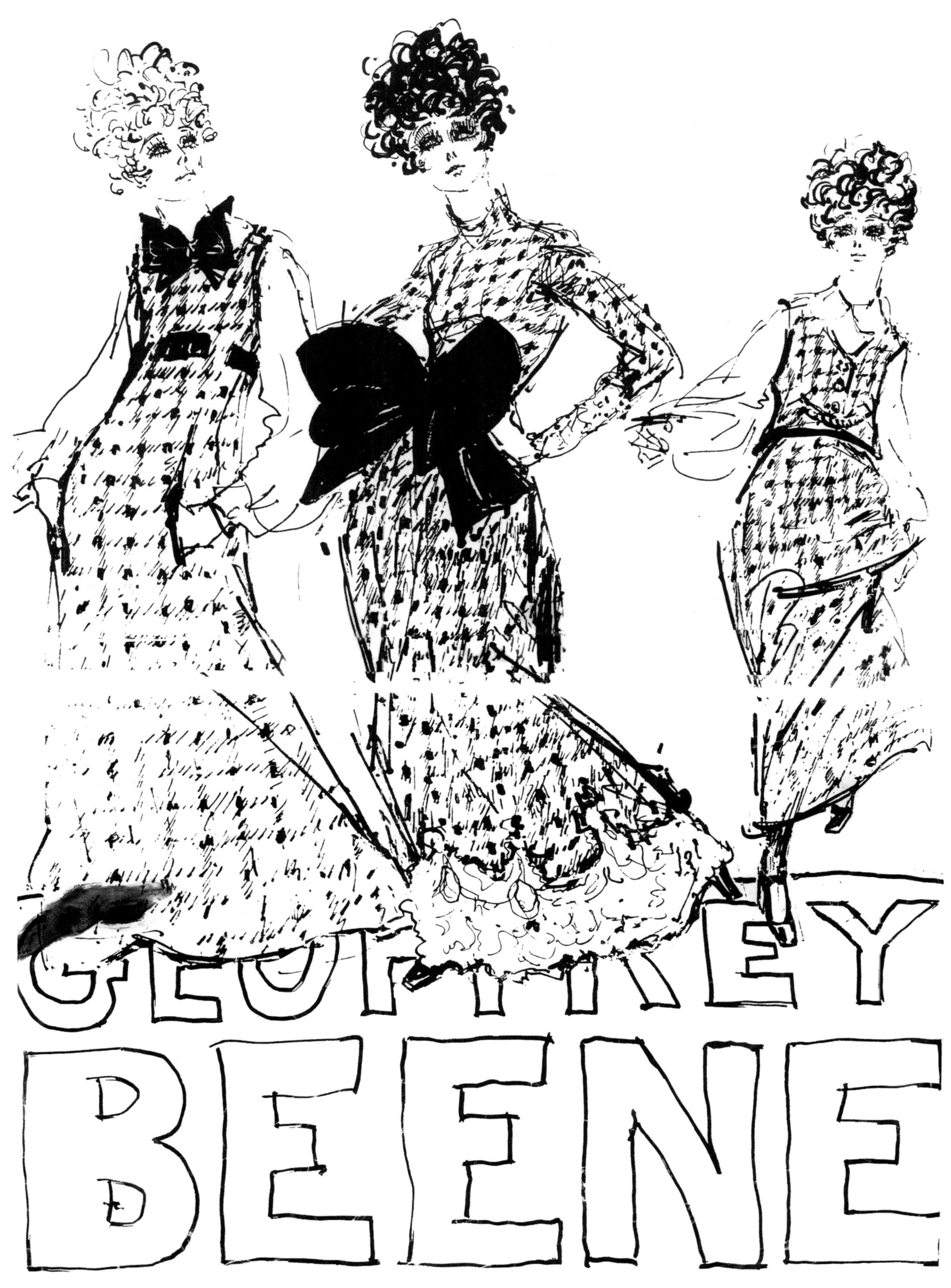

GEOFFREY
BEENE

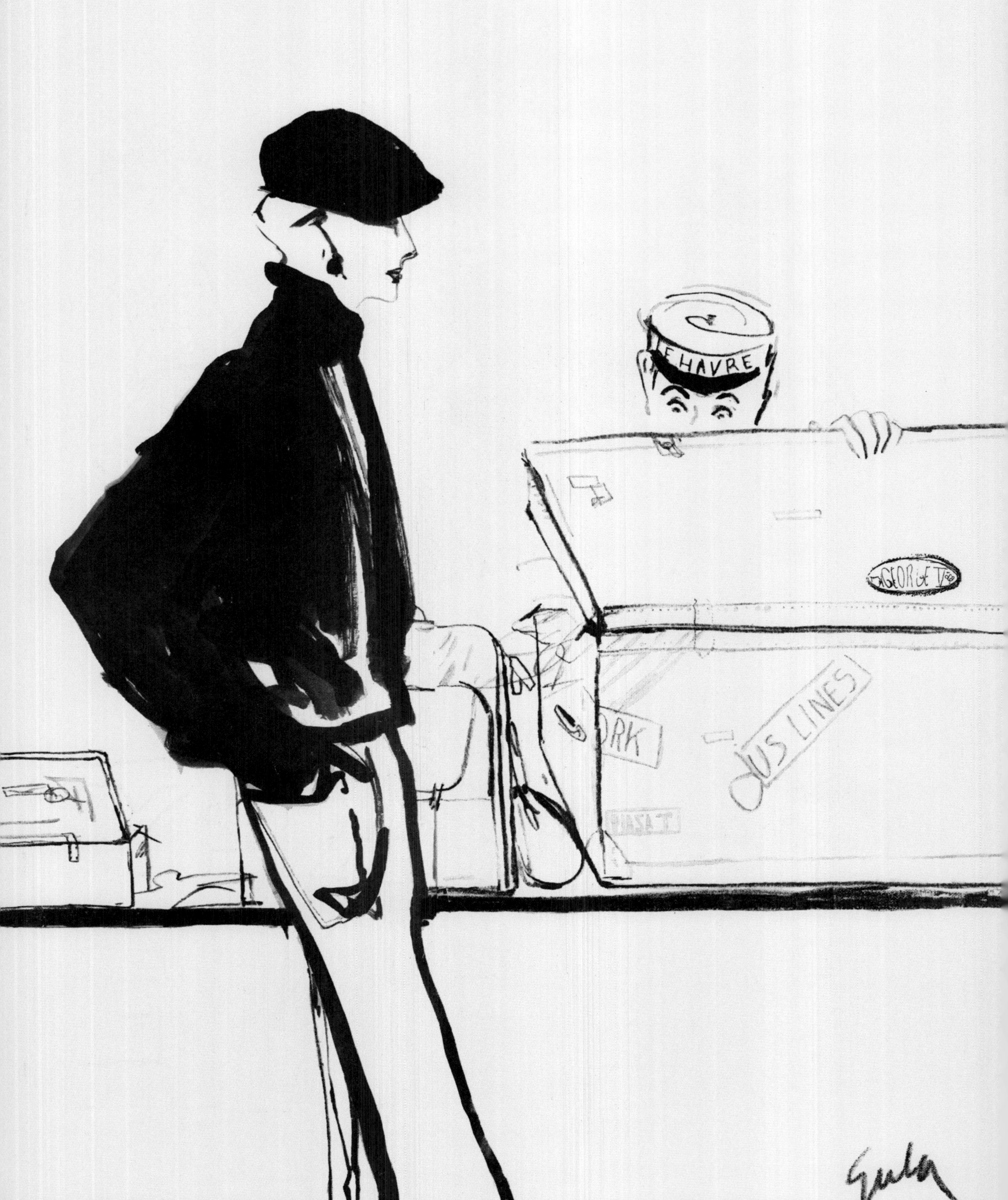

LE HAVRE
ORK
US LINES

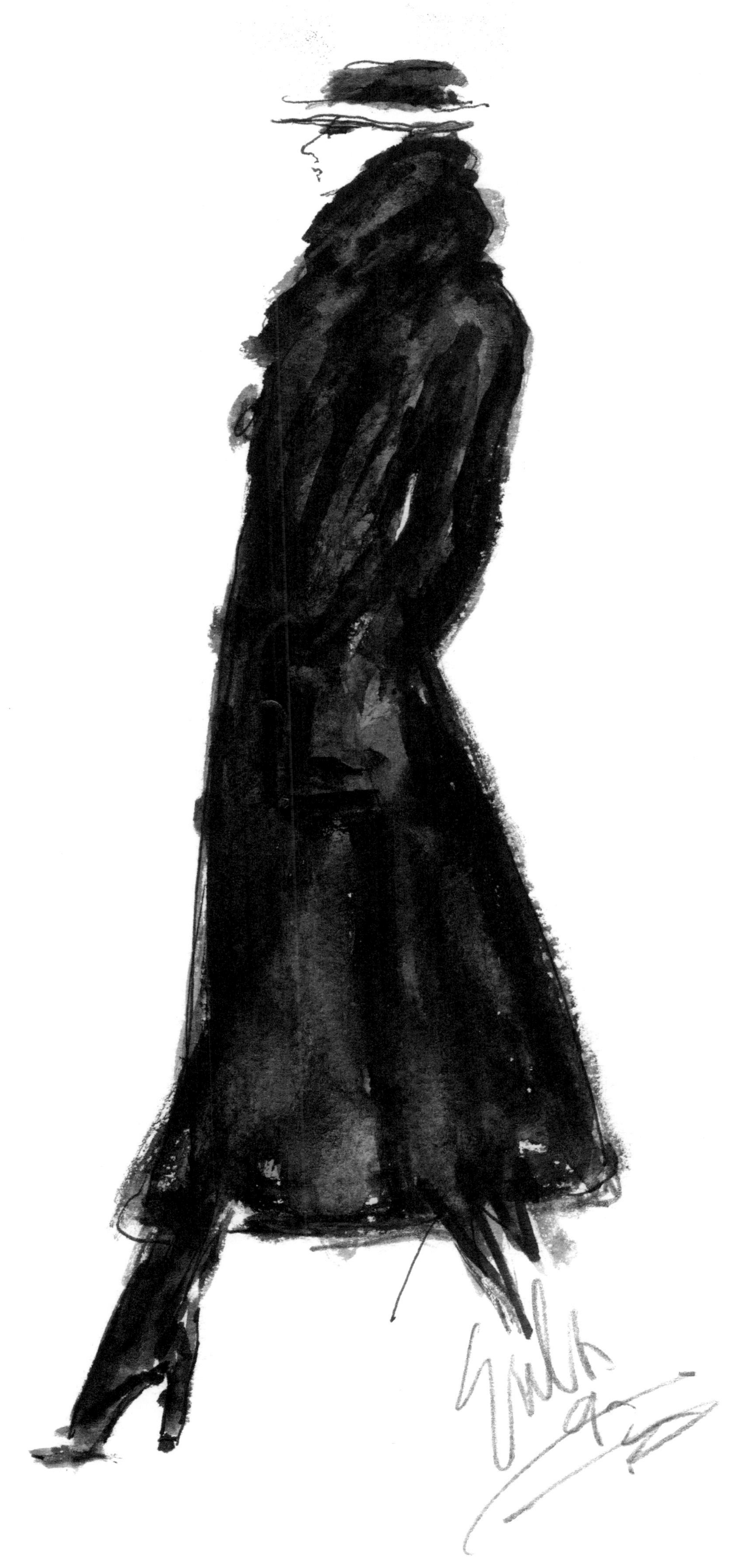

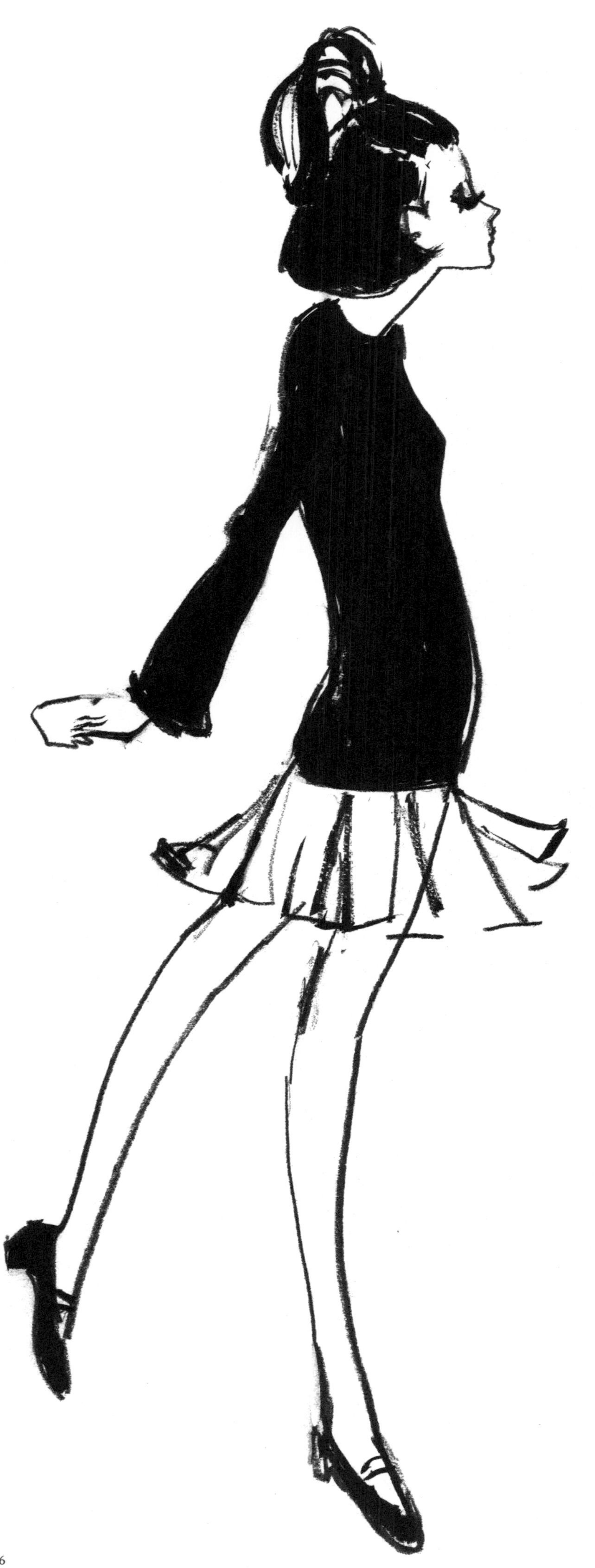

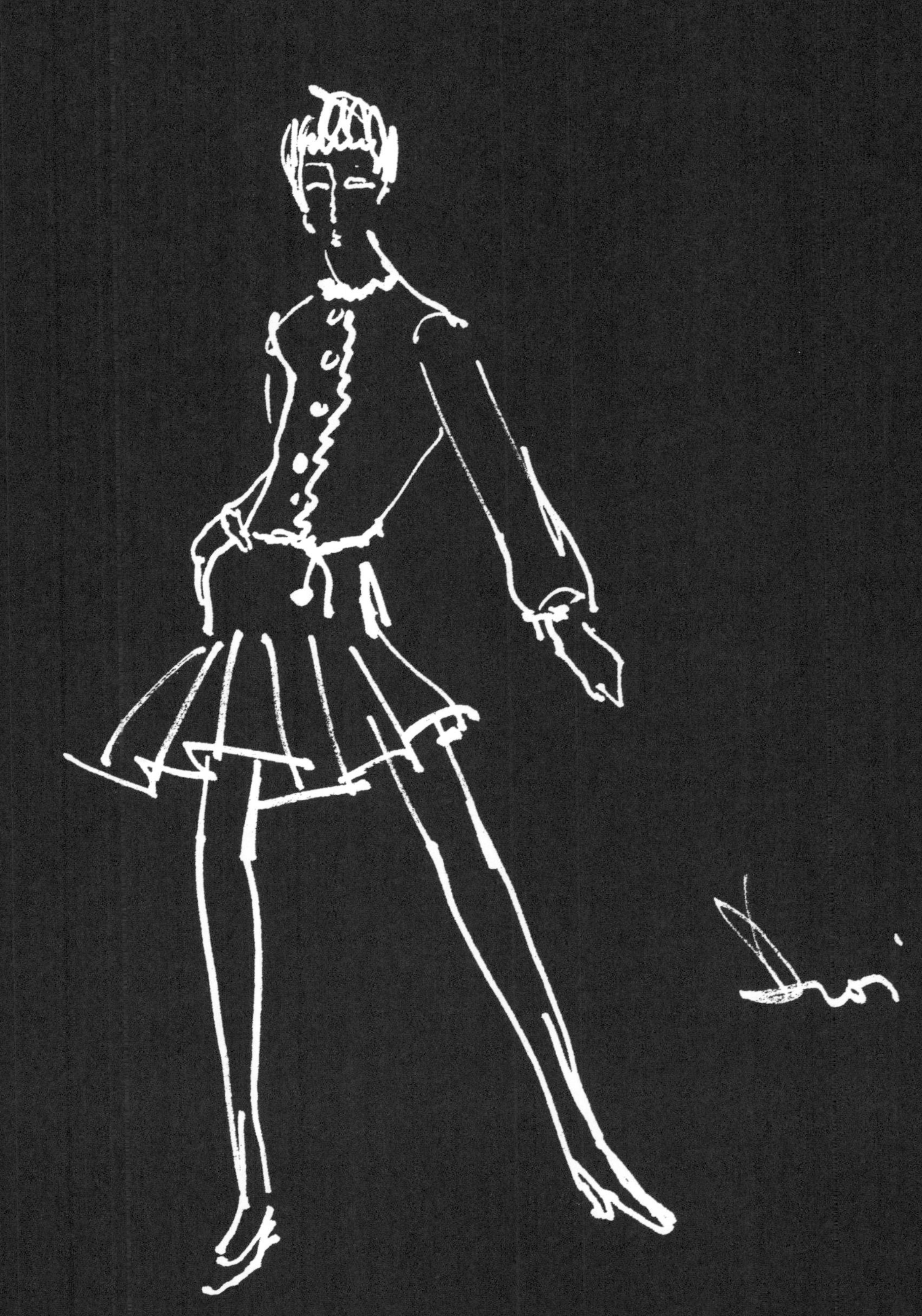

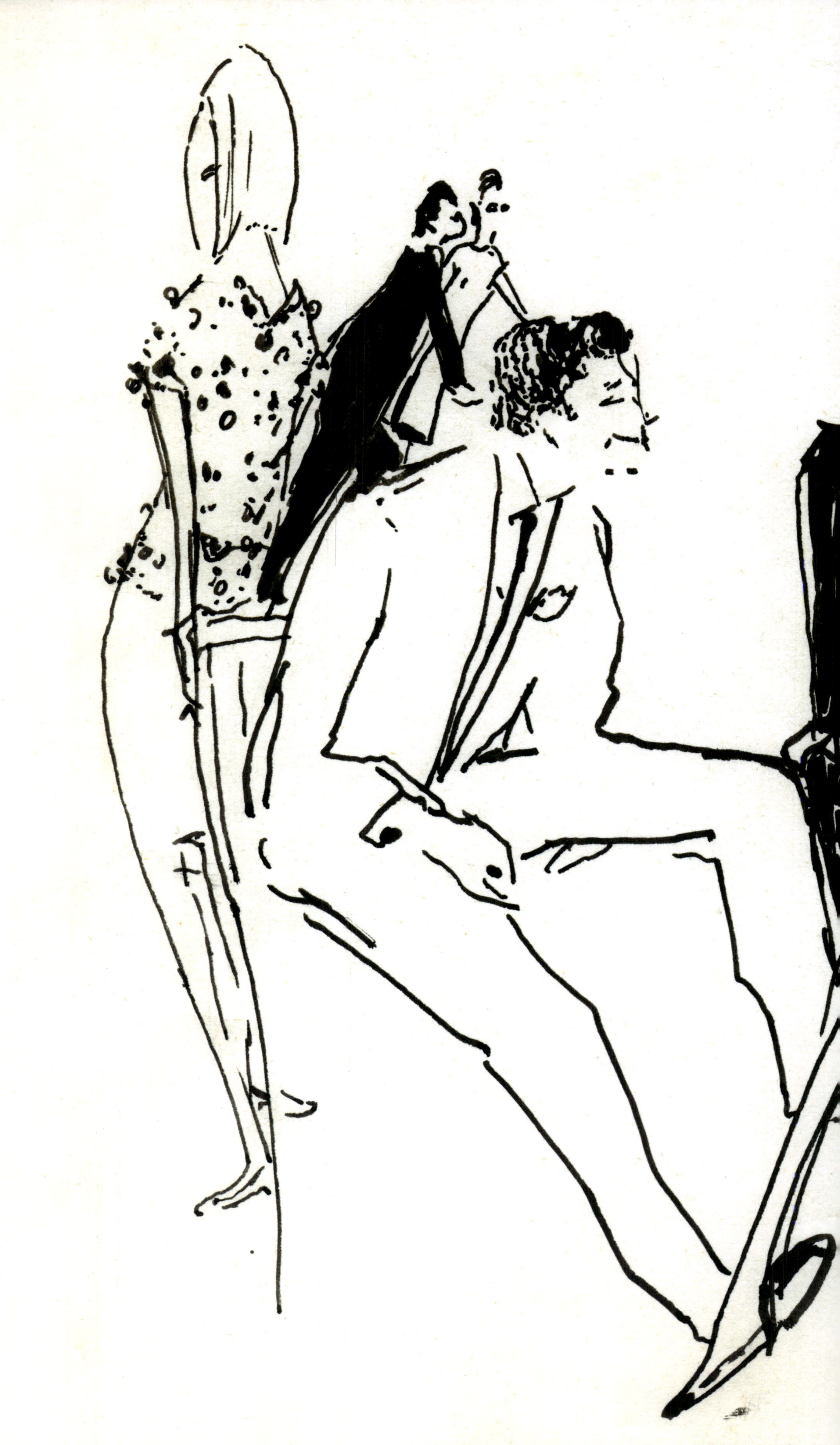

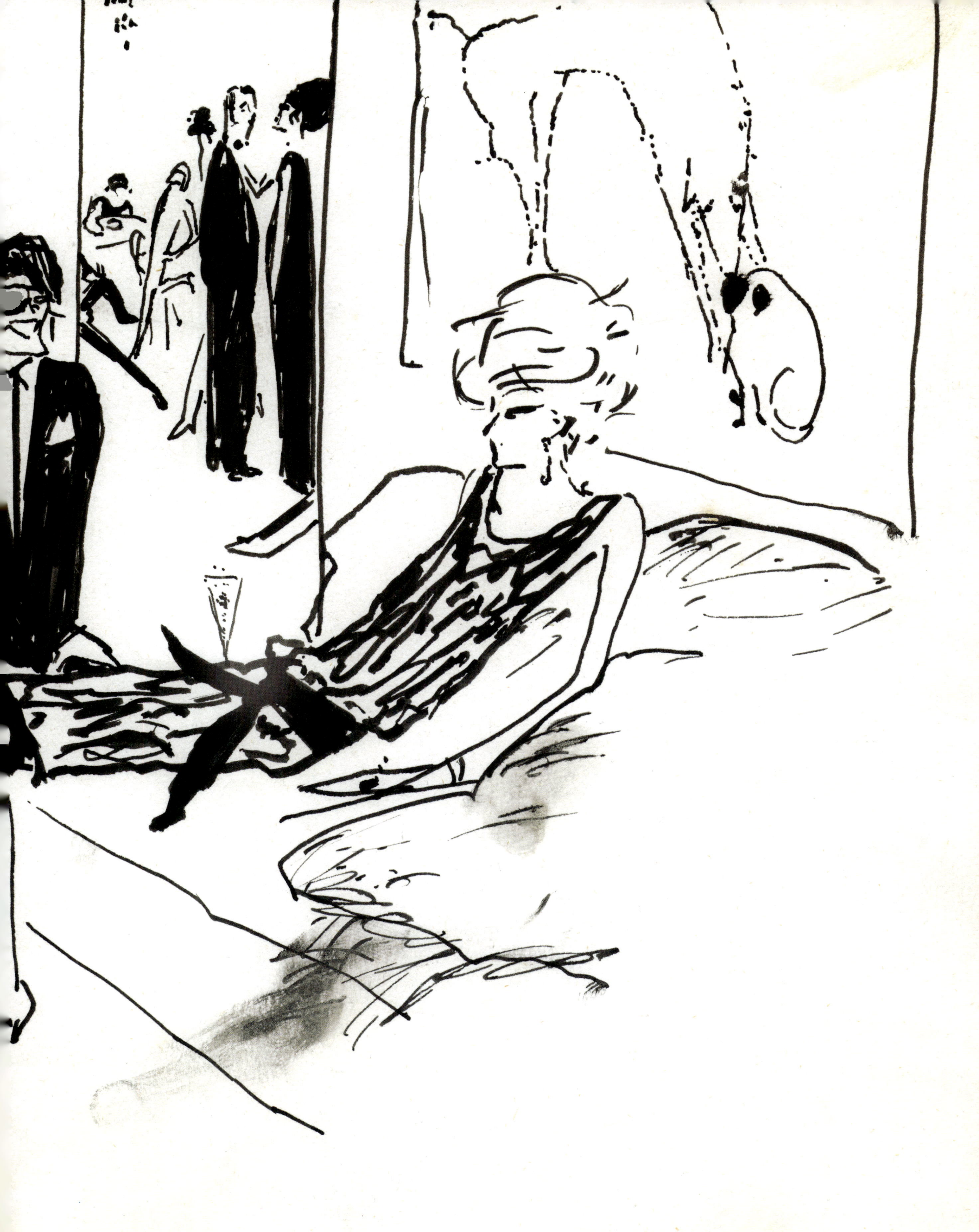

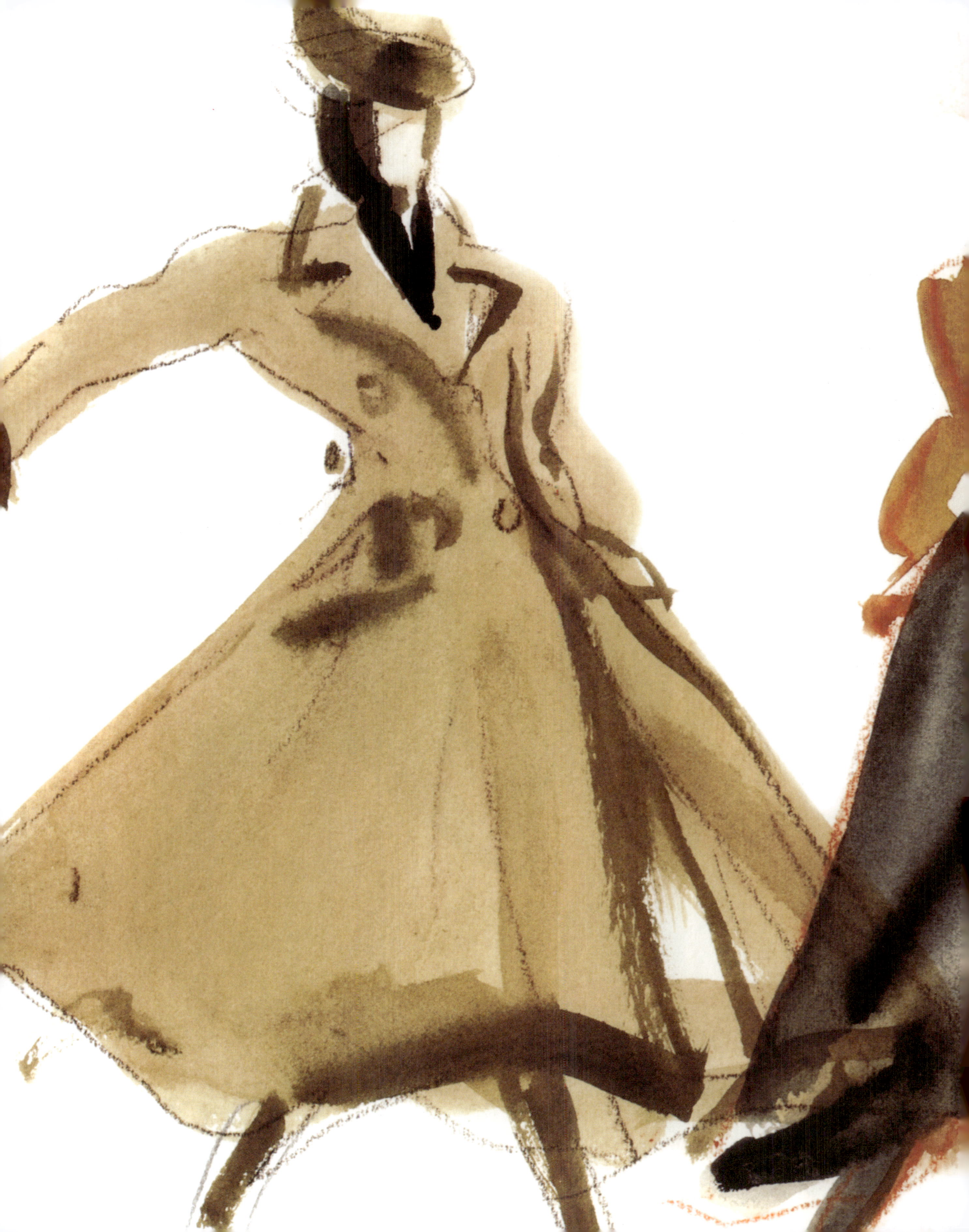

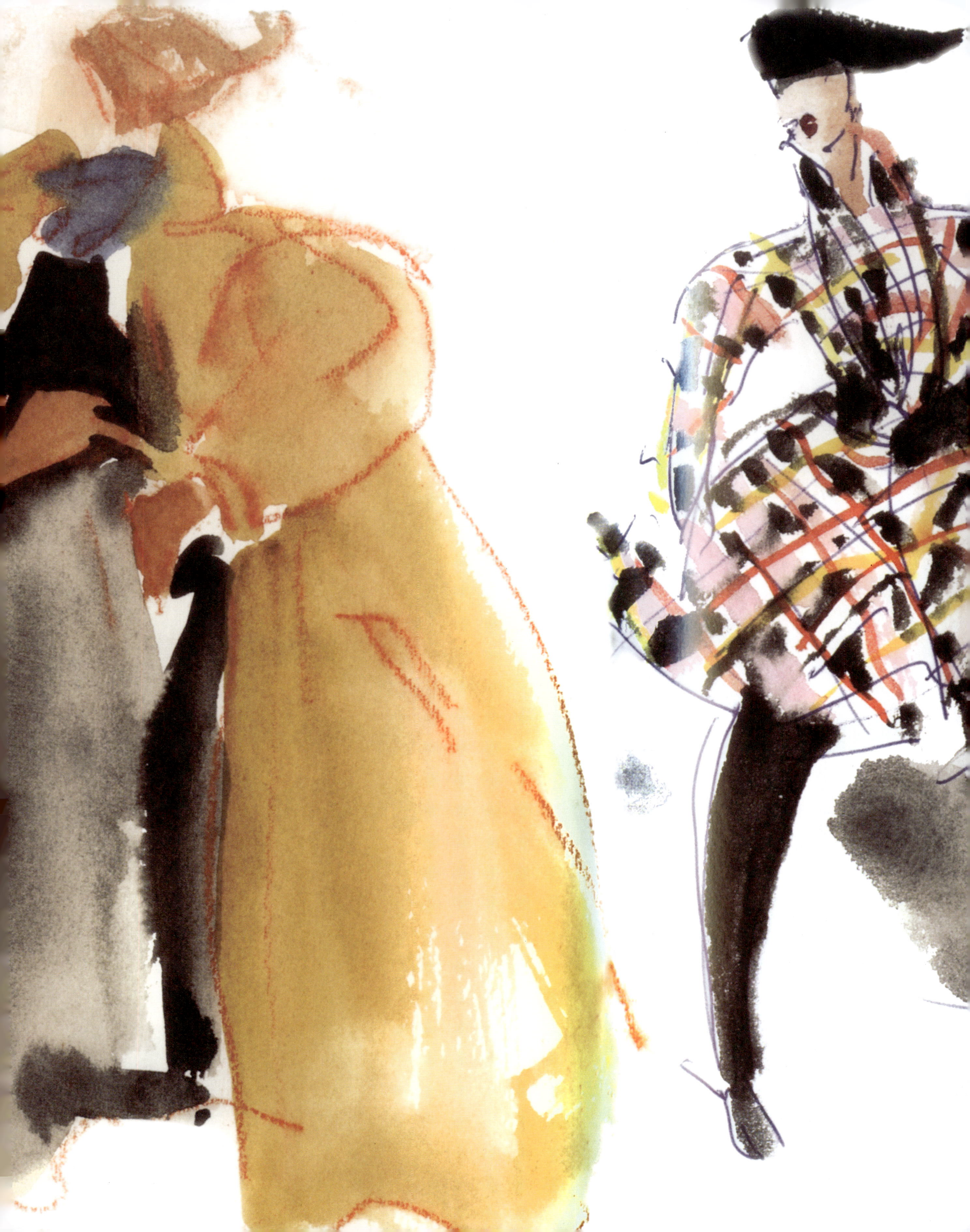

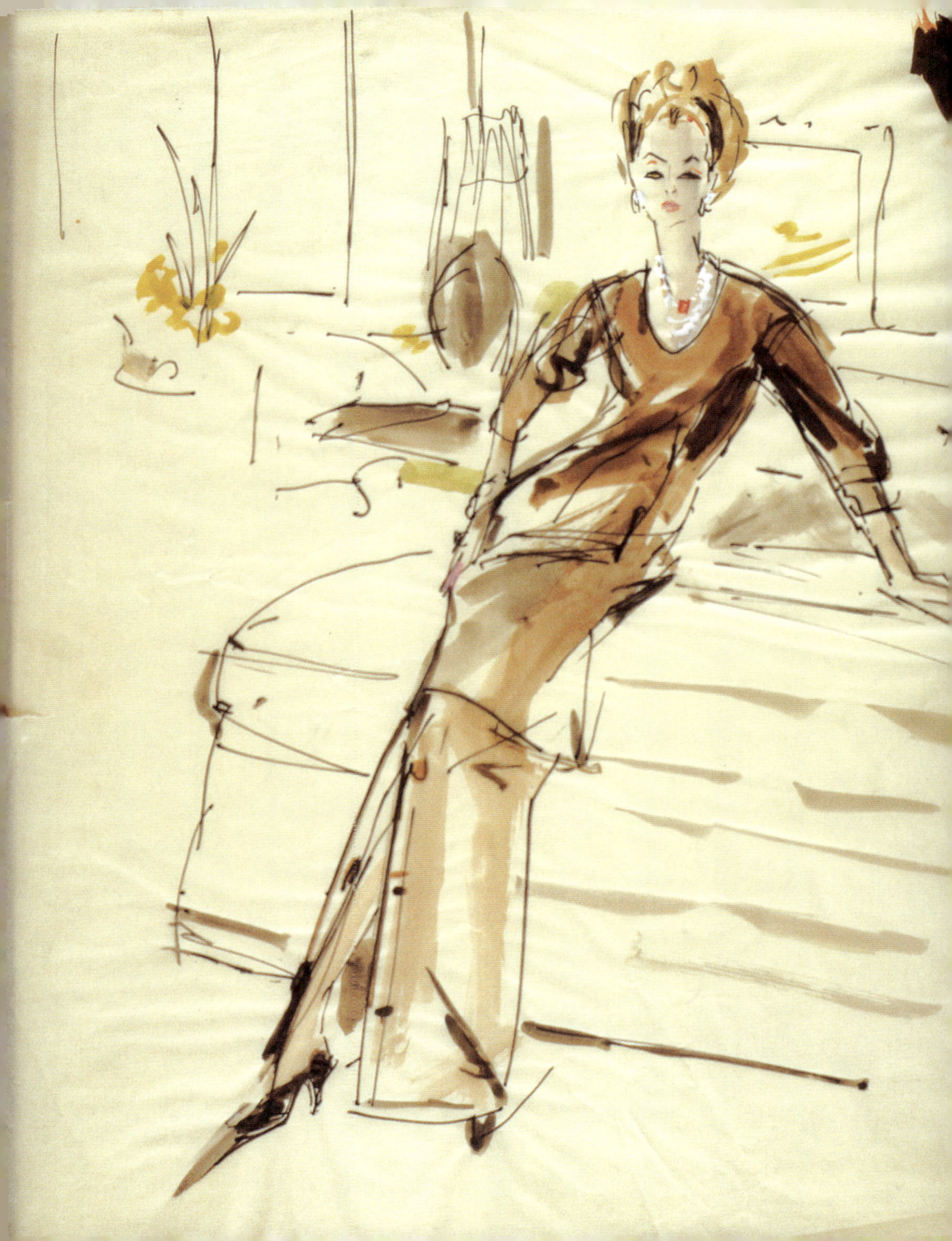

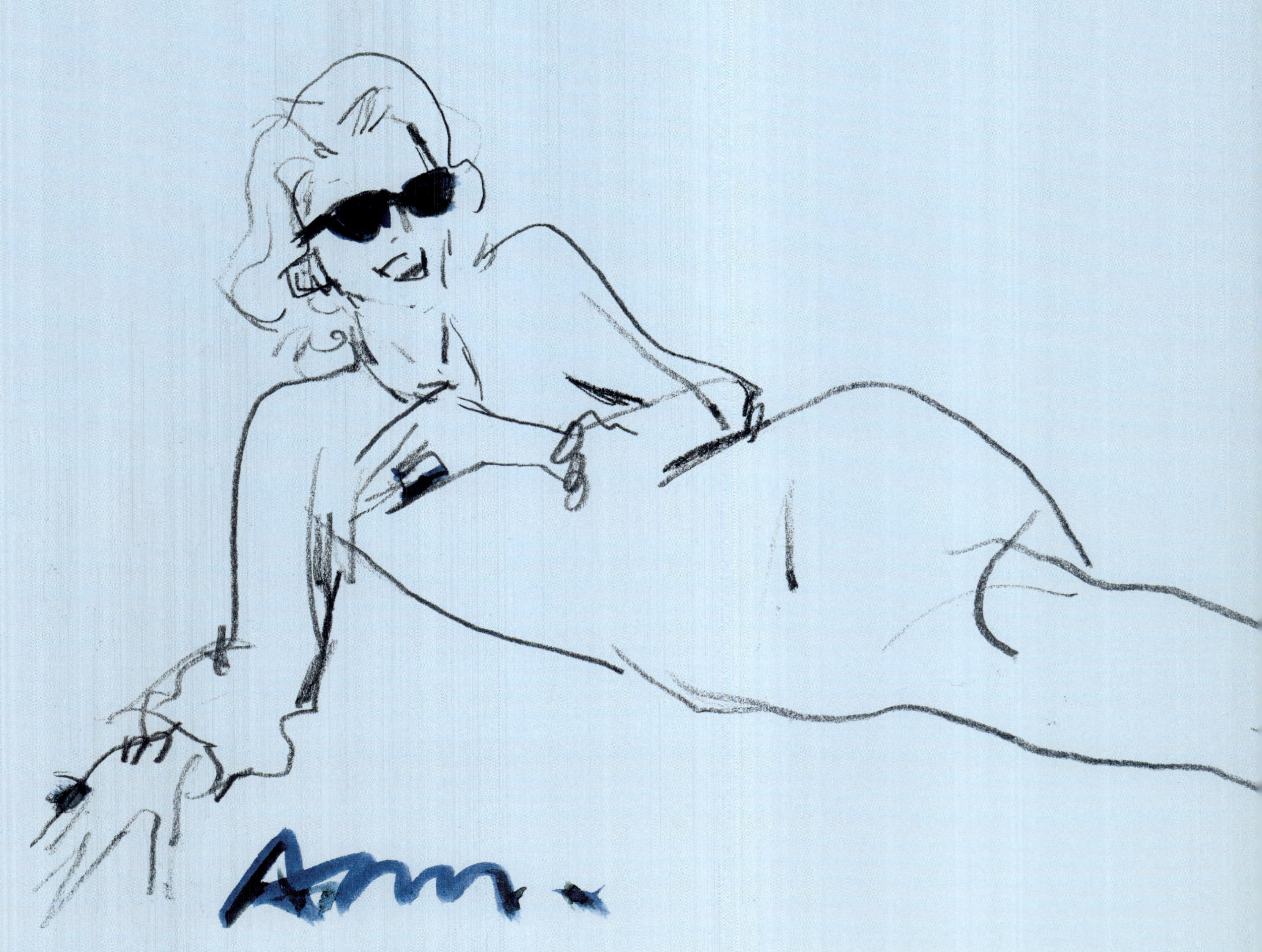

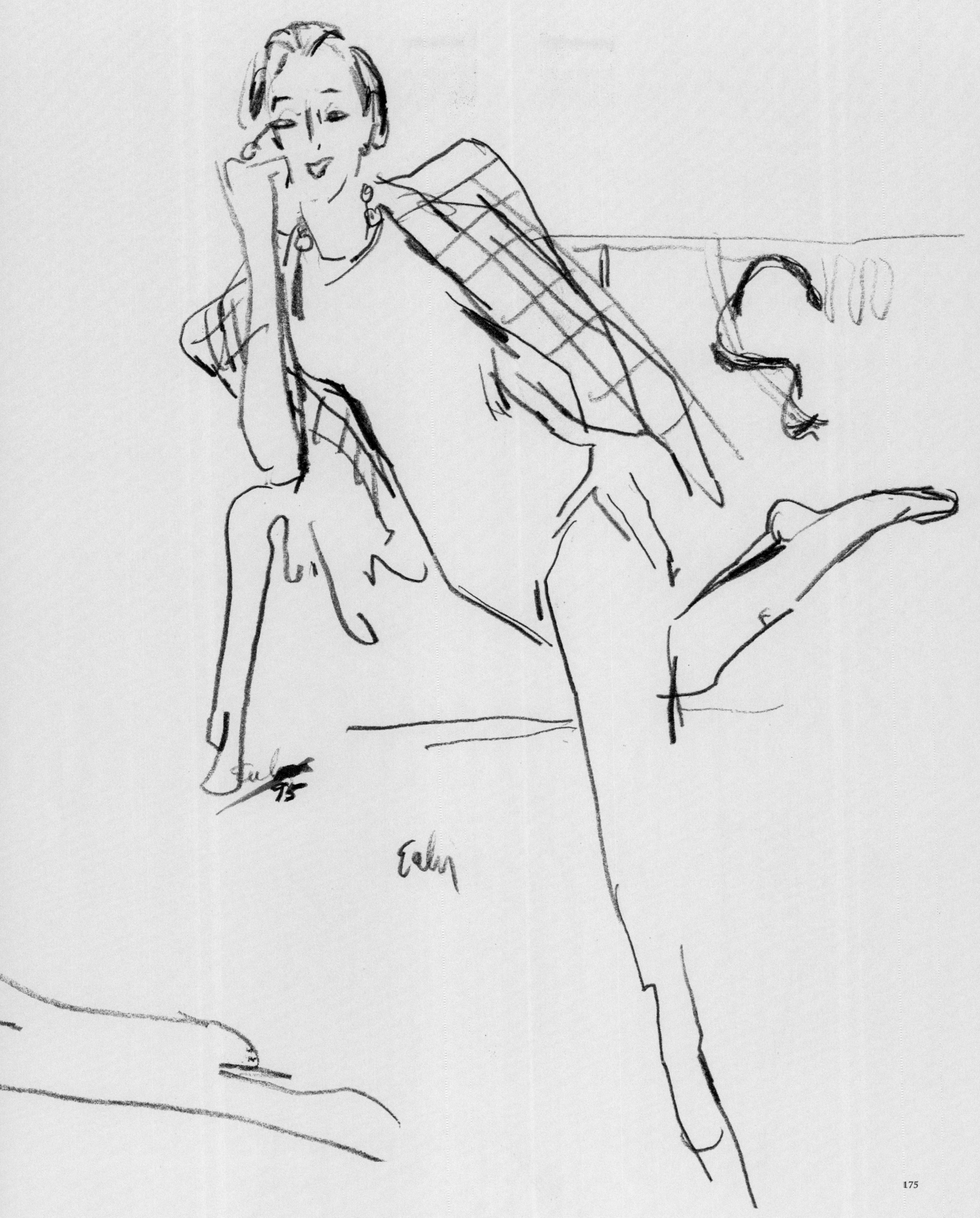

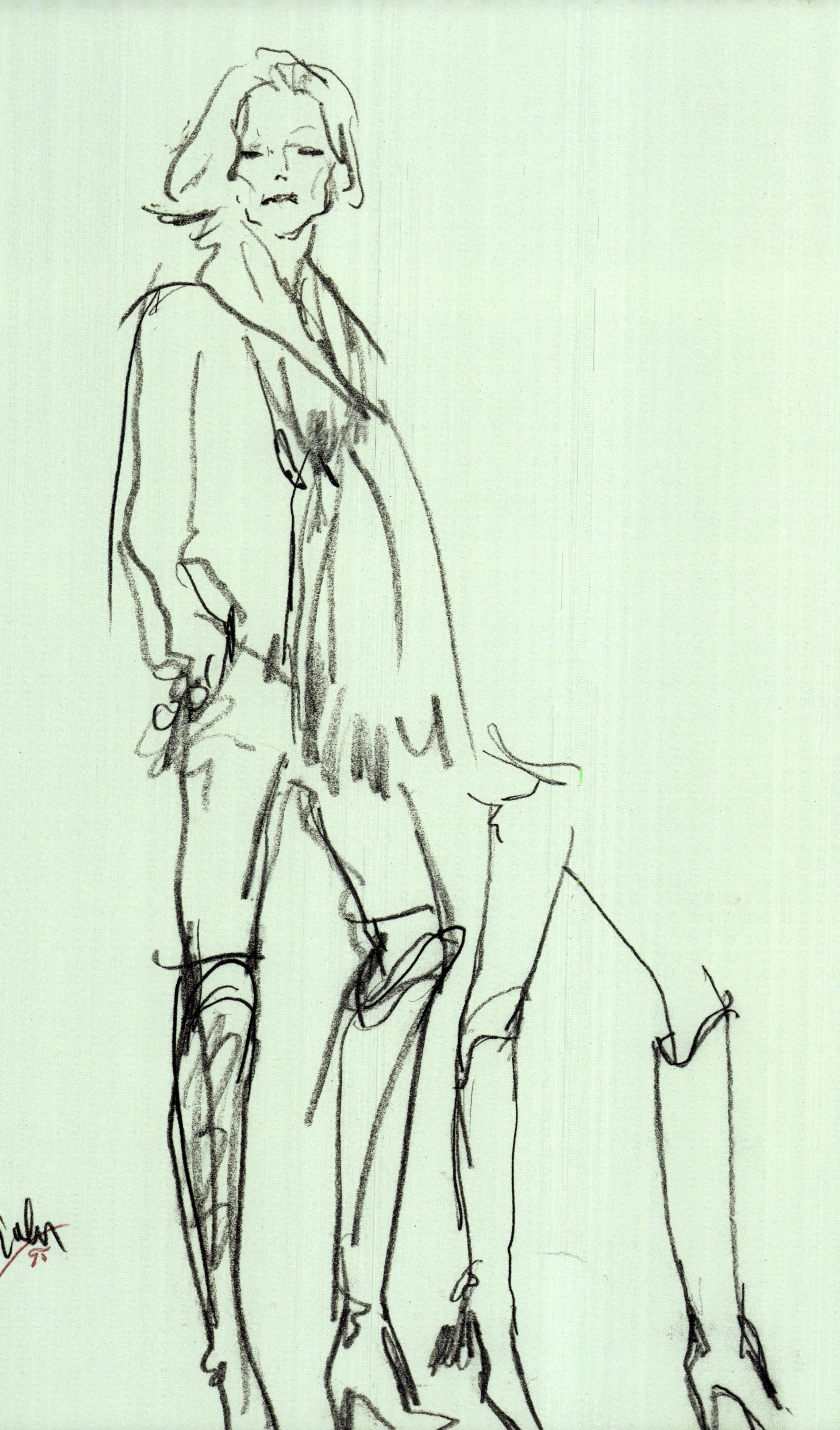

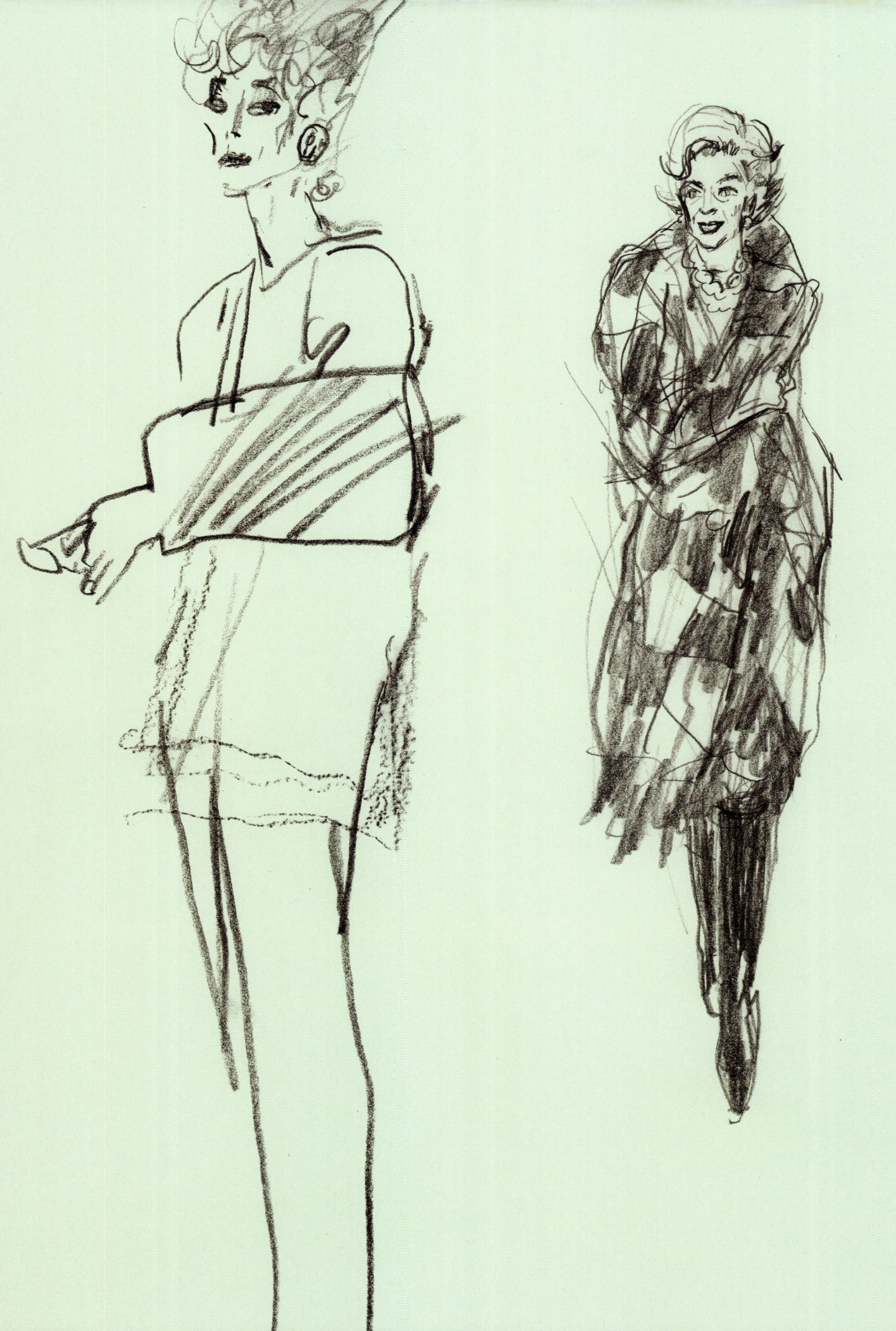

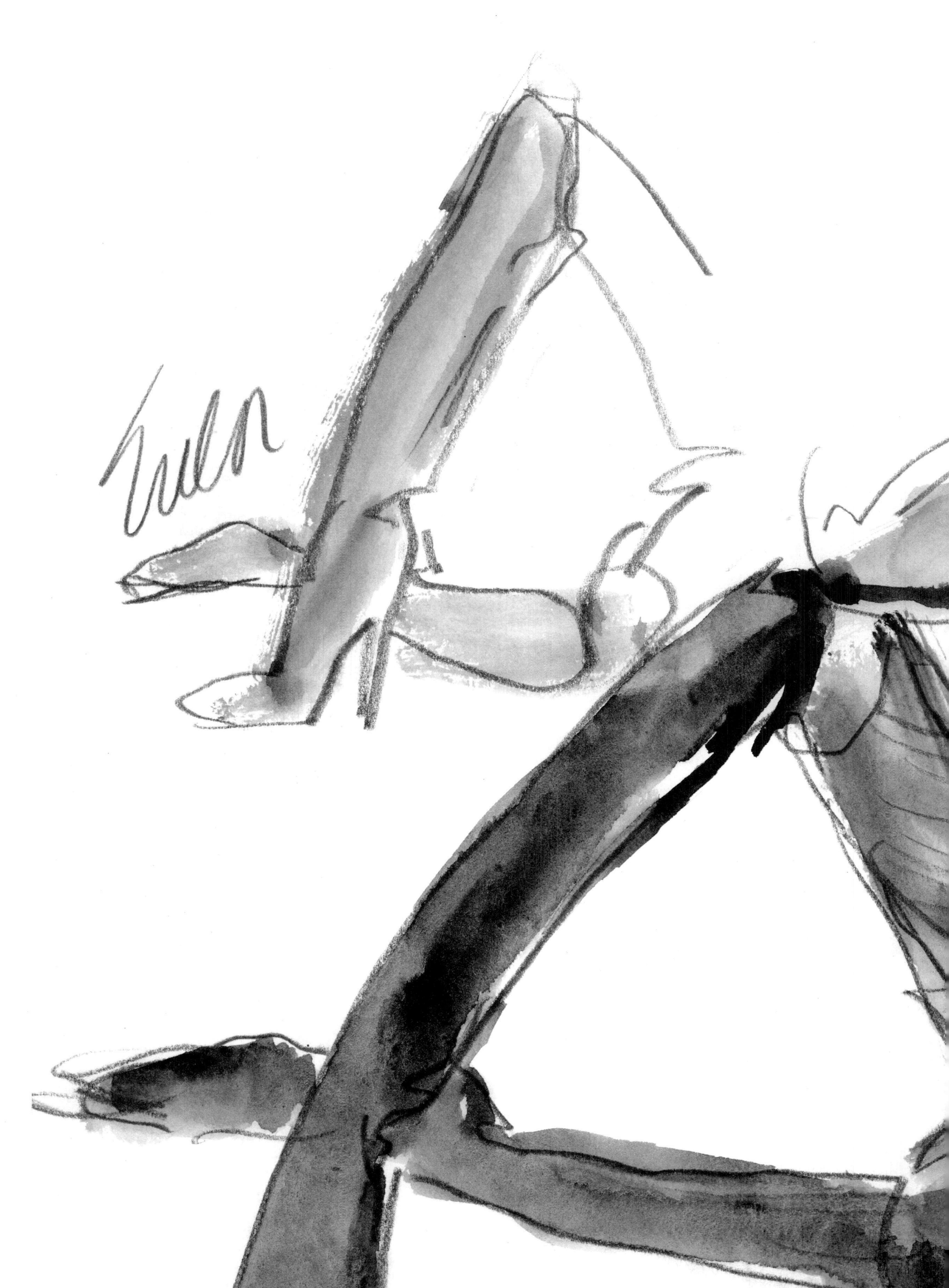

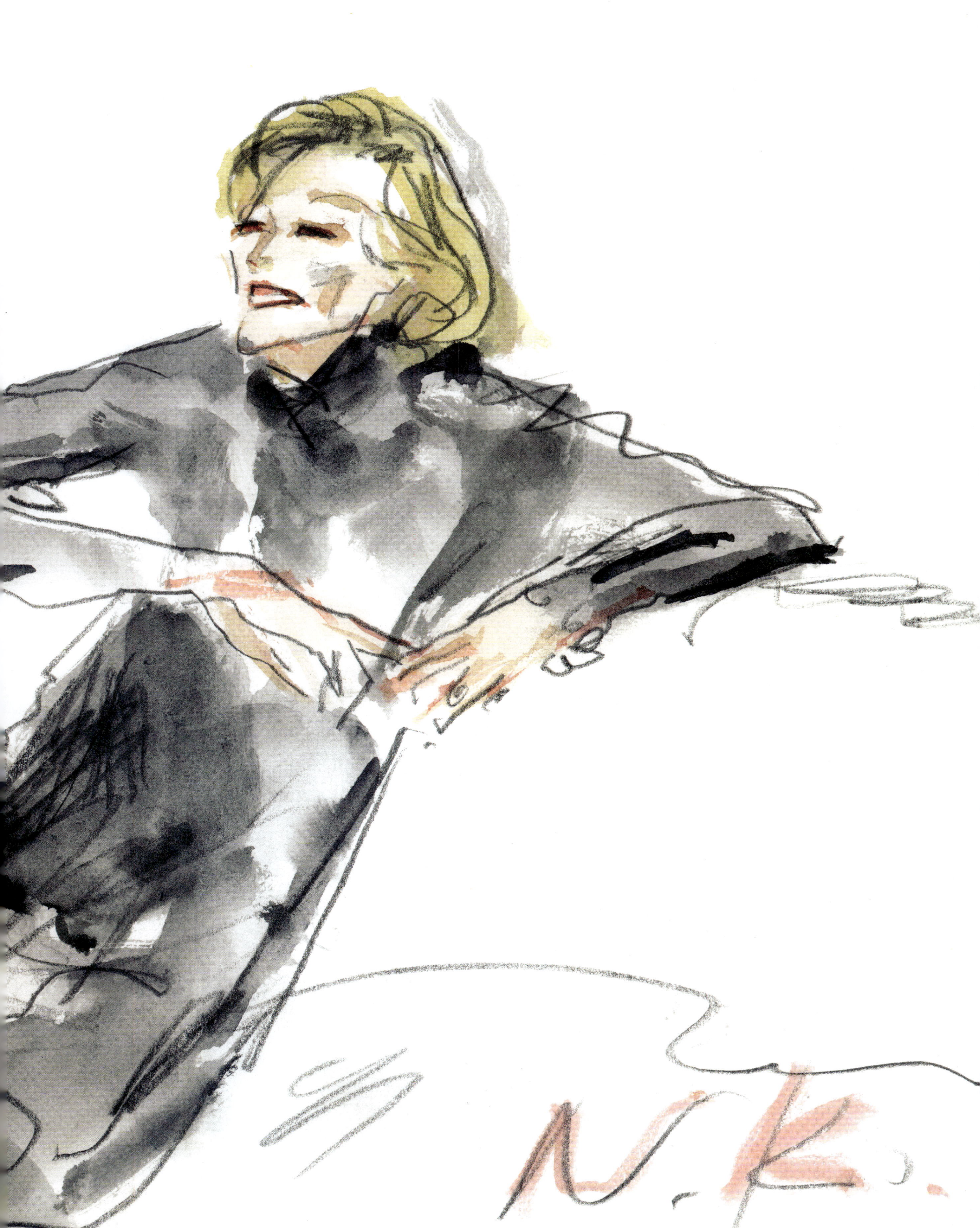
N.K.

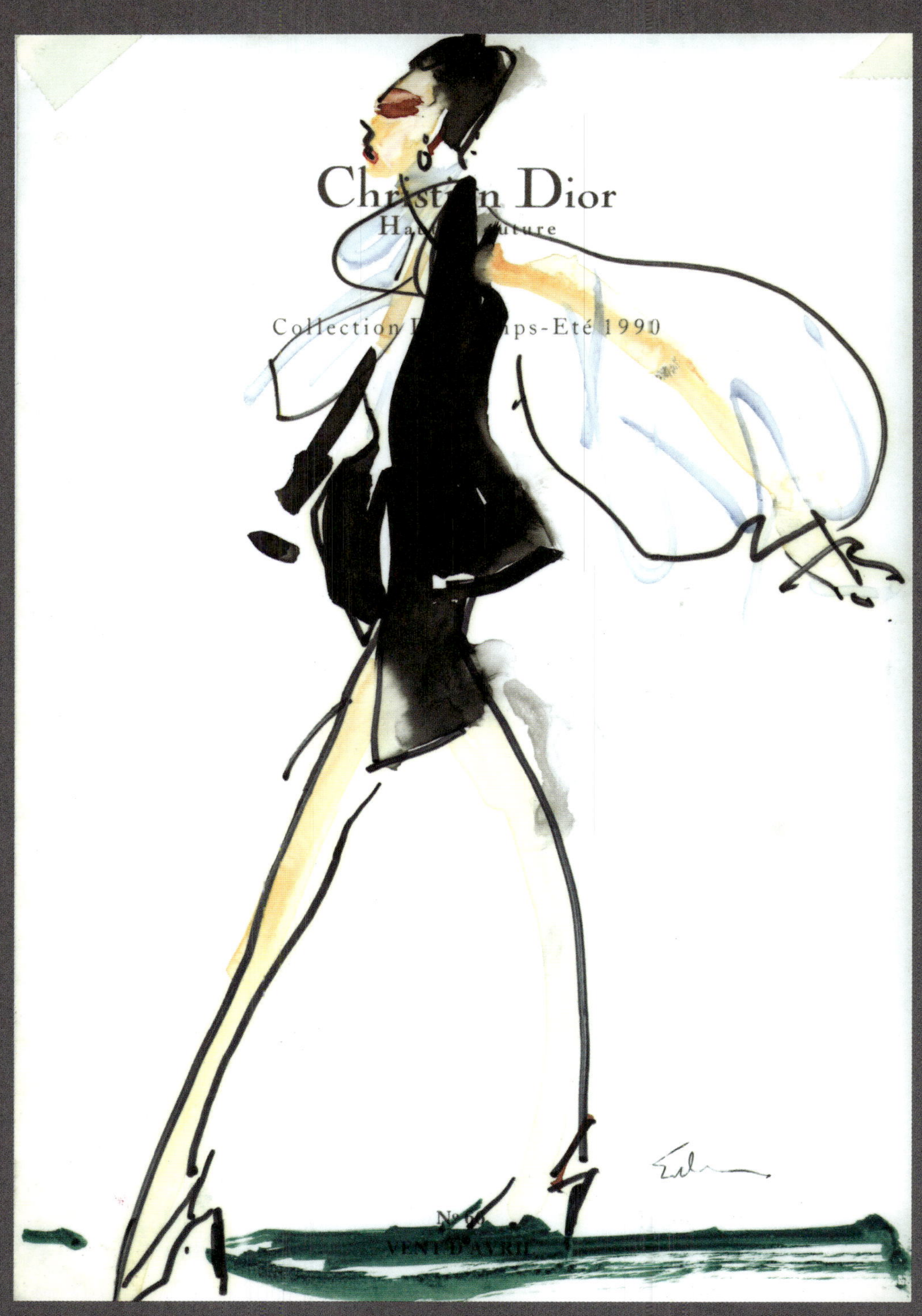

Christian Dior
Haute Couture
Collection Printemps-Eté 1990
VENT D'AVRIL

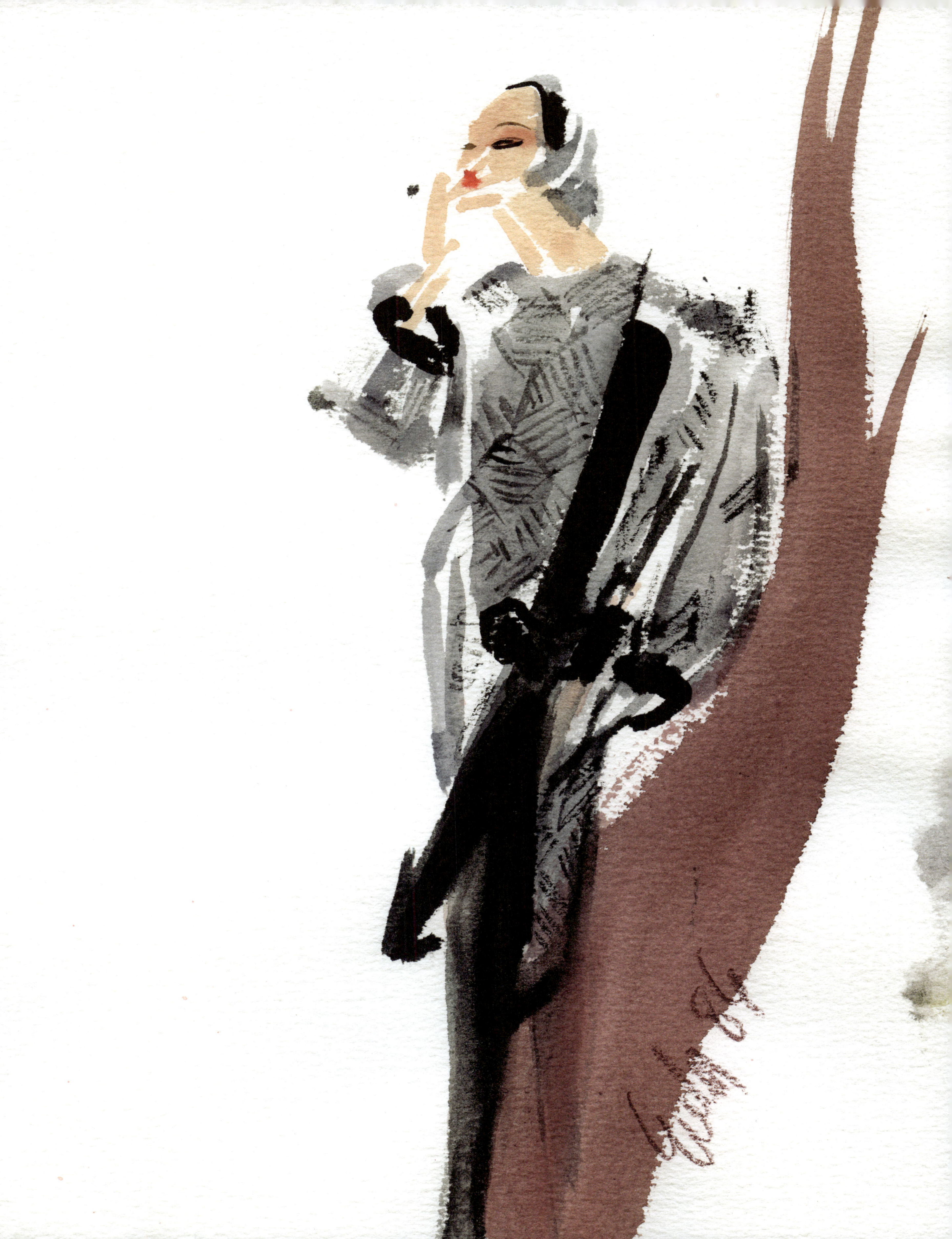

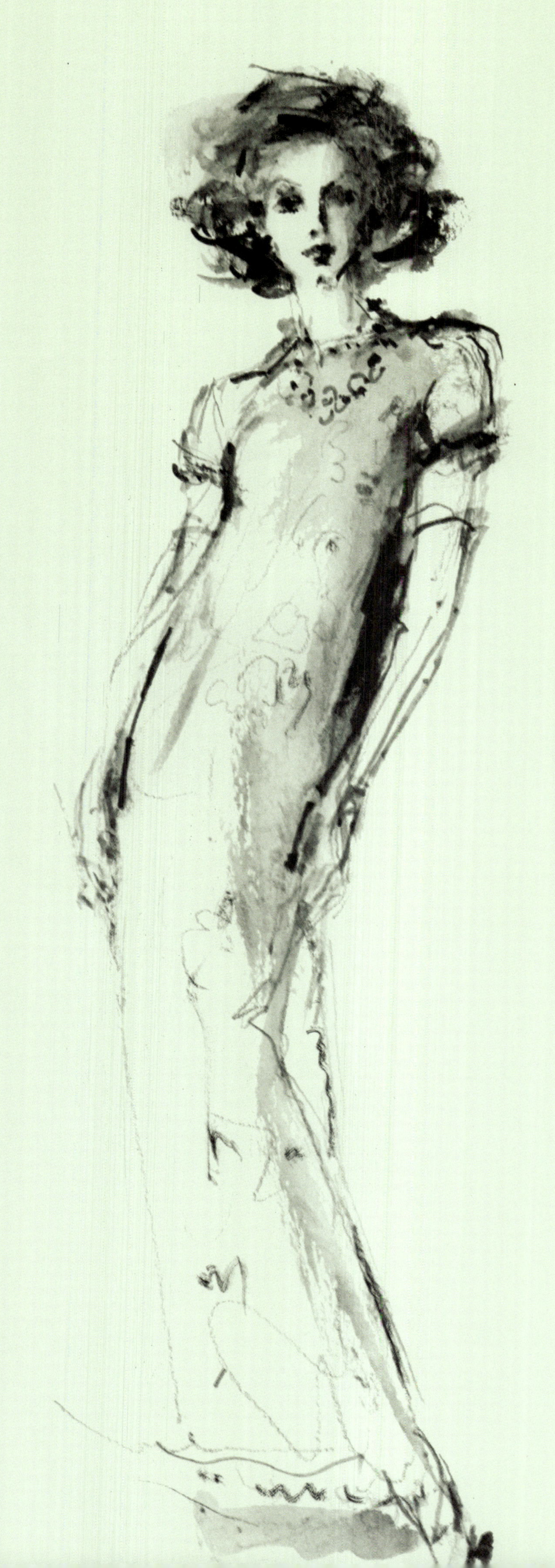

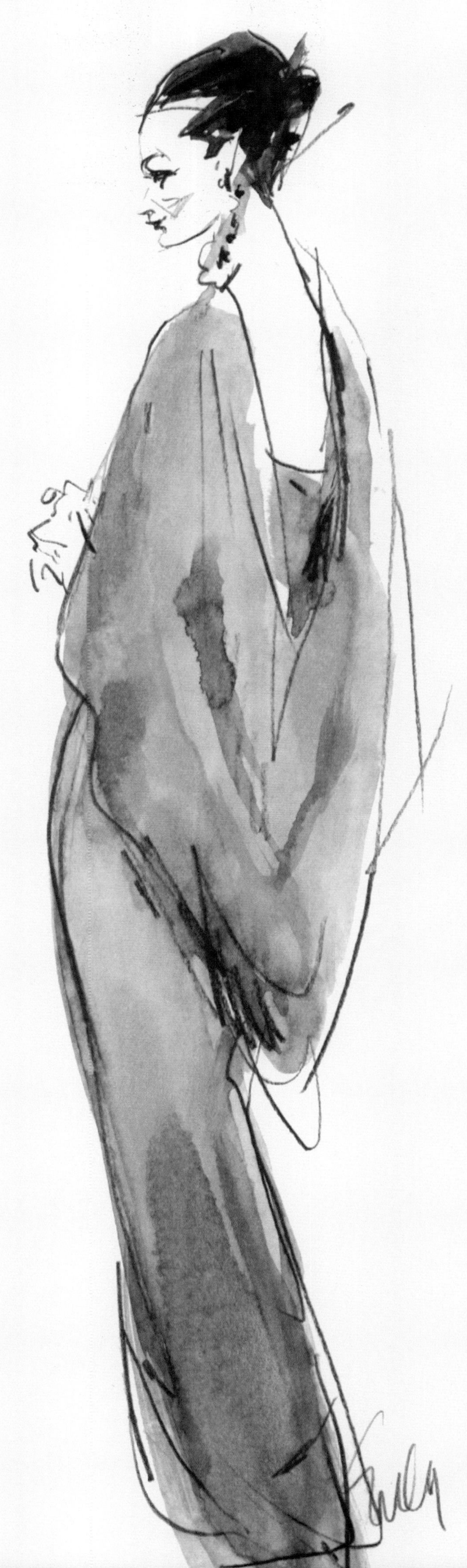

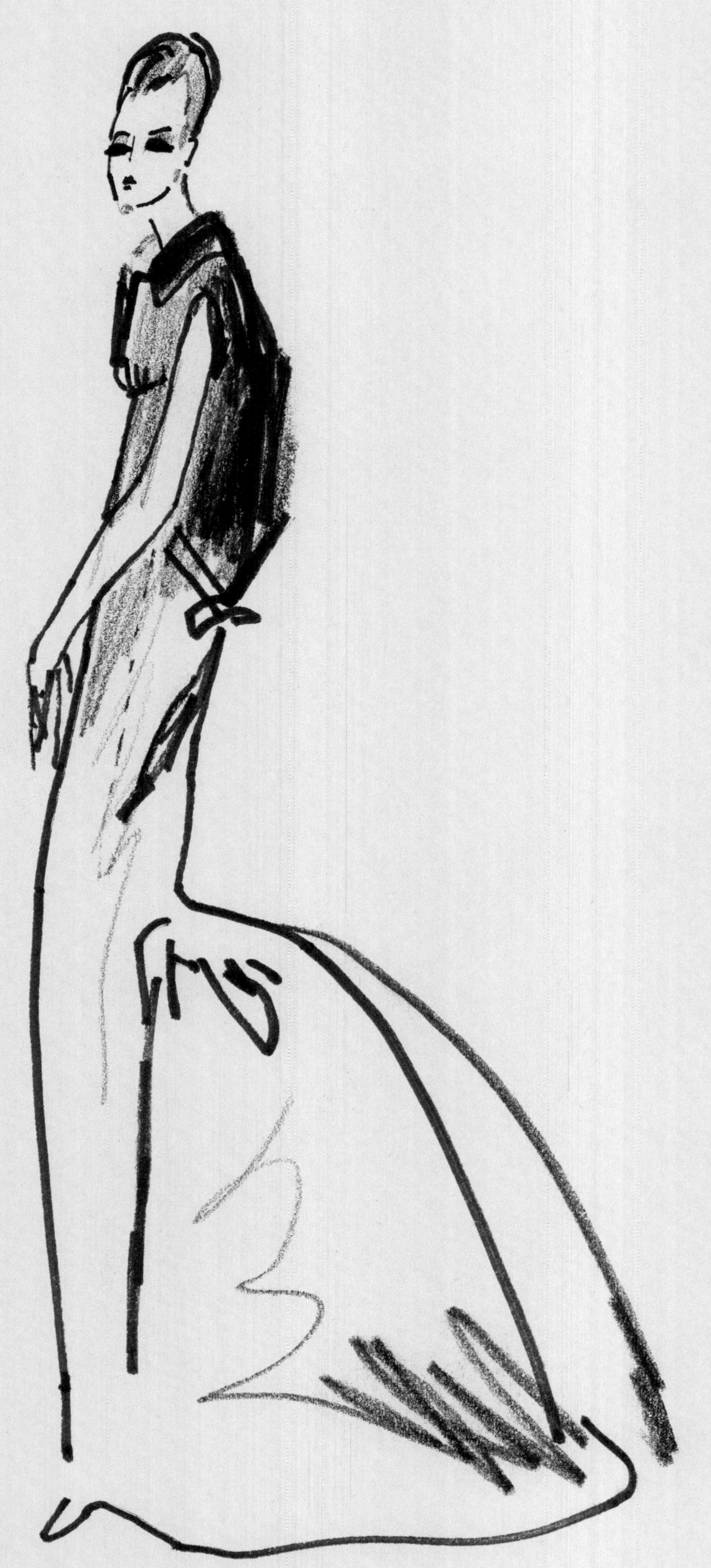

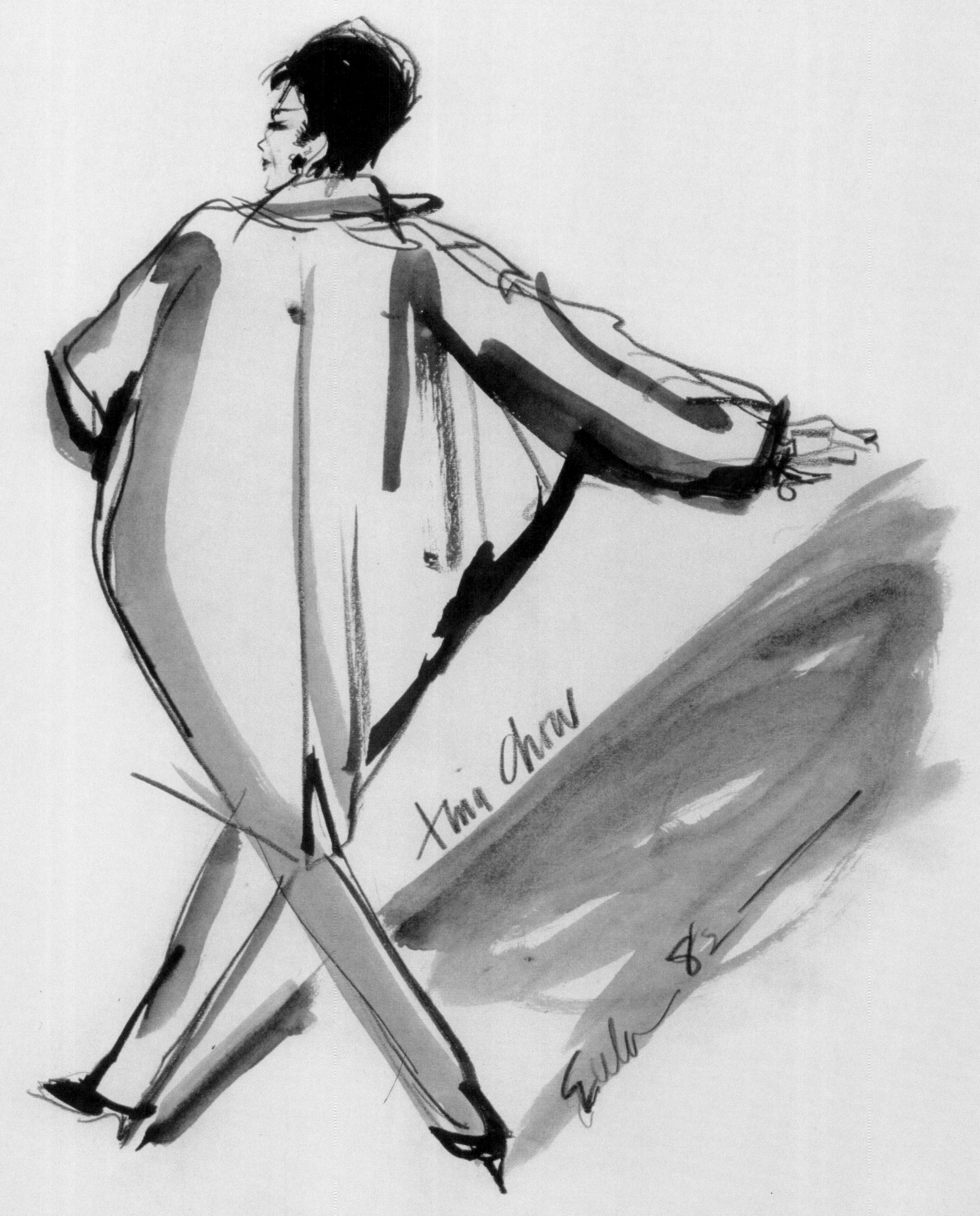
Anne Chow

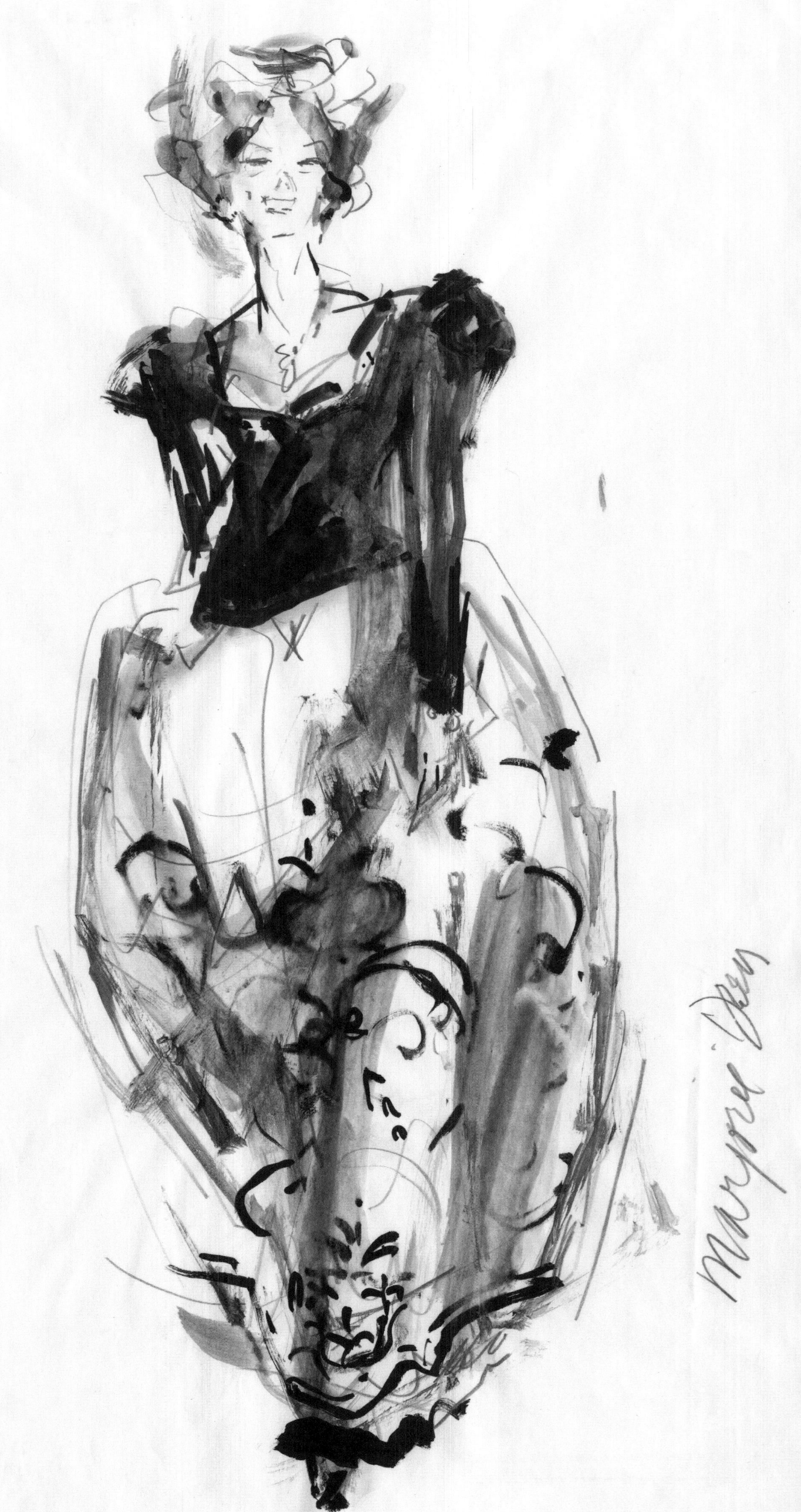
Margaret Dress

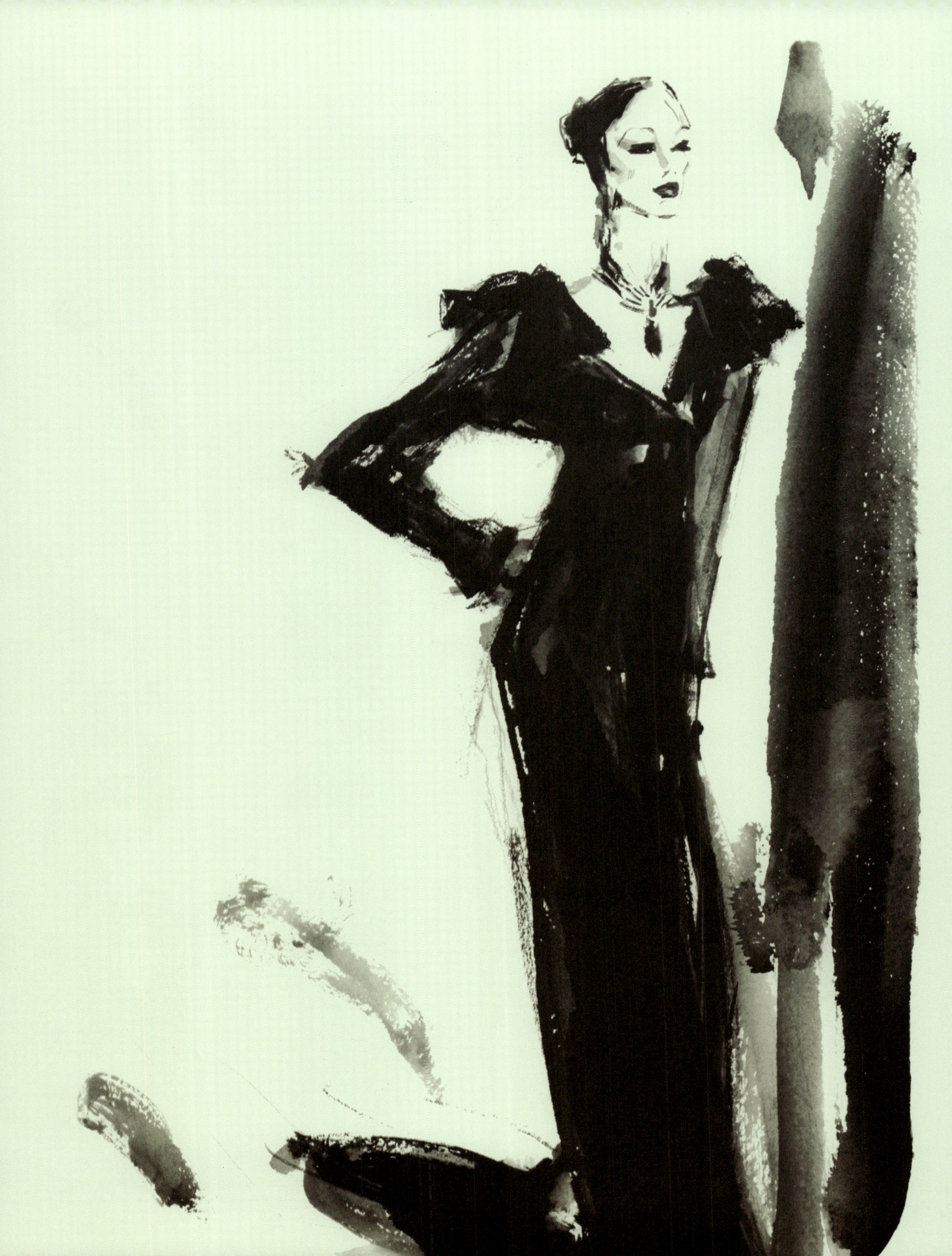

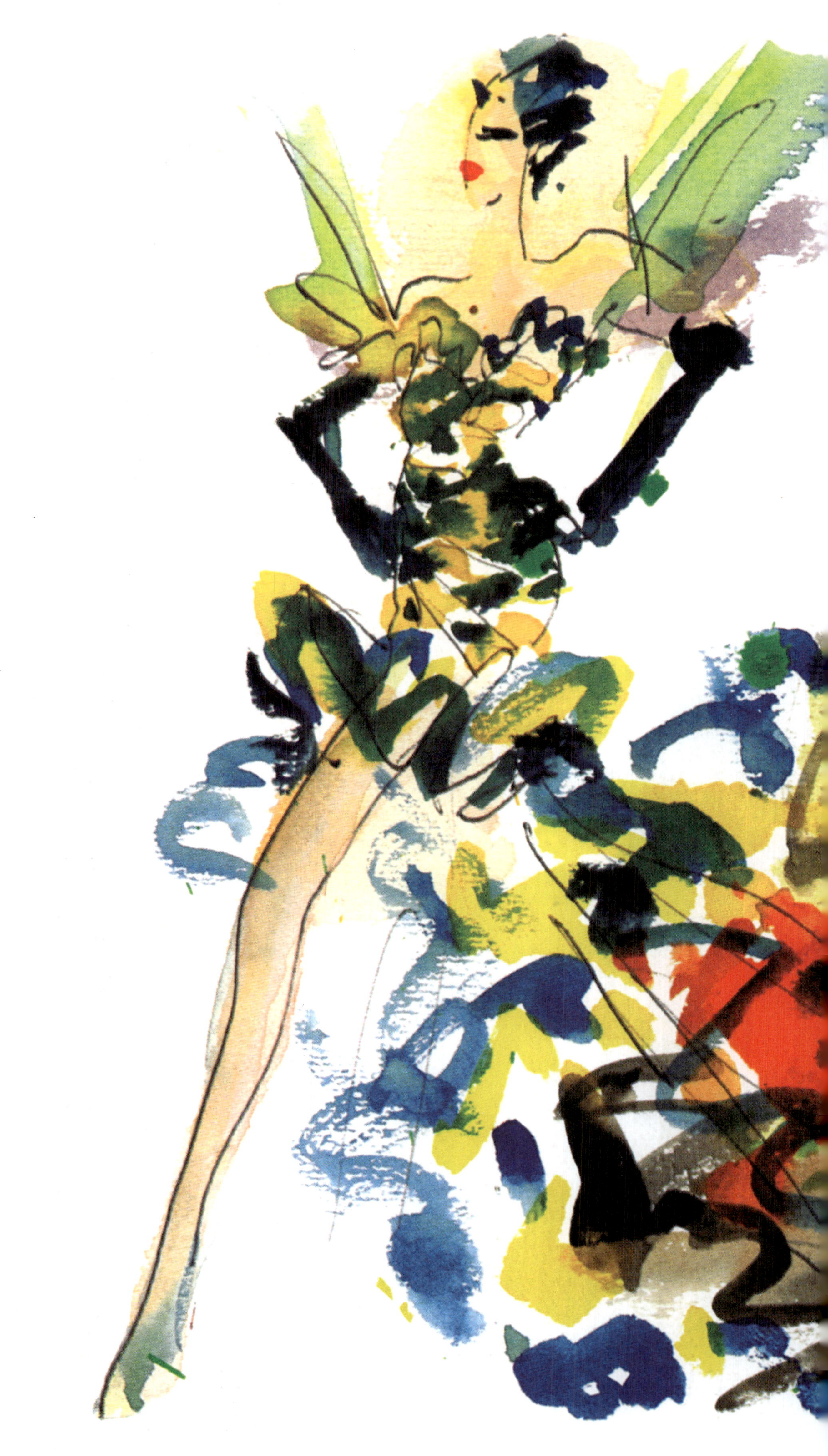

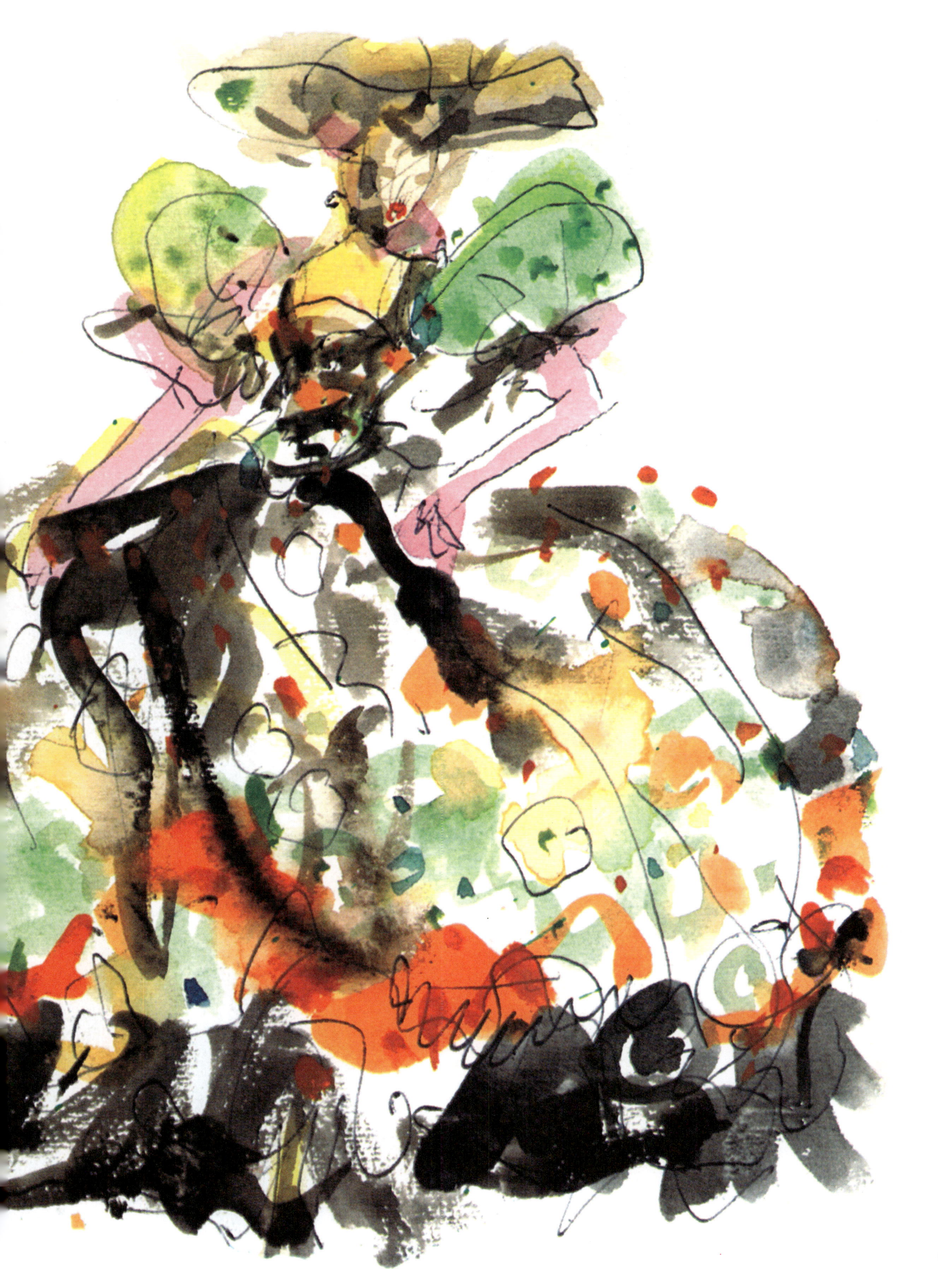

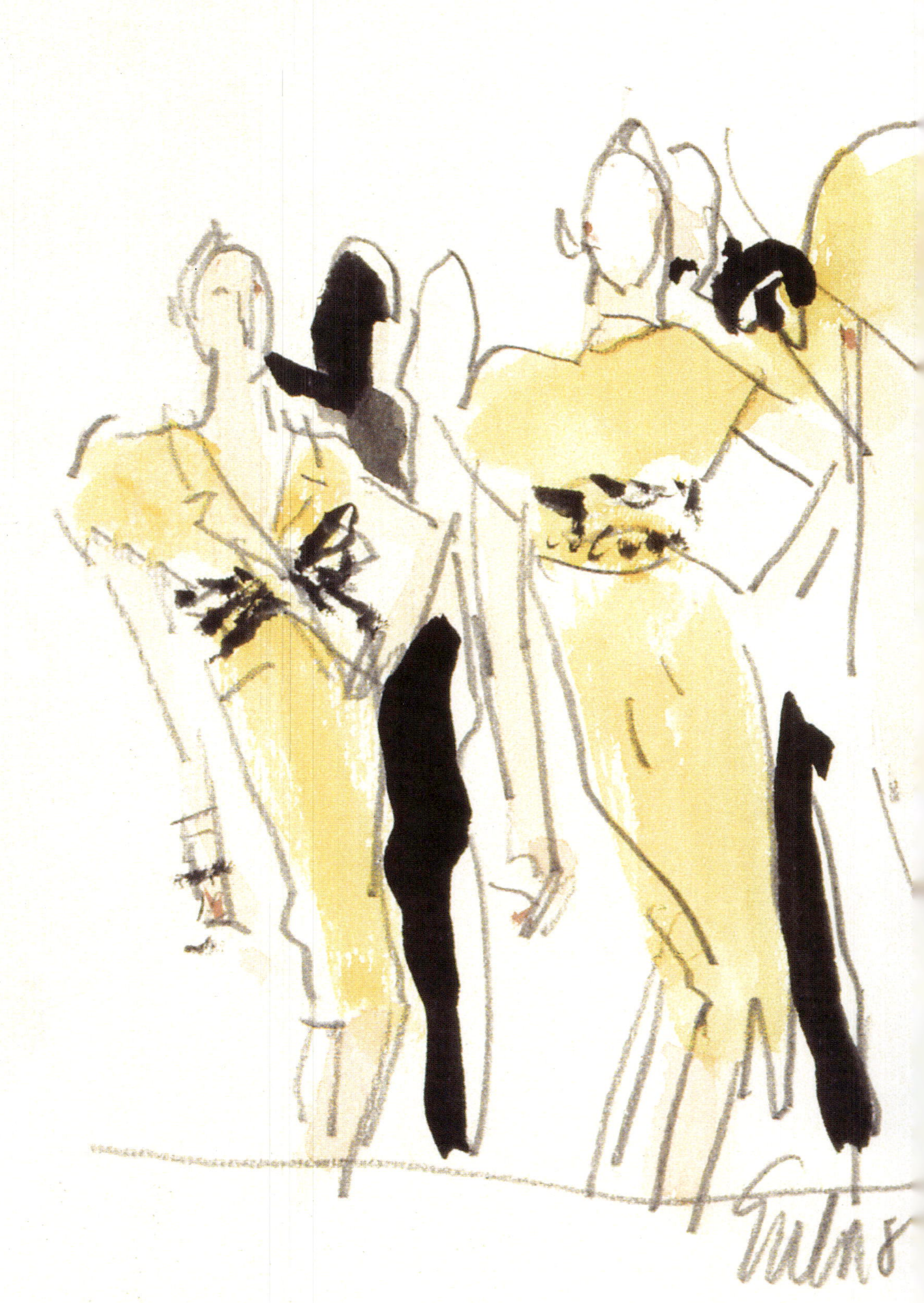

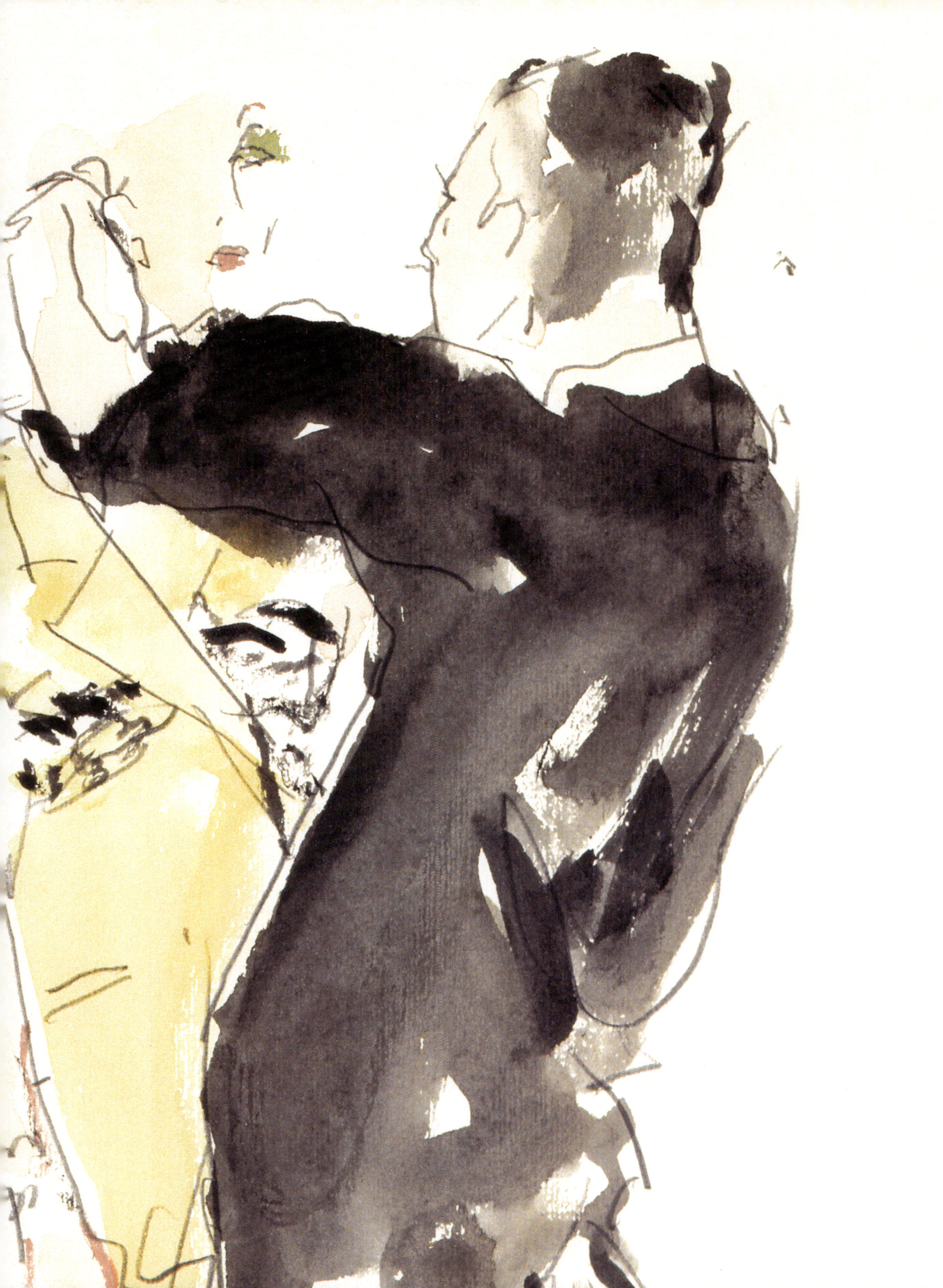

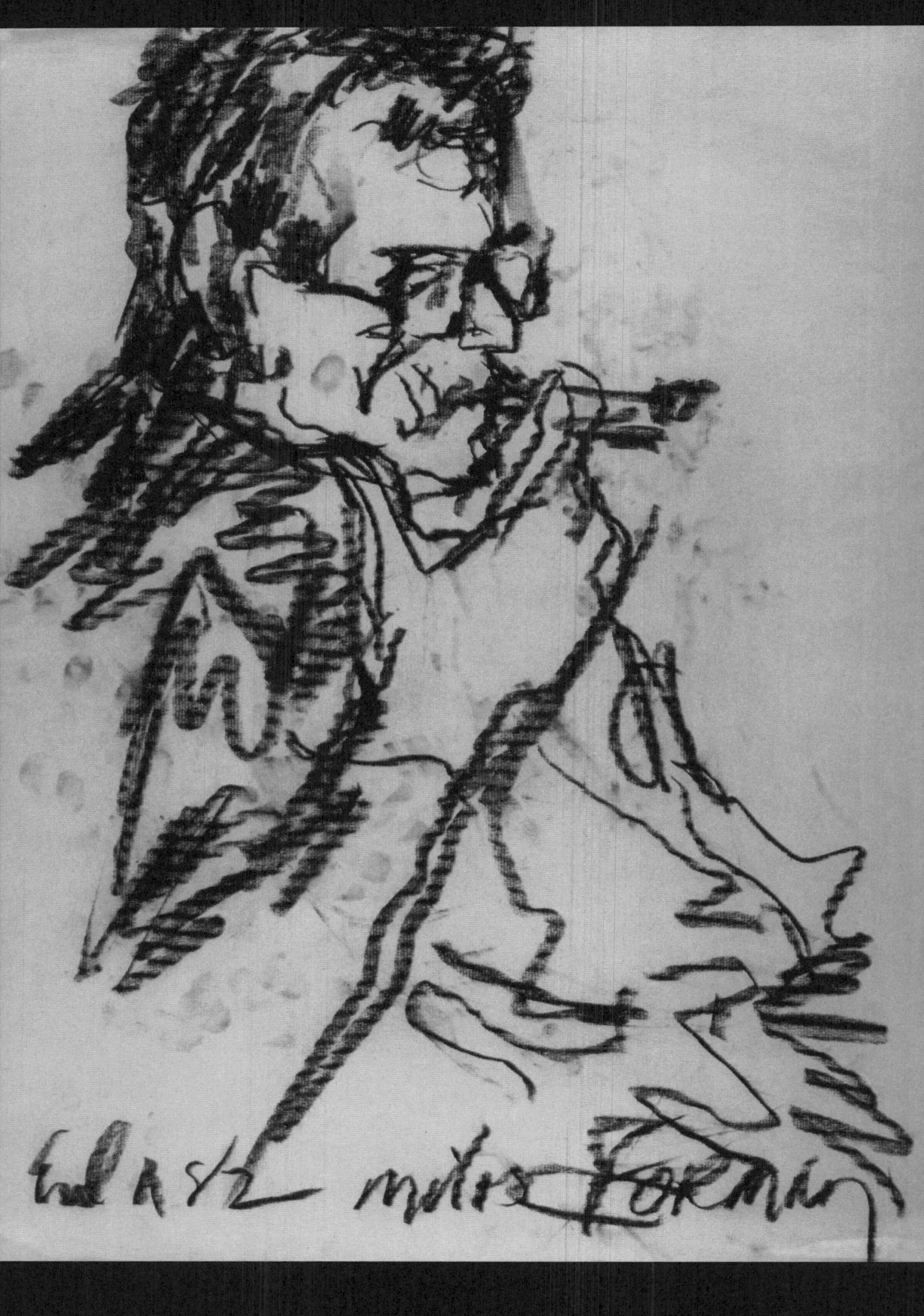

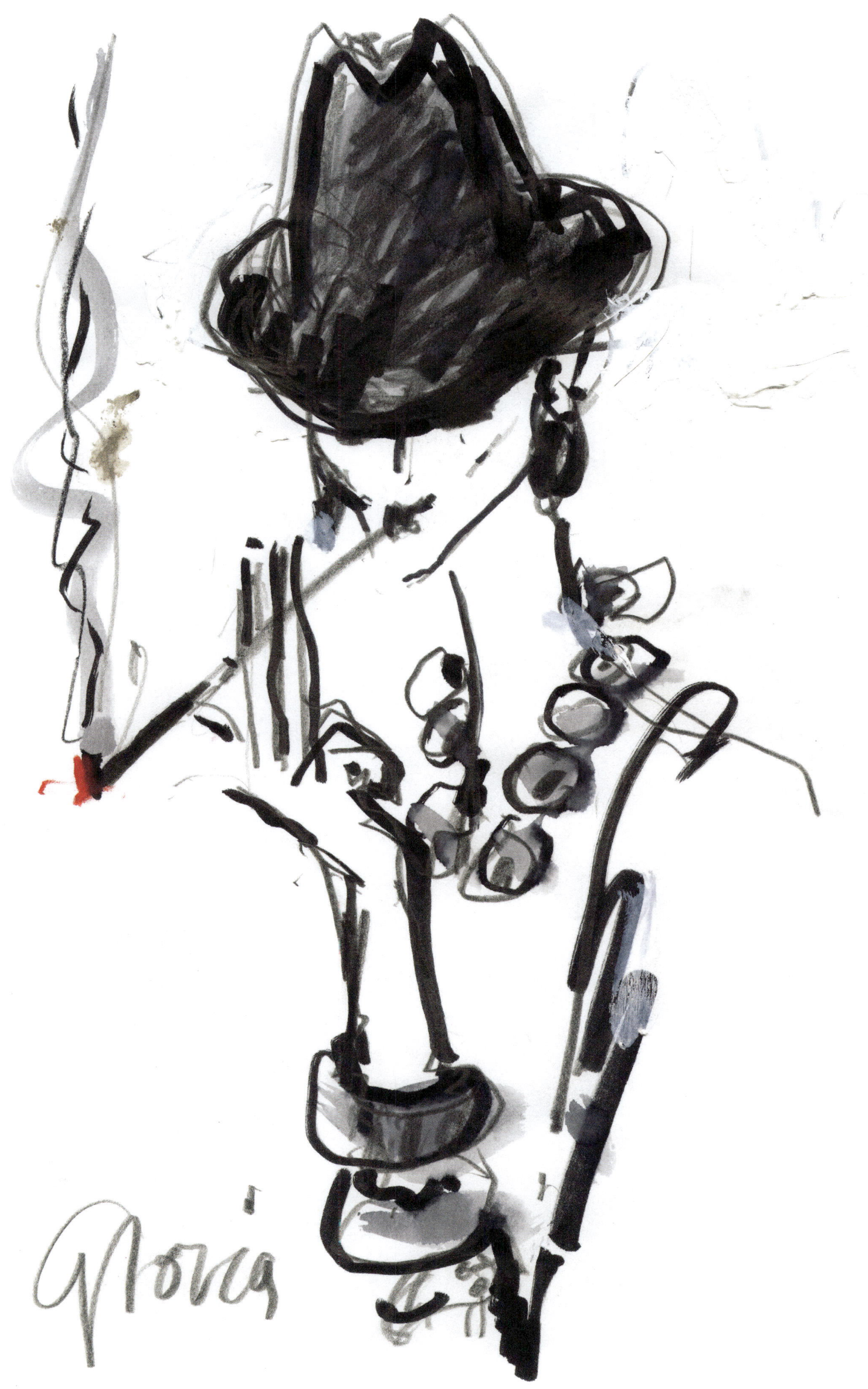

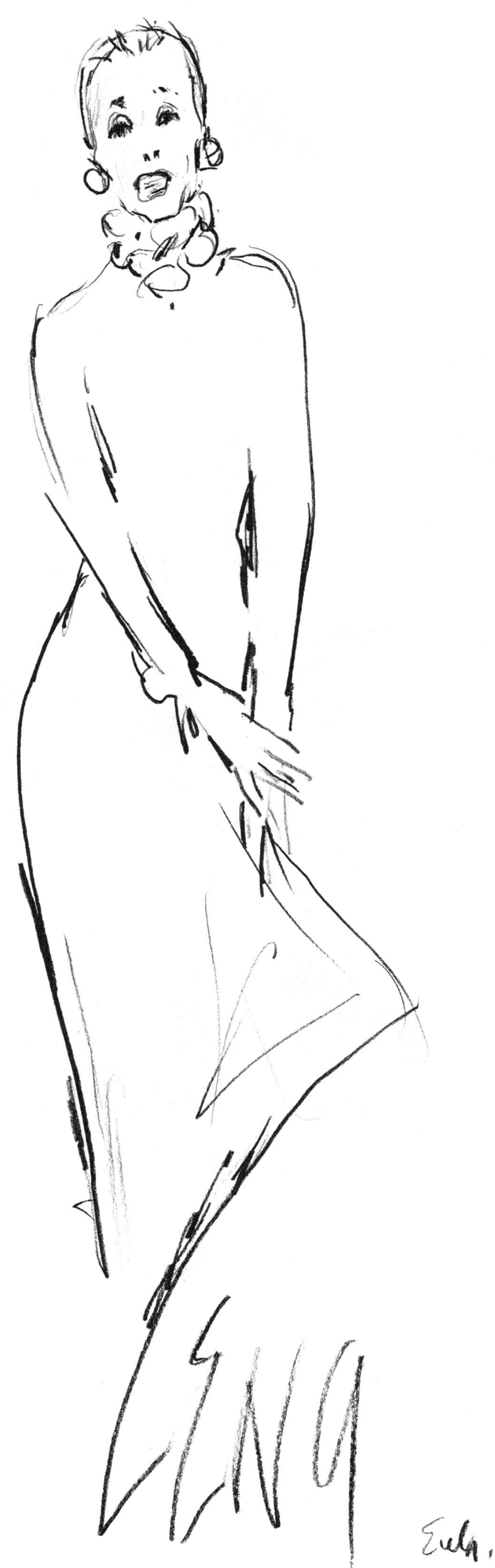

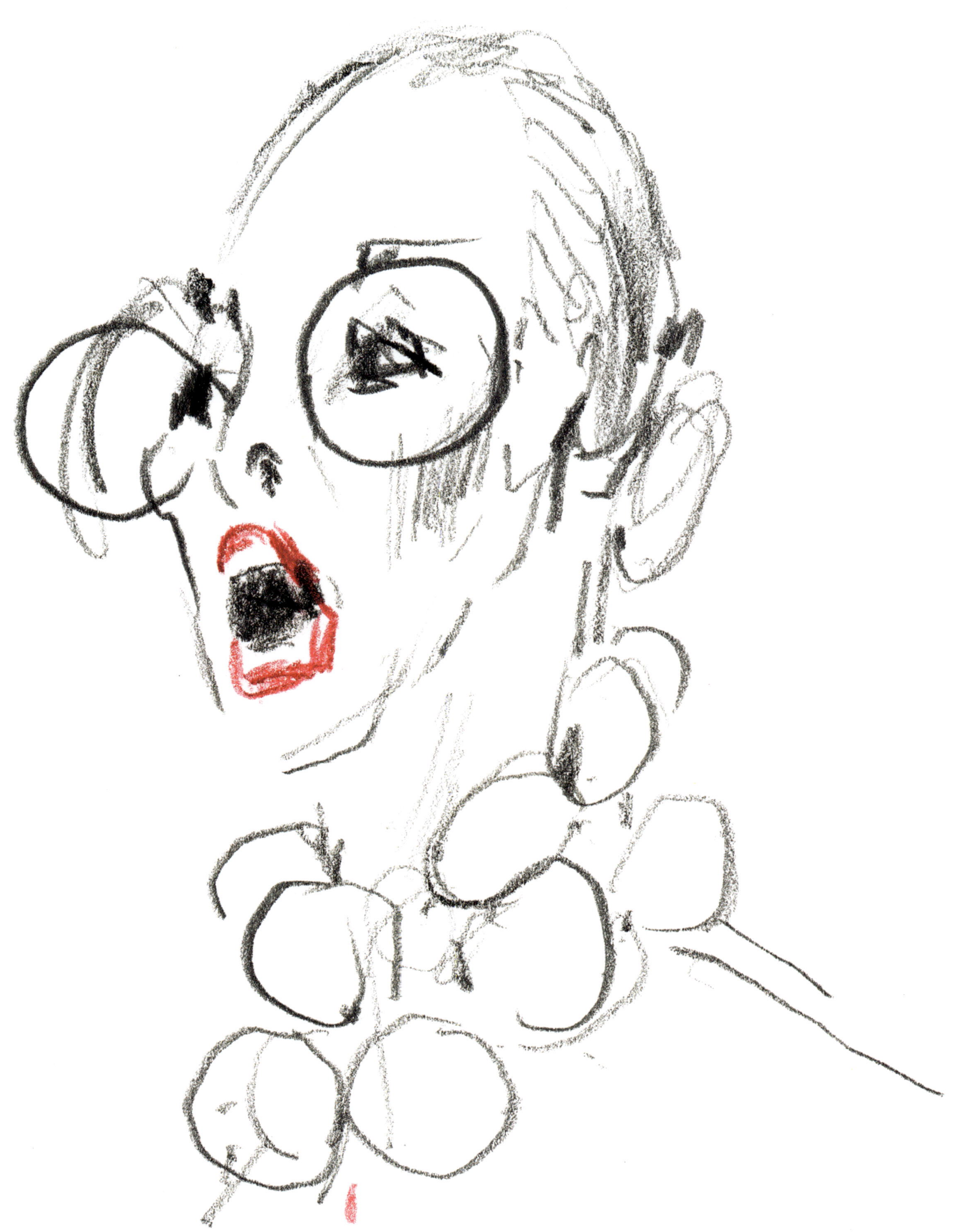

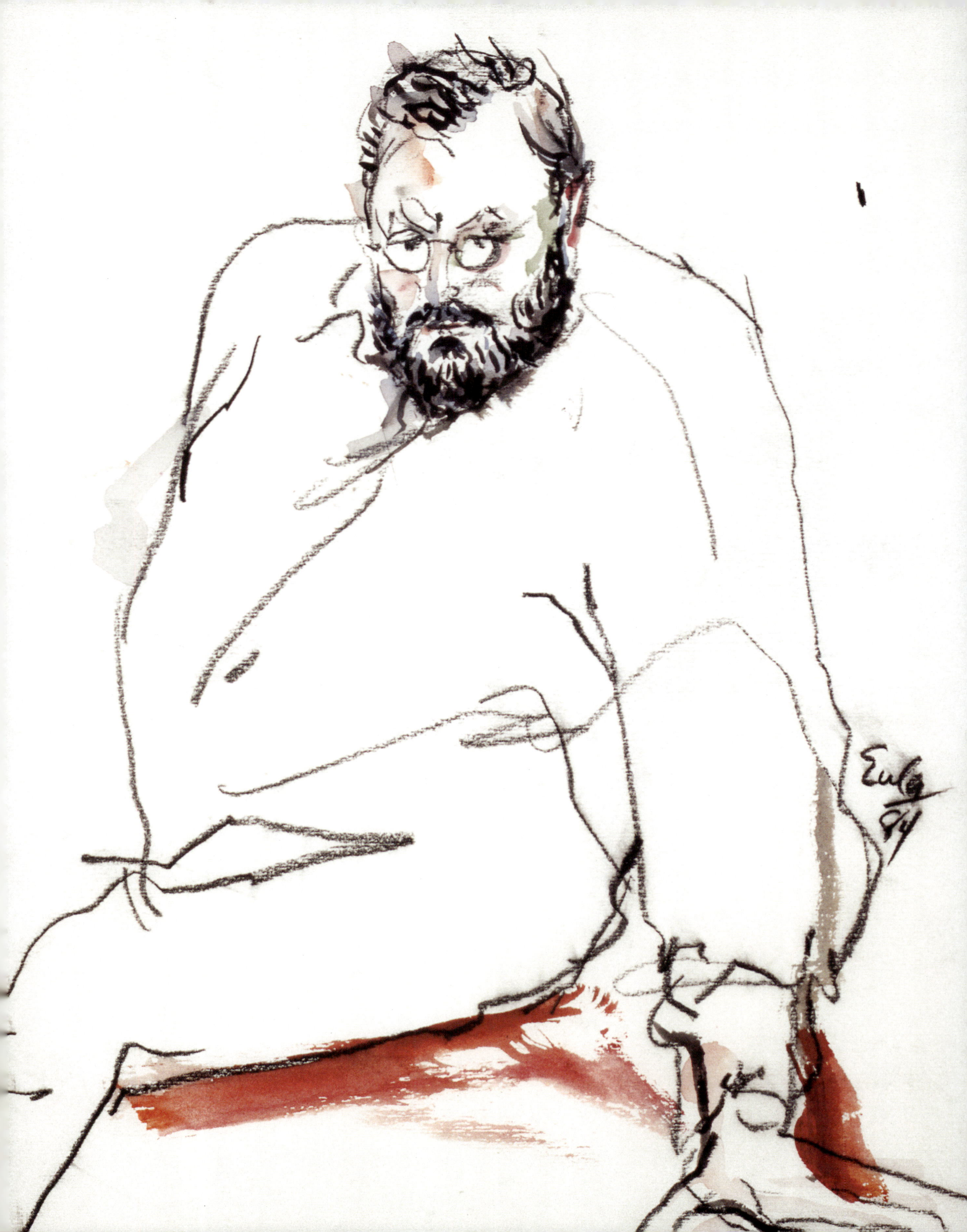

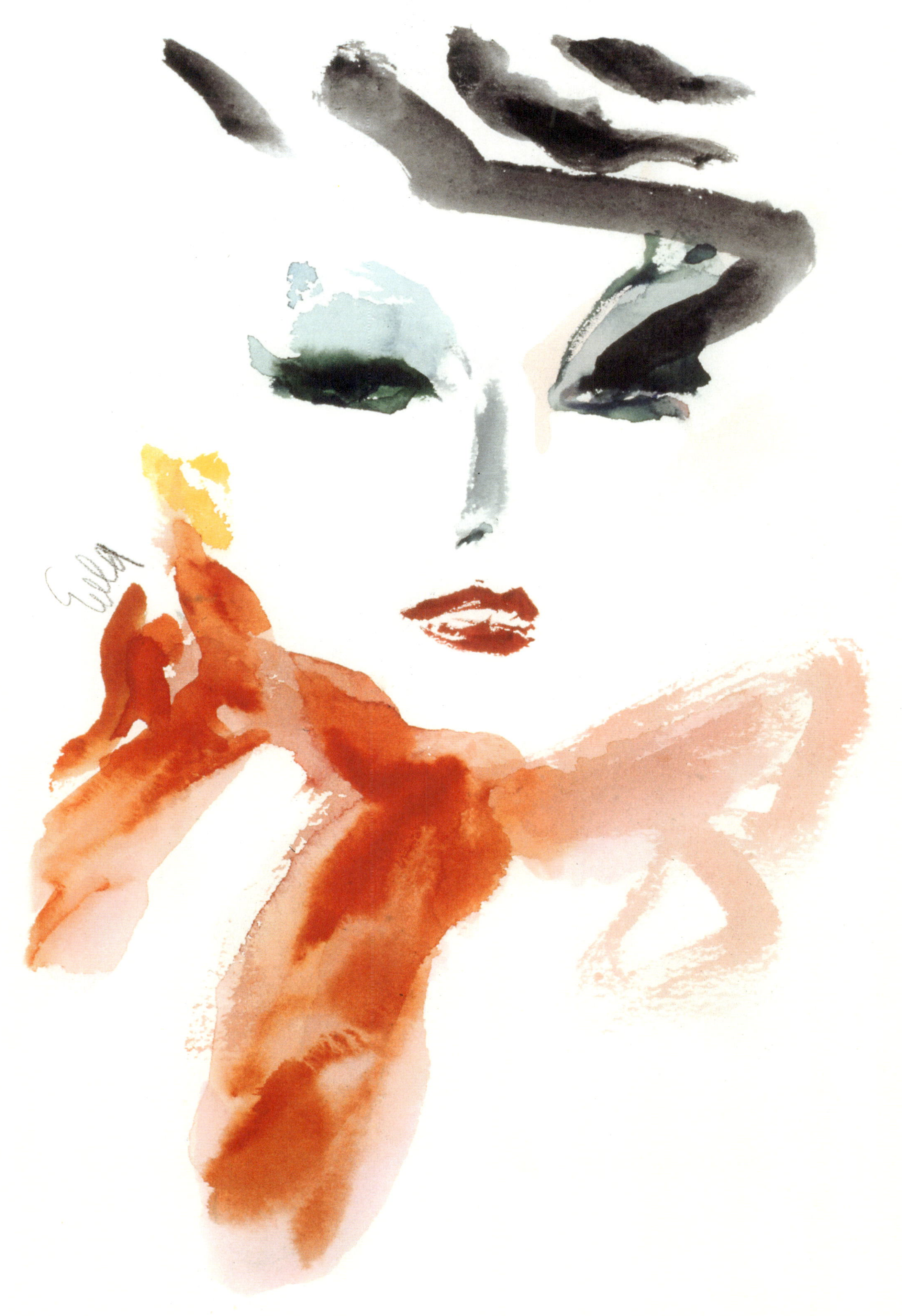

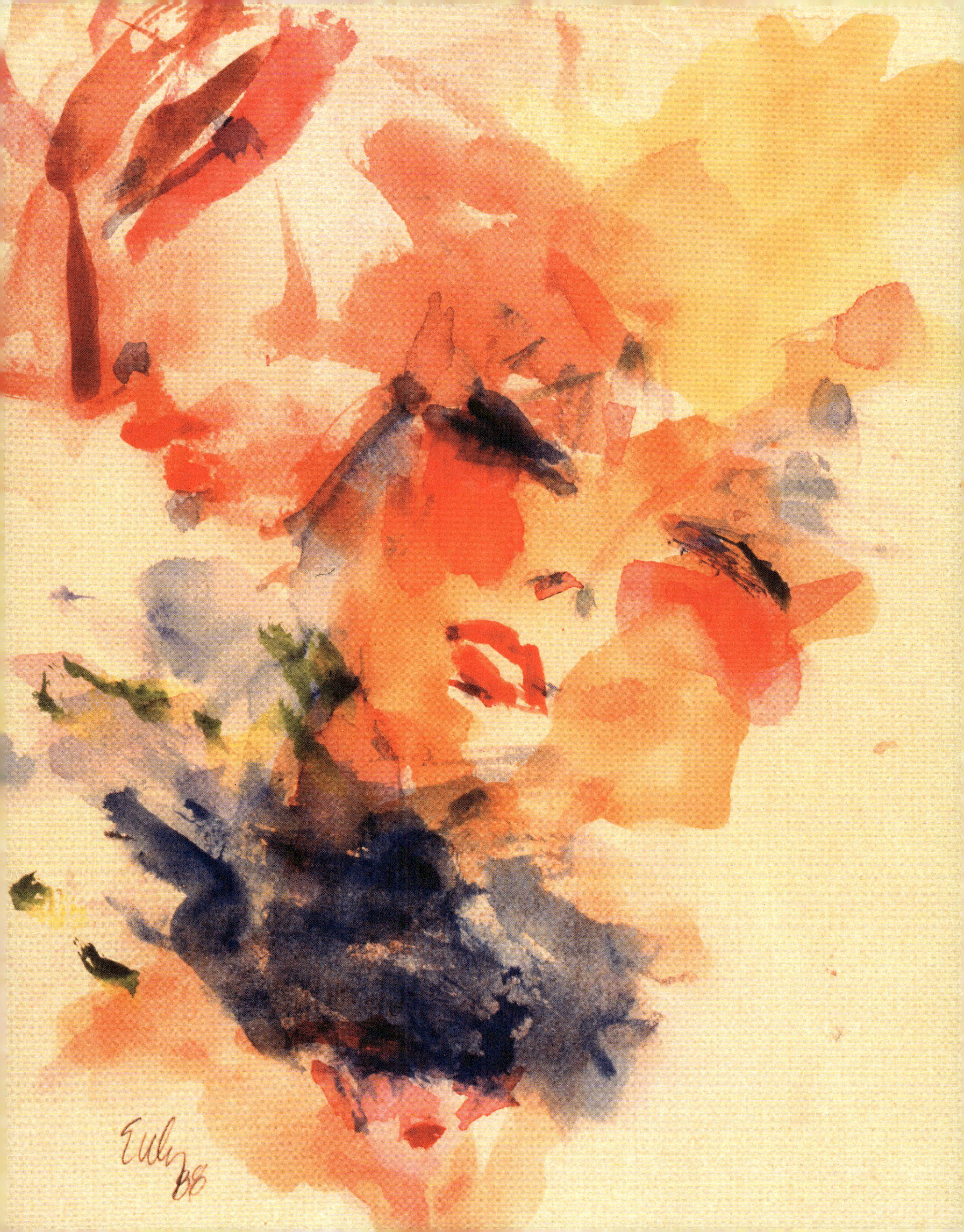

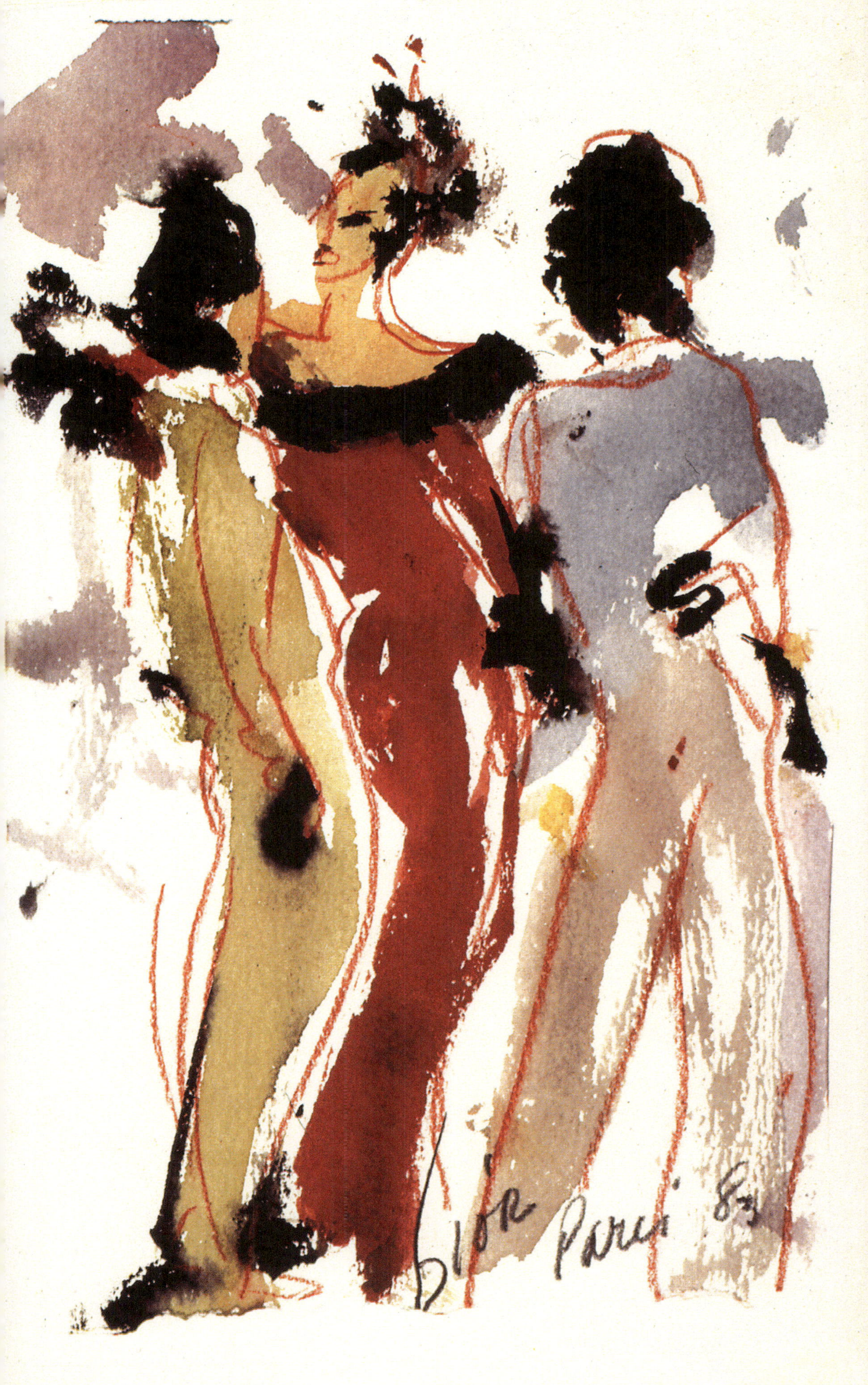

Dior Paris 8.

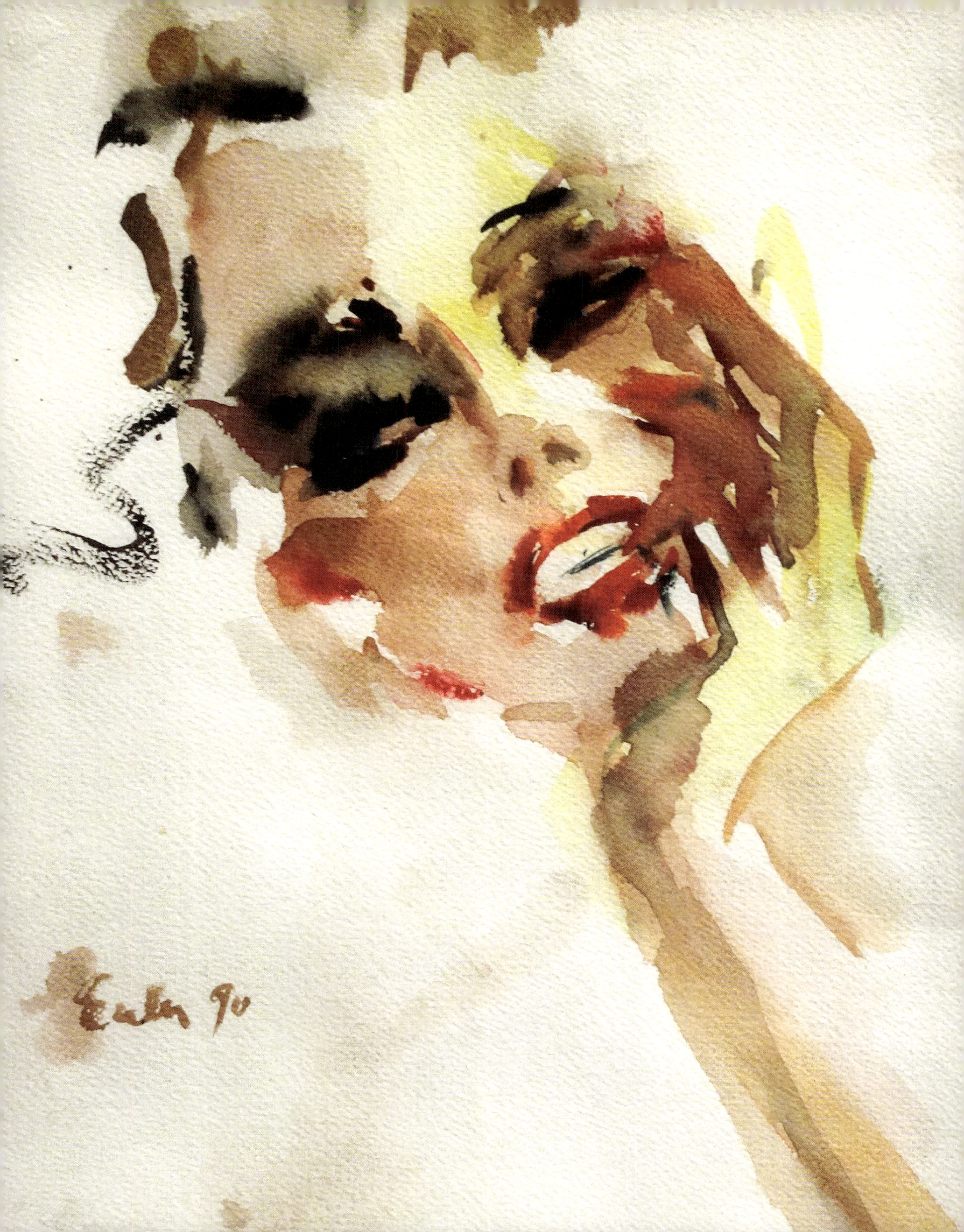

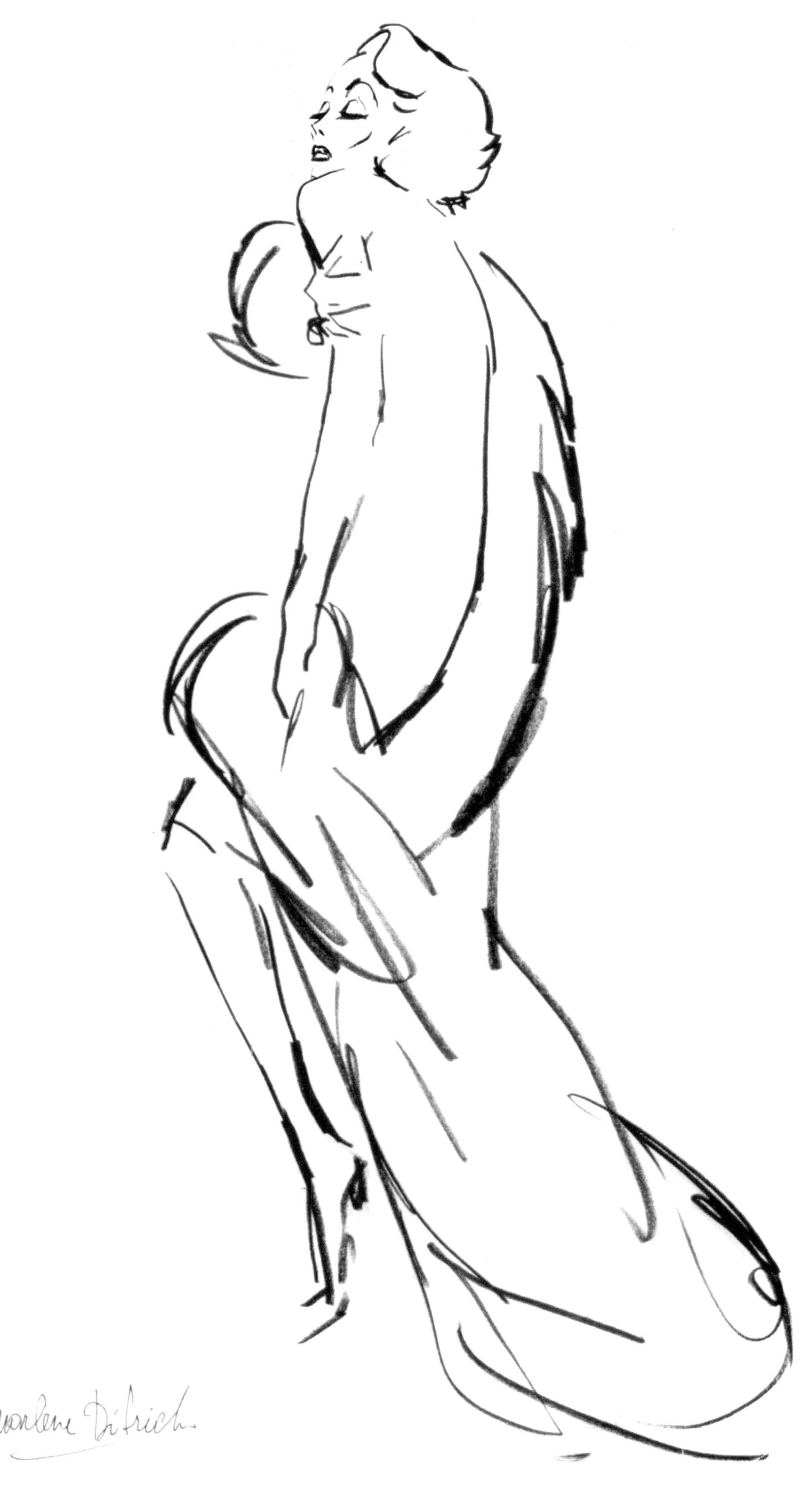

Marlene Dietrich

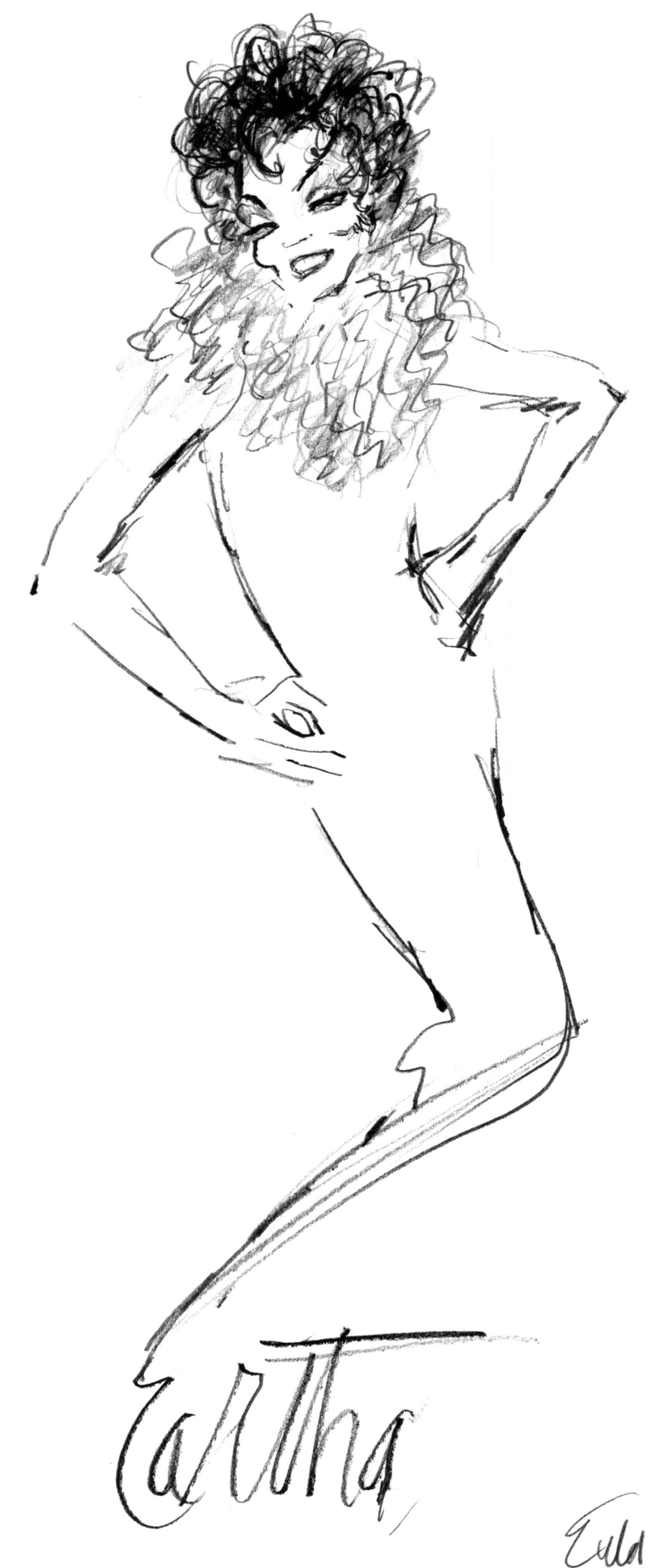
Eartha

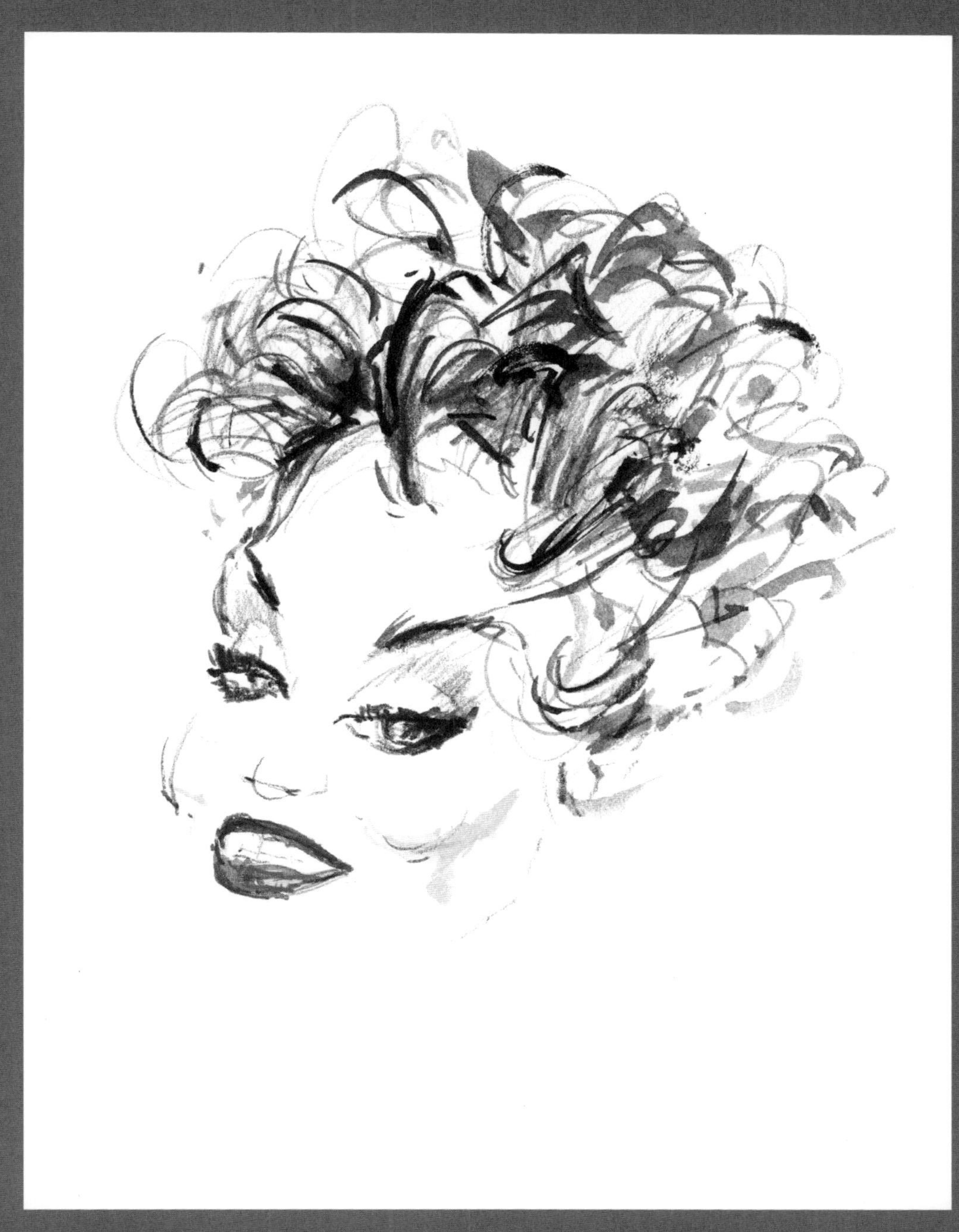

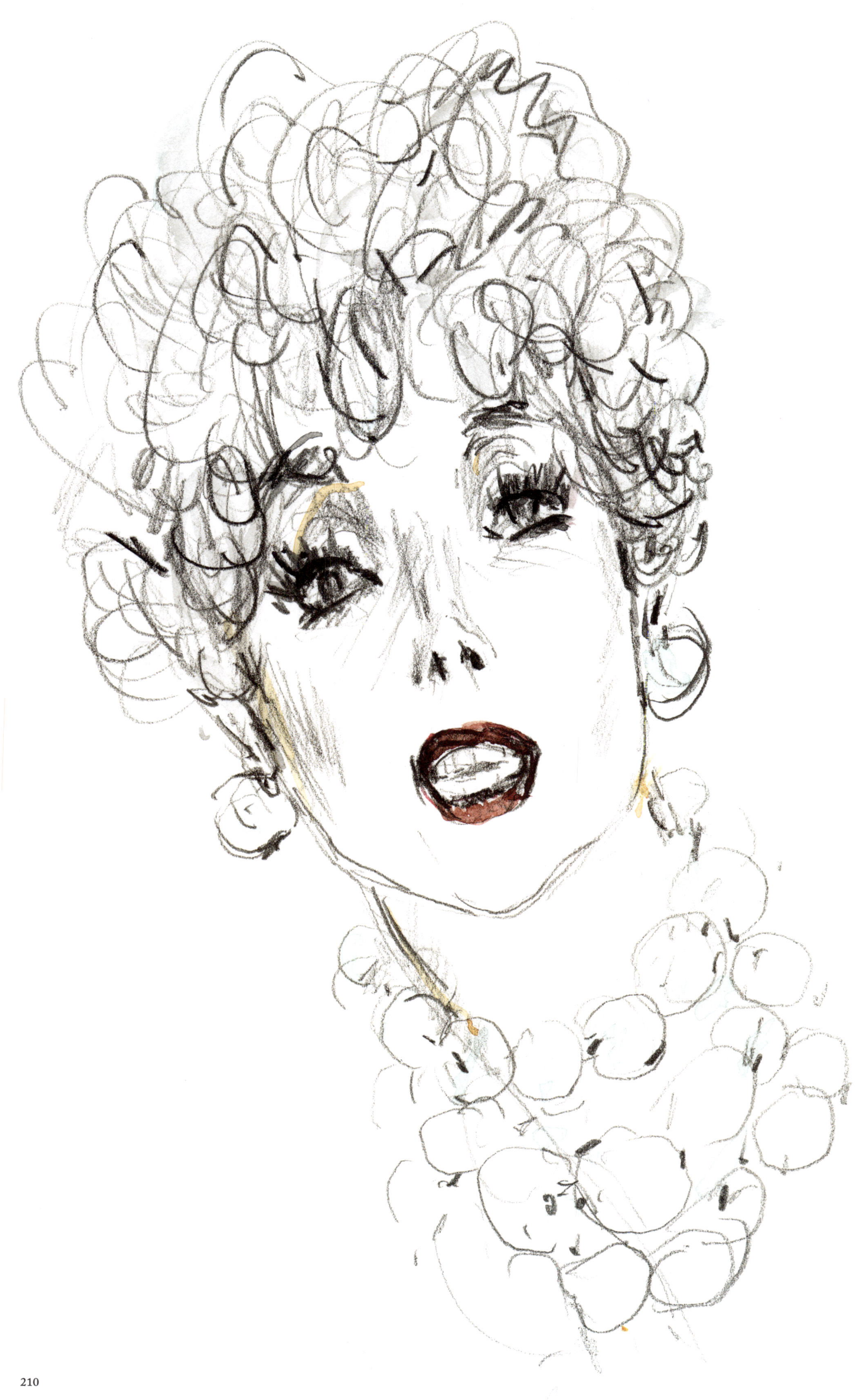

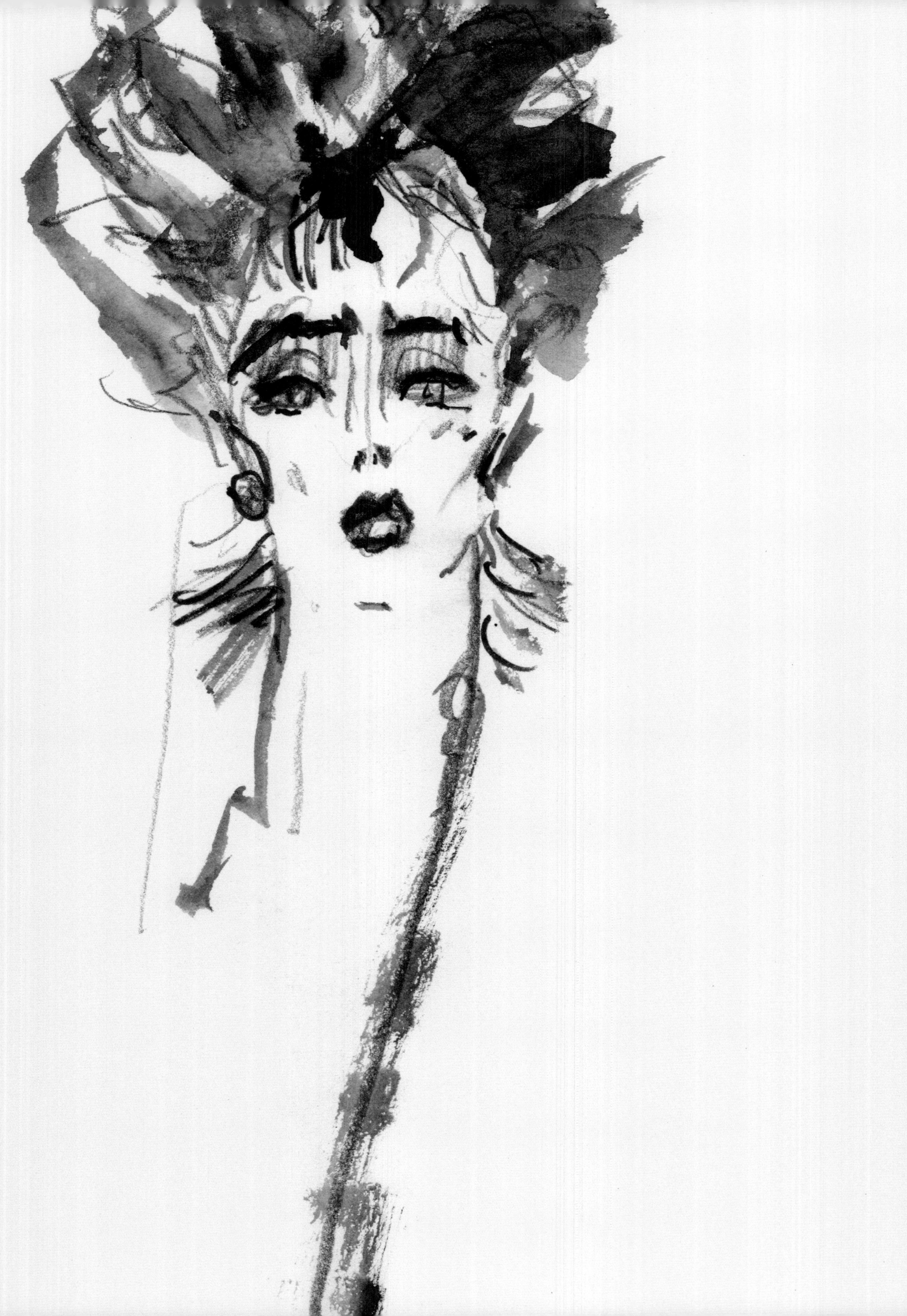

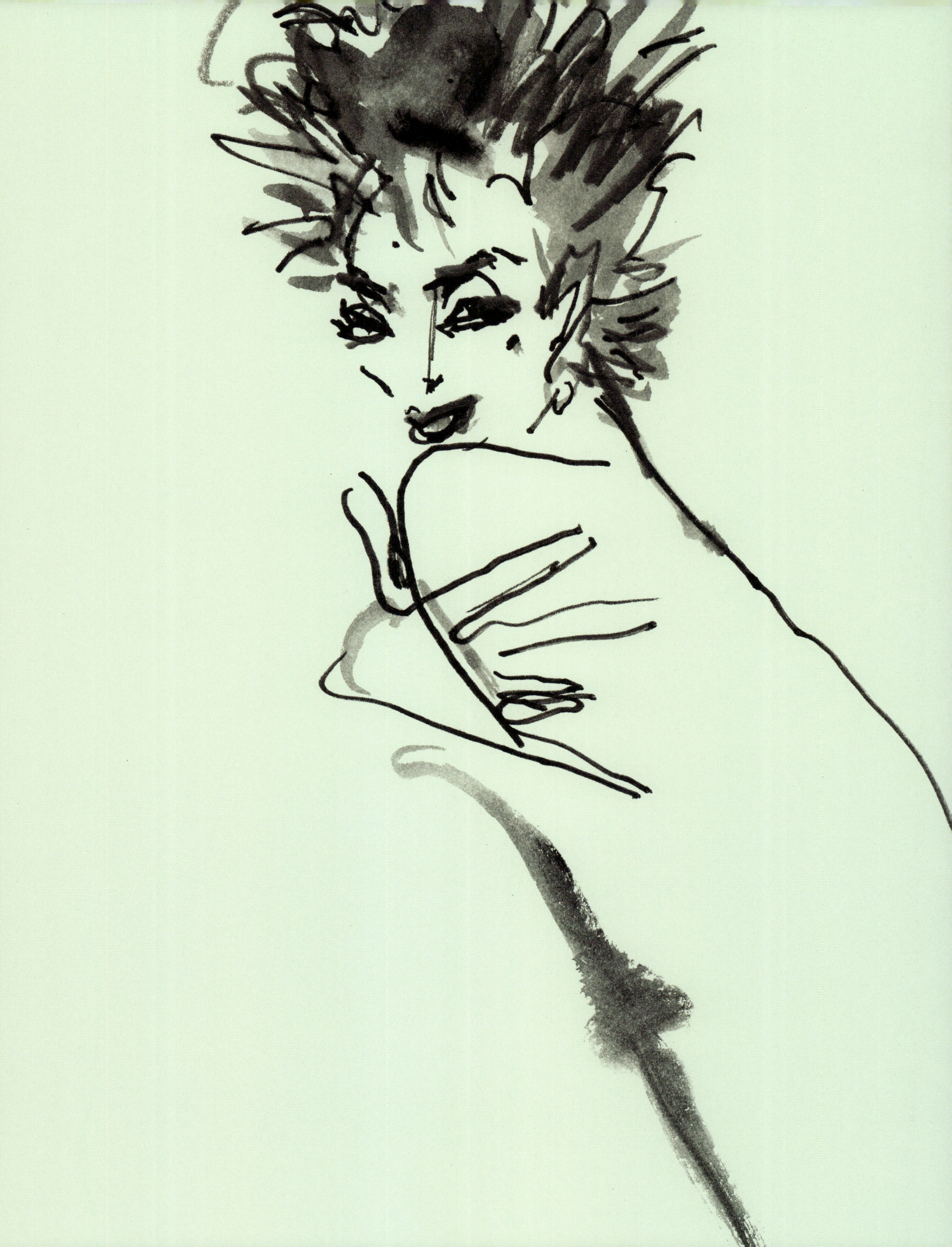

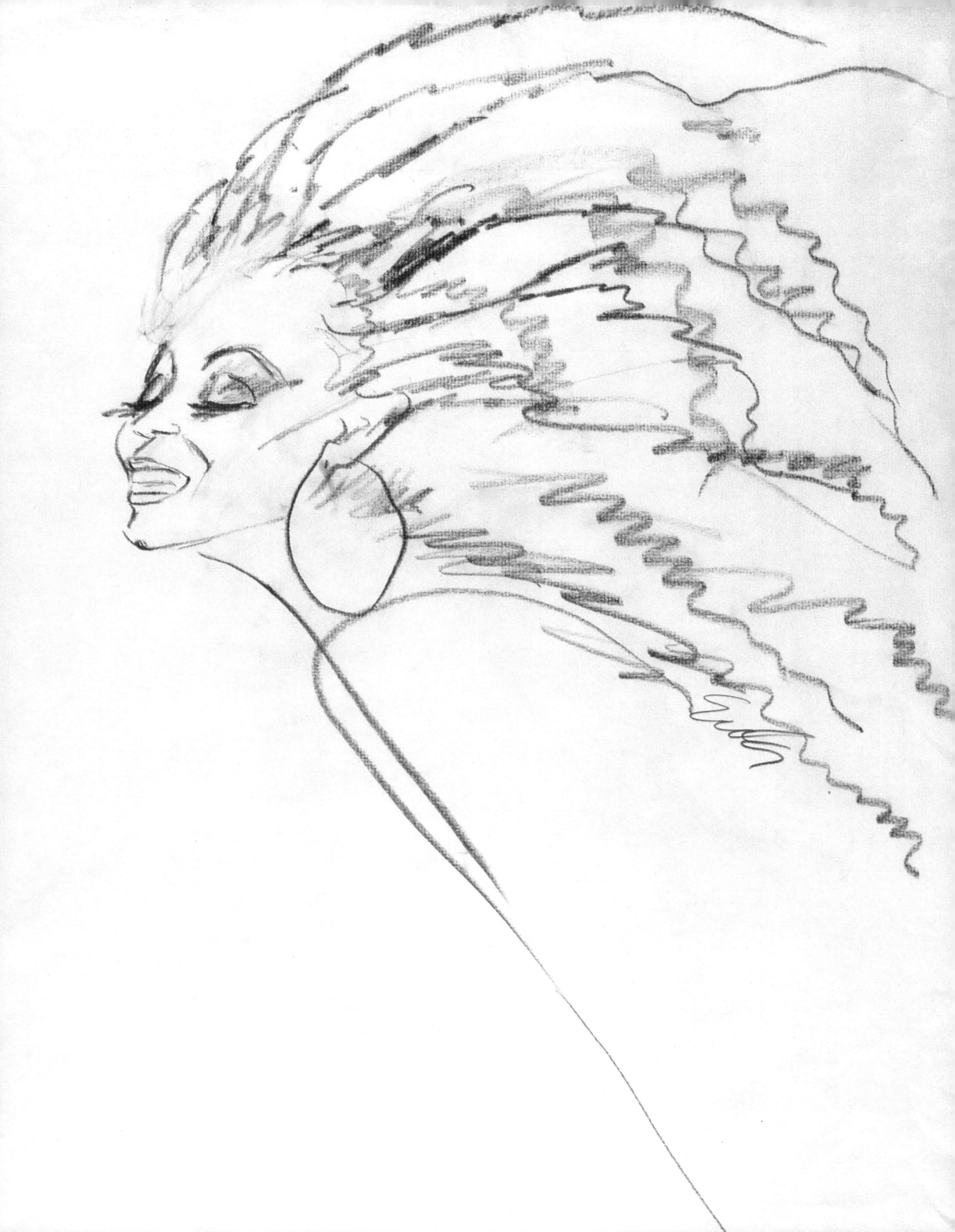

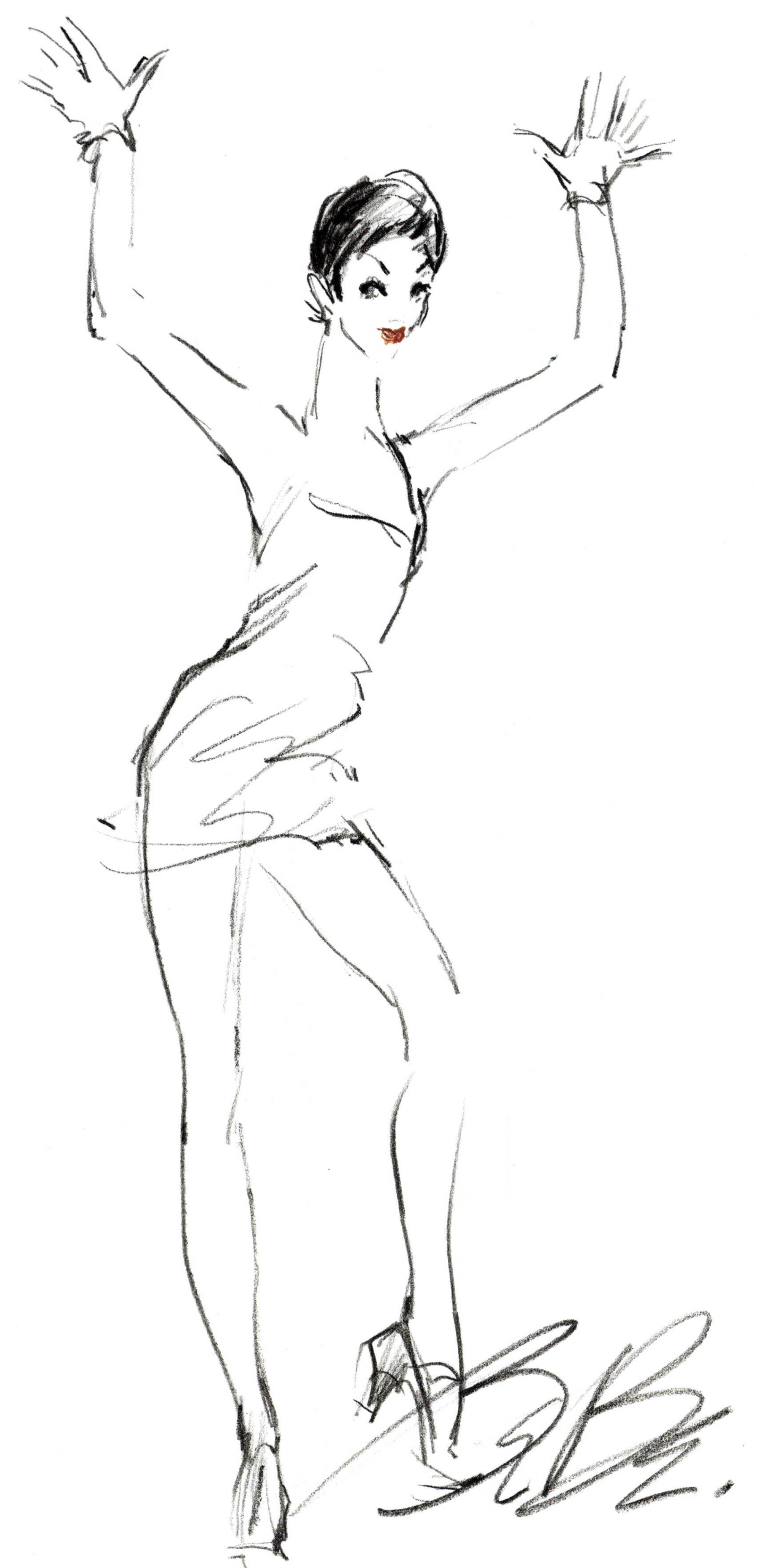

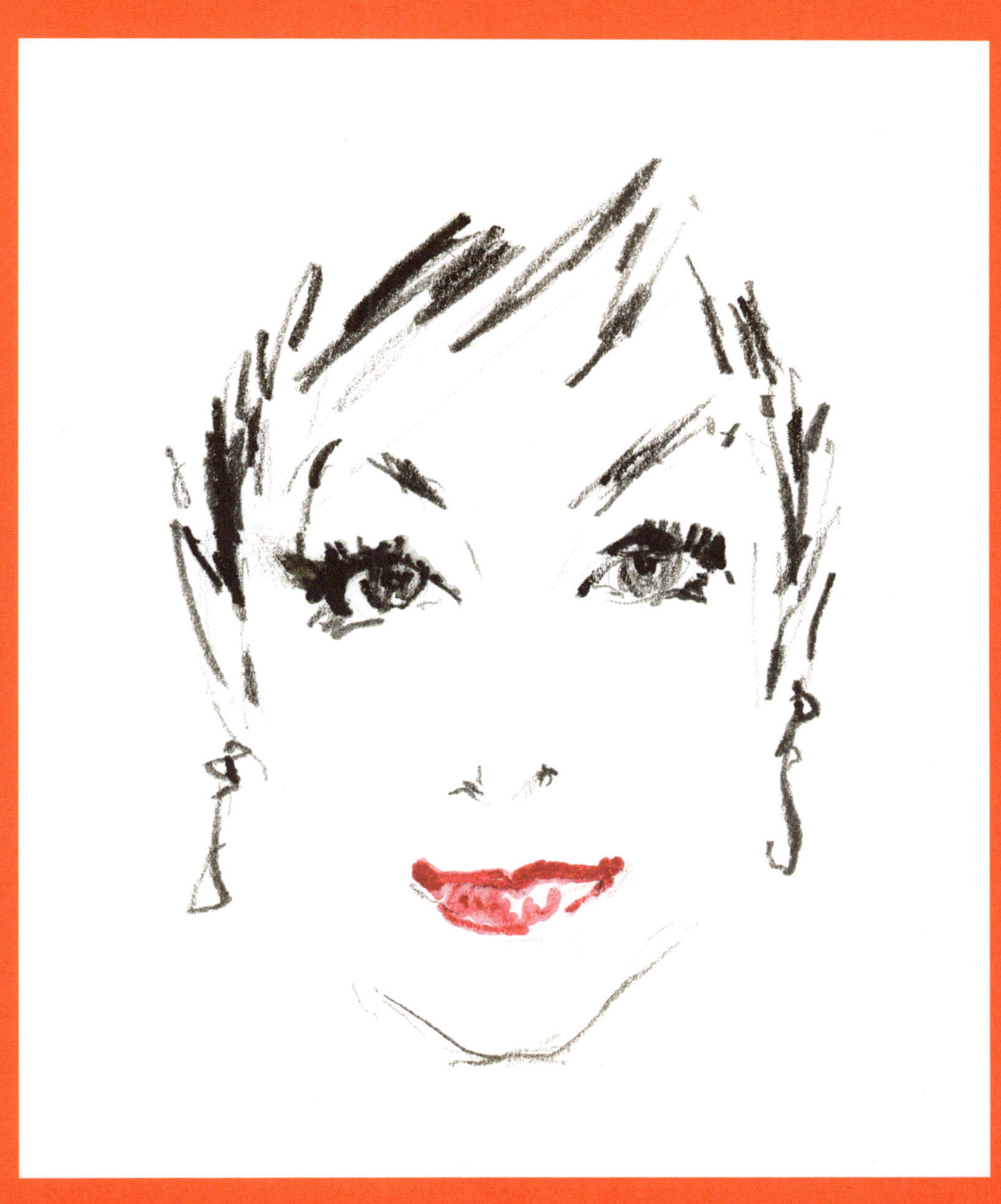

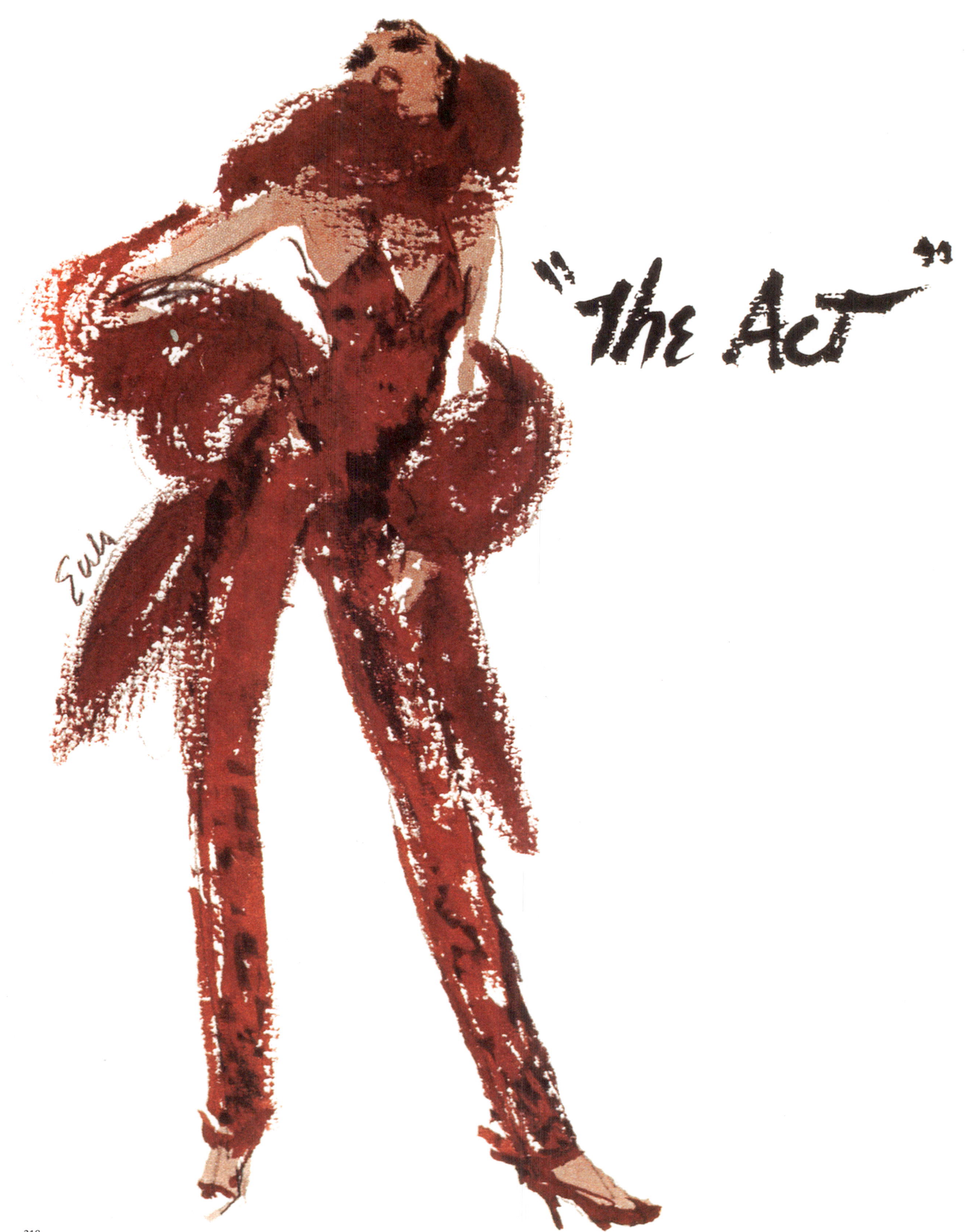
"The Act"

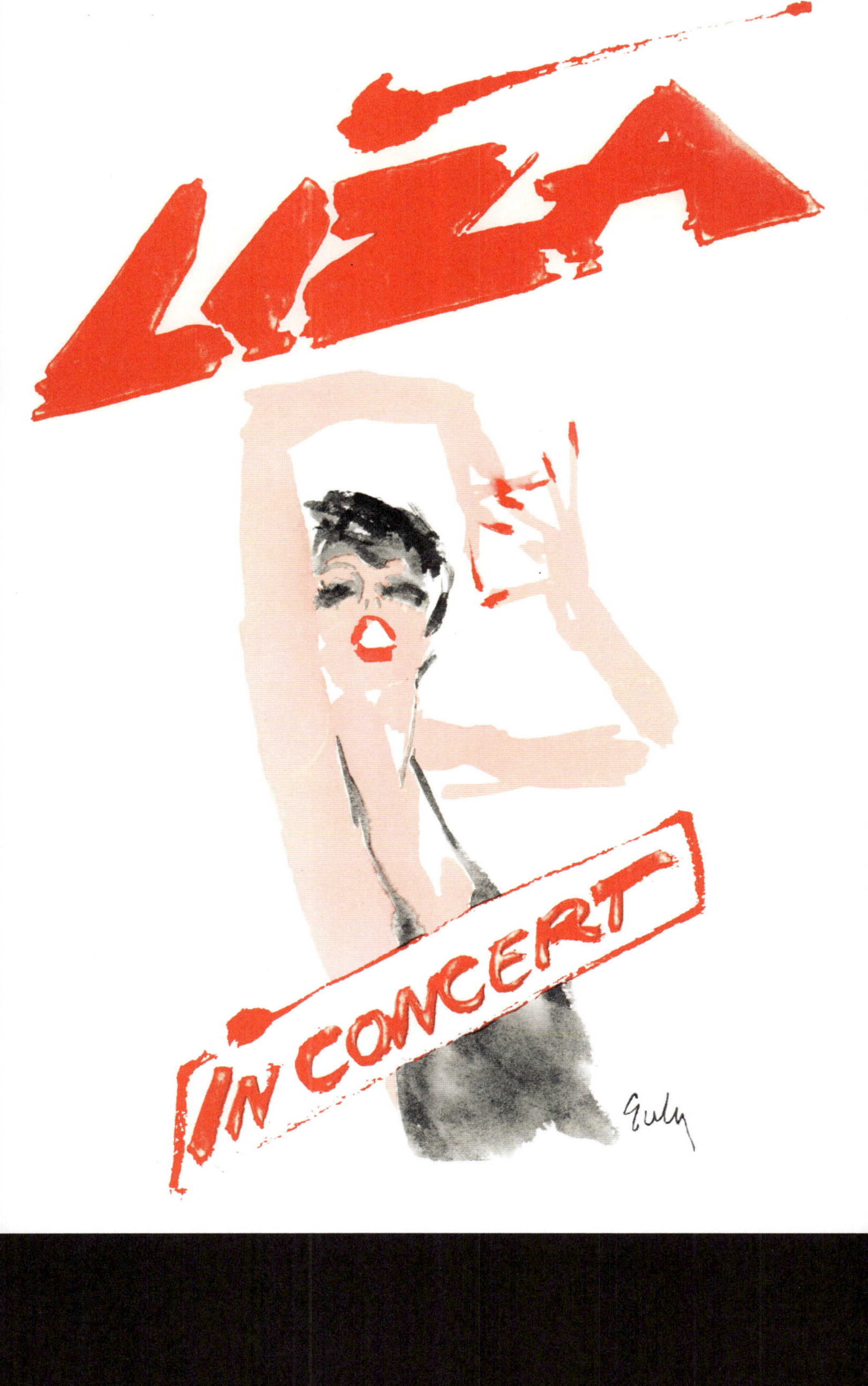

LIZA
IN CONCERT

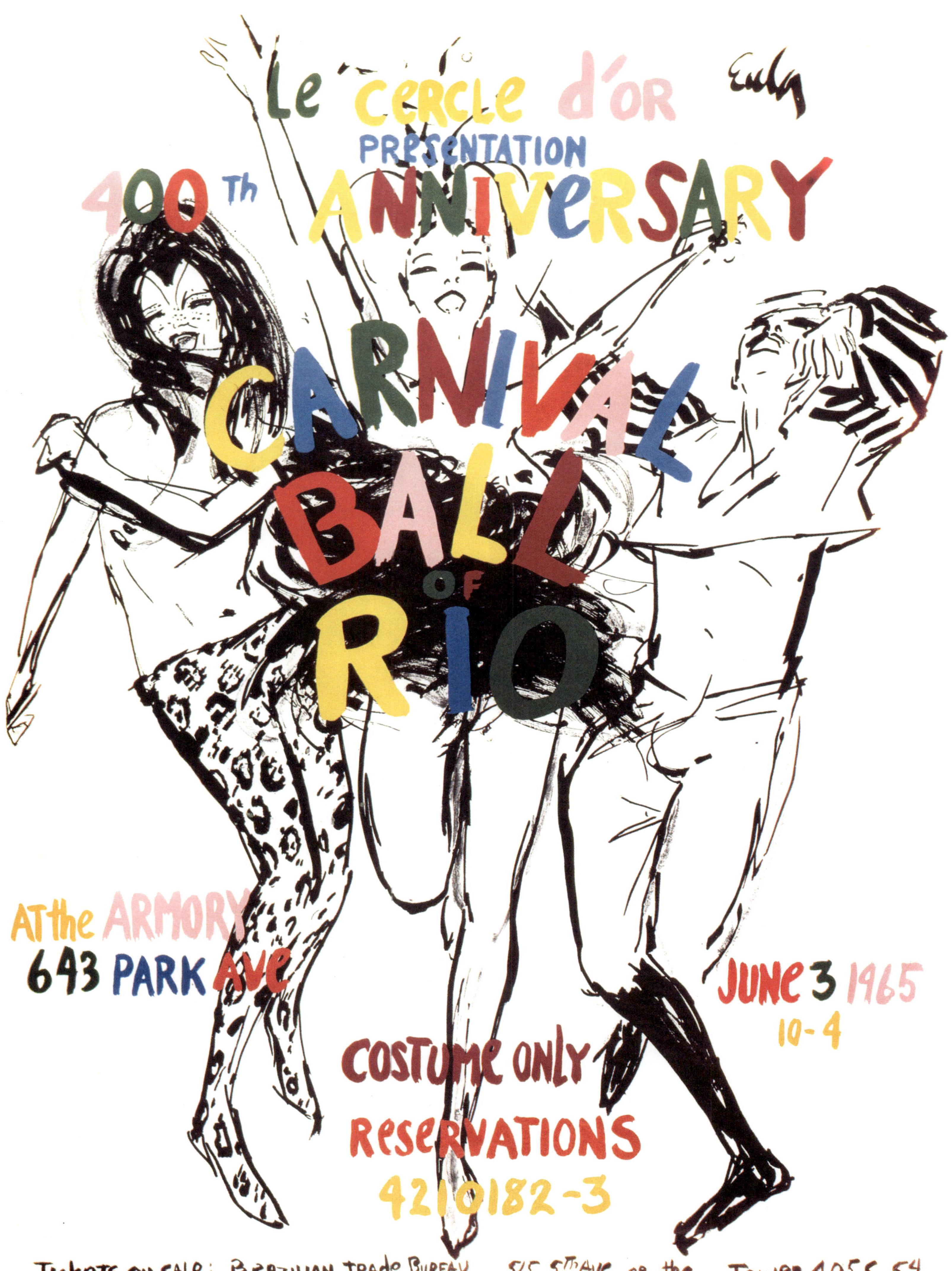

Le Cercle d'Or
presentation
400th Anniversary
CARNIVAL
BALL
of
RIO
AT the ARMORY
643 PARK AVe
JUNE 3 1965
10-4
COSTUME ONLY
RESERVATIONS
4210182-3
Tickets on sale: Brazilian Trade Bureau   515 5th Ave or the   Tower 405 E 54

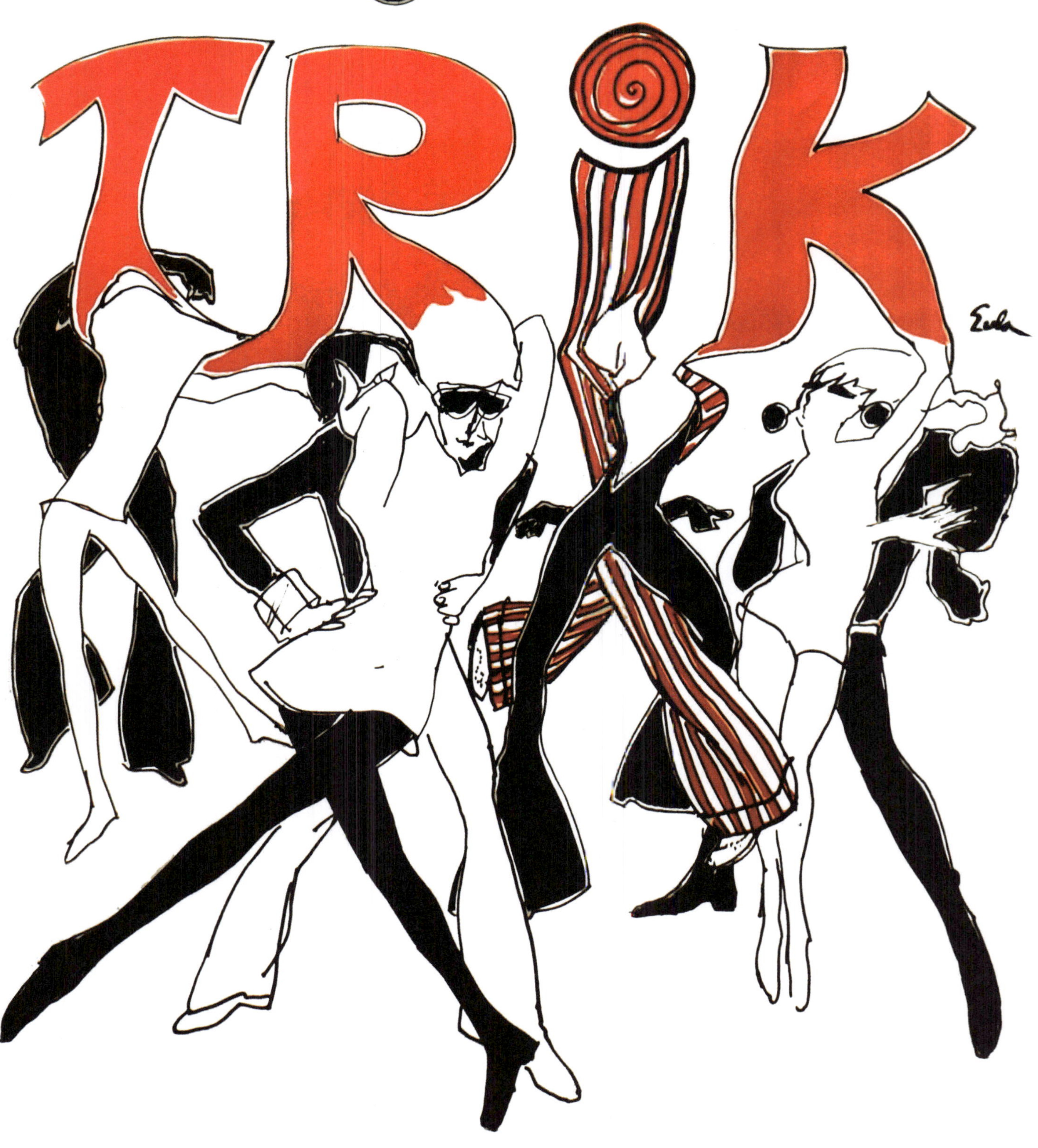

Trude Heller's new site
opening APR 20
on Brodway and 49
TRiK

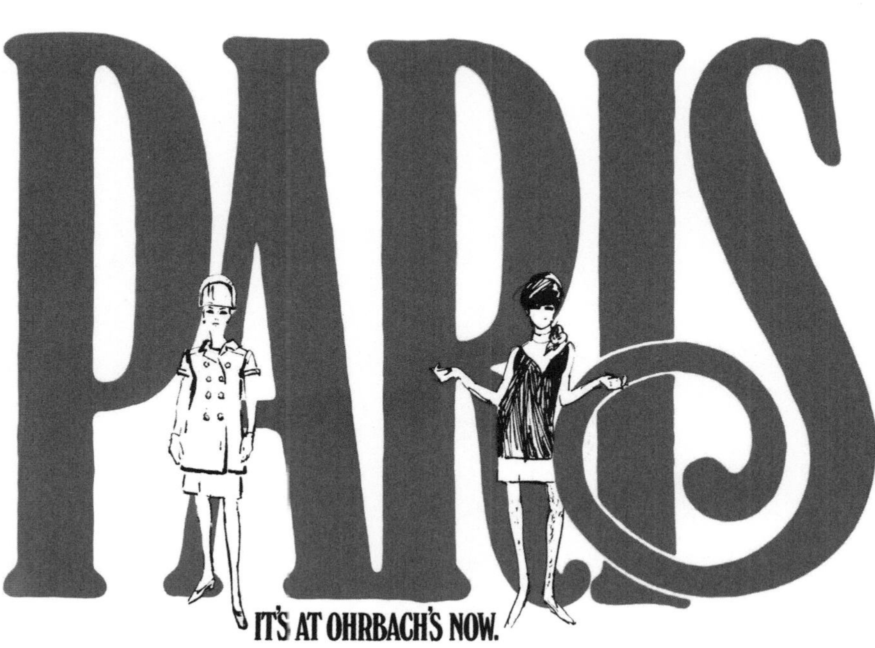

PARIS
IT'S AT OHRBACH'S NOW.
New York: 34th St. opp. Empire State Building. Newark: Market and Halsey. Westbury, L. I.: Old Country Road at the Raceway.

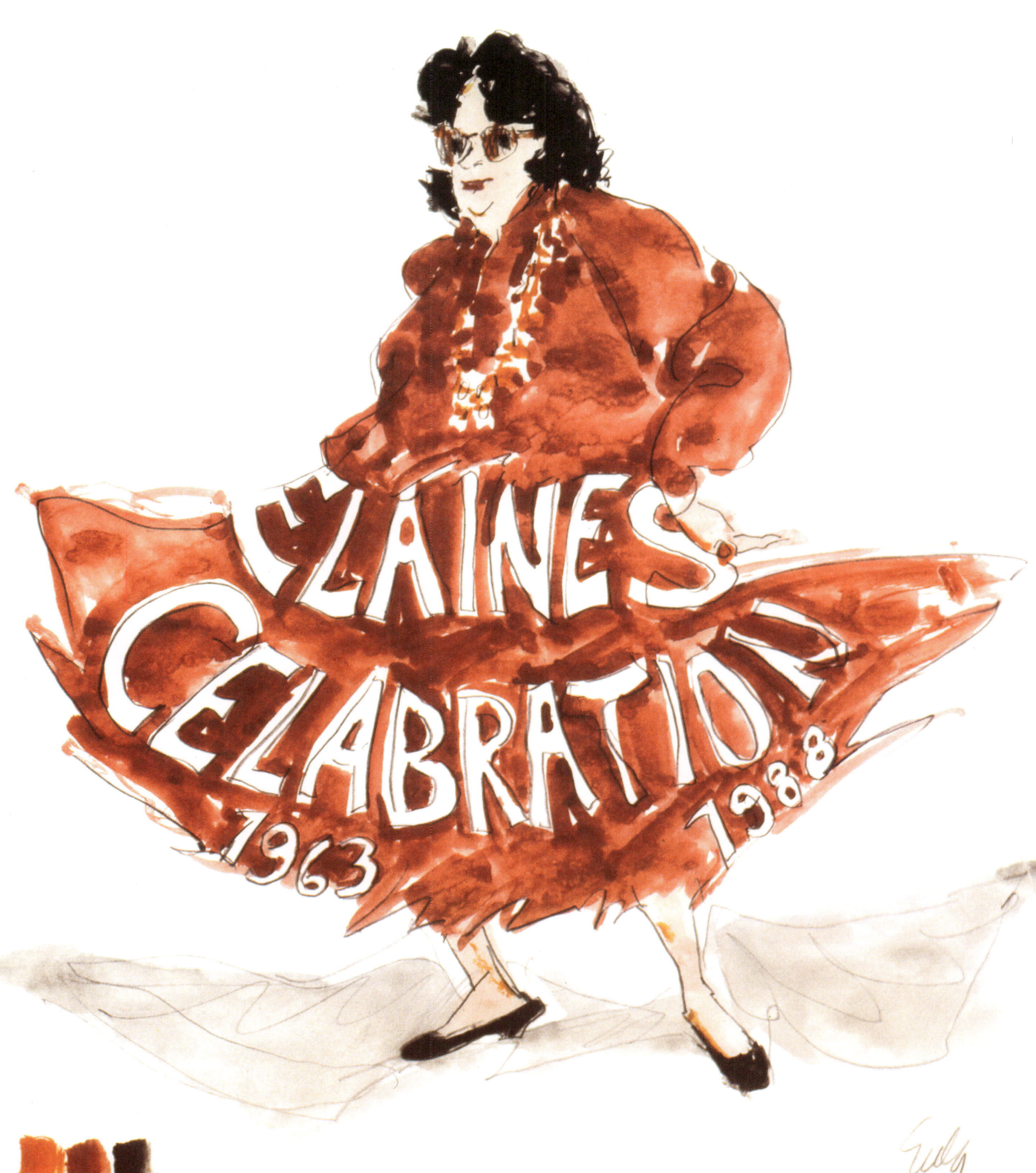
ZAINES
CELABRATION
1963   1988

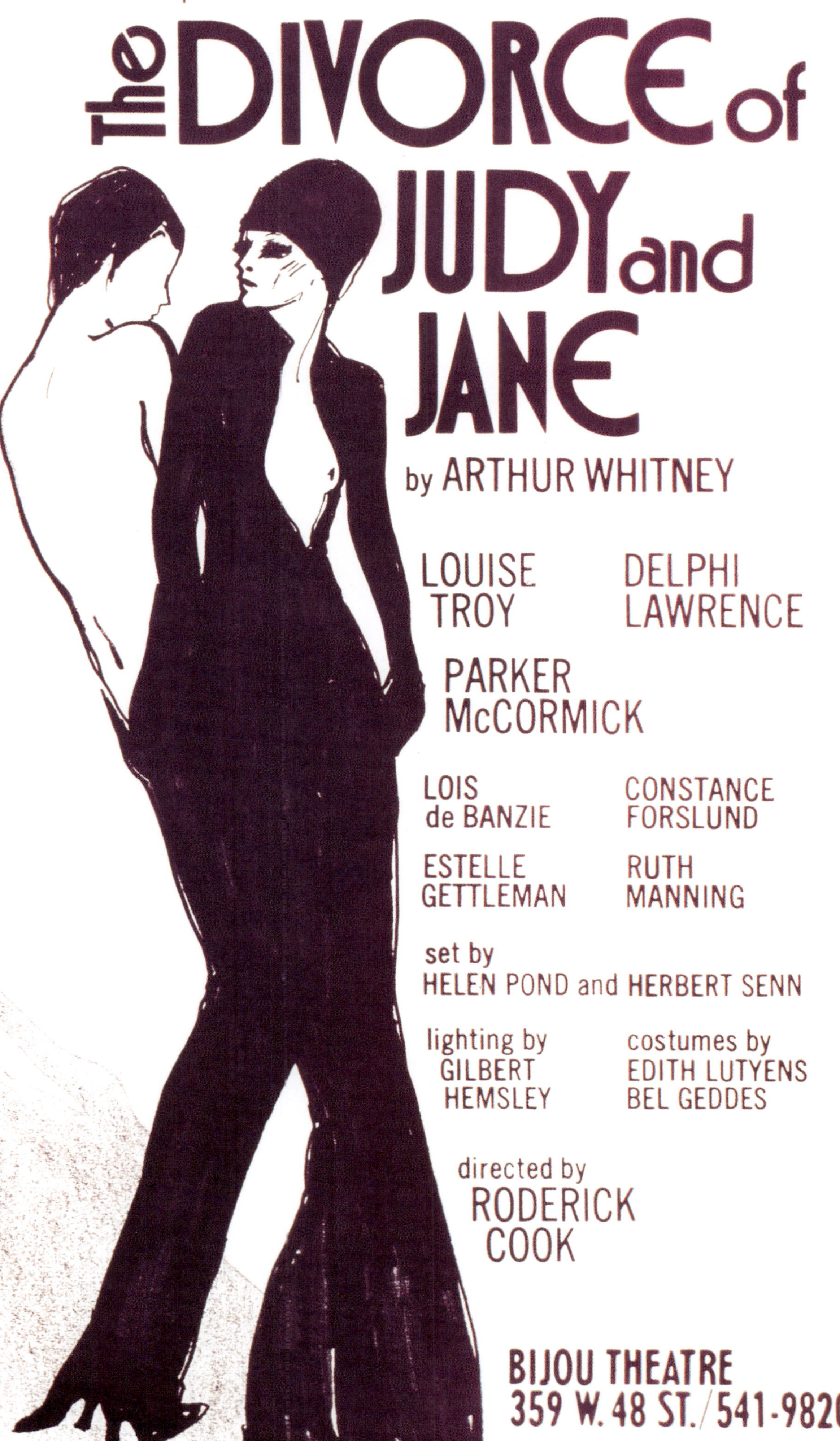
DUDLEY FIELD MALONE and VAN RAPOPORT
present

The DIVORCE of JUDY and JANE

by ARTHUR WHITNEY

LOUISE TROY

DELPHI LAWRENCE

PARKER McCORMICK

LOIS de BANZIE

CONSTANCE FORSLUND

ESTELLE GETTLEMAN

RUTH MANNING

set by
HELEN POND and HERBERT SENN

lighting by
GILBERT HEMSLEY

costumes by
EDITH LUTYENS BEL GEDDES

directed by
RODERICK COOK

BIJOU THEATRE
359 W. 48 ST. / 541-9820

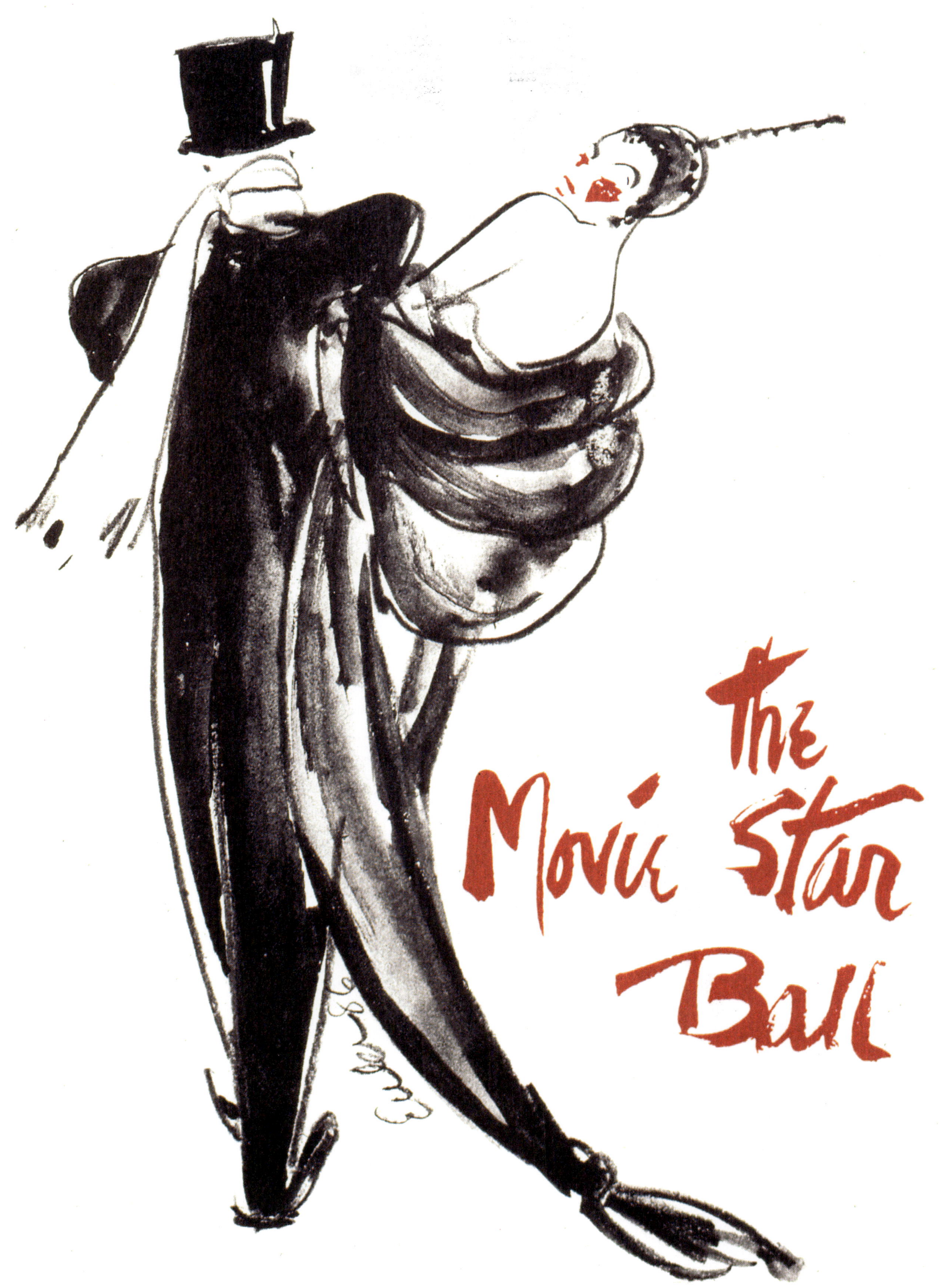
The
Movie Star
Ball

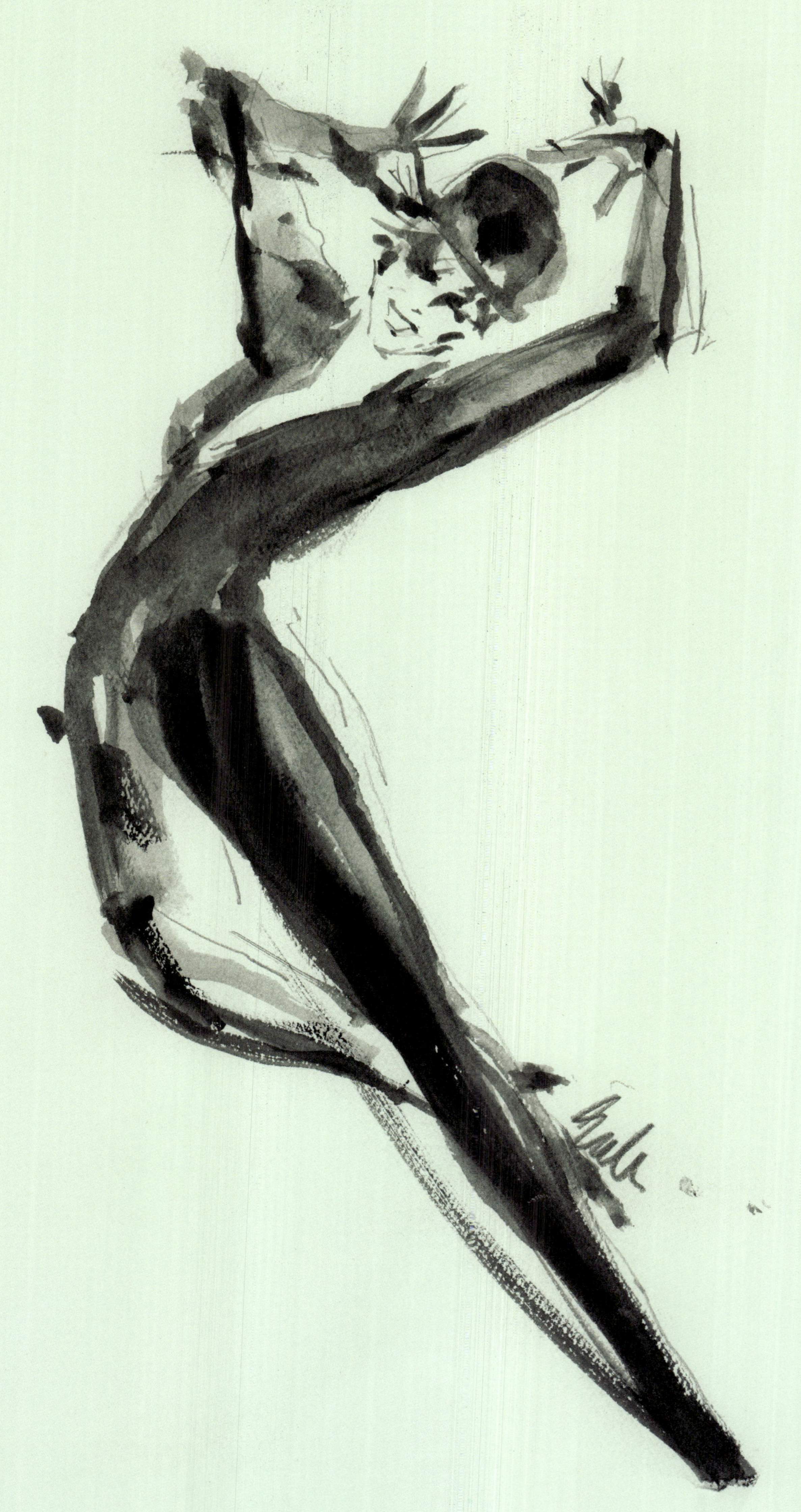

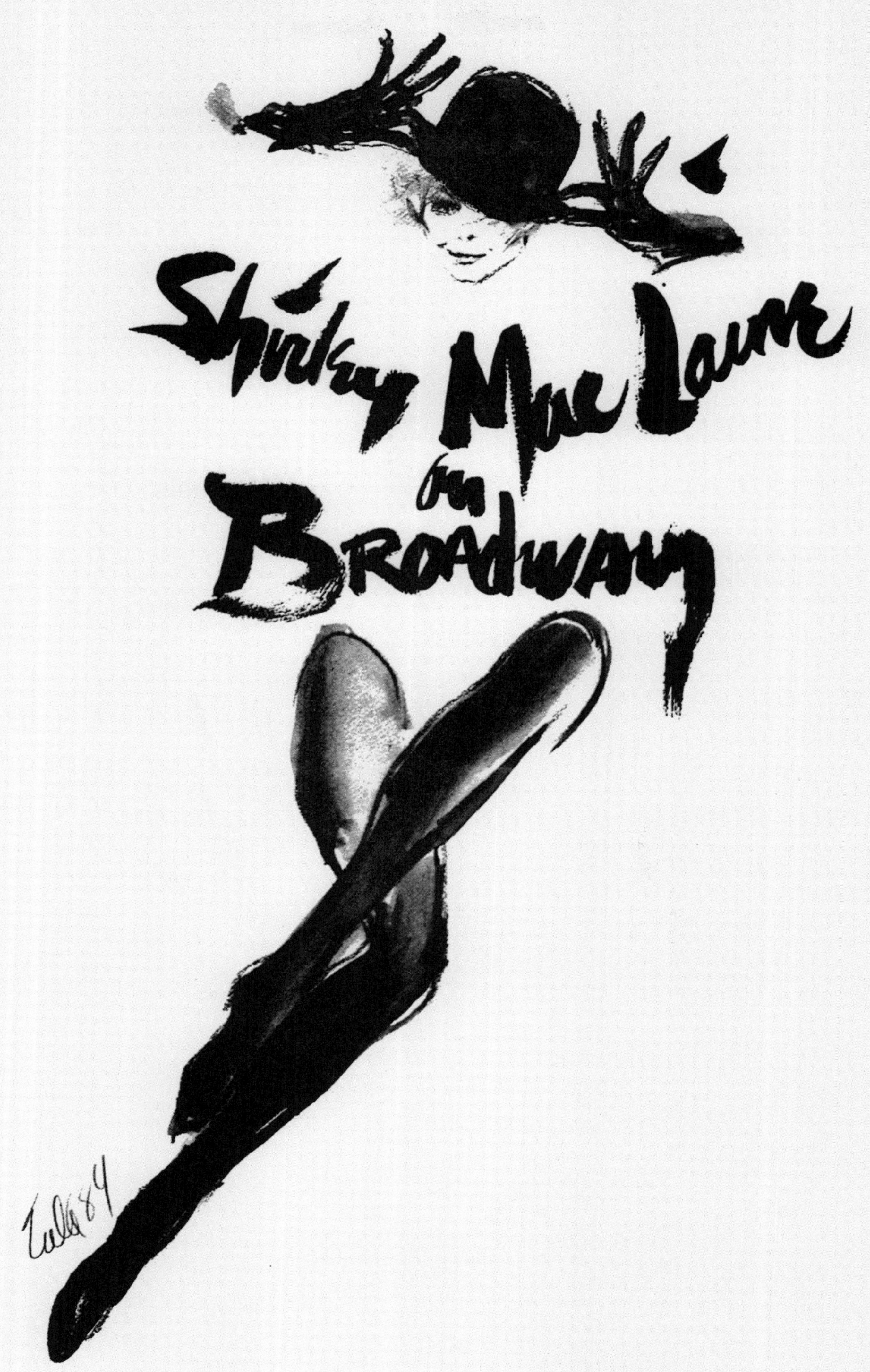
Shirley MacLaine
on
Broadway

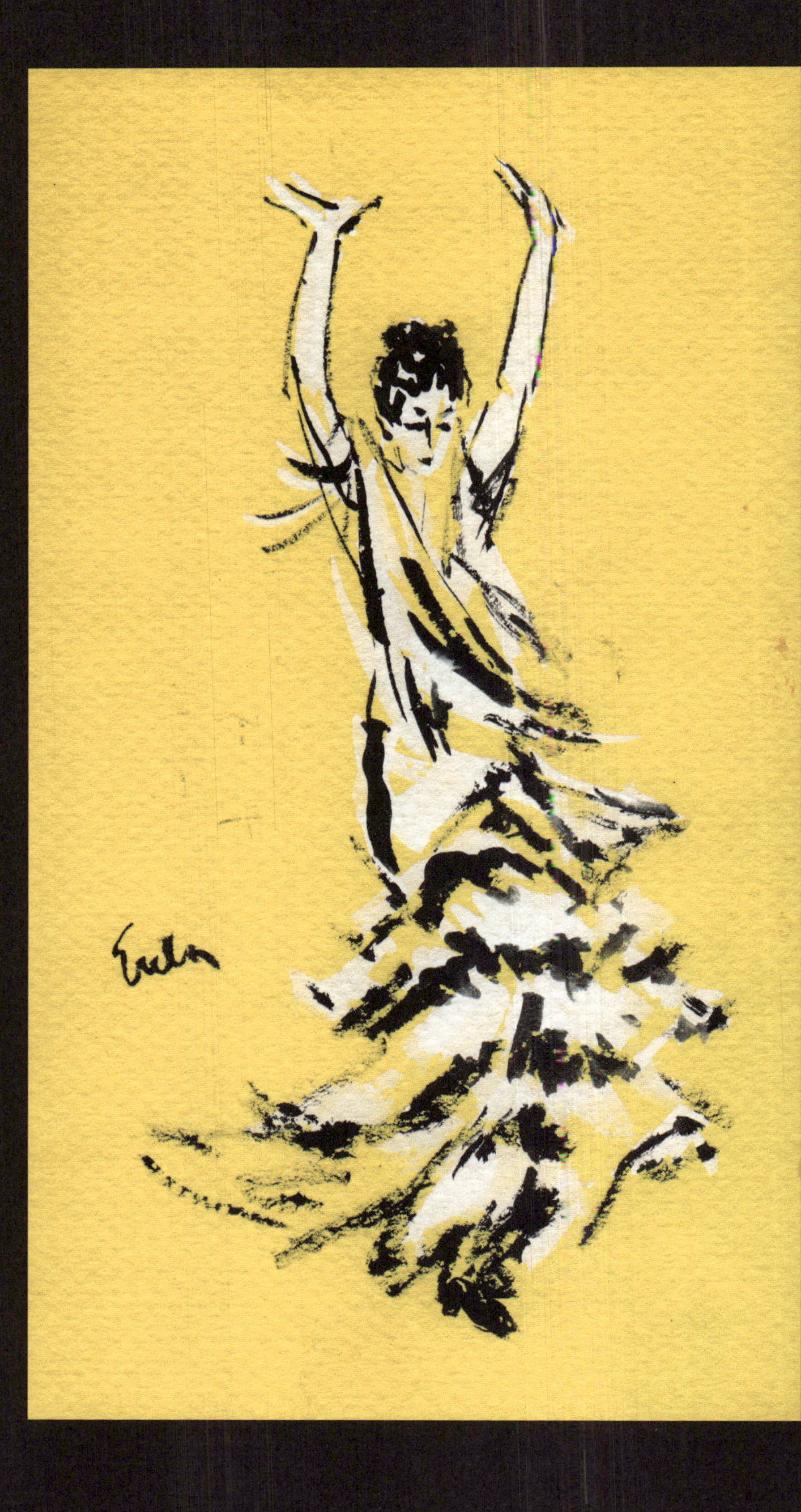

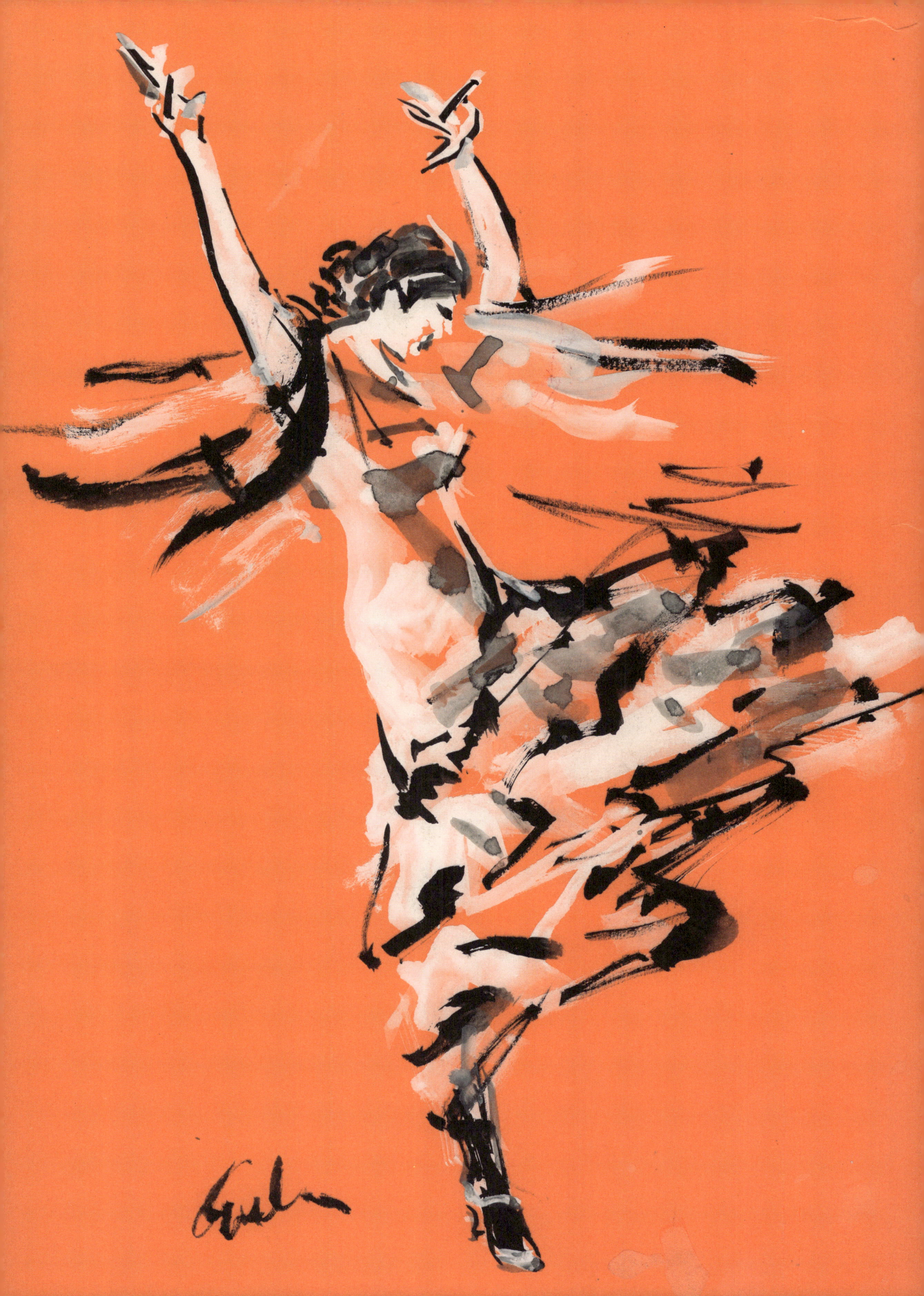

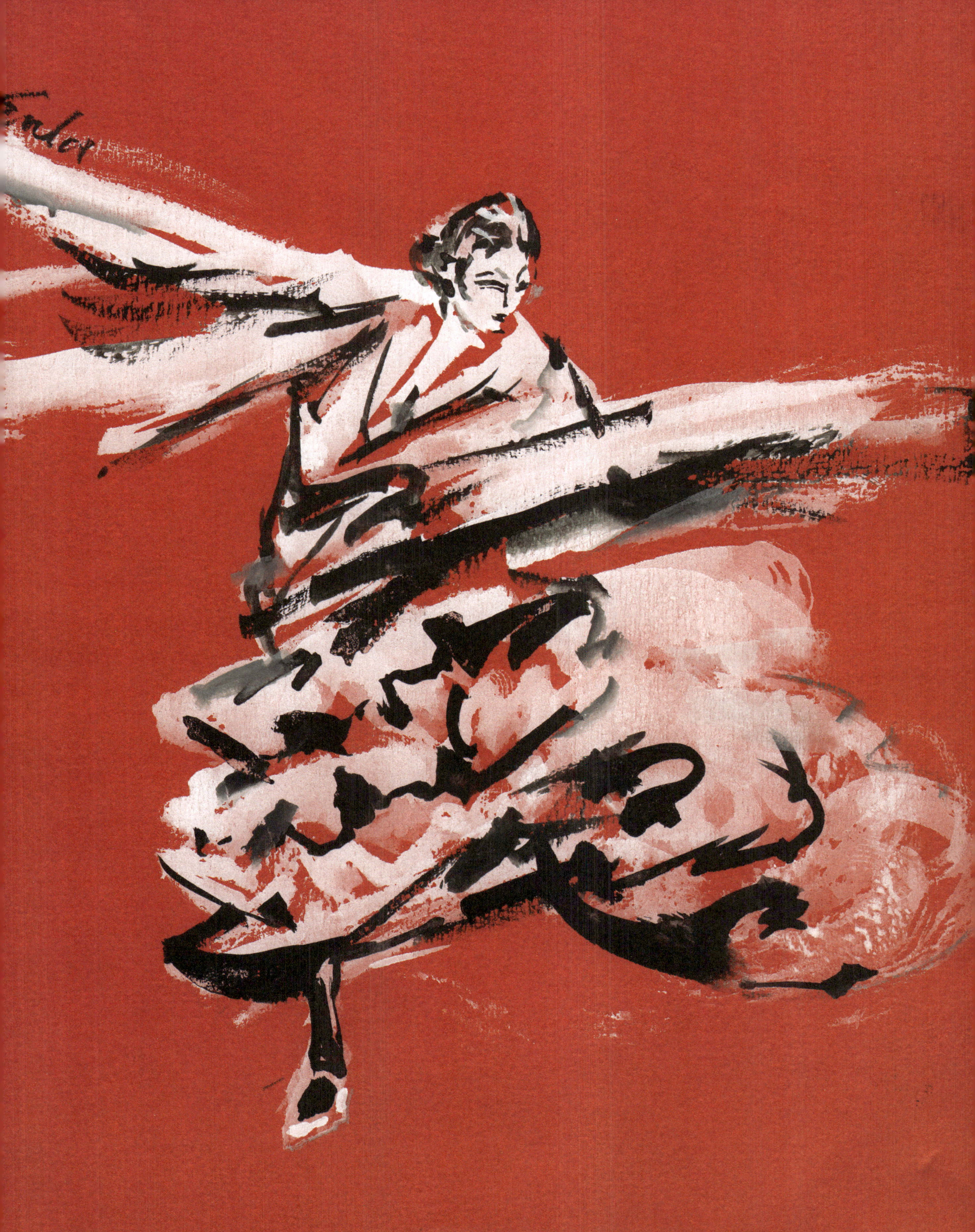

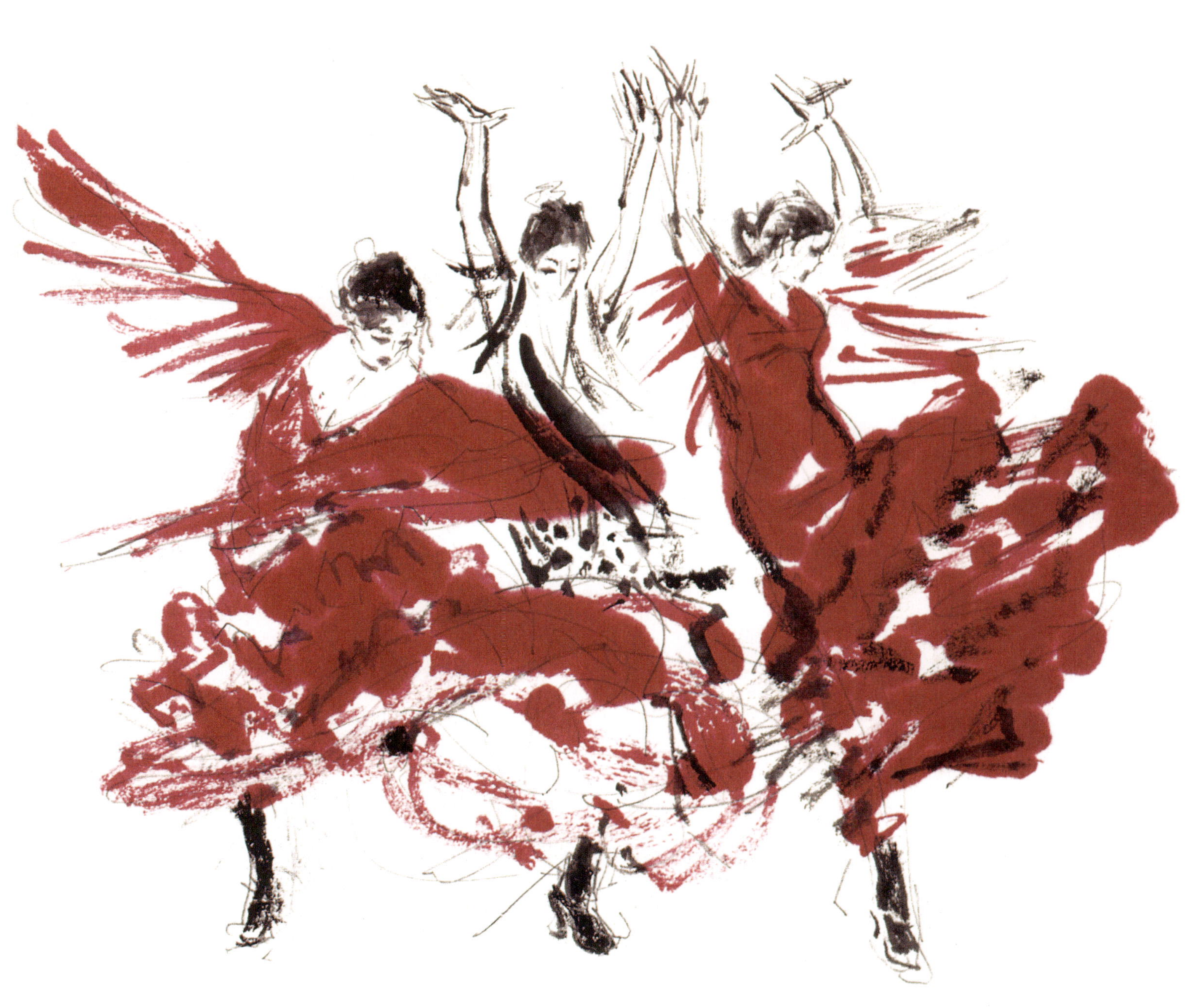

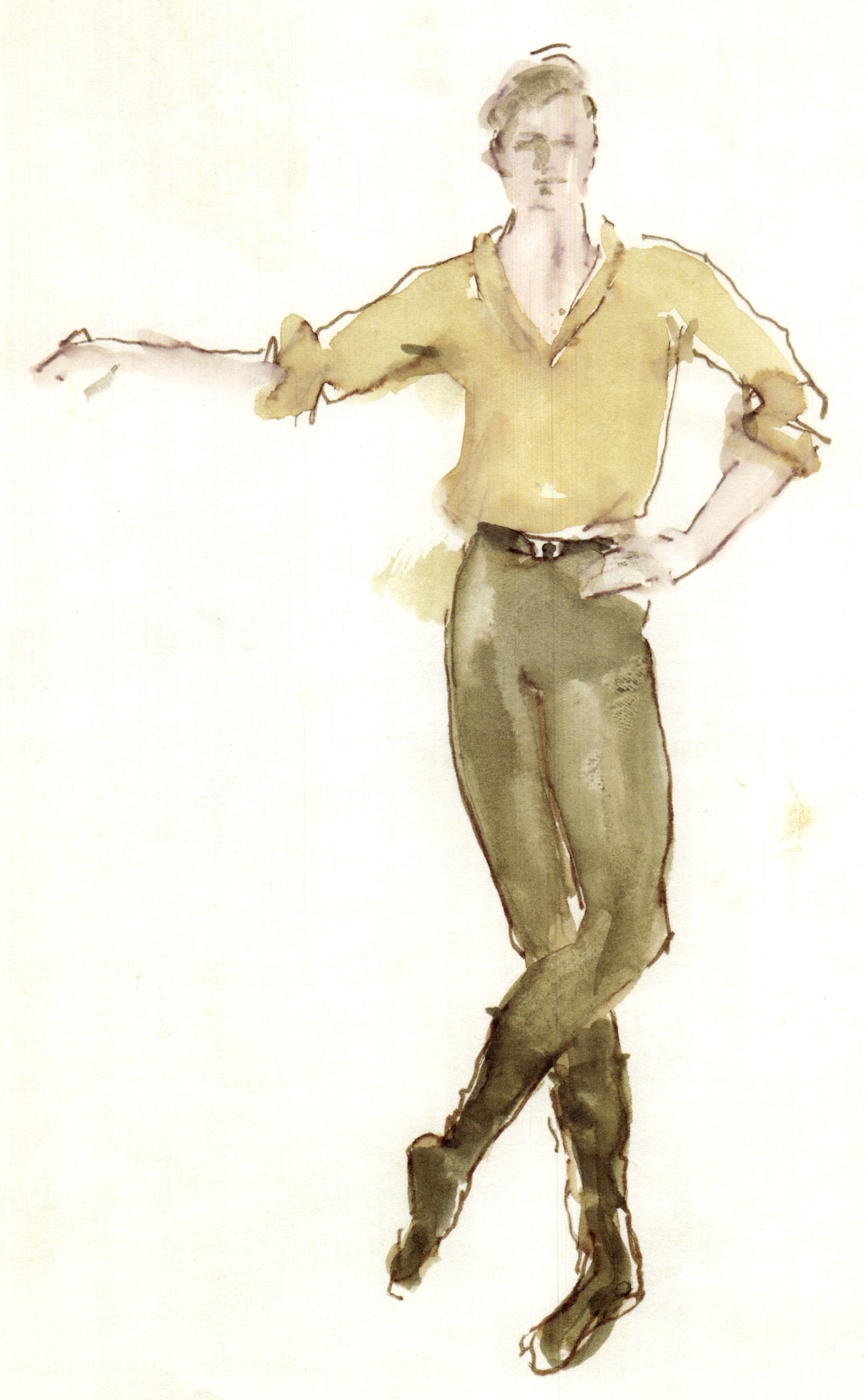

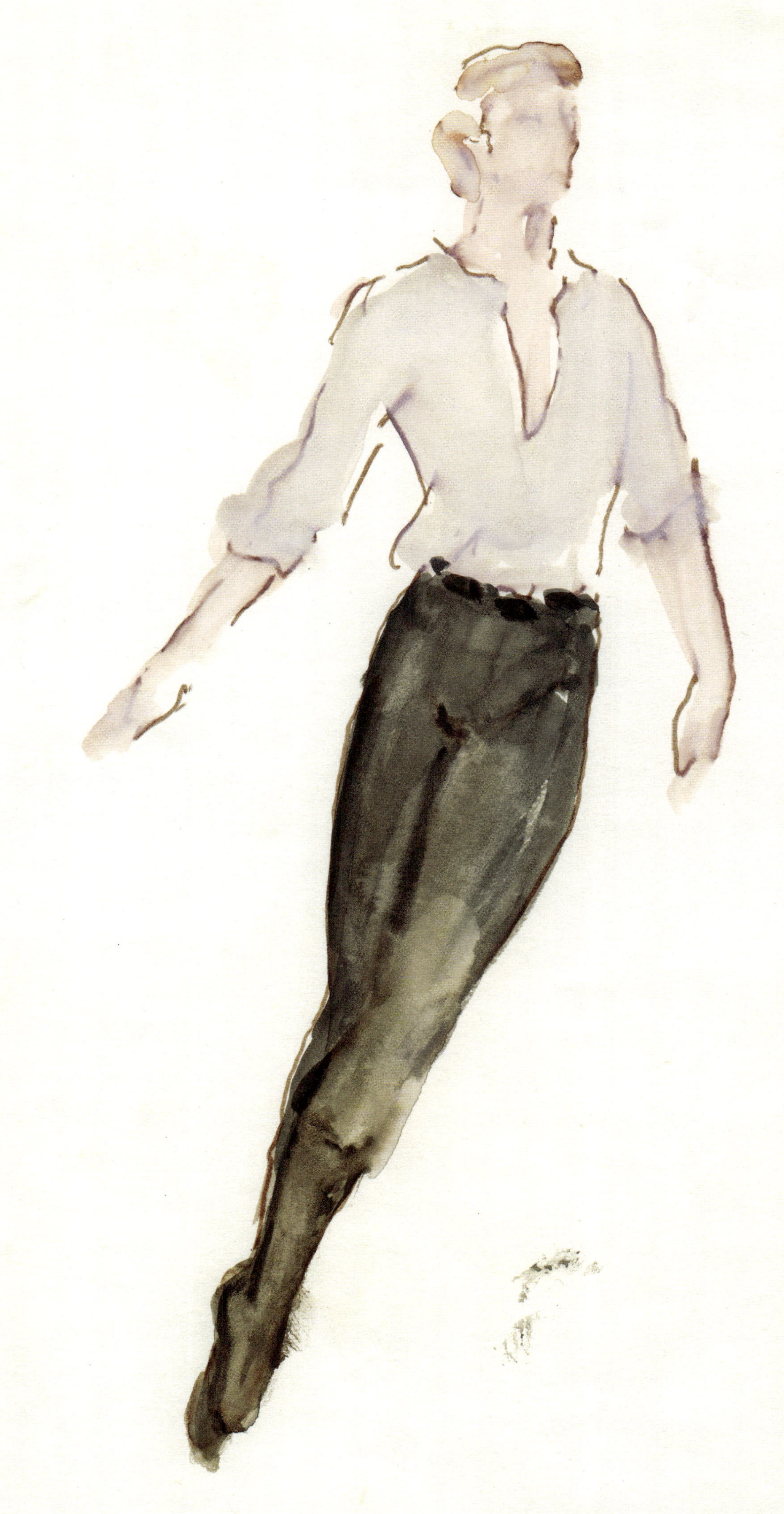

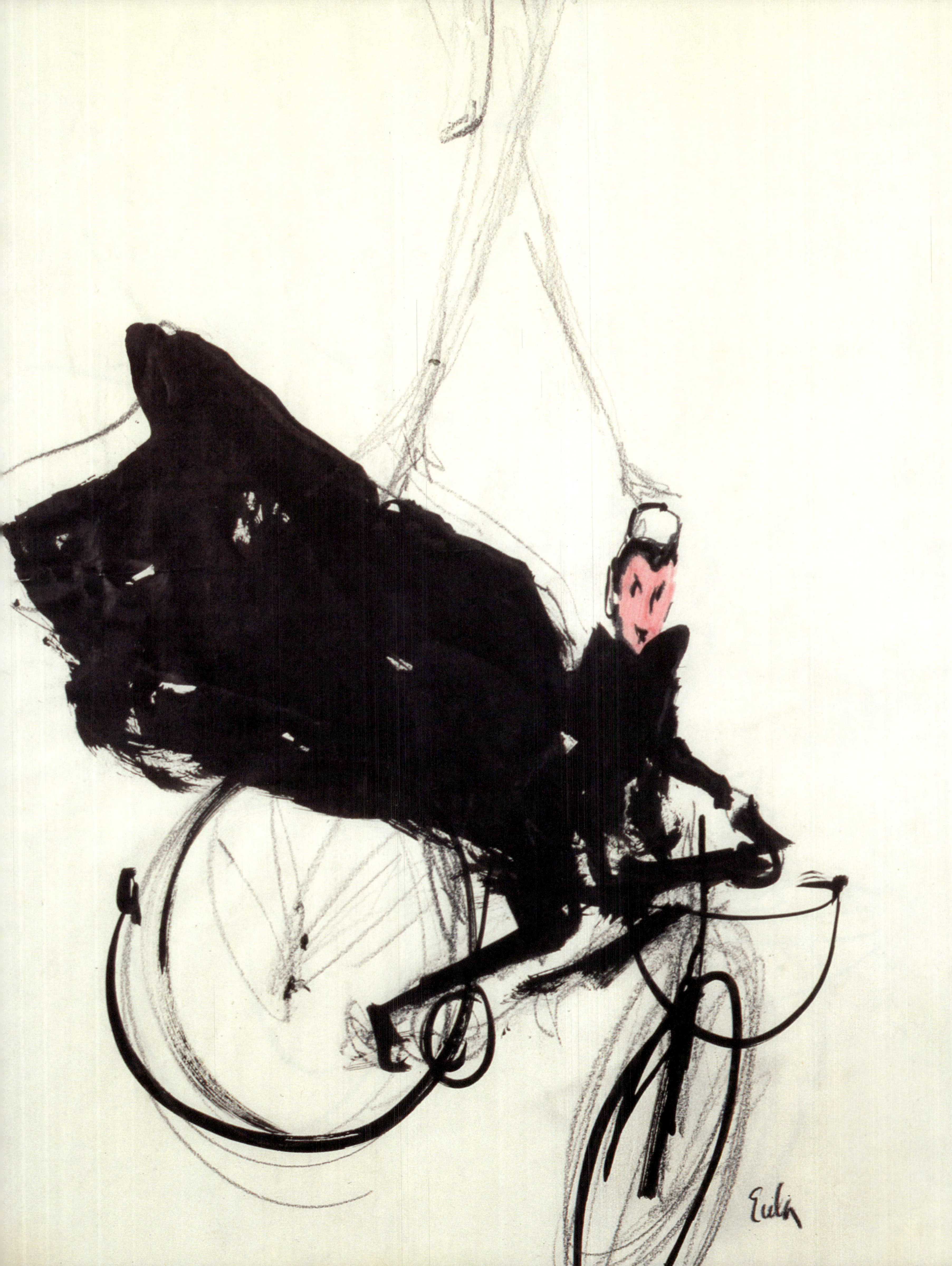

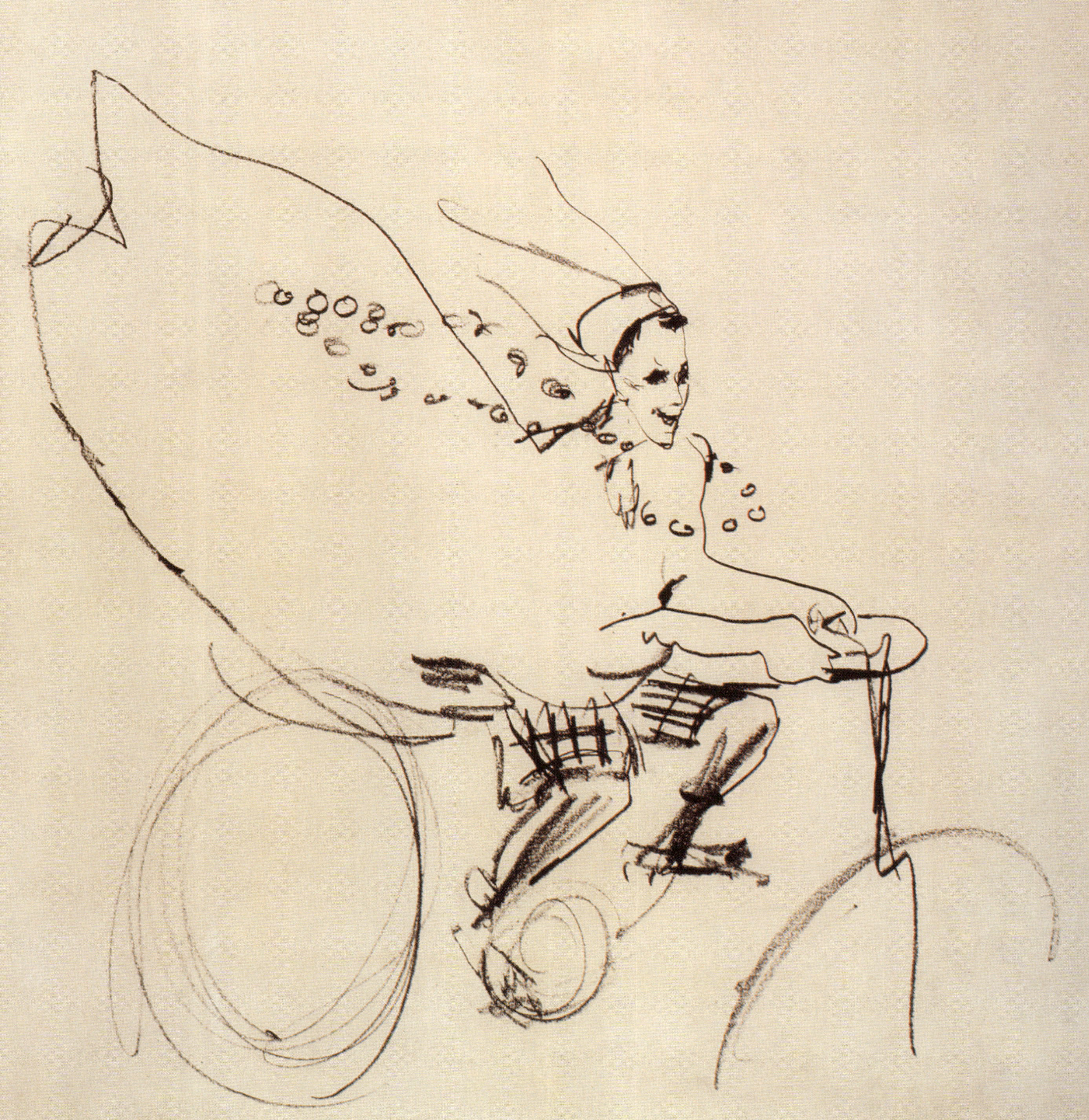

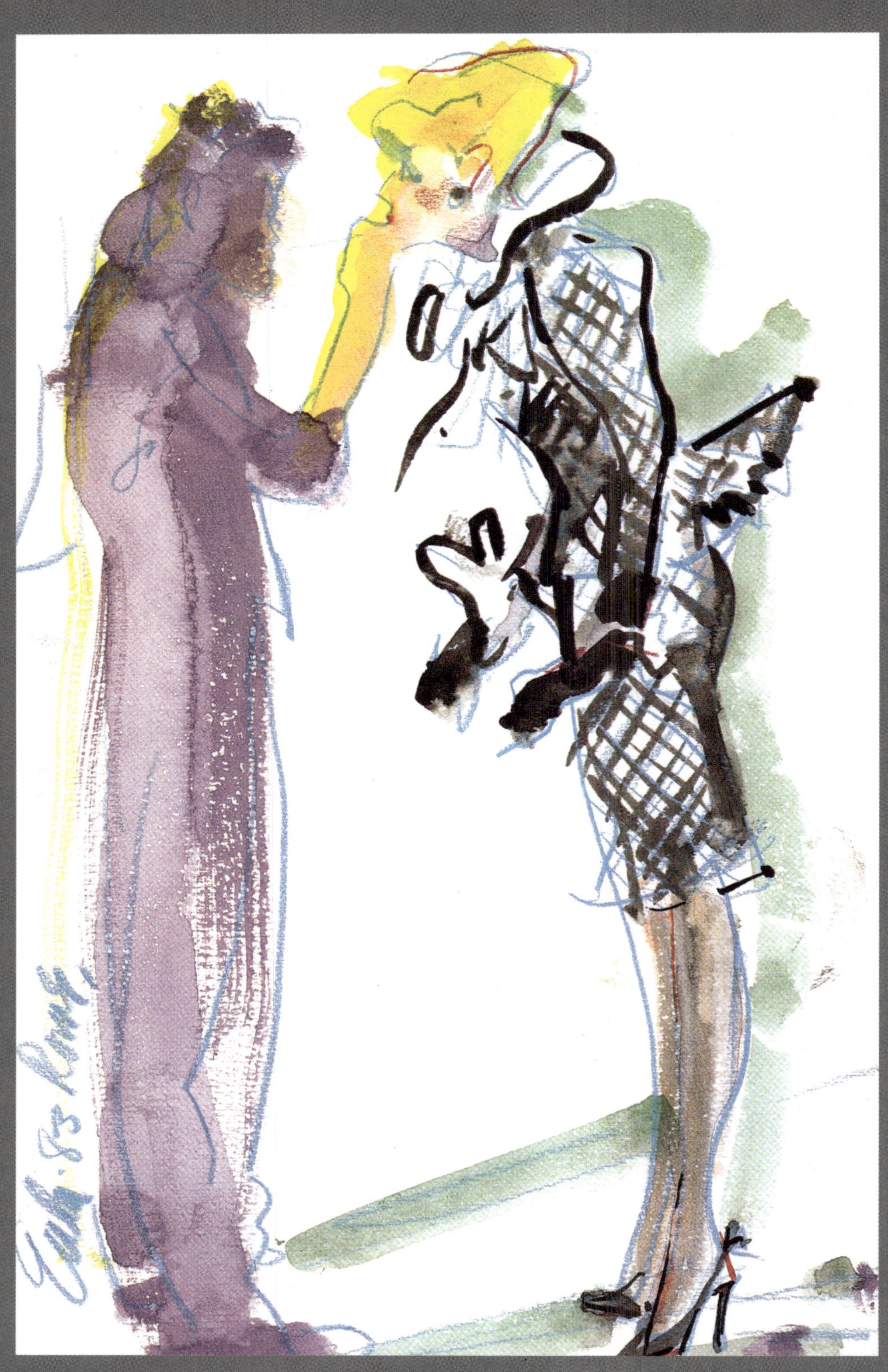

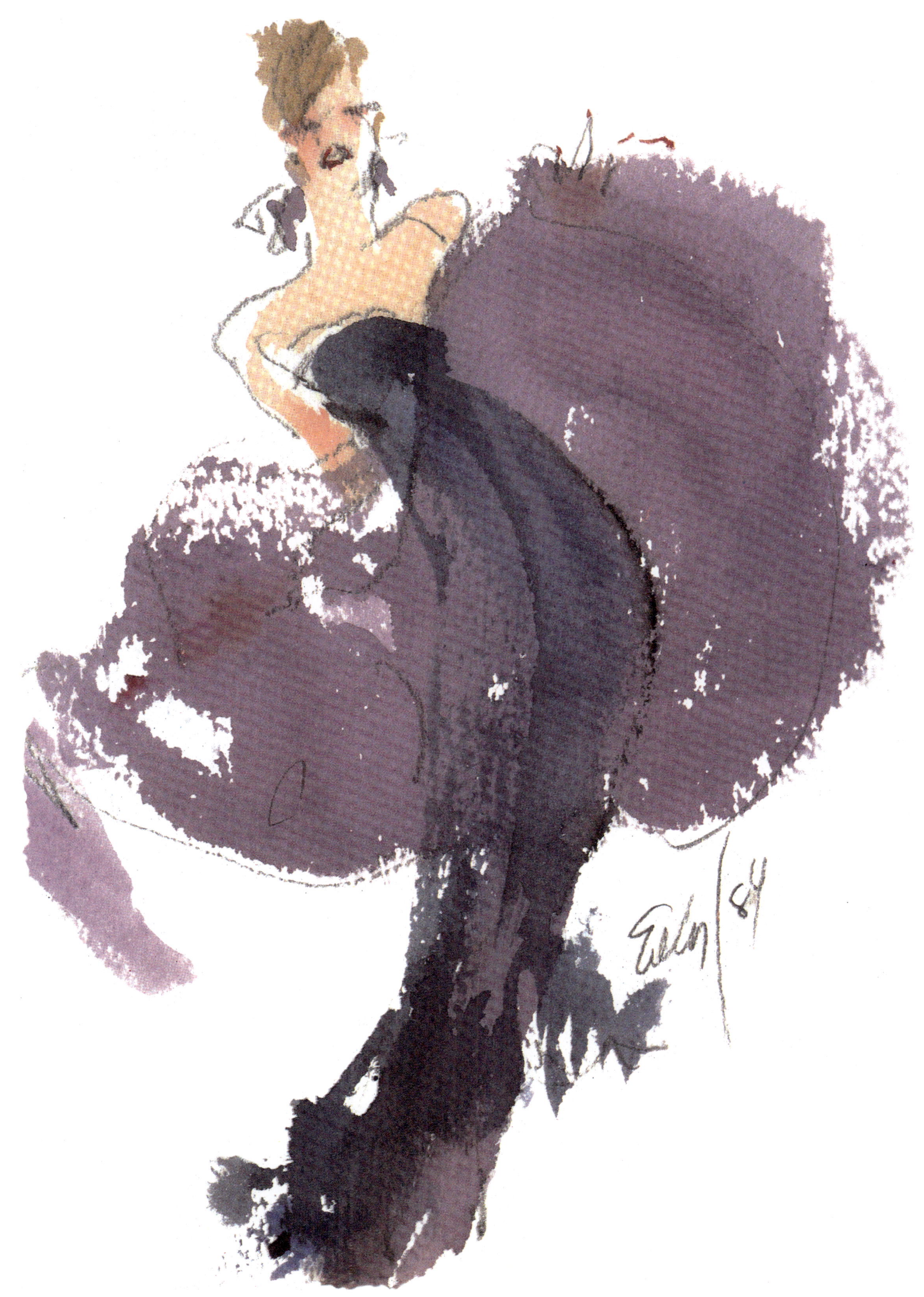

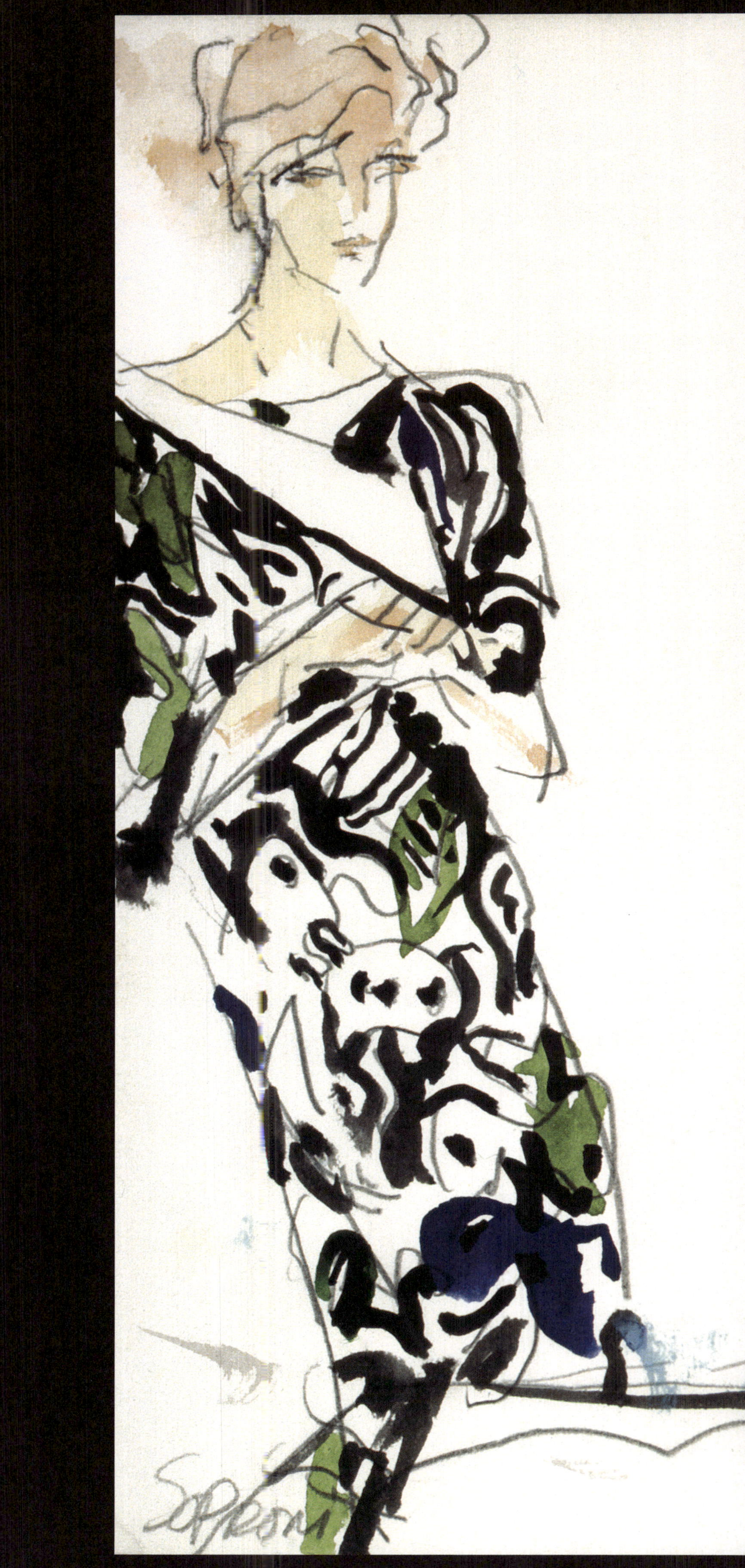

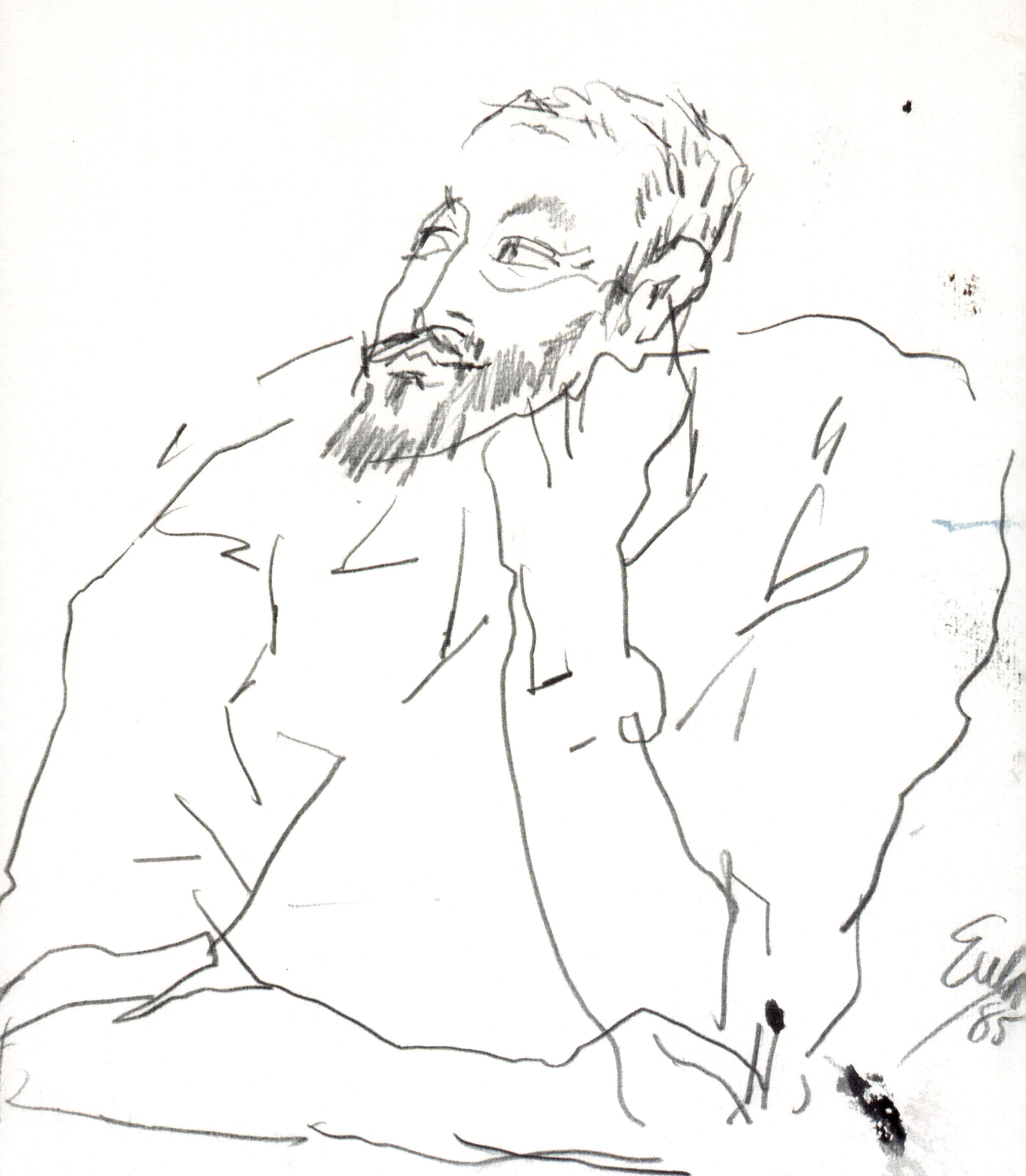

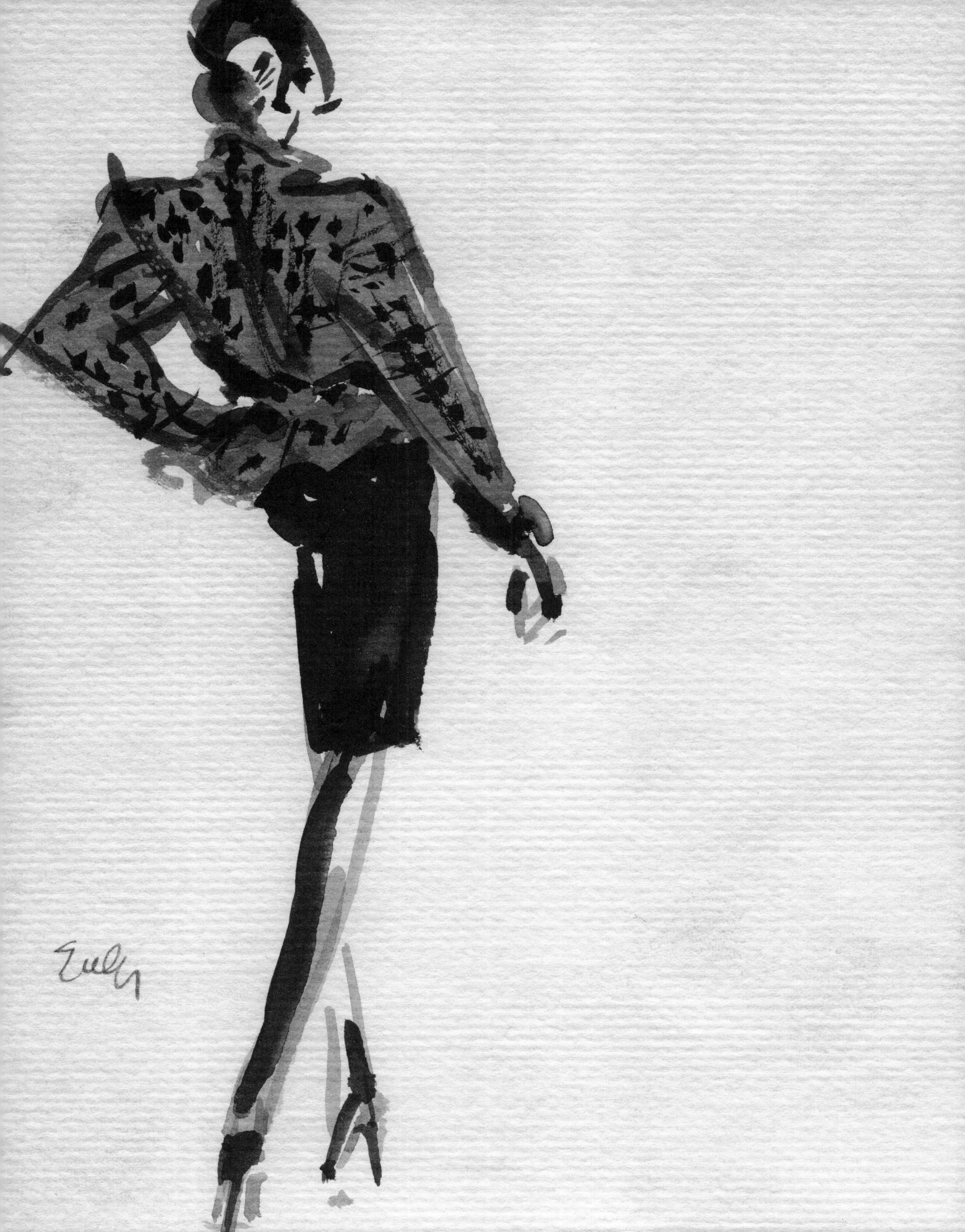

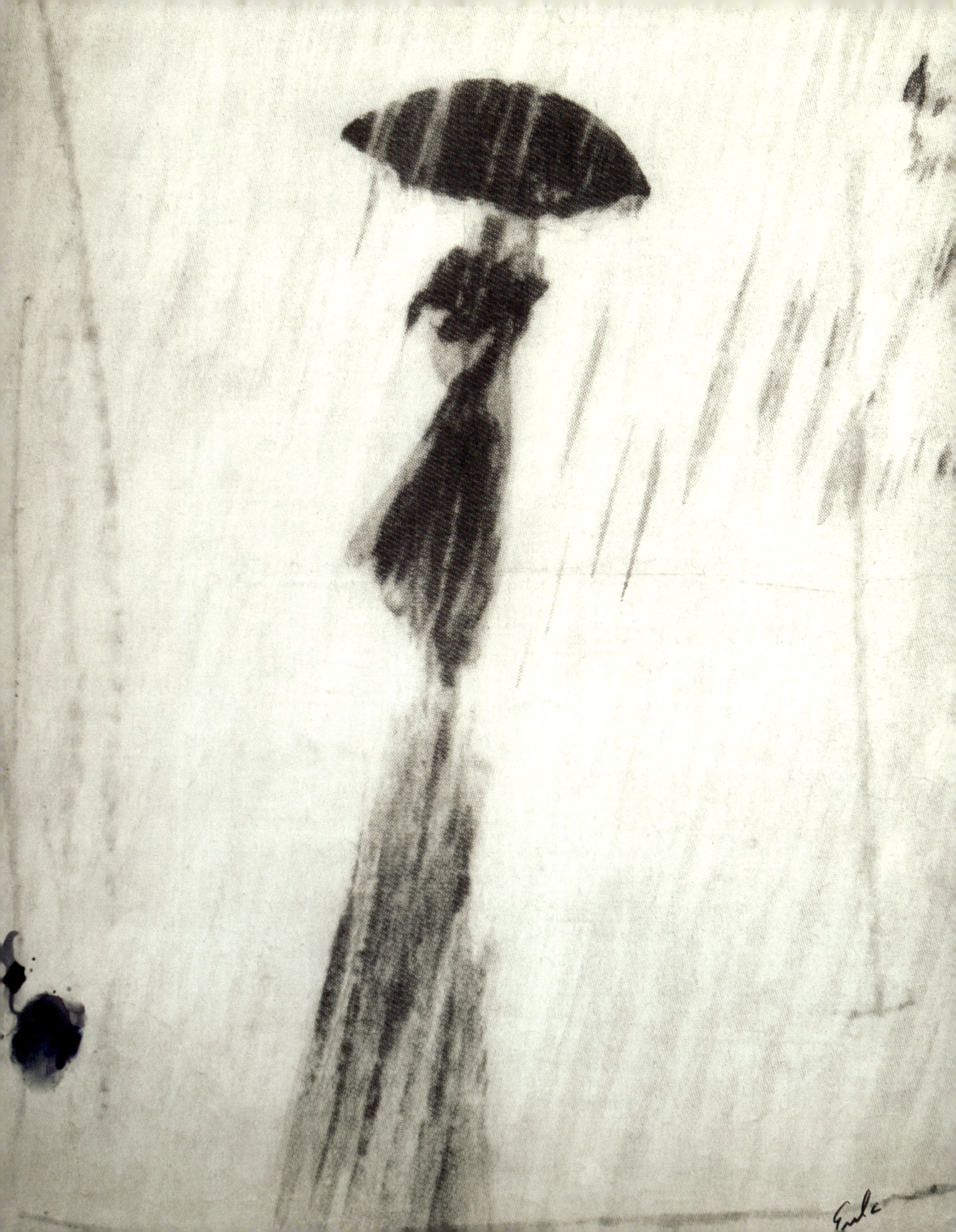

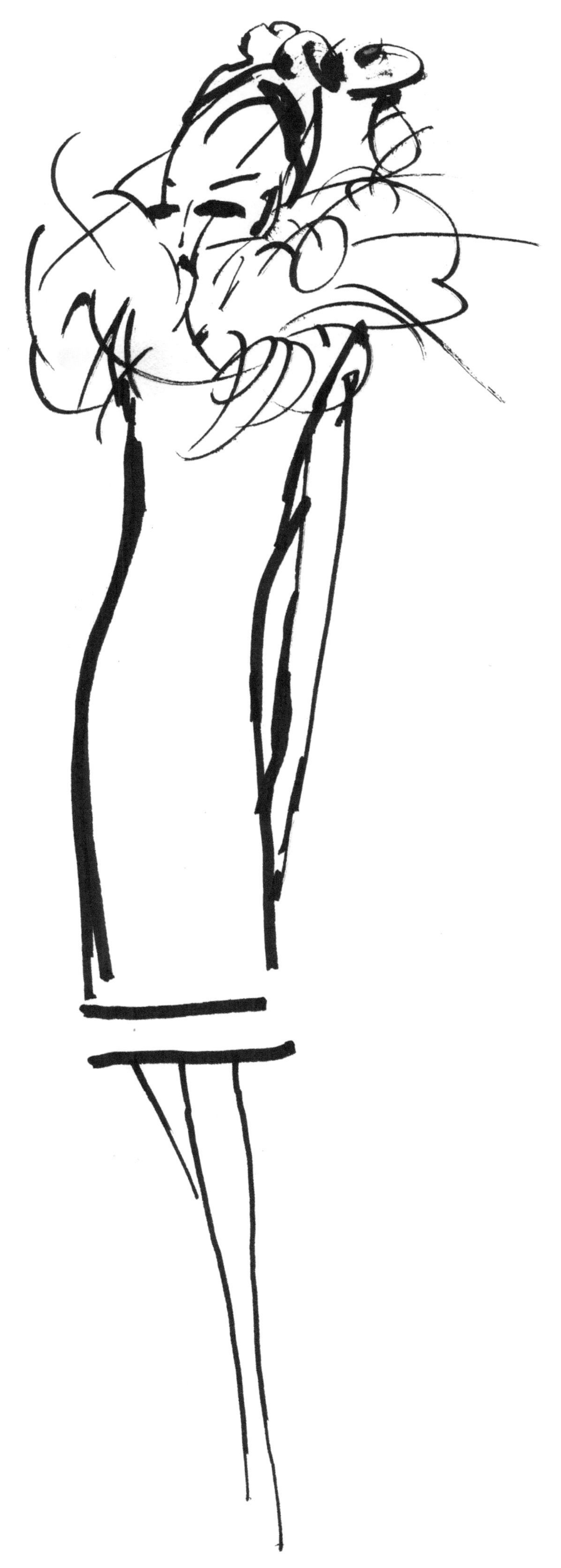

Page 111: Dior, late 1950s.

Pages 112–13: Dior, 1960s.

Page 115: Gianfranco Ferré for Dior, Paris, circa 1990.

Page 117: Chanel suit. Sketch for Eugenia Sheppard's column in the *New York Herald Tribune*, 1960s.

Pages 119 and 121: Pauline Trigère, 1960s.

Page 122: Sketch for Macy's, 1960s. Designer unknown.

Page 123: Dior, 1960s.

Page 125: 1950s. Designer unknown.

Page 127: 1980. Designer unknown.

Page 129: 1960s. Designer unknown.

Pages 130–31: Sketches for Eugenia Sheppard's column in the *New York Herald Tribune*, 1960s. Designer unknown.

Page 132: Sketch for Eugenia Sheppard's column in the *New York Herald Tribune*. Date and designer unknown.

Page 133: Robert Capucci, silver lamé tunic with blond banded mink trim, 1960.

Page 134: Balenciaga. Sketch for Macy's, date unknown.

Page 135: Dior, 1960s.

Page 137: Lauren Bacall in the play *Sweet Bird of Youth*, 1985.

Pages 138–39: Tiffany & Co., 1990.

Pages 140–41: Sketches for Eugenia Sheppard's column in the *New York Herald Tribune*, 1960s. Designers unknown.

Page 142: Duffel coat for *Town & Country*, date unknown.

Page 143: 1960s. Designer unknown.

Page 144: Jacques Tiffeau, early 1960s.

Page 145: 1960. Designer unknown.

Pages 146–47. Twiggy, date unknown.

Pages 148–49: Yves Saint Laurent. Sketches for Eugenia Sheppard's column in the *New York Herald Tribune*, 1960s.

Pages 150–151: Courrèges. Sketches for Eugenia Sheppard's column in the *New York Herald Tribune*, 1960s.

Pages 152–53: Rudi Gernreich. Sketches for Eugenia Sheppard's column in the *New York Herald Tribune*, 1960s.

Page 155: Sketch for Eugenia Sheppard's column in the *New York Herald Tribune*, 1960s. Designer unknown.

Pages 156–57: Bill Blass, date unknown.

Page 159: Gustave Tassell, 1960s.

Pages 160–61: Geoffrey Beene, date unknown.

Pages 162–63: Le Havre, Paris, 1960s.

Page 165: Mink coat. Designer unknown, 1992.

Pages 166–67: Dior. Sketches for Eugenia Sheppard's column in the *New York Herald Tribune*, 1960s.

Pages 168–69: Yves Saint Laurent (center) in his atelier, 1960s.

Pages 170–71: Designer(s) unknown. Watercolor for Italian *Harper's Bazaar*, 1980s.

Page 173: Babe Paley, date unknown.

Pages 174–75: Anne Slater (left) and Mica Ertegun (right), date unknown.

Pages 176–77: Nan Kempner (left), Pat Buckley (center), and Lynn Wyatt (right), date unknown.

Pages 178–79: Nan Kempner, date unknown.

Page 180: Gianfranco Ferré for Christian Dior, 1990.

Page 181: Watercolor for Italian *Harper's Bazaar*, 1986. Designer unknown.

Page 182: Portrait of unknown woman, date unknown.

Page 183: Chessy Rayner, date unknown.

Page 184: 1970. Designer unknown.

Page 185: Tina Chow, 1982.

Page 186: Portrait of unknown woman, date unknown.

Page 187: Marina Schiano, date unknown.

Pages 188–89: Christian Lacroix. Watercolor for Italian *Harper's Bazaar*, 1980s.

Pages 190–91: Designer unknown. Watercolor for Italian *Harper's Bazaar*, 1985.

Page 192: Miloš Forman, 1982.

Page 193: Gloria Guinness, date unknown.

Pages 194–95: Lena Horne, date unknown.

Page 197: Gianfranco Ferré, 1984.

Pages 199 and 201: Watercolors for Italian *Harper's Bazaar*, 1988.

Pages 202–03: Dior. Watercolors for Italian *Harper's Bazaar*, 1983.

Page 205: Melisa Gosnell, 1990.

Page 207: Marlene Dietrich, 1960s.

Pages 208–09: Eartha Kitt, date unknown.

Page 210: Phyllis Newman, date unknown.

Pages 212–13: Elizabeth Taylor, date unknown.

Page 215: Diana Ross, date unknown.

Pages 216–17: Bebe Neuwirth, date unknown.

Pages 218–19: Liza Minnelli, 1970s.

Page 221: Poster, Carnival Ball of Rio, 1965.

Page 222: Club poster for Trude Heller, 1960s.

Page 223: Poster for Ohrbach's department store, date unknown.

Page 225: Poster for Elaine's twenty-fifth anniversary, 1988.

Page 226: Poster, The Mod Ball, 1965.

Page 227: Poster, *The Divorce of Judy and Jane*, 1971.

Page 229: Poster, The Movie Star Ball, 1986.

Pages 230–31: Shirley MacLaine, 1984.

Pages 232–35: Flamenco Puro Dance Company, date unknown.

Pages 236–37: Costumes for the New York City Ballet, 1971.

Pages 238–39: Tammy Grimes in *High Spirits*, 1964.

Pages 240–41: Watercolors for Italian *Harper's Bazaar*, 1984. Designers unknown.

Pages 242–43: Luciano Soprani with unknown woman, 1985.

Page 245: Halston, 1979.

Page 247: Designer and date unknown.

Pages 248–49: Sketches for Eugenia Sheppard's column in the *New York Herald Tribune*, 1960s. Designers unknown.

Page 256: Joe Eula, 1950s. Photographer unknown.

Bibliography

BOOKS

Bender, Marylin. *The Beautiful People*. New York: Coward-McCann, Inc., 1967.

Blass, Bill. *Bare Blass*. Edited by Cathy Horyn. New York: HarperCollins, 2002.

Bluttal, Steven. *Halston*. New York: Phaidon Press, 2001.

Colacello, Bob. *Holy Terror: Andy Warhol Close Up*. New York: HarperCollins, 1990.

Downton, David. *Masters of Fashion Illustration*. London: Laurence King, 2010.

Greene, Amy, and Joshua Greene. *But That's Another Story: A Photographic Retrospective of Milton H. Greene*. New York: powerHouse Books, 2008.

Packer, William. *Fashion Drawing in* Vogue. London: Thames and Hudson, 1983.

Warhol, Andy. *The Warhol Diaries*. Edited by Pat Hackett. New York: Warner Books, 1989.

Watson, Steven. *Factory Made: Warhol and the Sixties*. New York: Pantheon Books, 2003.

ARTICLES

Eula, Joe. "Au Revoir, Yves." *New York Times Magazine*, March 31, 2002.

Gaines, Steven. "Got Tu Go Hustle: Presenting the Grand Man." *New York* magazine, June 25, 1979.

Grant, Robbie. "The Agony of Xtazy." *New York* magazine, December 18, 1978.

Horyn, Cathy. "Joe Eula, Fashion Illustrator, Dies at 79." *New York Times*, October 28, 2004.

Moore, Gaylen. "The Peretti Obsession." *New York Times Magazine*, February 26, 1978.

Profile of Joe Eula. Italian *Men's Bazaar*. January–February 1984.

Spindler, Amy. "Capturing the Energy and Beauty of Style." *New York Times*, April 25, 1995.

Taylor, Angela. "Elsa Peretti: Zany and Talented." *New York Times*, February 8, 1974.

UNPUBLISHED SOURCES

Eula, Joe. Proposal for memoir, 1989. Courtesy of the Estate of Joe Eula.

Eula, Joe. Selected wartime letters from Joe Eula to Lena Eula Paqua, 1945. Courtesy of Nick Eula.

Acknowledgments

I would like to dedicate this lovely book to my friend, artist Ron Ferri. Ron was Joe Eula's closest friend and certainly my biggest inspiration in bringing this project to fruition.

I would like to thank Jeff Franklin and Kate Lee, agents extraordinaire, who brought me to HarperCollins and to the creative genius of Elizabeth Viscott Sullivan, Lynne Yeamans, and their team.

My thanks to Elsa Peretti for sharing her photographs with us.

Thank you to the Eula family and Joe's many friends, who took the time to speak with Cathy Horyn; to Nino and Pamela Catuogno and Nicholas and Corinne Weil, for sharing their extensive collection of Eula works; to David Daines, Eugenia Masserini, and Mark Palmer, for letting us borrow their sketches; and to Joshua Greene, who not only shared his memories of Joe but also graciously lent both his father's and his own images to this book.

A special thank-you to a longtime friend of Joe's, James Devens, the creator of the Joe Eula Scholarship at the Art Students League of New York.

My thanks to Dagon James for his never-ending editing and genius style. I am also very grateful to Ms. Cathy Horyn.

—MELISA GOSNELL

About the Author

CATHY HORYN is the former fashion critic of the *New York Times*, where her work continues to appear. Her fashion reports and commentary have also been published in *Vanity Fair* and *Harper's Bazaar*. She first met Joe Eula in 2001 while working with Bill Blass on his memoir, *Bare Blass*. She lives in New York City.

About the Illustrator

JOE EULA (1925–2004) was the foremost fashion illustrator of the latter half of the twentieth century. Known as the fastest pencil in the field and a familiar fixture at international collections for more than sixty years, he captured the world of fashion and the essence of numerous renowned designers' visions with his quick, impressionistic, light-handed style. In the 1960s he shared a studio with photographer Milton Greene, collaborating on covers as well as news and fashion stories for *Life* magazine. In 1970 he became the creative director at Halston, where his work became a vital part of the house's legacy; he later worked extensively with Chanel, Givenchy, Versace, and Yves Saint Laurent. Over the course of his career, he created art, covers, and illustrations for numerous recording artists; designed sets and costumes for the New York City Ballet; drew posters for Broadway shows and portraits for many celebrities; and directed television fashion specials for Lauren Bacall and Candice Bergen. He created illustrations for numerous magazines and retailers, among them American *Vogue*, Italian and French *Harper's Bazaar*, *Town & Country*, Saks Fifth Avenue, and Tiffany & Co.

About the Archivist

MELISA GOSNELL is the executor of the art estate of Joe Eula. In 1978, she was a fledgling assistant Broadway producer when she was told about a job for an upcoming Broadway-bound play, *Got Tu Go Disco*, in the studio of Joe Eula, costume designer for that famed fiasco. Melisa found an immediate position in Eula's world. For more than thirty years she maintained order in the studio, and she kept company with the artist until his death in 2004. She is proud to realize his dream of publishing a book devoted to his work.

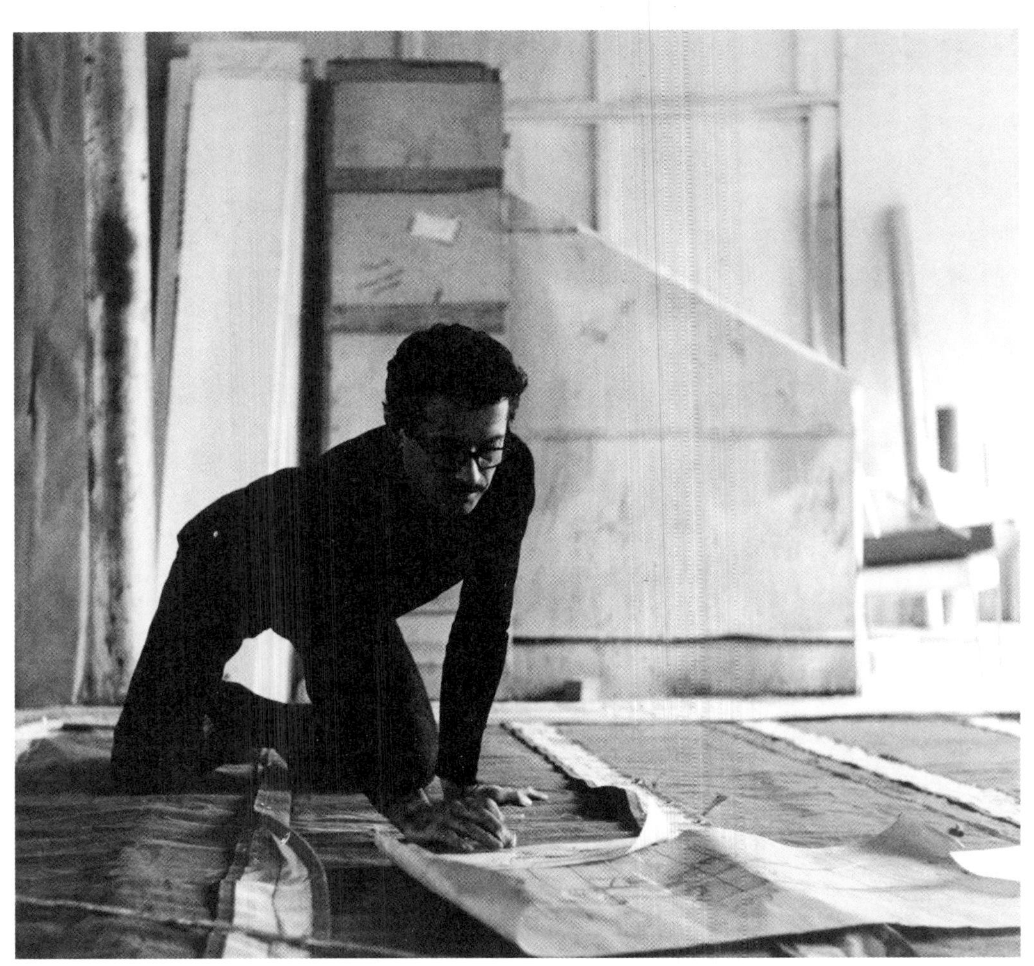